RENEWALS 458-4574
DATE DUE

WITHDRAWN
UTSA LIBRARIES

PERSPECTIVES IN
PSYCHICAL RESEARCH

This is a volume in the Arno Press collection

PERSPECTIVES IN PSYCHICAL RESEARCH

Advisory Editor

Robert L. Morris

*See last pages of this volume
for a complete list of titles.*

The Enchanted Boundary

By
WALTER FRANKLIN PRINCE

ARNO PRESS
A New York Times Company
New York – 1975

LIBRARY
University of Texas
At San Antonio

Editorial Supervision: EVE NELSON

———•◦∞◦•———

Reprint Edition 1975 by Arno Press Inc.

Reprinted from a copy in the Library of the
 American Society for Psychical Research, Inc.

PERSPECTIVES IN PSYCHICAL RESEARCH
ISBN for complete set: 0-405-07020-9
See last pages of this volume for titles.

Manufactured in the United States of America

———•◦∞◦•———

Library of Congress Cataloging in Publication Data
Prince, Walter Franklin, 1863-1934.
 The enchanted boundary.

 (Perspectives in psychical research)
 Reprint of the ed. published by Boston Society for
Psychic Research, Boston.
 1. Psychical research. I. Title. II. Series.
BF1031.P77 1975   133.8   75-7396
ISBN 0-405-07045-4

THE ENCHANTED BOUNDARY

The Enchanted Boundary

BEING A

Survey of Negative Reactions to Claims
of Psychic Phenomena
1820-1930

By
WALTER FRANKLIN PRINCE, Ph. D.
*Executive Research Officer of The Boston
Society for Psychic Research*

DECEMBER, 1930
BOSTON SOCIETY FOR PSYCHIC RESEARCH
346 Beacon Street,
Boston, Mass.

Copyright, 1930, by
Boston Society for Psychic Research,
346 Beacon Street, Boston, Mass.

TABLE OF CONTENTS

	PAGES
Preface	vii-x

PART I
BOOKS AND ARTICLES HOSTILE TO PSYCHIC RESEARCH

I.	Is Psychical Research Worth While?	1-18
II.	The Enchanted Boundary	19-133
III.	Some Sample Explanations	134-143
IV.	Houdini and Doyle	144-162
V.	Old Dogma and Later Statistics	163-197
VI.	Psychical Versus Visceral Hallucinations	198-206

PART II
DISCUSSION EVOKED BY A QUESTIONNAIRE

I.	A Hypothetical Question	209-222
II.	Belief in Psychic Events the Result of Pathological States	223-237
III.	The Argument from Negatived "Premonitions"	238-260
IV.	The Coincidence Argument	261-268
V.	Psychic (?) Incidents Explained	269-283
VI.	Then Why Has it not Happened to Me?	284-303
VII.	Miscellaneous Arguments and Opinions	304-329
VIII.	A Very Doubting Thomas	330-343
	Concluding Remarks	344

To
Mrs. Ellen A. Wood
and
Mrs. Harriet L. Hemenway,
Friends of Psychic Research.

PREFACE

Some will not like this book; they will say it is not psychic research, but only *about* psychic research. So it might be said that much written by Tyndall and Huxley—and can we ask better models?—was not science, but about science, clearing out the obstacles in the way of scientific understanding, removing prejudices and misconceptions, paving with the logic of science.

Some will not like this book, since it is made up of controversy; bring forward fresh evidence, they will say, and heed not those who oppose it. But controversy sometimes best clears up the fogs of thought, and leads to the appreciation of evidence. Look back and see if it was not so when the two great scientific leaders already named employed it in the nineteenth century.

Behold a wonder! For more than forty years a considerable group of persons of culture, learning and high scientific standing have been testifying to certain conclusions based, they declare, on evidence; opposed to these a much larger group, similarly made up of persons of culture, learning and high scientific standing, have been rejecting those same conclusions with peculiar scorn, and denying that they are supported by *any* respectable evidence! The vast majority of those who are qualified by intellect and training to be judges are silent, and we can only conjecture regarding them. But that the vocal should face each other in as uncompromising opposition as ever did the Greeks and the Persians is in itself a phenomenon which rivets attention and calls for explanation. This book pays the phenomenon the attention it merits, and professes to furnish the needed explanation.

Individuals may claim too much or deny too much and yet be in the main right. But when there are two opposing groups, one claiming that there exist facts of the order provisionally called "psychic" or "supernormal," the other denying that any such facts exist, one group must be right and the other wrong. No matter how learned, one side or the other must be ignorant of the facts or the nature of the facts in this field; one side or the other must be swayed by prejudice or infatuation; one side or the other must, in this particular field, be employing defective logic.

Certain scholars devoted the most or a large part of their time and energy for many years in the study of the facts under discussion, and came to the conclusion that a great number of them are entitled to be called " psychic " or " supernormal." Among the greatest of these scholars were Myers, Hodgson, Barrett, Podmore, Hyslop, and, still among us, Lodge and Mrs. Sidgwick. All of them, I say, agreed as to the rating of the facts, although not all sought to account for some of them by the same theory.

Undoubtedly a multitude of intelligent men and women have been mightily impressed by the spectacle of the larger group of scholars who have denied and deny the validity of the facts themselves, and principally on this ground favor opposition. Although the most which they have seen from the pens of the learned skeptics has amounted to little more than *ex cathedra* dicta or contemptuous ejaculations, they suppose that the authors, had they taken the trouble, could have justified the expressions overwhelmingly. Or, if they have read what purports to be an argument in refutal of evidence offered, they have trusted in its surface appearance of effectiveness, not thinking it necessary to ascertain whether the Case Reports have been met squarely and analyzed fairly, or have been garbled, nibbled about the edges, and treated with an evasion, sophistry and persiflage which would be deemed unworthy in any other field of discussion. Particularly readers not themselves informed could hardly suspect that any highly-esteemed scholar would rush to save the public from " superstition," so ill-equipped as to strew his course with blunders of fact which a little of the care that he takes in his own territory would spare him.

This book embodies the first attempt to appraise on a large scale writings hostile to psychic research. It seeks to deal fairly with persons who, through the course of more than a century, have expressed their disbelief in any facts " psychic " or " supernormal," according to the understood meaning of these terms. It proposes to ascertain with what degree of knowledge these persons are equipped to deal with the subject, to see whether the logic they employ is such as is employed in other types of investigation or is of a sort deemed good enough only for this, and generally to analyze and set forth their polemical methodology. All of these persons are respectable, and some of them illustrious, representatives of the classes to which they belong, physical scientists, psychologists, university and college instructors, physicians, clergymen, magicians and what-not. There are more than one hundred of these to be heard in this book.

Part One deals with writers of printed books, articles and letters from 1820 on, and embraces forty men and women, not counting **Doyle**, who finds place only because of a comparison made between him and Houdini. Dr. Head's statistics, it should be explained, were not alleged by him to argue against the validity of the apparitions of psychic research literature, but have been supposed by others to do so. Doubtless the list could be added to, but so far as the search for hostile writers in the English language was continued, not one was omitted from the survey.

Part Two is a by-product of a questionnaire whose direct results in the way of individual experiences will appear in a volume to follow this in a few months. One of the queries in that document was purposely framed to be coyly provocative, and won many expressions of skepticism in all the tones from mild compassion to acid contempt. I was really more interested in getting these reactions than I was in getting incidents, since masses of testimony to experiences have been collected and analyzed, but there has been no considerable collection and analysis of testimonies and arguments in opposition to the existence of psychic facts. Consequently, in terms of politeness which must mostly be omitted from this book (with the consequence that many of the letters appear brusque), an effort was made to induce the writers to develop the logic of opposition further, to state more explicitly the grounds of the negative certainty expressed. Some were willing to do this, others not. The views, whether or not supported by argument, of seventy-one persons, mostly of the professions, are the result. Names appear where this was expressly permitted. Certain paragraphs of my own letters, too hastily dictated, have been improved for printing; the letters of others are of course quoted with exactitude.

It would be a grave error to suppose that it is the aim of this book to lessen esteem for any of the hundred and eleven persons whose opinions, and their grounds, and the logic by which they are urged, are discussed in it, or that their general intelligence is doubted. It is the extremest test of human nature to be quite just and entirely governed by reason in relation to what one does not like. The zeit-geist, particularly in America, is at present unfavorable to psychic facts, and for many the vane is set, from childhood, against liking them. In some cases the dislike is so great that it prevents one from making any understanding examination of the evidence and at the same time betrays him into making declarations based on manifold misapprehension.

A writer is sometimes quite taken aback by learning that some expression of his which he had supposed perfectly luminous has been wholly misapprehended by one or more readers. His sensation then is that of the youth who, having remarked, " How tempus fugits!," was solemnly informed by a grave and reverend senior, "Young man, the Latin verb, present tense, third person singular, unlike the English verb, does not take the terminal s." I had better, then, explain to the ultra literal-minded, that the expression "Enchanted Boundary" does not stand for any serious theory of mine that a number of talented gentlemen are in the net of occult forces. It is only a playful invention, a device to account most charitably for the fact that they do not, in the discussion of matters relating to psychic research, seem to display all the intelligence which they undoubtedly possess.

Facts are sacred. At least as much as any man, Darwin taught us that, by his years of observing, testing and recording millions of facts, each conscientiously placed on the side of the ledger where it belonged. The many who assailed him by their prejudices, their reckless guesses, their dogmas and their fears for the edifices of thought which the past had reared, would have done better to have bared their heads before the saintliness of his intellectual rectitude. Facts cannot be destroyed. Like the stars in the sky, they shine on until the evolution of thought has proceeded so far as to compel their observation.

Although he himself did not always heed them all, three sayings by Huxley deserve to be engraved in the consciousness of every seeker after truth.

On the one hand:

Doubt is a beneficent demon.

And on the other:

I am too much of a skeptic to deny the possibility of anything.

And:

Nobody can presume to say what the order of the Universe MUST be.

PART ONE

BOOKS AND ARTICLES HOSTILE
TO PSYCHIC RESEARCH

I. IS PSYCHICAL RESEARCH WORTH WHILE?[1]

No cautious and intelligent person can or should be convinced by testimony that supernormal phenomena exist except on the basis of a great many case reports, nor can he take into consideration any case report which is not full, detailed and critical in the extreme. Therefore it would be quite hopeless for me to attempt, in the limits of one lecture, to convince any one by citing cases. I shall occasionally refer to one by way of illustration, and toward the close I may present one or two case sketches with the understanding that they are only "thumb-nail" sketches and that the full reports are available in print.

In the main, what I have to say will constitute a study in trends and reactions. What were the causes which led to the foundation of Societies for Psychical Research? What has been the effect of inspection and study upon the minds of persons apparently well qualified? Why is it that after nearly half a century Psychical Research Societies are still in existence and even multiplying? Have the methods of psychical researchers, to outward appearances, been cautious, logical and painstaking, or otherwise? How far has earnest and protracted psychical research, deserving of the name, resulted in making thorough skeptics? How far have opponents shown themselves qualified by experience or by study? On which side, among the most scientific leaders, is there the greater appearance of dealing with facts rather than dogmas, with logic rather than appeals to authority? What are some of the arguments against psychical research, and to what extent are other branches of scientific inquiry also liable to the weight of them? Is psychical research becoming more or less formidable with the passage of time? Are there sets of facts on which experienced researchers are practically agreed? If there are sets upon which they differ greatly, how is this to be explained? Has psychical research made, aside from the category of the supernormal, any worthy contributions to knowledge? In the main, this paper is, though I dislike the term, a study in behaviorism as related to psychical research.

1. Phenomena of the same nature as those which now form the

[1] From *The Case For and Against Psychical Belief*, Clark University, Worcester, Mass., 1927, by consent of Prof. Carl Murchison.

subject-matter of psychical research are witnessed to from the first records of the human race, apparently in all lands. They are in our Bible and other bibles. They are in ancient Roman histories and biographies. They are in the writings of the Christian Fathers, and so on to our day. Many of them are given at second-hand, many are doubtless distorted and curiously interpreted in the telling, yet the narratives witness to human belief in actual experiences. Oddly, we sometimes hear it said as a taunt that such beliefs were common in ancient times and are common among aborigines, which is exactly what we should expect would be the case if the phenomena to which they relate, correctly described, are integral to the human race.

2. Such testimonies may be found far more frequently in our own vaunted period of enlightenment than in any former period, now that effort is being made to collect them and it is comparatively an age of recording. They are not confined to the ignorant or the credulous, but are shared by the greatest intellects. Nor do they shun the lives of scientifically inclined men, though these tend to discourage them, discount them, and much less frequently to record than tell them to intimates.

I have noticed that if a small group of intelligent men, not supposed to be impressed by psychical research, get together and such matters are mentioned, and all feel that they are in safe and sane company, usually from a third to a half of them begin to relate exceptions. That is to say, man after man opens a little residual closet and takes out some incident which happened to him or to some member of his family, or to some friend whom he trusts, and which he thinks odd and extremely puzzling. I made a remark of this kind once when with six men of high standing in various professions. No sooner had I ceased speaking when a physicist whose name is known over the world told of something which happened to him when a young man—how he heard his father's voice pronouncing his name at the very hour, as it afterward proved, when his father died, hundreds of miles away. He ended: " That is something I never could understand." I do not think the physicist would forgive me if I revealed his name. Then, to my equal surprise, a very prominent physician, whose name is familiar to the profession all over the country, told stories of what seemed like telepathy in his own family. A noted editor and a well-known lawyer followed suit.

3. There is a large degree of homogeneity in the stories ancient, mediæval and modern, subject, however, to at least two disturbances even when told at first-hand. (1) Superadded interpretation, as when Luther said that he saw the devil, whereas had he lived in the twentieth

IS PSYCHICAL RESEARCH WORTH WHILE? 3

century he would have said he saw the apparition of a man, the notion that it was the devil being his interpretative addition. (2) Modification by the subconsciousness under the influence of the zeit-geist and the individual composite. As among the waving grass-blades shimmering in the morning light a pious child would be more likely to experience the illusion of a winged angel, and an ardent youth the illusion of a dancing girl, so, admitting that there are veridical apparitions, they are probably subject to modification by that strange mechanism, the mind, which at the same time is acted upon and acts upon itself. Thus, if one saw a vision of his deceased mother gazing pityingly upon him, a few moments after, as it proved, his far-distant father died, we might well, on the background of many similar cases, suspect a supernormal stimulus, but likewise suspect an intermixing memory stimulus to account for her being dressed in the familiar garb of years ago.

Nevertheless, many of the ancient and mediæval stories strikingly resemble the recorded and authenticated ones of our own time. Unbecoming as they may be in an age of science, dreams more complexly coincident with uninferrible events of the near future than any prophetic dreams in the Bible have been proved to occur in our generation. Lest some of my hearers should gaspingly turn for relief to Royce's theory of pseudo-memories, I add that I refer to dreams actually related to intelligent witnesses before the astoundingly coinciding events occurred. The raps which I studied in my own house, in my office and in the office of a New York physician lead back to the startling thumps which Luther heard in his monastery and in Wartburg Castle. The Apostle Peter's becoming aware of the messengers from Cornelius before they were in sight is analogous with the authenticated recent case of the lady who saw while awake a vision of a man of whom for a long time she had heard nothing, with his face tied up in a bandage, at the hour when her husband at a distance beheld with astonishment this man's face so bandaged as he lay in his coffin. The double incident of Peter and Cornelius is of a type with the recent authentic case of a New Jersey woman of culture who had a waking vision of her dead father and living foster-brother, which she immediately told to persons whose testimonies I have, it afterward proving that at that hour her brother, on a warship in the North Sea, as a torpedo was approaching, saw the apparition of his foster-father on the deck beside him. These were not beliefs, they were actual experiences, strangely coinciding subjective facts, which no so-called " logic of science " can annihilate.

4. The foregoing considerations determined a group of English

university men forty-four years ago [1a] to found a society for the investigation of such alleged incidents. One of the prime movers, Professor Henry Sidgwick, who has been called the "most incorrigible skeptic in England," nevertheless agreed that it was the scandal of science that it had never more than sneered at all this testimony of the ages, that it made no effort finally to determine whether there is or is not any fire back of so much smoke. At least it would be worth while as a study of folklore and of psychology, and would, if all was found illusory, have the effect of discouraging an epidemic which if it begins in the slums of human mentality, frequently enters the palaces thereof.

5. Forty-four years have passed since the Society for Psychical Research was founded. Several other worthy organizations have in the meantime arisen to engage in the same inquiry, not to give heed to less respectable ones. Some of the most eminent scientists on earth have taken part, some of the most brilliant intellects, some most familiar not only with pathological mentality, but also with the occasional queer mechanisms of the normal mind, not omitting some expertly conversant with the methodology of fraud in this field. If, after all, comparatively few with such varieties and combinations of equipment lent themselves to the work, it really seems as if there were enough and the time elapsed enough to have already proved to approximate certainty that only superstition and credulity, illusion and delusion, infantilism and mental aberration underlie these million stories, if such indeed is the case. But the forty-four years have not had this result. If I could go no farther, this would be a striking announcement. After thousands of years science at last turned its critical eye upon the matter, men of learning, intellectuality, logic and familiarity with critical procedure took hold, some of them with the full expectation of showing that the whole class of beliefs was without rational foundation, and—they have not succeeded.

6. More than this, a number of species of claims formerly almost universally derided by intellectuals so far as their *public* announcements were concerned, have been placed upon a firmer basis than ever before. And, *mirabile dictu!* a not inconsiderable number of eminent scientists, men of brilliant intellects, adepts in logic and critical procedure, trained detectives in the jungle of human illusion and delusion, have actually become convinced on the evidence, that more or less types of supernormal claims are valid. It would appear that, if it was worth while in 1882 to begin an organized attempt to study the phenomena alleged, there is now ten times the motive to continue that study.

[1a] This lecture was delivered at Clark University in 1926.

IS PSYCHICAL RESEARCH WORTH WHILE?

7. Let us not lose sight of the significance of the fact that many of these convinced men started their quest as materialists, and that the training and prepossessions of the scientific fraternity were adverse to the claims under consideration. And yet as honest analyzers and reporters of the facts they have declared their conviction that certain species of hitherto discredited claims are, as a matter of fact, justified.

To cite one example, if any man was fitted by mental constitution and by equipment to build a road clear across the bog, assuming that the whole region of psychical research is a bog, Dr. Richard Hodgson, the academic product of two great universities, lecturer in one of them, seemed to be the man. Of keen and logical intellect, author of historic exposures of fraud, co-author of the finest demonstration of the possibilities of mal-observation and memory aberration in existence, unusually versed in the methodology of fraud and deception, he was regarded as the arch skeptic, and his appointment to the head of Psychical Research in this country was hailed by its opponents with approval. After years of study, particularly with Mrs. Piper, he became convinced that several types of mental supernormal claims were valid, and that certain phenomena were best explained by the spiritistic hypothesis. Therefore it is now dogmatically asserted that he was all the while a victim of the " will to believe," although for years manifesting the very opposite symptoms.

8. As intimated, the favorite jeer of scientific opponents is that such men as Lodge, Barrett, Crookes, Myers, Hodgson and Hyslop, were victims of a " will to believe." If uttered in good faith this cry is simply a tabloid of desperate superstition,—superstition because it is a belief irrationally grounded and desperate because beyond it is the deep sea of utter inability to explain the conviction of those qualified men who have most laboriously and protractedly studied the phenomena, without admitting that they probably obtained some respectable evidence. Of course no man is absolutely without bias, and it is possible that some man even of the caliber of those I have named was not inwardly displeased to find evidence in favor of supernormal claims, exactly as it is very possible that a scientific opponent allows the scales of his thinking on the subject to be weighted by a will to disbelieve. But prior to his study of the evidence the man with the hypothetical will to believe may have seemed to keep it in good subjection. If he secretly longed to live after bodily death, in some cases he neither went to church nor read nor conversed much on religion. It really looks as though, with most men, actual present advantages rather than those of a hypothetical future world are more influential.

We don't know what inner craving for continuance a given psychical researcher may have had (for aught I know, most scientific men, *pro* and *con*, if their lids could be taken off, would reveal at least a vestige of such an instinctive craving, and if so the fact would be to a degree evidential), but we do know, and he knew, that his reputation for sanity and judgment, that his scientific standing, that his very job, would be less secure if he announced that a claim to the supernormal was established. It is certain that such motives to create a will to disbelieve would press upon him as they do on those who announce themselves as opposed, while the slogan that a Lodge or a Hodgson is actuated by a will to believe is purely a dogma, as fully as that of the philosopher's stone. But, equally enamored of this comforting dogma and of the Freudian technique, an eminent gentleman undertook to reconstruct the biography of a living man, encouraged by lack of response from dead worthies subjected to a similar process. Sir Oliver Lodge, said he, is convinced of survival because he is getting to be an old man who doesn't wish to lapse from being, and because he wants to see again his son who was killed in the great war. How evident that, instead of yielding to the logic of observed facts, Sir Oliver gravitated toward the fulfilment of his wishes! Only—Sir Oliver was not an old man when he arrived at his convictions, long before the war, and his son was yet a boy. But why should facts be allowed to spoil a fine theory?

9. For the most part all this talk about a "will to believe" is beside the mark and foolish. What if Columbus did have a will to believe that if he sailed westward far enough he would reach land—the essential thing is that he proved his belief correct. As Tyndall has told us, there comes a point in a man's investigation of an obscure phenomenon when he legitimately employs his "scientific imagination" to picture a cause or concurrence of causes which would satisfactorily explain the phenomenon. From the time that he has so framed his theory, and so long as it continues to form the most economical and adequate solution, he can hardly help wishing that it may prove to be the true one. That must have been the case with Galileo, Kepler, Newton, Faraday, Darwin and all the rest. Who cares for that? The only question is, what was their evidence and what their argument founded thereon.

10. A man reaches his convictions in any one of three ways. (1) In the main by the intellectual route, through study and reasoning, or (2) partly by this route but also partly through his emotions, his prejudices and likings, or (3) mainly through these emotional by-ways. Whatever class he belongs to can be pretty well gauged by the way he

IS PSYCHICAL RESEARCH WORTH WHILE? 7

writes or talks. It is certain that many advocates of supernormal phenomena and theories belong to the last class. Their reports of cases are full of leaks, their inductions are hasty and fragile, they rush to defend cases of another continent against the judgment of the actual and competent observers, their language is heated and hortatory, they display a degree of zeal becoming to an apostle but not to an investigator of facts. There are also the half-way class, those who have had and set forth some evidence, but mix with it so much indiscrimination, incaution and intemperate zeal as also to make them ineffectual except with the unthinking and as marks for their adversaries. Mesmer in his time announced a new and very important fact to the world, but in his ignorant zeal invested it with so much extravagant nonsense as to delay its scientific reception for half a century. Nevertheless it was the reproach of science that it turned away in disgust and did not go directly to the dust-heap and lay hold of the valuable thing therein hidden, as a similar course is a reproach to it today.

But there have been and are persons whose works show them to have been careful, intelligent and patient observers, experimenters, analyzers and synthesizers of evidence. Fully as much as Darwin or Huxley or Tyndall or Spencer, do such leaders minutely collect, examine, weigh and classify their facts. They are fully as conservative, paving their way as they go, their language is as temperate and they as seldom give vent to exclamations of impatience at the impudent and vacuous volubility of their adversaries. They set forth the facts and the conditions in detail, they dodge no difficulties, and calmly discuss the various possible theories to account for the facts. They have built up a precautionary methodology from which many a psychological laboratory, as Dr. F. C. S. Schiller has shown,[2] might borrow hints to make its inferential errors less frequent. Hence the spectacle of such men, standing up before a taunting scholastic majority and calmly announcing that they have reached, severally, one or another stage of conviction that supernormal facts actually exist, is a profoundly impressive one.

11. Now let us apply the same test, analysis of modes of discussion, to the physical scientists, psychologists, physicians and others who have written books and articles attacking the whole domain of psychical research, including telepathy. I make a statement which will seem incredible, but which defies confutation. Every one of them, by the application of the test is shown to belong, *when he enters the field*

---

[2] *Proceedings* S. P. R., Part 35, pp. 361-364.

of *Psychical Research with general hostile intent*,[3] to the third class, that composed of persons whose conclusions *in that field* are actuated mainly by their emotions, by manifest bias and prejudice, rather than by calm reasoning on the basis of careful study; persons who *react irrationally to particular subjects which for some reason are obnoxious to them*, and evidence the fact by generalities, *a priori* assumptions, refusal to squarely face and calmly discuss main issues, attacks on men of straw, weird logic which they would deride were it employed in their own special field, indulgence in wild and unsupported hypotheses in regard to the intellects of all their opponents, exhibitions of ignorance of their subject matter by frequent blunders of fact, exclamations of disgust and sundry marks of emotionalism. So emphatically is this true that I wrote for a London magazine [*Psyche*] an article exhibiting these traits in the printed output of fifteen prominent writers, under the title "The Enchanted Boundary." I am fairly familiar with the literature on this subject of the last forty-five years, and have been searching in vain for a case where a hostile spear, however effective outside, did not turn to a reed when it crossed the border of this region of inquiry, and where this cannot easily be shown. No rejoinder came from one of my fifteen subjects of demonstration, because the facts were irrefutable when once pointed out. One could recite instances for hours; how opposers of psychical research pick out, for attack, incidents which the original reporters for honesty's sake did not omit but expressly stated were not evidential, while carefully avoiding the real evidence; how they mutilate and do malpractice on records they profess to summarize; how they ludicrously misconceive and misstate the problems and opinions of those whom they criticize; how in juvenile awe of scientific assumptions which are continually altering and enlarging they undertake to demolish facts by

---

[3] The reader is asked to take account of every word in this italicized passage. I do not accuse scientific men in general of being emotional or unfair, or the particular men referred to of being so characterized in other fields than that of psychical research, nor even men who have written against the spiritistic theory, endeavoring to account for the facts by telepathy. Nor is my statement based upon conjecture. It is an induction drawn from an actual survey of books and articles which indiscriminately attack all alleged supernormal facts and theories. Most scientific men lack both interest and time to pay attention to psychical phenomena—and write little or nothing relating thereto. Such as do have the interest and time to study the facts tend to become impressed by what they find and either to express to one or another degree their favorable interest or at least to refrain from careless disparagement. But a comparatively small number, to whom psychical research is as the traditional red rag to the bull, turn their attention to it, mainly to collect material for polemic purposes and betray insufficiency of their acquaintance and departure from a scientific spirit by the characteristics of their writing. It is solely to the last class that I refer in the text.

IS PSYCHICAL RESEARCH WORTH WHILE? 9

dogmatic pronunciamentos; how they boast of their unwillingness to get first-hand knowledge by patient experiment, and betray their lack of acquaintance with the works of those who have done so by childish blunders of fact (I counted six in one short paragraph); how they sweep away hosts of authenticated actual cases by one oracular dictum as intelligent as that of the farmer who, when he saw a giraffe, said, "There ain't no such animal"; how they betray emotional bias as in the case of the psychologist of whom Dr. Hyslop said that if he was so actuated he ought to join the Salvation Army.

Even Huxley lapsed from his logical rectitude when he said that the only good of a demonstration of "Spiritualism" was to furnish an argument against suicide. If he had heard some one in or out of Texas say that the only good of a demonstration that men are biologically related to apes is to furnish an argument *for* suicide, I can imagine his acid retort that facts do not pay heed to emotional repulsions. I myself have a decided prejudice against biting and stinging insects, and my feelings declare that my world shall not contain them, but now and then in my travels I am painfully reminded that it nevertheless does. Suppose it proved that all subconscious twaddle of a medium comes from heaven and that the indications are that we all become idiotic when we reach that region, still facts would be facts, whether blissful or otherwise.

Think of Dr. Hyslop, who had his human subjects for experiment introduced after the psychic was in trance, had them sit behind her and keep silent, reported every word, and even every time the pencil fell from the writing medium's hand, then think that a Doctor of Philosophy attempted to demolish him in a book which mutilated, distorted and misrepresented every incident which she professed to quote, without exception, and finally think that an eminent educator, not without interest to Clark University, was so unguarded *in this field* that in its preface he expressed the hope that the now forgotten book would prove to be "the turn of the tide!"

12. Or take my own case as that of one convinced of several types of supernormal phenomena, and supremely unconvinced of certain other claims. Put me under the microscope as the bug some people think I am. Excessively cautious, and regarded by the Spiritualistic religious cult as a hard-hearted skeptic; formerly thoroughly skeptical all along this line; always occupied during a curiously varied career, from the boyhood days when no mechanical or other puzzle was ever given up unsolved, in the analysis and resolution of one kind of a problem or another, in history, sociology, abnormal psychology,

etc., up to psychical research; one to whom accuracy is a religion and minute analysis an obsession so that it is an agony to terminate the testing process and write a report; intolerably detailed in reporting and in presenting the subject in hand at every possible angle; alive by experience and study to the various pitfalls of illusion, delusion and deception—all this has made me a kind of a scrutinizing, analyzing and rationalizing monster, quite unpleasant to the tender-minded. For years I have been inviting any man in the world to face squarely such affirmative reports as I have been willing to make, and to discuss them fairly; to point out precautionary measures overlooked, serious flaws in scientific method and weaknesses in reasoning. Few have made any appearance of opposition, none has more than entered mere formal *a priori* objections or uttered a few oracular and evasive generalities.

Is this boasting? Not at all, the very point is that if so humble and plodding a student as myself, whose main intellectual merit leans to the side of a failing—that of being scared to death of being caught in an error—can present his facts in such a way that no one seriously attempts to refute them, how strong must be the case for psychical research! For years I have tried to find a man who would take any one of a number of reported cases in psychical research which I will name, and make a critical attack upon it as a whole, show that any of the necessary precautions were lacking, that the method of investigation was scientifically defective, that the reasoning from it was not sound. No one has done so, though one professor of psychology, at once my friend and my forensic opponent,[3a] is notably voluble on the subject. Several declared that they *could* do it. One promised that he *would* do it and was furnished with all the materials which, after four years, he has yet. I predict that on his deathbed he will murmur: "I could have done it if I only had had time." (By the way, I think that my friend, the voluble professor, may have the Saul of Tarsus complex. You remember that Saul, knowing nothing in particular against the Christians, imagined that they were a bad lot, and having no official functions which required him to persecute them, went out of his way to obtain an official license to do so. We know he listened to Stephen at the time of that martyr's execution, and it well may be that he was half convinced that the Christians were right. He verily thought, as he tells us, that he was doing God service in harrying them, and yet all the time it was probably a subconsciously initiated psychological defense against his own heretical tendencies. There is nothing

---

[3a] Joseph Jastrow, now professor emeritus of the University of Minnesota.

IS PSYCHICAL RESEARCH WORTH WHILE? 11

in my friend the professor's official functions which calls upon him to tour the country and enrich the magazines with his attacks upon psychical research, within which his revelations of knowledge are not very profound. Have certain facts like winged arrows pierced the joints of his armor, and is he, actuated by the Saul of Tarsus complex, fighting for the preservation of his own academic orthodoxy? It is an interesting psychological question.)

13. Even rational men, unable to cope with facts against which they have an emotional complex, frequently react irrationally, set up an illusory dogma and cling to it as a pillar of safety. So we hear that psychic or supernormal facts are " impossible " by the " logic of science," are contrary to the laws of nature, and destructive to the principles of universe. Psychologists, much more than physicists and biologists, are apt to cherish the delusion that science has reached the point where it can perfectly delimit between the possible and the impossible, that its principles and final concepts have been perfectly and fully ascertained. Science has been in our own time a changing panorama, continually enlarging the circle to introduce facts formerly regarded impossible, tearing down old and erecting new theories and altering some of its very foundation principles. Was it not Lord Kelvin who said that hypnotism was half fraud and half malobservation? Certainly it was denounced by many eminent men as gross humbug. Edison's electric light was declared by several scientists, when the newspapers first reported it, impossible. The phonograph was impossible. The flight of heavier-than-air machines was impossible. So the catalogue could be extended indefinitely. Hence Von Helmholz's dictum to Sir William Barrett was not quite final, great a scientist as he was: " Neither the testimony of all the Fellows of the Royal Society, nor even the evidence of my own senses, could lead me to believe in the transmission of thought from one person to another independently of the recognized channels of sensation. It is clearly impossible." As impossible is a word which admits of no comparative degree it follows that since some " impossible " things have nevertheless been found true, others probably will be. And thus far the universe has not suffered from the establishment of " impossible " facts.

But, more than this, the formulas, the theories, some of the very so-called laws relating to the origin, and constitution of and relations existing between material things have changed. As Will Durant has lately said [*Harper's* Magazine, December, 1926]: " To what distant star has our famous nebular hypothesis flown? . . . Where are the laws of the great Newton now, when Einstein and Moskowski and other disreputable foreigners have upset the universe with their unintelligible relativity? Where is the indestructibility of matter and the conservation of energy in the chaos and dispute of contemporary physics. . . . Where is Gregor Mendel now that 'unit characters' are in bad odor with geneticists?" And again, such queries could be extended. Nor do they breathe contempt for science, whose noble building grows in solidity and grandeur, albeit it undergoes many alterations, some of them so radical as to change its appearance and parts of its very structure. It is only when a scientist becomes a philosopher, and adopts the philosophical theory of mono-materialism, that psychic facts seem impossible in the scheme of things. Let these facts reach to the indisputable stage and the scientists' philosophy of the universe will alter to include them, and they will composedly smile at the perturbations of their predecessors.

14. But is it not a fact that the field of psychic research extends back through centuries of gross and silly superstitions? Superstitions are often wrong interpretations of facts. But there certainly is very much of superstition in the sense of irrational and unfounded occult beliefs and practices perceptible in our glimpses of ancient times, and amongst cultured peoples of the present age. Think of the fact that some newspapers still print daily "horoscopes," despite the fact that no scientific investigator in the world credits the absurdities of astrology. And of the host of generally intelligent people who have respect for the theory that human destiny is portrayed by the lines that folds of flesh happen to make in the palm of the hand. Or for that moronic superstition called numerology, or for a machine which will determine from your autograph whether you have a cancer or the chickenpox and what was the religious belief of your father. But other sciences also have had their history and have today their disreputable camp following of superstition. Chemistry was largely born out of alchemy, and astronomy out of astrology. Shall we flout the science and art of medicine for the hotbed of superstition in which it was nurtured and for the queer theories which accompanied its main current of progress, as well as for the grotesque doctrines and practices which hang to its skirts still? Is the hypnotism of today to be twitted with Mesmer the charlatan? So psychic research is not so very lonely. It is a science, later to develop, like the others, order and discrimination in the midst of chaotic and heterogeneous materials.

15. Next a question, supposed to be quite deadly, is put: "Have not psychical researchers, even scientists among them, been fooled by phenomena which turned out to be illusive?" Certainly, some have

IS PSYCHICAL RESEARCH WORTH WHILE? 13

blundered in certain cases. Has it not been so elsewhere? So Bastian, a scientist, claimed to have produced living creatures in hermetically sealed jars devoid of life, and wrote a book about it which Tyndall refuted, but biology remains a science. And a German geologist was fooled into accepting as genuine fossils, weird manufactures by waggish students, and published a monograph on them, but geology still survives. Charcot fooled himself into thinking that hypnosis always proceeds by three described stages; his observations were deceptive, but hypnotism is yet a fact!

Now and then a scientific man, a psychologist, or whatnot, gets logically impressed by a case where the conditions are both as fully under his control and as adequate for judgment as those of a laboratory, particularly a case of mental character. Then, in his newly-awakened interest he attends a sitting of so-called "physical phenomena," where the conditions are mostly prescribed for him on the basis of alleged "psychic laws," which correspond closely to the precautions which hinder the detection of fraud, where in short everything is almost the precise opposite to his familiar laboratory. In darkness or near darkness, his hands probably held, listening to the suggestions around him (and even college professors and laboratory experts are human), knowing little of the great area of conjuring possibilities under such conditions, and in some cases feeling a knightly unwillingness that an appealing medium shall be less innocent than she looks—under these conditions, when things occur quite outside of his familiar experiences—he sometimes becomes, as Samson did when his hair was cut, "like any other man," and goes forth to give his favorable opinion, though it be counter to that of investigators of twenty times his experience. These tragedies will become less and less in number with the passage of time, as in other branches of research equally blundering conclusions are already infrequent.

16. "But," again it is urged, "psychical researchers do not agree in their theories to account for the facts. A particular class of facts is accounted for by some on the basis of spiritism, by others on that of telepathy, while 'cryptesthesia'—whatever that is—is the watchword of another, and we even hear of the Cosmic Mind as the explanation. How can we be expected to pay attention to your alleged facts until you come to some agreement in the interpretation of them?" If such a demand had been enforced by the thinking world upon other sciences, there would be little science today. Look at the past history of every science and see the record of conflicts of opinion, and the skeletons of perished theories which line the road.

Does chemsitry still explain combustion on the theory of phlogiston? Would medical men today bleed George Washington for pneumonia? Psychical research is almost the youngest branch of scientific exploration, and of course there are differing theories. This is the very sign that it is alive and that opposing schools agree on a large basis of facts, although not yet on all classes of alleged facts.

It is not a century since psychology was nothing more than a theoretical discussion of the three formal categories of the " soul," intellect, sensibility and will. It is not fifty years since William James said that he did not see that it had any practical use. It has enormously developed, various methods hitherto undreamed of are applied to its investigation, and it is of use in various ways for various practical ends. But is there unity of theory; do all psychologists agree in interpretation? I need only to mention the psychology of James, or of McDougall on the one side and of that obstreperous young scoffer Behaviorism on the other, or Freudism—and anti-Freudism. Wundt at one period held that psychology is merely a branch of physiology, and later reversed his position, lamenting the wild oats of his youth, but he remained a pioneer of psychological method.

No general test should be applied to psychical research, in order to ascertain its validity, which would not be regarded as equally significant if applied to other branches of science.

17. But was not Podmore a keen and indefatigable psychical researcher, and did he not combat the spiritistic theory? Only pausing to remark that there is much in psychical research besides spiritism, I answer that he did, but did so by urging, with extreme ingenuity and multiplied minor assumptions, the claims of telepathy. That is, he combated one theory of supernormal character by another. It must not be forgotten that telepathy, if it exists, is a supernormal fact, that is, it is not within the present " logic " of the science most commonly accepted,—it means that thought passes from one person to another by some process unknown and other than by the recognized channels of the senses. The opponent of the authenticated facts of mediumship is between the devil and the deep sea, either he must resort to telepathy, usually abhorrent because fatal to his materialistic philosophy, or he must pretend that the evidence does not exist, and, covering his eyes, murmur for the safety of his hypothetical soul formulas and shibboleths about the " logic " and the " laws " of science, " animistic tendencies " and the " will to believe." Dr. George M. Beard was frank when he wrote that to face the evidence appeared so deadly that " for logical, well-trained, truth-loving minds, the only security

IS PSYCHICAL RESEARCH WORTH WHILE?

against spiritism is hiding or running away."[4] Incredible as it may seem, these are the actual words printed by an opponent of psychical research.

18. Do psychical researchers all agree that any types of phenomena are supernormal? If I may be allowed to define a psychical researcher as a person of evident intelligence and cultivation, whose writings reveal acquaintance with and employment of critical method, and who has had much experience in this field, and who is interested in the fixation of facts and not in propaganda, religious or other, I answer in the affirmative, and will name four types upon which I think that there is practically unanimous agreement, nor is the list necessarily exhaustive.

(1) Telepathy is generally agreed to by psychical researchers, on the basis of numerous experimental series, and on spontaneous cases of extraordinary character. One instance of the latter class is the fact that the naturalist John Muir, not having seen his friend Professor Butler for years, nor having heard from him for a month, in a letter which contained no hint that he thought of going to California, was impressed, while high up on a plateau of the Yosemite Valley, by the feeling that he must go down and find his friend, descended thousands of feet and found Butler lost and about to be benighted among the rocks. The facts were testified to by both gentlemen. Several incidents almost as remarkable occurred in my relations with a single person.

(2) Veridical (truth-telling) apparitions. The English Society gathered a large list of cases, from which it eliminated all but the most thoroughly authenticated, then applied the mathematical method with the result that some of the most critical minds in England were convinced that a relation, other than chance, exists between the seeing of such apparitions and the deaths of the persons whom they represent. I think there is practical agreement on this.

(3) Mediumistic deliverances. There is agreement that experiments by stranger sitters under scientific management, with more precautions than opponents have ever thought to suggest, and with absolutely complete records of every word by any one in the room, have produced series of facts pertinent to sitters, and provably unknown to the medium, far, sometimes millions of times, beyond the probabilities of chance. Such instances can be exhibited convincingly only in this totality, but I may mention one detached incident. . . .

---

[4] *North American Review*, July, 1879.

[The illustrative example summarized in the lecture is omitted here, because found elsewhere in this book.]

(4) Psychometry. This is the unfortunate name of the phenomenon, confined to an exceedingly small number of persons, of being able to recite, during contact with a strange object, a series of facts true of a person connected with the object, facts not inferrible from the object itself. I discovered one remarkable psychic of this kind, a person in private life who had never been so experimented upon. The results were immediate and astounding, case after case, and they have been reported in detail, without other response than a few oracular remarks about "the logic of science," "impossibility" and my "will to believe." She got impressive results in about half a dozen tests made before she joined a church which stopped experimentation, and the evidential weight of one of the successes was so enormous that a hundred following failures mathematically would have affected its cogency exceedingly little. . . . [Again the illustrative summary of an experiment is omitted because printed elsewhere in this book.]

I have not time to mention other agreements among psychical researchers, or to go to the other end of the spectrum and detail the alleged phenomena, such as "spirit slate-writing," which nearly all psychical researchers as I have defined them regard as always spurious, and "spirit photographs," which all cautious investigators regard as dubious.

In general I may say that the greater certainty and unanimity has been attained in the field of mental than that of physical phenomena, unless certain supernormal sounds, especially raps, some of which at least appear to be physically initiated. In other words, the simpler and more open the conditions, the more it is a matter of experienced common-sense and logic, the more certitude. Some apparently very cautious observers have been convinced of movements of objects without contact, but probably no one can be quite convinced short of opportunities for personal observation. Many scientific men on the continent of Europe, some of whom had no previous predilections in favor of such things, have been convinced of ectoplasm. I have never seen any exhibition of it on this side of the water, or heard any careful description, which was in the least convincing to me, nor did Drs. Hodgson and Hyslop ever discover any impressive samples. . . .[5]

---

[5] Nor were my subsequent experiments with three of the most noted physical mediums in Europe any more convincing. (See *Bulletin* VII of the B. S. P. R.) But they have their strenuous defenders still, to whom I listen with respect, regretting that my "vibrations" are so inhibitive as is alleged.

IS PSYCHICAL RESEARCH WORTH WHILE?

19. Amateur acceptance and non-acceptance in this field is often delightfully naïve. There is only one thing that we can predict in the case of the "hard-headed business man," and that is that he will never read through one of our elaborate reports, nor listen to reason on the subject. What impresses students will probably make no dent on him, but he may say, "Here was something that was certainly genuine," and relate the wonders of a platform-code-"telepathist," or of a "billet-switching" conjuror. And I, who was a clergyman, may be permitted to say that what clergymen will do only God can predict, for some of them, after remaining prudent in the face of masses of scientific evidence, fall easy victims to ingenious fakery protected by darkness. One of the most learned clergymen that Boston ever boasted, who during successive seasons discussed science in his Monday lectures, in an hour of weakness was beguiled by a slate-writing conjuror, and wrote a statement witnessing to the passage of matter through matter.

On the other hand, acceptance of the usual "explanation" exhibited in public is about equally naïve. I have seen a movie picture demonstrate the methods of fraudulent mediums, which amused me more than a comedy, for, while there are fraudulent mediums enough, probably none of them ever used the means shown since the world began. I have seen at least two magicians demonstrate how things are done, and both of them were mainly faking the fakers. . . .

20. Finally it is well to mention some of the by-products of psychical research, as they should be taken into account in the effort to ascertain if it is worth while. Here I can do no better than to summarize and in part quote Mr. H. Addington Bruce [*Unpopular Review*, Oct.-Dec., 1914]: "It is safe to say that no scientific movement ever set on foot has, in the same length of time, contributed so much toward the advancement of knowledge as psychical research." Granting great credit to Wundt and his disciples for the marvelous development of psychology after 1885, very largely the stimulus was derived from "those 'dabblers in the occult,' who, like Sidgwick, Myers and Gurney in England, and Janet and Richet in France, thought it not beneath their dignity to study table-tipping, alleged telepathy, and the disputed phenomena of the hypnotic trance. To them, incontrovertibly, we owe the foundation-laying of abnormal psychology, with its manifold implications." Hypnotism had not ceased to be an "occult" subject when the psychical researchers Janet and Gurney did much to lay the foundations of its use both for the study of the human mind and for therapy.

Dr. Morton Prince, and probably others who have become prominent in mental therapeutics, was directly inspired to specialize therein by the researches of Edmund Gurney, psychical researcher. And there have been fresh springs; for example, the Emmanuel method of mental therapeutics which has had a large and, when its principles have been adhered to, salutary influence, originated with Dr. Elwood Worcester, a psychical researcher.

Psychical researchers such as Janet, Gurney and Myers, Hyslop and others since have done much to explore and enlarge the boundaries of the subconscious mind. Myers is the man who invented the term " subliminal."

Psychical researchers contributed the oft-quoted Ansil Bourne Case of dual personality, the Brewin Case, the Doris Case of Multiple Personality, and the Heinrich Meyer Case to the literature of abnormal psychology.

And psychical researchers have accomplished these things and more because, from Myers to William James and from James to Hyslop and the present, they disdained not to handle what others thrust aside with contempt, because, like anatomists, they searched down to the entrails of human experience, and because, after they had observed and tested and verified and studied, with unflinching honesty they declared the facts which they had found.

II. THE ENCHANTED BOUNDARY

And so they set forth toward the region which they had vowed to conquer, a band of gallant knights, all bedight in massy armor and bravely bearing lances and swords, all seated on steeds which were both swift and sure. But as soon as the first had crossed the border of that region his weapons became like rotten wood, the joints of his armor began to gape widely, and his proud steed altered to a sorry jade, which stumbled at every pebble in the way. And thus fared it with every knight as he crossed, for lo, it was an enchanted boundary.

Thus begins a tale which still continues. For the knightly band is made up of sundry learned and professional men, the region which they set forth to harry is that of psychical research, and verily, it seems to have an enchanted boundary, for it happens to them when they cross it even as has been said. In other fields they are prudently silent until they have acquired special knowledge, but they venture into this with none. Elsewhere they test their facts before they declare them, but here they pick up and employ random statements without discretion. Elsewhere they use a fair semblance of logic, but here their logic becomes wondrous weird. Elsewhere they generally succeed in preserving the standard scientific stolidity, but here they frequently manifest and confess a submission to emotions ill befitting those who sprang from the head of Brahm. Elsewhere they observe the knightly etiquette of the lists, but in this field think it no shame to decline the fair encounter, and, from the safe shelter of the barrier, to jeer about the presumptive quality of their opponents' brains.

I am not here defending anything within the debatable region, I am only pointing in wonder to the effects of the enchanted boundary upon those who cross it with deadly intent. Be it remembered that all, or nearly all of these are as hostile to telepathy as to the theory of spirit communication. With a full sense of responsibility, I assert in regard to these that:

1. None have squarely faced and fairly discussed the real evidence. They either avoid the great evidential cases altogether, or they make a travesty of them, usually picking out incidents for dissection which no psychical researcher would think of putting forward as proof, and

passing by or maltreating those which the psychical researcher does emphasize as significant of some species of supernormal acquisition of information.

2. Most of them are frequently guilty of absurd blunders in matters of fact which are comparatively easy of reference.

3. Some of them seem unable to quote correctly.

4. Many of them give evidence of lacking acquaintance with the literature of psychical research (other than by special cramming) by queer spelling of proper names familiar to students.

5. They fall into curious solecisms of logic such as would expose them to universal laughter in any other field.

6. Generally, they exhibit impatience, "loathing," and other emotional aberrations such as ill befit those who sit as voluntary judges.

7. Especially, they are inclined to the logical fallacy of entrenching themselves behind the barrier of supposed scientific maxims which beg the very questions of fact in dispute.

8. Particularly of late, they manifest a tendency to exchange argument for technical billingsgate, applying to their opponents expressions of which the shorter and plainer equivalents are " cranks " and " simpletons."

FARADAY, TYNDALL AND HUXLEY

MICHAEL FARADAY was a great chemist, but when he consented to investigate the claims of D. D. Home, it was on conditions of which one was as follows:[1]

" If the effects are miracles, or the work of spirits, does he [Home] admit the utterly contemptible character, both of them and their results, up to the present time, in respect either of yielding information or instruction, or supplying any force or action of the least value to mankind? "

Suppose that the American Geographical Society had reluctantly consented to examine Peary's claim that he had discovered the North Pole, on conditions parallel with those which Faraday demanded in advance from Home:[2] " Will Admiral Peary ' admit the utterly contemptible character ' of his reputed discovery, in the way of supplying anything ' of the least value to mankind '? " Do such terms represent the spirit and the logic which science applies to the determination of facts?

---

[1] *Modern Spiritualism*, by Frank Podmore, II, 145.　[2] *Ib.*, II, 145.

Podmore, who was very suspicious of Home, nevertheless justly comments:[3]

"From the whole tone of the letter it is clear that Faraday had made up his mind that the phenomena were delusive or fraudulent, and Home an impostor, and that he had no desire to conceal his opinion. Whether Faraday's conclusions were justified or not, no philosopher was justified in undertaking an inquiry of which he had so ostentatiously prejudged the issue; nor could the subject of the proposed inquiry have been fairly blamed for declining a trial in which the judge had already pronounced sentence. As a matter of fact, it appears that the proposal was declined by Robert Bell, the intermediary in the matter, without even consulting Home.

"The letter was of course altogether unworthy of Faraday's high character and scientific eminence, and was no doubt the outcome of a moment of transient irritation.[4] The position taken was quite indefensible. It would have been reasonable for Faraday to plead that his time was too much occupied with his proper work to undertake a task of this kind; or that he was not qualified for an investigation which confessedly led or might lead beyond the limits of the physical sciences. But to enter upon a judicial inquiry by treating the subject-matter as a *chose jugée* was surely a parody of scientific methods. Faraday either had grounds sufficient for condemning Home, or he had not. In the former case an inquiry was superfluous, and could only be mischievous; in the latter, Home and his manifestations were alike entitled to strictly neutral treatment."

JOHN TYNDALL was a great physicist, but he also lost his scientific pose when once he put his foot beyond the enchanted boundary. For when he gave out to the world [5] the fact that Faraday had been invited to examine the manifestations of Home, he said that the arrangement had fallen through because the conditions made by Faraday were not accepted. That was true but misleading, since the reader would suppose that Faraday had made fair conditions and that Home had backed out. But supposing that Home had phenomena which he believed of utmost importance,—how could he be expected to admit, as a preliminary to the examination of his "effects," that they were "utterly contemptible," both in themselves and in any of their implications for mankind? That would be to admit prior to examination that there

---

[3] *Ib.*, II, 145-6.
[4] This was the view taken at the time by Mr. F. T. Palgrave (*Pall Mall Gazette*, May 16) and the editor (*Pall Mall Gazette*, May 22, 1868).
[5] *Pall Mall Gazette*, May 5, 1868.

was nothing worth examination. Suppose that Fulton, before his steamboat was built, or his predecessor, had been told by one of the scientific men of his day: "Yes, I will examine your sketches and ideas, if you will first admit that they are utterly contemptible and can never be of use to mankind." Would Fulton have ever conceded to such a stipulation? Even the worst knave and the most arrant cheat, if he is to be tried at all, deserves a fair trial.

Later [6] Tyndall attempted to justify Faraday's demand, although surely in any other field of research he would have seen how insolent it was, and declared that he was willing to investigate "in the same spirit."

So deadly is the blinding power of prejudice, Tyndall not only justified Faraday's demand that a creed should be acknowledged as a condition prior to examining facts, but his own acts and remarks in connection with the only psychic experiment he ever witnessed were so at variance with the scientific procedure which characterized him in his own proper field that even so resolute a critic of the spiritistic hypothesis as Podmore is obliged to condemn them.[7]

THOMAS H. HUXLEY was a great scientist, and, like Faraday and Tyndall, disposed to reach decisions by calm examination of facts. But when he was invited by the Committee of the London Dialectical Society to assist in its investigations,[8] he could make such reply as this:[9]

"Sir,—I regret that I am unable to accept the invitation of the Council of the Dialectical Society to coöperate with a Committee for the investigation of 'Spiritualism'; and for two reasons. In the first place, I have no time for such an inquiry, which would involve much trouble and (unless it were unlike all inquiries of that kind I have known) much annoyance. In the second place, I take no interest in the subject. The only case of 'Spiritualism' I have had the opportunity of examining into for myself, was as gross an imposture as ever came under my notice. But supposing the phenomena to be genuine—they do not interest me. If anybody would endow me with the faculty

---

[6] In *Pall Mall Gazette*, May 18, 1868. See *Modern Spiritualism*, II, 145-6.
[7] *Ib.*, II, 147.
[8] One of those invited was the philosopher George Henry Lewes, and in his letter of declination he said (Report, 230): "When any man says that phenomena are produced by *no* known physical laws, he declares that he knows the laws by which they are produced." Surely, Mr. Lewes's logic was affected by the enchantment. If a scientist, traveling in the heart of Africa, finds tracks which he says are produced by no known animal, does he thereby declare that he knows the animal by which they were produced?
[9] *Report*, edition of 1871, 229-30.

of listening to the chatter of old women and curates in the nearest cathedral town, I should decline the privilege, having better things to do.

"And if the folk in the spiritual world do not talk more wisely and sensibly than their friends report them to do, I put them in the same category.

"The only good that I can see in a demonstration of the truth of 'Spiritualism' is to furnish an additional argument against suicide. Better live a crossing-sweeper than die and be made to talk twaddle by a 'medium' hired at a guinea a séance."

A scientist objects to "trouble and annoyance"! Besides, he had examined just one case, and that was an imposture! So a man might report when told that off a certain shore rock-cod were plenty: "But I put my line in once, and caught a sculpin." Not even the most bigoted Spiritualist had ever denied that there were impostors. And did the scientist mean to say that if a machine were invented that should enable him to hear conversations in the nearest cathedral town, and that were no nearer, say, than twenty miles, he would take no interest, in case what he heard was the chatter of old women and curates? And what contempt Huxley or Darwin would have felt for the man so under the spell of emotional repulsion against the mere thought that he could be biologically related to apes as to exclaim, "The only good I can see in the demonstration of such a claim is to furnish an additional argument for suicide, in order to get beyond the sight of such unpleasant relatives." If they had patience to answer such a piece of inconsequence at all, would they not have remarked, in substance, that facts are neither determined nor abolished by one's emotions in relation to them?

T. B. MACAULAY

Referring to his *History of England*, the *Encyclopædia Britannica* says that Macaulay "spared no pains to ascertain the facts." And some biographer has told of the miles he would travel and the pains he would take to be sure he committed no error of fact. But when he came to write about that man who, perhaps more than any other Englishman of the eighteenth century, approached the standard of a psychical researcher of our day, the magic of the boundary paralyzed his zeal for exactitude, and with the book which might have taught him better, Boswell's *Life of Samuel Johnson*, before his eyes, he could write such statements as these:

"Johnson, incredulous on all other points, was a ready believer in miracles and apparitions. He would not believe in Ossian, but he believed in the second sight. He would not believe in the earthquake of Lisbon, but he believed in the Cock Lane Ghost.[10]

"He once said, half jestingly we suppose, that for six months he refused to credit the earthquake of Lisbon, and that he still believed the extent of the calamity to be greatly exaggerated. Yet he related with a grave face how old Mr. Cave, of St. John's Gate, saw a ghost, and how this ghost was something of a shadowy being. He went himself on a ghost hunt to Cock Lane, and was angry with John Wesley for not following up another scent of the same kind with proper spirit and perseverance. He rejects the Celtic genealogies and poems without the least hesitation; yet he declares himself willing to believe the stories of the second-sight." [11]

But Boswell had made it emphatically plain that Johnson did not believe in the Cock Lane Ghost, but, on the other hand, was one of the group which discovered the imposture, and the very man who sent to the press its first exposure. He says:[12]

"Churchill, in his poem entitled 'The Ghost,' availed himself of the absurd credulity imputed to Johnson, and drew a caricature of him under the name of 'Pomposo,' representing him as one of the believers of the story of a Ghost in Cock Lane, which, in the year 1762, had gained very general credit in London. Many of my readers, I am convinced, are to this hour under the impression that Johnson was thus foolishly deceived. It will therefore surprise them a good deal when they are informed that Johnson was one of those by whom the imposture was detected. The story became so popular that he thought it should be investigated, and in this research he was assisted by the Rev. Mr. Douglas, now Bishop of Salisbury, the great detector of impostures, who informs me that after the gentlemen who went and examined into the evidence were satisfied of its falsity, Johnson wrote in their presence an account of it which was published in the newspapers and *Gentleman's Magazine*, and undeceived the world."

There is no evidence that Johnson *believed* in second-sight, as affirmed in the first quotation from Macaulay. The version in the second quotation that Johnson was *willing* to believe, is correct. But what did Johnson mean when he said that he was willing to believe? That he cherished a will to believe? That he was even anxious to believe? No, simply that he was open-minded to evidence and was

---

[10] Essay on Ranke's *History of the Popes*.
[11] Essay on Boswell's *Life of Johnson*.
[12] *Life of Johnson*, II, 72-73. Edited by Augustine Birrell, Philadelphia, 1901.

courageous enough to say so. As a matter of fact, he never reached the point of conviction. He thus sums up his examination of "second sight":

"There are against it the seeming analogy of things confusedly seen and little understood, and for it the indistinct cry of natural persuasion, which may be perhaps resolved at last into prejudice [in the sense of *prepossession*] and tradition. I never could advance my curiosity to conviction, and came away at last only willing to believe." [13]

And Boswell says:[14]

"The real fact then is that Johnson had a very philosophical mind, and such a rational respect for testimony, as to make him submit his understanding to what was authentically proved, though he could not comprehend why it was so. Being thus disposed, he was willing to inquire into the truth of any relation of supernatural agency, a general belief of which has prevailed in all nations and ages. But so far was he from being the dupe of implicit faith, that he examined the matter with a jealous attention, and no man was more ready to refute its falsehood when he had discovered it."

There is no evidence for Macaulay's allegation that Johnson "was a ready believer in miracles and apparitions," but, on the contrary, all indications which we discover either in his own works or in Boswell's *Life*, one of the most unsparingly candid biographies ever composed, are that he was not easy to convince of "miracles and apparitions." It should be remembered that much which he uttered on such subjects was drawn from him by the queries of Boswell, who was so eager to test his mental reactions that he once asked the philosopher what he would do if he found himself shut up in a tower alone with a new-born baby. Thus we know that if Johnson had seemed to see and hear an apparition, this would not by itself have convinced him of its objective reality.

"We talked of belief in ghosts. He said, 'Sir, I make a distinction between what a man can experience by the mere strength of his imagination, and what imagination cannot possibly produce. Thus, suppose I should think that I saw a form, and heard a voice cry, "Johnson, you are a very wicked fellow, and unless you repent you will certainly be punished," my own unworthiness is so deeply im-

---

[13] *Works of Samuel Johnson*, 1825, IX, 107.   [14] *Life of Johnson*, II, 72-73.

pressed upon my mind that I might imagine I thus saw and heard, and therefore I should not believe that an external communication had been made to me. But if a form should appear, and a voice should tell me that a particular man had died at a particular place and a particular hour, a fact which I had no apprehension of, nor any means of knowing, and the fact, with all its circumstances, should afterwards be unquestionably proved, I should in that case be persuaded that I had supernatural intelligence imparted to me.'"[15]

Again we are told that he said "we could have no certainty of the truth of supernatural appearances unless something was told us which we could not know by ordinary means, or something done which could not be done by supernatural power."[16] He required proof, as does a hard-headed psychic researcher today, only the latter would say *supernormal* rather than "supernatural."

Boswell asked him if there was not a story about the ghost of Parson Ford. He replied that there was; "according to the story," a waiter saw it twice while going down cellar, not knowing that Ford was dead, and came down with a fever; that after he had recovered he said he had delivered a message from the spirit to some women which had a startling effect upon them; that "Dr. Pellet, who was not a credulous man," investigated the story and was convinced, and that Mrs. Johnson made inquiries and was also convinced. Did he say that he himself was convinced? Far from it; this is his own reaction: "To be sure the man had a fever, and this vision may have been the beginning of it. But if the message to the women and their behavior upon it were true as related, there was something supernatural. *That rests upon his word*, and there remains."[17]

What was there in relating the story of the ghost at St. John's Gate to convict Johnson of credulity? He did not say, as one might suppose from Macaulay's language, that Mr. Cave *did* see a "ghost," but that Mr. Cave said he did, and that Mr. Cave was an honest and sensible man.[18] Mr. Podmore later told many stories of people who had seen "ghosts,"[19] yet he did not believe in their objective reality. It was not Johnson who said that the ghost was "something of a shadowy being," but Cave, and Johnson simply responded to Boswell's desire to know how Cave described "the appearance." Macaulay's "yet he related with a grave face" is sheer imagination. He was born sixteen years after Johnson's death, knew nothing about the incident except what he read in Boswell's *Life*, and had no right to pin

---

[15] *Ib.*, II, 72. [16] *Ib.*, III, 8. [17] *Ib.*, V, 52-3. [18] *Ib.*, III, 36. [19] *New View of Ghosts*

THE ENCHANTED BOUNDARY

any particular expression upon Johnson's countenance to suit his own prejudices. It is just as likely that Johnson's face wore a quizzical smile. Or he may have answered Boswell quite casually—not gravely —between sips of his eternal tea.

But we are told that he "was angry with John Wesley for not following up another scent of the same kind [as the Cock Lane Ghost] with proper spirit and perseverance." Certainly one's impression from these words would be that it was Johnson who believed in this case, and probably Wesley who did not. And that in Boswell's *Life* there could be found evidence that Johnson became enraged with Wesley about it. What does Boswell really say? Johnson had been talking about Wesley, and Boswell inquired: " Pray, sir, what has he made of the story of the ghost? "

" Why, sir, he believes it, but not on sufficient authority. He did not take time enough to examine the girl. It was at Newcastle, where the ghost was said to have appeared to a young woman several times, mentioning something about the right to an old house, advising application to be made to an attorney, which was done; and, at the same time, saying the attorney would do nothing, which proved to be the fact. ' This (says John) is a proof that a ghost knows our thoughts.'

" Now (laughing) it is not necessary to know our thoughts to tell that an attorney will sometimes do nothing. Charles Wesley, who is a more stationary man, does not believe the story. I am sorry that John did not take more pains to inquire into the evidence for it.

" Miss Seward (with an incredulous smile) : ' What, sir! about a ghost.' Johnson (with solemn vehemence) : ' Yes, madam; this is a question which, after five thousand years, is yet undecided; a question, whether in theology or philosophy, one of the most important that can come before the human understanding.' " [20]

First we note the difference between being " sorry " and being " angry." Next we observe that, while he is interested in John Wesley's story, he cannot accept it, for—

1. The proof is insufficient; Wesley did not take time to examine the girl who told it.

2. The supposed prediction may easily have been a mere guess with a large chance of fulfilment.

3. Charles Wesley, who is more inclined than John to be conservative, disbelieves the story.

---

[20] *Life*, IV, 299-300.

Yet he regrets that John Wesley did not examine the evidence better. It would have been worth while. For—

(a) The question is undecided after [at least] 5,000 years.

(b) It is one of the most important, whether of theology or philosophy, which can come before the human understanding.

All this is in perfect harmony with the principles and prevailing practice of our modern psychical researchers, though of course the majority of *savants* still think it not at all important to decide the question whether there are in the experiences, still repeating themselves after the testimony of ages, any grains of supernormal truth, since they have already, to their own satisfaction, answered the question by·fiat.

In the first passage quoted from Macaulay it is affirmed without qualification that Johnson " would not believe in the earthquake of Lisbon." In the second it is acknowledged that Johnson said this " half jestingly, we may suppose." Then why bring up the remark, if it was made half in jest? And without examination of the first reports in the press, we cannot know that they were not exaggerated, terrible as the disaster actually was. There was hardly more justice in bringing forward the remark than there would be in assuming that Johnson was serious in his standing pretense to a dislike of Scotland and Scots. He was always joking about them, but this was only a pose. He had a sense of humor so unruly that it intruded even into his *Dictionary*. Witness his definition of *oatmeal:* "A grain used in England as food for horses, in Scotland for men," and of *lexicographer:* "A harmless drudge." But it is said that the assistants he chose to help him compile the *Dictionary* were mostly Scots, and his familiar friend and accepted chronicler " could not help " being born in Scotland.[21]

It is now plain that the historian's prejudices unfitted him to deal justly with psychic research, so far as that subject, not yet entitled, developed itself in writings and utterances of Samuel Johnson.

We may fitly finish this section with a few paragraphs from this mighty thinker, which will still further show how falsely Macaulay pictured him. They were not originally directed to the discussion of the questions embraced in what is now known as psychical research, but are peculiarly applicable to these discussions. It would be well if all parties to the great debate laid them to heart.

---

[21] But does coupling Johnson's disbelief in the Ossianic myth with his " half jesting " skepticism in regard to the actual earthquake of Lisbon, indicate that Macaulay himself *did* believe in MacPherson's account of the antiquity of his poem?

The first bids us remember that the negative side of a question can always manufacture arguments against evidence, however overwhelming.

"It is always easy to be on the negative side. If a man were now to deny that there is salt upon the table, you could not reduce him to an absurdity. Come, let us try this a little further. I deny that Canada is taken, and I can support my denial by pretty good arguments. The French are a much more numerous people than we; and it is not likely that they would allow us to take it. 'But the ministry have assured us, in all the formality of the Gazette, that it is taken.' Very true. But the ministry have put us to an enormous expense by the war in America, and it is their interest to persuade us that we have got something for our money. 'But the fact is confirmed by thousands of men who were at the taking of it.' Ay, but these men have still more interest in deceiving us. They don't want that we should think the French have beaten them, but that they have beat the French. Now suppose you should go over and find that it is really taken, that would only satisfy yourself; for when you come home we will not believe you. We will say you have been bribed. Yet, sir, notwithstanding all these plausible objections, we have no doubt that Canada is really ours. Such is the weight of common testimony." [22]

Objections, he goes on to say, may be raised against anything, even each of opposites, one of which must certainly be true.

"The human mind is so limited that it cannot take in all the parts of a subject, so that there may be objections raised against anything. There are objections against a *plenum* and objections against a *vacuum;* yet one of them must certainly be true."

The professional critic and objector can argue against the most firmly established positions, but by constantly seeking to evade the force of evidence, reason is violated and its machinery gradually thrown out of gear.

"I never spoke but to contradict. . . . I sometimes exalted vegetables to sense, and sometimes degraded animals to mechanisms. . . . Having demonstrated the folly of erecting edifices like the Pyramid of Egypt, I frequently hinted my suspicion that the world had been long deceived, and that they were to be found only in the narratives of travelers. . . .

---

[22] *Life,* II, 92-93.

"Having now violated my reason and accustomed myself to inquire, not after proofs, but objections till my ideas were confused, my judgment embarrassed and my intellect distorted. . . .

"Engaging reason against its own determinations. . . . Argumental delirium." [23]

The resolute doctrinaire, who opposes experiments which refute him, will ingeniously invent all sorts of subterfuges to becloud the clearest demonstration and the will to contend becomes at length befuddlement and sincere infatuation.

"I have heard of one that, having advanced some erroneous doctrines in philosophy, refused to see the experiments by which they were confuted, and the observations of every day will give new proofs with how much industry subterfuges and evasions are sought to decline the pressure of resistless arguments, how often the state of the question is altered, how often the antagonist is wilfully misrepresented and in how much perplexity the clearest positions are involved by those whom they happen to oppose. . . .

"There is yet another danger in this practice: men who cannot deceive others are very often successful in deceiving themselves: they weave their sophistry till their own reason is entangled and repeat their positions till they are credited by themselves; by often contending they grow sincere in the cause and by long wishing for demonstrative arguments they at last bring themselves to fancy that they have found them." [24]

PROFESSOR SIMON NEWCOMB

Professor Simon Newcomb, head of the department of Astronomy in Johns Hopkins' University, director of the United States Naval Observatory, editor of the *American Journal of Mathematics*, etc., published an article in *Nineteenth Century* for January, 1909, in the course of which he said:

"The volumes of *Phantasms of the Living* might be continued annually without end, could all the cases be discovered. The few hundred cases published are actually fewer than what we should expect as the result of known conditions. There is therefore no proof of telepathy in any of the wonders narrated in these volumes, and in the publications of the Psychical Society."

---

[23] *Rambler*, Feb. 12, 1751, Essay on the "Prejudices and Caprices of Criticism."
[24] *Ib.*, Essay of July 3, 1750. For a fuller discussion see my article entitled "Samuel Johnson as a Psychic Researcher," *Journal* A. S. P. R., XI, 701-19.

In the course of his extended comments on this article, Dr. J. H. Hyslop said:[25]

" In the usual courts of science a man is supposed to stick to his last, and would not venture to express an opinion outside his special department. But it seems that any man is qualified to speak on psychic research, though it is much more complicated than normal psychology, on which Professor Newcomb would not think of speaking."

Farther on, Dr. Hyslop said:[26]

" The kind of objections presented to the alleged evidence are the commonplaces of the subject, and Professor Newcomb does not tell the reader that he perhaps owes his whole knowledge of them to the very men whose conclusions he criticizes and rejects. He speaks as if he were instructing mere boys on the precautions necessary against illusion in judging these phenomena. Of course, this is all that a man can do who intends to repudiate telepathy. To treat it, seriously, as a probable truth, would be to minimize the usual limitations of the evidence, and opposition would have nothing to rest upon. We all know, at this period, what objections lurk in the possibilities of chance coincidence, guessing, illusion, hallucination, etc. But if we cannot at least mention that the authors of the work quoted had tested chance coincidence on the most liberal assumptions, and rejected it in terms that have never been disputed by the calculus of probabilities we ought not to discuss the problem at all. Professor Newcomb only indulges in the most palpable generalities in this matter, and one would imagine that no one had ever thought of the specific questions that had to be investigated in the case. But the *Phantasms of the Living* exhausted the limitations of the evidence, and the method and conclusion were repeated in the *Census of Hallucinations*,[27] whose conclusion was that the apparitions of the dying, even after eliminating the majority of cases collected, and limiting the calculation to only 52 cases out of 350, were not due to chance, and that the calculus of probabilities were such that this view was proved. Professor Newcomb should have met this by much more definite proof than the general and unsupported assertion that *a priori* expectation—as if science could tolerate the *a priori*—would favor a much larger number."

Professor Newcomb was the first President of the first American

---

[25] *Journal* A. S. P. R., III, 256. [26] *Ib.*, 270-71. [27] *Proceedings* S. P. R., Vol. X.

Society for Psychical Research, founded in 1885. In order better to appreciate the spirit in which he occupied the chair of an organization whose expressed purposes were the same as those of the Society for Psychical Research in England, established three years earlier, let us read an extract from the inaugural address of Prof. Henry Sidgwick, the first President of the English Society.

" We are all agreed that the present state of things is a scandal to the enlightened age in which we live. That the dispute as to the reality of these marvelous phenomena,—of which it is quite impossible to exaggerate the scientific importance, if only a tenth part of what has been alleged by generally credible witnesses could be shown to be true, —I say it is a scandal that the dispute as to the reality of these phenomena should still be going on, that so many competent witnesses should have declared their belief in them, that so many others should be profoundly interested in having the question determined, and yet that the educated world, as a body, should still be simply in the attitude of incredulity.

" Now the primary aim of our Society, the thing which we all unite to promote, whether as believers or non-believers, is to make a sustained and systematic attempt to remove this scandal in one way or another. Some of those whom I address feel, no doubt, that this attempt can only lead to the proof of most of the alleged phenomena; some, again, think it probable that most, if not all, will be disproved; but regarded as a Society, we are quite unpledged, and as individuals, we are all agreed that any particular investigation that we may make should be carried on with a single-minded desire to ascertain the facts, and without any foregone conclusion as to their nature."

The address of President Newcomb [28] was not characterized by this fair and open-minded spirit. While he formally agreed that it might be well to investigate claims of psychic phenomena, he argues throughout against the likelihood that any of them will prove valid. He paid attention especially to claims of thought-transference and dealt with them in a disparaging fashion, comparing attempts to ascertain whether they are ever valid to attempts to discover whether there is in existence gold of a different density than that of the gold with which science is acquainted. He hinted that the two inquiries are equally foolish, though some useful by-products might accrue from the first-named.

Referring to alleged incidents of persons experiencing the " visual

---

[28] *Proceedings* A. S. P. R., July, 1886.

image of some absent friend or relative in a state of suffering, or the voice of a speaker calling aloud," he continues:

"Such is the order of events as commonly described; but, if described as they actually come to knowledge, they would appear in a different form. The experience of the observer would be: 'I heard that my friend was dead or that he had met with an accident and cried aloud. After inquiring when the death or accident occurred, I remembered that about that time I heard this very exclamation or saw his image before my sight.'"

Very well, if it was settled that such visual or auditory experiences, dreams, etc., are never recorded or related before the coincidental event is learned, then it would be equally foolish to spend pains upon such claims. Professor Newcomb does not expressly say this, but no other conclusion can follow.

He proceeds to allege that he himself frequently was unable to tell whether some memory was of a dream or of an actual occurrence. Of course the inference from this autobiographic testimony was that because he was frequently puzzled to distinguish past real occurrences from dreams, everyone else must have the same difficulty, and because he never directly recorded or related a dream which for some reason stood out as exception, so as to fix its verity, no one else ever does so.

The last and cryptic sentence is:

"I even venture to say that, if thought-transference is real, we shall establish the reality more speedily by leaving it out of consideration, and collecting facts for study, than by directing our attention directly to it."

He did not explain how we are to collect facts on telepathy and study them without "taking them into consideration."

Professor Newcomb was a mathematical expert, yet when he entered the field of psychical research to discuss what he knew little about, he was capable of supposing that there is one chance in a million of drawing from a bag containing one million grains of corn, the one black grain which it contains. Abstract mathematics is one thing, however, and additional considerations have to be taken into account in applied mathematics. Dr. J. H. Hyslop showed [29] that, to contain that number of grains, a bag would have to be of more than

---

[29] *Journal* A. S. P. R., III, 272-76.

three bushels capacity, and if the black grain were at the bottom one would have no chance whatever of drawing it, since his arm would not reach so far; whereas, if it happened to be on top, the chance would be much greater than one in a million.

Again, Professor Newcomb said that if the black grain were drawn at the first attempt " we should justly claim that there was some unfairness in the proceedings." The fact is that we would have no right to claim this as a fact, since there would be as much chance (provided all the grains were equally accessible) of drawing the black one at the first trial as at the hundred thousandth or the millionth. It would be indeed very unlikely that it should be drawn at any particular trial, which is precisely what I mean when I say of a mediumistic statement which is correct against the chances of 100,000 to 1, that this is unlikely as the result of chance. But I have never said, and no careful psychical researcher would say, that any one such instance would be such that a ".claim" could be based upon it. Perhaps Professor Newcomb is only unfortunate in his language, for he continues: " If, on a thousand of trials of this kind, the black grain were drawn several times, our suspicion would ripen into a practical certainty." That, substantially, is the situation in many of our psychical cases, and such is the foundation of my practical certainty that (all normal knowledge having been excluded) chance is not the explanation in some of the cases with which I have had to do and which I have mathematically appraised. So many hits in the same group, a part of them against enormous odds, achieve practical certainty. No human being has yet hinted at any possible leak in the network of precautions surrounding the utterances of the *Mother of Doris*.[30] Let us suppose there is none in the corn-drawing experiment, and that every grain were equally accessible, and then compare the cases.

Professor Newcomb says that " several " successes in a thousand trials would amount to practical certainty that the explanation was not chance. Three drawings would be " several," and certainly Professor Newcomb would have admitted that five were sufficient to convince him to that effect. Every drawing of the black grain out of the million in a thousand trials would defeat chance expectation in the ratio of 1,000 to 1. Five successes would defeat chance expectation 1,000,000,000,000,000 to 1. But the sum total of the *Mother of Doris* statements concerning the past, plus one interjected purporting to be from Dr. Hodgson, were, as has been elaborately shown, against

---

[30] See *The Mother of Doris* (*Proceedings* A. S. P. R. for 1923, 8-17) for the precautionary measures, and 184-216 for the mathematical evaluation.

chance expectation in the relation of 4,500,000,000,000,000,000,000,-
000,000,000,000. If, in spite of all the precautions displayed in the
printed report not to overvalue any of the items which entered into
the problem, it be thought—though no one has yet suggested this, in
print or orally—that some may have been overvalued, then divide the
enormous figure by 1,000,000,000,000,000,000, and the result will still
be more than four times what to Professor Newcomb, the mathematician, meant, and very properly meant, " practical certainty."

Without any such unjustified division, the figure in the *Mother of
Doris* case is more than four billion times a billion times larger than
that which sufficed for practical certainty in the case of the corn.

My results in one single experiment, lasting not half an hour and
with every word uttered taken into account, that experiment being
with Mrs. King,[31] were exceeded by chance expectation five quadrillions
to one. As we have seen, a result combining to make one quadrillion
to one was a " practical certainty " to the mathematician and
astronomer.

DR. AMY E. TANNER

Amy E. Tanner, Ph.D., in 1910 published a book entitled *Studies
in Spiritism*.[32] Since she was for three years the " research coadjutor " of Professor G. Stanley Hall, President of Clark University, and
was pronounced by him " an able and indefatigable worker "[33] and
author of an excellent work on child psychology, we would expect to
see in these studies in a new field marks of the scholastic virtues
ascribed to her. But alas! it happened to her exactly as in the parable
with which this article begins. The result was one of the most awful
travesties of analysis and criticism ever seen. Dr. Hyslop reprinted
in the *Journal* of the A. S. P. R.[34] every word which Dr. Tanner wrote
in reference to incidents of his sittings with Mrs. Piper, and confronted them with the facts in the record which she had consulted.
The exhibit is almost terrifying. It appears beyond question that she
persistently avoids the strongest incidents; that she persistently picks
out a few details of the incident which she deigns to notice, in order to
deride them, while silent upon important particulars and avoiding
altogether collective significance, that in many cases she materially
mis-states, or even reverses the facts; that she persistently distorts
the relation of the facts; that she repeatedly misrepresents Dr.

---

[31] See *Proceedings* A. S. P. R., XVIII, 204-18. [32] D. Appleton & Co., 1910.
[33] *Studies in Spiritism*, p. xxxiii. [34] January, 1911.

Hyslop's arguments and opinions; that she repeatedly declares that he regarded a particular incident as evidential when he, by express statement, did not; that she repeatedly declares that he regarded a statement by a "communicator" as correct, when he did not, but the contrary; and that she discounts the conditions of the sittings by sheer flights of imagination, without any basis for so doing in the record she is studying, or even in defiance of what it says. I give one incident as Dr. Tanner reports it, and it is a fair sample. The facts are placed in brackets.

"James McClellan said that his brother John would be there soon, the context indicating plainly that his brother would die soon and join him. It turned out, however, that John had already died, nearly a year before [*False; the record plainly stated that he died more than nine months afterward*] and of course the control proceeds to explain his ambiguous phrases, and Hyslop accepts the explanation [*No such explanation was made and, consequently, none such was accepted*].

"The same control said that the same John had had a sunstroke from which he never fully recovered [*False; he said that John's brother David had had the sunstroke*]. After much labor, Hyslop found that he [*No, not John, but a David*] had been a little overcome by the heat, but had never suffered permanently from it, and yet this statement is regarded as correct." [*Doubly untrue, since Dr. Hyslop stated that it was another David related to John who was affected by heat, and also that according to the children of this David, there had been no permanent effects, though doctors declared that one never fully recovers from even slight sunstroke.*]

The following is all that Dr. Tanner reports of a complicated group of statements in the mediumistic record:

"The father spoke of visits to Hyslop's brother which Hyslop did not remember. But do not most fathers visit their children? Any one could make such a reference without knowing anything whatever about a family."

[*Who would dream from this that the "visit" was correctly related to a previous trip west, that the visit was not to one but to two brothers, that the brothers were correctly named, and that the communicator correctly stated that he went west to live after the visit?*]

Instances of the constructive use of imagination are found in such statements as these: that Dr. Hodgson took no stenographic records, that Hyslop said that in some sittings he himself spoke no word, that "minerals are something practically every child makes a collection of at one time"—all untrue, and the last false as tested by every reader's recollection.

In the *Proceedings* of the S. P. R.[35] Mrs. Sidgwick politely demonstrates Dr. Tanner's perverse analyses, her reckless misstatements and her singular logic, and says that she could "multiply instances of inaccuracy and misrepresentation." One is found in the "attempt to provide a common train of thought in three automatists to account for cross-correspondences on the words 'cup' and 'Diana,' and (in two of them) references to Macbeth." Miss Tanner says that she got a clue "in the fact that Henry Irving played 'Macbeth' and 'The Cup' in London that winter." But the facts were that Irving died a year or more before "that winter," and never acted in the two named plays in the same year.

I myself, for the sheer fun of it, compared many other of Dr. Tanner's summaries of incidents with the original records, and found them almost without exception atrocious to the point of becoming comic. It seemed to me that she was incapable of grasping the salient points in any paragraph more than two inches in length. Dr. Hyslop found in the 27 incidents from his record 148 misstatements, and a host of omissions of important particulars, while she was silent on 38 incidents more significant than any she treated in her fashion.

I have referred above to summaries by Dr. Tanner examined by myself. A single example out of scores will be given. It is to be found on page 119 of *Studies in Spiritism*, and is supposed to represent the facts of an incident told in *Proceedings* S. P. R., Vol. XX, pages 209-10, and as the original narrative comprises but a page and a quarter, this should not have been a difficult task for a doctor of philosophy. Here is the way Dr. Tanner puts it:

"Mrs. Thompson had asked Mrs. Verrall to try for writing on a certain evening between nine and ten. At this time the script wrote: [*sic*] 'There is someone with Mrs. Thompson, another woman, taller and slighter—she helps her to write—the message is not clear to you. I do not know the house. I cannot take you there.' A week later, and before she had heard anything from Mrs. Thompson, the hand wrote, 'Mrs. Thompson named a name, but not yours—Nelly could help if she could come—she finds it hard to write but would easily speak.'

"Later, Mrs. Verrall heard that on the first evening Mrs. Thompson had with her a friend answering to the description, and that Mrs.

---

[35] XXV, 102-108.

Thompson had referred by name to Mrs. Verrall's daughter, but we are left ignorant as to whether the place of the sitting was an unknown place, or whether from the way Mrs. Thompson made her request, Mrs. Verrall did not have some reason to infer that someone would be with her while she was sitting. Of course, the description of the woman is too indefinite to have value."

Inexcusable Omissions

Dr. Tanner, while quoting Mrs. Verrall's script of April 22, closing with the words, " I do not know the house. I cannot take you there," obviously signifying that the communicator was not able to identify the house where Mrs. Thompson and the other woman were, omits her important script of April 24, which apparently does profess to identify the house. On that date, after " Wensday " [*sic*] there came: " the case has been identified—but they wait for more about the room. There is a portrait hanging near the fire. Edmund Gurney books in cases in the room—no colored picture." She omits Mrs. Verrall's statement that " those who know the rooms in Hanover Square [rooms of the S. P. R.] will recognize the intention in the above." She omits the fact that Mrs. Thompson and the woman did sit in the rooms of the S. P. R. to write. She omits to note that the mention of Wednesday in connection with those rooms corresponds with the fact that it was on Wednesday that Mrs. Thompson and the woman wrote in them. Although she quotes the fact that Mrs. Thompson asked Mrs. Verrall to try for writing between nine and ten on a certain evening [April 22], she omits that while Mrs. Verrall then expected that Mrs. Thompson would also write at that hour, she had no expectation that the latter would do this in the S. P. R. rooms or other than her home. She omits Mrs. Verrall's declaration that she fully expected that Mrs. Thompson would be alone. Quoting Mrs. Verrall's script of April 30: " Mrs. Thompson named a name, but not yours," she omits the fact that, as stated, Mrs. Thompson's script did not, as would perhaps have been expected, name Mrs. Verrall. Admitting the fact that during Mrs. Thompson's experiment, Mrs. Verrall's daughter was mentioned, Dr. Tanner omits what makes this significant, the fact that Mrs. Verrall's daughter sat with her mother at the experiment of April 22. She omits that Mrs. Thompson had no knowledge that Mrs. Verrall's daughter was to sit with her, or that the daughter had also experimented with her own automatic writing.

Contradictions of Mrs. Verrall's testimony

Not only was Dr. Tanner guilty of all these vital omissions (as if a man should go through a house, tearing out part of the foundation wall and ripping away sills and braces and rafters here and there, then complain that the house is not sound), but she makes statements directly contrary to Mrs. Verrall's express testimony.

1. " We are left ignorant as to whether the place of the sitting was an unknown place "—*i. e.*, the rooms of the British Society at Hanover Square, where Mrs. Thompson and her friend sat on April 22.

Whatever this statement means, it is untrue. We are not "left ignorant " as to Nelly the control, for she said, " I do not know the house." As to Mrs. Thompson, if she did not know the place she would not have gone there for the sitting. Mrs. Verrall, being a member of the Council of the Society, certainly knew the place. But Dr. Tanner probably means that we are left ignorant as to whether Mrs. Verrall knew or suspected that Mrs. Thompson would sit in that place. But this is untrue. Mrs. Verrall expressly says, " I . . . fully expected that at the hour arranged she would sit alone and at her own house." What more could Mrs. Verrall affirm to lift the cloud of Dr. Tanner's ignorance respecting this point?

2. " We are left ignorant as to . . . whether from the way that Mrs. Thompson made her request, Mrs. Verrall did not have some reason to infer that some one would be with her while she was sitting." It is wholly incorrect to say we are left ignorant when a statement has been made explicitly covering the point. Mrs. Verrall says: "As we were parting, Mrs. Thompson asked me to try for automatic writing between 9 and 10 in the evening of April 22," and again, " I . . . fully expected that at the hour arranged *she would be alone* and at her own house." How could Mrs. Verrall more forcibly have declared that she had no " reason to infer that some one would be with her? " It is true that we cannot depend upon the positive statements of some people. For instance, I should be justified in suspecting that any given page, yet unexamined, in Dr. Tanner's book contains misstatements, since nearly every page I have examined contains such. But Mrs. Verrall was not only a highly accomplished woman, but her whole treatise in which the incident we are discussing is found shows her to have been a critical and cautious one, aware of the pitfalls which psychical research must keep in mind, and decidedly disposed to present any possibly explanatory particulars. It is not intelligent to treat her as though she were an ignoramus of careless speech, and to intimate that besides what she declares was said, something else was said whose vital importance Mrs. Verrall had not the sense to recognize.

Illegitimate reasoning

1. To suppose that Mrs. Thompson actually hinted that she was not only going to be accompanied but that the person would be a woman, and that the woman was taller and slighter than herself, that Mrs. Verrall received this information, and that neither of the ladies had any recollection that the information had been given, when one of them, at least, was so keenly aware of the criteria of evidence, is rather brazen. But even if Mrs. Verrall had inferred or guessed that " someone would be with " Mrs. Thompson, it would not follow that the someone would be (a) a woman, (b) taller and (c) slighter than Mrs. Thompson. Dr. Tanner's wheelbarrow breaks down with this load. The woman was unknown to Mrs. Verrall, so that even the mention of her name would not have suggested her description.

2. " Of course, the description of the woman is too indefinite to have value." This is an illogical declaration. Suppose the person with Mrs. Thompson had been a man, thicker and shorter than herself, would not Dr. Tanner have seized upon the discrepancies? The agreements, then, have value. They are not conclusive, of course, but they have value, as far as they go.

DR. G. STANLEY HALL

That distinguished psychologist must also have been affected by the magic of the enchanted boundary, else he would not have given his imprimatur to such a book as we have described, in a lengthy Introduction, ending with the words:

" It is significant, too, that the chief works of the English Psychic Research Society have never before had a searching, impartial, critical estimate, often as they have been worked over by believers. Those with skepticism enough to have been impartial have never been able to arouse interest enough to treat these studies thoroughly. Thus, I cannot but hope that this book will mark a turn of the tide."

A row of exclamation points ought to come after each of these sentences in turn. What bewitched Dr. Hall that he took all of his assistant's analyses on faith, and never looked up the original in a single case? Or did he, and was the spell even then too much for his discernment? To think that the book which he endorsed and which he piously hoped would mark a turn in the tide, has now been for years the laughing-stock of all who know the facts! There is evidence that the spell was really upon him, for he could not even get the title of the

Society for Psychical Research correctly, and actually intimated that to be skeptical is the preparation for impartiality.

Dr. Hyslop showed that Dr. Hall, while suspecting without cause the completeness of the records made by psychical researchers, by his own admission was guilty of making incomplete records of his own sittings with Mrs. Piper. Mrs. Sidgwick points out his faults of experimentation, which psychical researchers have learned to avoid. And Andrew Lang [36] makes merry with "the method and logic of your contributions to the book of Dr. Tanner." One funny instance which he mentions is where the ostensible communicator Hodgson complained with reason of Dr. Hall's "awful whoppers," says "I think I told you so before," and Dr. Hall remarks, in the book, "which he certainly had not." And yet he certainly had, as any reader of the book can see.[37] Mr. Lang turns Dr. Hall's words back on him: "It is *you* who here 'display the inability that we should expect from a secondary personality.'" What is this but another way of saying that the erstwhile alert psychologist, having crossed the fateful boundary, has fallen under the spell of an enchantment?

In a later fulmination against Sir Oliver Lodge,[38] a typical piece of oracular generalization, Hall begins by calling Sir Oliver a "nobleman," which he is not, and saying that he was "once of high standing as a physicist," as though he had ever fallen from his estate. He asks, "Who ever heard of an up-to-date psychologist of the normal who advocates spiritism," "unless we except Mr. Myers?" And why should we except him—presumably because to accept spiritism made him not "up-to-date"! And yet later he has to regret the "profoundly sympathetic attitude of William James," but then, "he died before the psychoanalytic movement was felt in this country," so cannot be called "up-to-date." To say nothing of the fact, to be adverted to later, that psychoanalysis cannot in the nature of things solve the problems which exist, I happen to know of three psychoanalysts, one of them of wide repute, who are interested in the appearances as of supernormal information in crystal gazing, psychometry, etc. But this very fact would probably make them old fogies to Dr. Hall, who scorns telepathy as he does spiritism. He affirms that psychologists believe that coincidences and the similarity of structure and function of the minds of friends and relatives are sufficient to explain all so-called telepathic phenomena. Friends and relatives are unnecessarily lugged in, as the phenomena are not limited to these as

---

[36] *Proceedings* S. P. R., XXV, 90-101. [37] *Studies in Spiritism,* Cf. 255 with 228.
[38] Boston *Herald*, Feb. 12, 1920.

agents and percipients. But even in cases where they were—think of attempting to explain in this way the following: the agent imagines " Dostoievsky writing in a very bare room, I think in France, and hearing the bailiff people banging at the door, and pretending he is not in the house," and Professor Gilbert Murray says, " I think it is out of a book—it's Russian—it's a man inside a house and the people beating and beating on the door outside—and he's keeping quite still so they shan't know he is there—it's a big sort of a bare room and he is a writer—seems a mad sort of person—don't somehow feel as if I was going to get it—I think it is in France—but he must be Russian—I don't feel as if they were going to murder him at all—I should think it is a story of Dostoievsky, that I can't get—I have a feeling that I can't be right—are they bailiffs?" [39] Will Dr. Hall say that he believes that this result came about through coincidences and the similarity of structure and function of the minds of relatives? Let him say that a marvelous degree of hyperæsthesia is the explanation, let him declare that there was a general conspiracy of S. P. R. officials and others to defraud, but let him not foist upon us the similarity-of-structure-and-function formula, for it is not only incredible, but fairly unthinkable in application to such a result.

Dr. Hall ends his article with the words: " I insist that there is no single golden grain of truth in all this mass of spiritualistic dross which will stand the assay of modern psychology. If there is, as so many affirm, what is it? " But where is the evidence that he has ever attempted the assay of any case upon which psychical researchers place emphasis? Or that he has ever experimented himself, except to prove that suggestion can paint upon the subconscious of the psychic all sorts of pictures, which no psychical researcher worthy of the name questions? If he is willing to attempt the assay of one case which covers not more than fifty printed pages, and to print his explanation, he has only to say so, and the documents will be placed in his hands.[40] This case has been recommended to a number of psychologists and others who use confident language similar to that just quoted, since it is one of comparative brevity, and the attendant circumstances singularly easy to appraise, and they all dodge it. There is one exception, a psychologist did promise to undertake the task and to publish his explanation; he has a copy of the record still, after nearly three years,[41] but has unfortunately been " unable to find time."

---

[39] *Proceedings* S. P. R., XXIX, 109.
[40] Dr. Hall (1846-1924) was living when the article in *Psyche* was printed.
[41] Now nine years.

HUGO MUENSTERBERG

The late Professor of Psychology at Harvard University wrote an all-round attack upon psychical research which Dr. Hyslop answered in the *Journal* of the A. S. P. R.[42] Therein he garbled records,[43] though not so badly as Dr. Tanner had done. He scattered wild and random statements which are not even consistent with each other. He declared that in what professed to be communications from Dr. Hodgson through Mrs. Piper "there is nothing characteristic of the man who purports to speak," though his knowledge of Hodgson's characteristics was exceedingly limited; that "everything is characteristic of the woman," though he did not know Mrs. Piper and refused opportunities to study her; that Hodgson's "idioms blended with her memory of the man," although he had just declared that the messages contained *nothing* characteristic of him. He depicted Dr. Hodgson as having been "absorbed by one passion" for many years, "to understand the conditions of existence after death—devoting his whole scholarly career to this one group of problems and discussing them a thousand times with his most intimate friends," though Dr. Hodgson had no such passion, the conditions of existence after death were never his quest, and he never discussed them once with one of his most intimate friends, Dr. Hyslop.[44] Finally Muensterberg blurted out the

---

[42] January, 1908.

[43] Dr. Hyslop's condemnation of this procedure is scorching. "One of the most inexcusable acts of a man pretending to be scientific and to be fairly discussing his opponent's facts and theories is to quote the part of his evidence which the writer does not value and to omit that which he does value. It is amazing to see the evasion involved in the treatment of one of the cross-references. Professor Muensterberg wants to ridicule certain passages and selects those to which I attached no value at all and neglects to tell the reader what I did value. The passage I have in mind is the one on pages 129-132 of the *Journal*. Professor Muensterberg quotes only what he finds on page 129!! Of course he did not dare quote the rest of it and make such assertions as he wanted to make in a newspaper article. We should apply his instrument for getting people to tell the truth in such situations. He escapes being convicted out of his own mouth only by a policy of prevarication. A list of a hundred words here ought to make him stammer like the poor girl whom he found to have been eating chocolate candy and lying about it. . . . Professor Muensterberg does not quote a single incident to which I attached importance. He garbles what I said and allows the reader to think that there are no better facts in the record than those to which I myself gave no evidential value alone."

[44] This is what Muensterberg said:

"Fancy a scholar, through many years of his life, absorbed by one passion,—to understand the conditions of existence after death—devoting his whole scholarly career to this one group of problems, and discussing them a thousand times with his most intimate friends. And now he enters into the land of eternal mystery; all the secrets which no living man has ever grasped are unveiled to him, and, with full consciousness of personal identity he at last attains the power of direct communication with his friends; he can be the first to convince mankind and to transform the hopes of millions into a certainty,—and in this glorious position he speaks, or rather gossips about the most trivial and most insignificant matters!" Again:—

truth, that his hostility to any possibility of there being evidence of the existence of spirits was in major part due to emotion. "Behind the mere argument of reason stands more powerfully still the argument of emotion," he says, " his [the psychologist's] whole being abhors this repellant caricature of immortality," etc. Since science utterly discards emotion as a test of objective fact, what brought Professor Muensterberg so completely under its vitiating influence, and caused him even to confess the fact without shame, if not the magic of the enchanted boundary?

Another article by Dr. Muensterberg, entitled "Psychology and Mysticism," was answered by Dr. F. C. S. Schiller, of Oxford University, in what I take to be one of the finest pieces of polished satire in the language, as well as one of the most unanswerable expositions of the folly of scientific obscurantism in reference to the subject matter of psychical research.[45] He shows the erstwhile astute Harvard professor floundering in a morass of blunders, fallacies, and "ridiculous and incoherent reasonings"; that he impresses uninformed or careless readers through a show of academic authority, sheer dogmatic assertion, juggling with definitions and terms, and even by a smoke-screen of metaphysical unintelligibility. He compares the onslaught against psychic research with the famous prosecution of Dreyfus.

"Perhaps in a critical age, such *ex cathedra* pronouncements, even of the greatest scientific dignitaries, are not as safe nor as effective as the lofty and scornful silence affected by most of his *confrères* on the General Staff of the Army of Science. The Goliath of Authority cannot stalk forth into the field of debate without a risk that a little pellet of reason may pierce through the thickness of his skull and put an end to his pretensions. For too often the effect of authority is impaired by argument, and the impressiveness of a judgment is destroyed by divulging the reasons on which it was based. Professor Muensterberg

---

"And even if he were unskilful in proving his existence, he would have furnished his friend Hyslop at least with some new insight into the wonders of the over-world which they discussed so often."

This is a part of Hyslop's reply: "It was not Dr. Hodgson's one absorbing passion to understand the conditions of the existence after death. Professor Muensterberg, with his one conversation on hypnotism, was not likely to discover what that passion was, especially as he admits they both carefully avoided conversation on it! I happen to know that it was not. I had sixteen years of intimate acquaintance and frequent conversation with him, and we never once even talked about the subject. His passion was for evidence that there was such a world, not what it was like, and he accepted precisely the same view of what is evidence for it that I hold, and spent his intellectual efforts in finding it. He did not waste time on investigating what such a world was like."

[45] *Proceedings* S. P. R., XIV, 348-65.

should have remembered Lord Mansfield's advice to the man who undertook the job of judging what he did not understand, or, as one must say in Professor Muensterberg's case, what he *would* not understand. For Professor Muensterberg's inability to grasp the nature of the case for Psychical Research is manifestly of an emotional rather than of an intellectual character, and affords as fine an example of the effect on the mind of a passionate ' will to disbelieve ' as I have had the pleasure of meeting. I am accordingly confident of expressing only the sentiment of every psychical researcher when I thank Professor Muensterberg for the interesting light he has (however inadvertently) thrown on the psychology of psychologists, and the nature of the fixed ideas by which they seem to be obsessed.

"And, personally, I owe Professor Muensterberg a debt of gratitude also on account of the undesigned, exquisite, and almost ideal illustration which his remarks yield of the aptness of a comparison I ventured to institute in reviewing Mr. Podmore's book in the pages of *Mind*,[46] when I called ' psychical ' phenomena ' the Dreyfus Case of Science.' I then pointed out that they had never received a fair and open trial, *coram populo*, that the evidence on which they had been condemned had never been published, and could not be produced, that their banishment from the society of scientific fact and their relegation to the company of the Devil had been effected by a secret and nameless court-martial, which made no serious pretence of examining the evidence, and that for nearly two centuries the authorities who professed to speak in the name of Science had, when questioned, done nothing but invoke the sanctity of the *chose jugée*, and intimidate inquirers with solemn prophecies of the absolute ruin that would overtake the whole scientific order if any investigation or revision of the matter were to be attempted.[47]

" I also drew attention to the fact that, in spite of all discouragements and threats, a demand for ' revision ' had grown up, which was supported by an increasing number of ' intellectuals,' who were not afraid of being maligned as the hirelings of ' a conspiring syndicate of all the superstitions.' But I could not anticipate that Professor Muensterberg would simultaneously have been goaded into divulging the contents of the secret *dossier*, of which we have heard so much and seen so little, that he would have exhibited to an astonished *urbi et orbi* the ridiculous documents on which he relies to substantiate his case."

---

[46] For January, 1899. No. 29, N. S.
[47] Professor Muensterberg, of course, trots out this old bugaboo also. Courageous confidence in the ability of science to deal with every order of fact—with " the psychology of spirits, angels, and demons, if such things there be, as well as with that of men and beasts " (as I said in *Mind*), he declares to be " *wrong and dangerous from beginning to end.*" Can it be that he has a lurking fear that if he attempted to investigate demons, they might fly away with him?

Dr. Schiller's paper should be read in its entirety. But the temptation to present one more sample is irresistible.

"It is a relief to turn from such excursions into 'the vast inane' to the pleasant side-lights Professor Muensterberg sometimes throws on his personal characteristics. He is a very Galahad among psychology professors. He has never, he assures us, 'taken part in a telepathic experiment or in a spiritualistic séance.' But he once had a thrilling adventure 'with two famous telepathists in Europe,' who had discovered 'a medium of extraordinary powers' at a distance, unfortunately, which would have involved him in '15 hours' traveling'— no slight journey even for a well-girt man. For a moment the professor wavered in his decision, and his mighty mind was nigh o'erthrown. But, before he had started, the telepathists had discovered the fraud. A most providential escape, surely; for if the professor had come and seen, he might have been conquered, and then a flood of superstition might have swept us all back into the Middle Ages! But, after all, his (and our) escape was not, as he confesses, so much due to his scientific caution as to his dilatoriness; the virgin purity of his scientific character was preserved unsullied only by his professorial slowness in packing his trunks![48] Perhaps his readers would have been more interested to hear the reason why he has never expended a couple of hours and of 5-cent car fares and, fortified only with, say, a couple of bags and a choice selection of psychological instruments, tried his luck with Mrs. Piper! After such heroic readiness to pack his trunks for a 15-hour journey, that seems a little strange.

"The reason, doubtless, lies in his sense of the surpassing innocency of his character. He is in very deed 'the Israelite in whom there is no guile' we read of in the Scriptures. 'Why do I avoid these séances?' he asks pathetically. 'It is not because I am afraid that they would shake my theoretical views and convince me of mysticism, but because I consider it *undignified* to visit such performances . . . and because I know I should be the last man to see through the scheme and discover the trick.'

"And, after an appeal to the effete old *ignava ratio* that a conjurer and not a scientist is the proper person to detect trickery,[49] he

---

[48] Note the *plural*.
[49] This seems a truism *a priori*, but is not borne out by experience. For such experts have often most unreservedly admitted the supernormal character of many of the disputed facts—even where the scientists subsequently discovered trickery. The explanation, of course, is that the expert is quite as liable (or in some cases, because of his conceit of knowledge, even more liable) to be deceived by trickery on lines which are unfamiliar to him. And, as Messrs. Hodgson and Davey have shown, the subtler sort of spiritistic fraud really rests on a higher plane than ordinary con-

proceeds to commend himself, and his science, for his lack of detective insight. As an experimental psychologist he is by his whole training 'absolutely spoilt for the business of a detective.' He does not know 'another profession in which the suspicion of constant fraud becomes so systematically inhibited as it does in that of the scientist.' Daily work in a scientific laboratory he regards 'as a continuous training of an instinctive confidence in the honesty of one's co-operators.' . . .

"Now, of course, we must accept Professor Muensterberg's description of his own idiosyncrasy. I am quite ready to believe that he is as easy to deceive as he is difficult to convince. But on the other points of this argument I take leave to differ.

"I think he exaggerates the incompetence of other scientific men in psychical research when he judges them by himself. They are, of course, not born experts in psychical research, but become such by a pretty severe training, in the course of which they may often fall into error. For they are no more infallible in their observations than in their *a priori* convictions. An instinctive insight into the possibilities of fraud comes to them, as to the detective, only as the fruit of long experience. (That is just why I am not impressed by the authority of scientists whose qualifications resemble Professor Muensterberg's.) But they can make themselves very fair judges of trickery, though perhaps they would do well, both before and after investigating, to consult with a real expert with the long and varied experience of, *e. g.*, Dr. Hodgson. And it is just because isolated investigation is so hazardous, because experience and special study are so valuable, that it is so desirable that the S. P. R. should have the means to employ dozens of trained investigators, who 'know the ropes,' and are fully alive to all the difficulties of the subject, instead of one. For our science here stands shivering on the shore of an 'unharvested sea' of unknown dimensions.

"Again, I am a little reluctant to accept Professor Muensterberg's account of the experimental psychologists' superhuman guilelessness. This may in part be due to the unfortunate outcome of my only attempt to enlist an experimental psychologist's coöperation in a 'psychical' experiment. He took advantage of the opportunity to secure the failure of the experiment. No doubt his scientific conscience permitted, nay, persuaded, him to protect 'science' against the possible inroad of 'superstition' by such means, but after this I naturally incline to guard myself against the possibilities of deception on *both* sides. For it is decidedly humiliating to have escaped the wiles of the

juring. It rests not so much on the deception of the senses by apparatus and prestidigitation, but on the fact that the spectator is induced to *deceive himself* by lapses of attention and errors of interpretation. Hence his mental processes present far subtler, more complicated and interesting psychological problems than those of the conjurer's audience.

professional mediums only to fall a victim to the excessive zeal of a professorial psychologist, whose good faith one had taken for granted!

"Further, and this is a contention which has a wider scope, I would maintain that, whatsoever may be the natural and acquired guilelessness of psychologists *de facto*, they have no business to pride themselves on it and to cultivate it *de jure*, and that if Professor Muensterberg's account of the mental attitude of himself and his 'experimental' *confrères* is correct, it *pro tanto* unfits him, and them, for the prosecution of delicate psychological inquiries."

Finally, a number of brilliant and irrefutable paragraphs show that, as respects the pitfalls which lie in wait for the psychic researcher, the position of the experimental psychologist "*is precisely analogous, only he does not appear to know it*," whereas the former has to a large extent developed a technique for their avoidance. Why did the brainy Muensterberg, whenever he wrote on a certain subject, immediately begin to drool blunders and inconsequences, to quote unfairly, and to wind in and out in his logic, if he was not smitten by a magic spell?

DR. CHARLES A. MERCIER

In 1917, Dr. Mercier, a specialist in insanity, published a book entitled *Spiritualism and Sir Oliver Lodge*. A considerable part of this is made up of a discussion of general principles, good enough, though elementary, to psychical researchers, and delivered in a tone of oracular finality worthy of one who at the end of his book announces that he is preparing " courses of study and books " on " Witchcraft," " Criminology," " Psychology," " The Grounds of Belief—what we ought to believe, to disbelieve, and to doubt, and why," " Explanation —A Course of Instruction in Principles of Explanation and Causation," " Conduct—A Course of Study in the right conduct and regulation of action in all the circumstances and relations of life," " Thinking and Reasoning," etc. We would say that one who knew all that could afford to be oracular.

But when it comes to the field of psychical phenomena, there is an appearance as though Dr. Mercier had never heard of it until somebody sent him *Raymond* for review. He says that this astonished him so that he sent for *The Survival of Man*, by the same author, of which he apparently had never heard, and was still more astonished by that. And then, according to his own account, he made inquiries, and found that such ideas had attained a very wide vogue. Having come out of his Rip Van Winkle sleep of thirty-five years to this extent, he read the two books by Lodge, and was prepared to blight the whole disgusting business of alleged psychical phenomena by the light of pure reason. In experiments conducted by Sir Oliver, Dr. Mercier can, by the telescope of imagination, discover all manner of defects which were invisible to the scientist of greater fame who was actually present. And yet he himself is so naïve as to say that if a man " has been seen to raise a full pint pot to his mouth, and if when he lowered it the pot was found empty, that is proof that he has had a drink." Yet I have seen a conjurer duplicate that performance, and he had not had a drink.

Mercier apparently thinks that all the evidence for telepathy is in *The Survival of Man,* and that collusion is the explanation of all that is perplexing in it. If he had any acquaintance with the many sets of experiments, with their conditions varied and imposed upon the principals, he might not be so dogmatic, or he might, after all. Perhaps he might intimate that Professor Murray's remarkable feats were the result of collusion between himself and others.[50]

But he is not fair to the evidence given by Sir Oliver Lodge. He finds fault because Sir Oliver had experiments (which the latter did not hold were conclusive) with the agent and percipient in the same room. But the experiments between Miss Miles and Miss Ramsden, a brief account of which directly follows, is completely ignored, although they were twenty miles apart and the conditions were such as utterly to shut out collusion. There was enough about these experiments to incite a man who really wanted to get some notion of the evidence for telepathy to go to the *Proceedings* of the S. P. R., Volume XXI. There he would have found that on October 17 Miss Miles, at the hour set, mentally proposed " SPECTACLES," and that at the same time Miss Ramsden thought " spectacles," and " sense perception "; that at the next experiment Miss Miles thought " SUNSET OVER THE ORATORY," this being suggested by the fact that a Mr. MacNab called her attention to the sun setting over Brampton Oratory, and she saw it with his head illumined by its rays, and that Miss Ramsden wrote " First it was the sun with rays and a face peering out of the rays," etc.; that at the next experiment Miss Miles thought the name of a lady and Miss Ramsden thought a lady's name, but not the right one; that at the next experiment Miss Miles thought " HANDS," and Miss Ramsden first thought of Miss Miles going upstairs and putting

---

[50] This has since been suggested, though not by Dr. Mercier.

on a wrap, which apparently had no relevance, and next of "a little black hand." Take these four experiments in unbroken succession, to say nothing of the rest, some of them failures, some complete or partial successes—why did Dr. Mercier not face them?

He attacks the cross-correspondences between Mrs. Verrall, the accomplished scholar of Newnham College, and Mrs. Forbes. He mentions but two of these, one in the following terms:

"Again, on December 18, attempts were made in Mrs. Forbes' script to give a certain test word, 'Dion' or 'Dy,' which it was stated, 'will be found in Myers' own . . .' Mrs. Verrall interpreted the test word at the time, for reasons given, as 'Diotima,' and a description of the same part of the Symposium, including the mention of Diotima, did occur in *Human Personality* (by Myers), which was published about three months later. This is quite as convincing as the bricks in Smith the weaver's chimney which 'are alive this day to testify it; therefore deny it not.'"

Here Dr. Mercier is more reckless than even Dr. Tanner. She did look through the original report of the incident; all that Mercier did was to quote what are hardly more than references to the incident, and treat them as though they were complete. She stated a number of other details of importance in the "Diotima" incident, threadbare as her recital is; he states particulars which in comparison with the mass which make up the entire incident are like the facts that Smith wore a derby hat and was seen standing on a certain corner at 10 p. m., in comparison with the mass of circumstances which convict Smith of murder. Mercier quoted from Lodge, but Lodge was not summing up the evidence for cross-correspondence, but illustrating its nature, as one would discuss two or three bones of a dinosaur. Mercier, like the unlettered peasant, sneers at the isolated bones, and will not take pains to go and look where the entire skeleton is set up on view. He leaves his reader to believe what is not true, namely, that the two incidents which he cites are substantially set forth. One of them, which his quotation sums up in seven lines, fills nearly seven large pages in the original printed record. He declares that "there are very few of these so-called cross-correspondences," probably because he thinks that Sir Oliver mentioned them all; whereas there are many, and even many between Mrs. Verrall and Mrs. Forbes alone. He quite neglects the cumulative effect of so large a percentage of correspondences in a series, which is exactly what strikes the scientific unbiased mind most forcibly. This was probably not from *malice prepense*, but from sheer

THE ENCHANTED BOUNDARY

ignorance and such haste to demolish Lodge that he could not wait to learn more.

Psychic researchers who did not need to be told that fraud exists, and malobservation and credulity, and who had no respect for bad logic and innuendo, reviewed *Spiritualism and Sir Oliver Lodge* somewhat contemptuously, almost apologizing for noticing such a piece of inconsequence at all. Apparently stung, " Charles A. Mercier, M.D., F.R.C.P., F.R.C.S., sometime Examiner in Psychology and Mental Diseases in the University of London, Lecturer in Insanity at Medical Schools of the Westminster Hospital, Charing Cross Hospital and the Royal Free Hospital," as he stunningly announces on the title page, issued a little book called *Spirit Experiences*, which descends a step lower, in that it is nothing but burlesque. It may be, indeed, that the doctor did try a telepathic experiment with his two daughters, allowing one to choose her own subject with full opportunity for collusion with the other; it may be that he really was puzzled by their rapping and tossing things about and by one of them telling what card he was thinking of after she had got him to say in which row vertically and which horizontally it was; it may be that he was taken in by the pea-under-the-thimble trick. If so, we can willingly laugh at him; if he is lying we can laugh with him over the droll yarns; in neither case have they any more bearing upon or relation to the methods of psychic research than has grimacing or thumbing one's nose. But even in a *tour de force* of humor one ought to observe some degree of accuracy in his allusions to history or legend. One's appreciation of drollery on the subject of the pyramids would be jarred by locating the pyramids in Rome. It is so when Dr. Mercier says that Chicago is " famous for the manufacture of wooden nutmegs," when *tout le monde* knows or ought to know that the glory of that legend belongs to the State of Connecticut.

EDWARD CLODD

We now turn to Edward Clodd, who has written a book called *The Question: If a Man Dies, Shall He Live Again?* [51]

The general reader, who cons statements set down with an air of authority about cases and materials with which he himself is imperfectly acquainted quite naturally supposes that the cases and materials have been canvassed with critical care, and that the statements can be

---

[51] London, 1917.

trusted. But the general reader, if shown that a writer makes blunders in the simplest matters of fact, on which cyclopedias and other easily accessible books of reference could set him right, must see that the same person will inevitably be still more likely to be untrustworthy when dealing with complex and intricate matters, and abstracting from lengthy records.

Dr. Hyslop pointed to the blunder of saying that the real name of "George Pelham" was Pennell. Even less pardonable is the inaccuracy of changing the name of Daniel Dunglas Home to David Dunglas Home, as is done on page 41. There are other blunders in the same passage. "Home or Hume" is said to have been the name. There was no "*or* Hume" about it, as might have been seen from Mrs. Home's biography of her husband.[52] "Home always wrote his name 'Home,' but he retained the ancient Scottish pronunciation of that name, '*Hoom.*'" She calls the spelling Hume "a mistake made by many persons." But there was no reason why Clodd should have repeated the mistake, if he had had any desire to be accurate. Again, we are informed that Home, "in his seventeenth year . . . came out as a medium, finding support in that profession from a group of spiritualists." But Home himself, who ought to know, tells us that this took place in the month when he was eighteen.[53]

Clodd is not more fortunate in his reference to the Rev. Dr. Phelps and the "Stratford rappings" in his house. He calls that gentleman a "Presbyterian minister," which is no insult, but the fact was that he was a Congregationalist. And he says: "As for the Stratford disturbances, the report of them is practically valueless, because it was not set down by a son of Dr. Phelp's [*sic*] till *thirty years later*, and then at secondhand, since he was no witness of what he affirms happened." If the Stratford disturbances are not worth consideration it is not for the reason assigned. Does Mr. Clodd think that there were no newspapers in the United States in 1850? On the contrary, the house was visited by editors and reporters, as well as by other persons, and accounts, some of them lengthy, were printed in many papers while the events were in progress; notably in the *Daily Derby Journal* and the *New York Sun*, but also in the *Journal, Palladium* and *Register* of New Haven, Connecticut, the *Bridgeport Standard, Hartford Times, New Britain Advocate, New York Tribune, New York Journal of Commerce*, etc. The intimation that the story was solely dependent on

---

[52] *D. D. Home: His Life and Mission*, 31.   [53] *Incidents in My Life*.

what a son of Dr. Phelps wrote thirty years later is a laughable perversion of the facts.

There is as poor luck with quotations as with concrete facts. Relating an incident told by Sir William Crookes about Home, Mr. Clodd says, using quotation marks and claiming to take the words from Crookes's pen, that Home " folded a handkerchief, and putting his left hand into the fire took out a red-hot cinder and put it on the handkerchief, which remained unburnt." The incident is told by Crookes in the English *Proceedings*, VI, 103-104, and the statement is that Home " folded it up and laid it on his hand like a cushion [he does not say which hand], putting his other hand [he does not say which] into the fire, took out a large lump of cinder red-hot at the lower part and placed the red part on the handkerchief." How does Clodd know that Home put his *left* hand in the fire? What is worth while stating so particularly is worth while having authority for.

Again, he declares that " Sir William tells us that on another occasion Home ' took a good-sized piece of red-hot coal from the fire, put it in his right hand and carried it with the other hand.' " This, too, counterfeits a direct quotation. But what Sir William wrote was this:[54] " took out a red-hot piece nearly as big as an orange, and putting it on his right hand, covered it over with his left hand.". Clodd goes on with his vain attempts to quote Crookes: " Then ' he blew the small furnace thus extemporized till the lump was nearly at white heat,' " in place of " then blew into the small furnace thus extemporized until the lump of charcoal was nearly white hot." Small divergences, but what Clodd says that Crookes wrote, Crookes did not write.

Other quotations are misapplied. He speaks of the cold air, sometimes amounting to a decided wind, " which frequently preceded the manifestation of the figures " [materializations]. But Crookes did not mention this in connection with materializations. He was talking of Home's phenomena, in which materializations bore little part, and particularly of the movement of objects without contact. His language was:[55] " These movements (and indeed I may say the same of every kind of phenomena) are generally preceded by a peculiar cold air, sometimes amounting to a decided wind." The reports by Crookes are short, and if Clodd cannot get them straight, what ability would he be likely to have of dealing correctly with, or of even understanding (if we are to acquit him of dishonesty), the voluminous Piper records?

Insinuation often takes the place of argument, and a peculiarly

---

[54] *Proceedings* S. P. R., VI, 103.
[55] *Notes of an Enquiry into the Phenomena Called Spiritual.*

vicious form of insinuation which dares not face the facts of record. Referring to the famous experiments with the spring balance, he slyly suggests that a hair may have been used. But the pull indicated was sometimes $3\frac{1}{2}$ pounds. If Mr. Clodd has in mind a human hair, he might have experimented and found that no human hair will bear such a weight. If he means a horsehair, not only would that increase visibility, but he should, to be fair, have shown how, in a good light, with five investigators watching him, it would be possible for a man at one and the same time to have the fingers of his hands touching one end of a board three feet in length and be pulling down the other end of the board with a hair, without detection. The sneer that Crookes was too short-sighted to be trusted is unworthy, even if Sir William Ramsay stooped to it. In the first place, there were four other observers present. In the second, Crookes used spectacles, and it is the nature of these to correct defects of sight. The late Theodore Roosevelt, without his spectacles, was exceedingly near-sighted, but with them he could detect the markings of forest birds at a distance as well as John Burroughs himself. I have no objection to any intelligent criticism of Crookes's experiments, but this juggling with the facts, this mere carping and insinuating, is nauseating. It is the same with the talk about the mythical *Blue Book*, of which "the Boston section alone contains, we are told, seven thousand names." Granting this were true, suppose that a particular inhabitant out of some 700,000 in Boston paid a visit to a medium for the first time, how large a chance would she have of finding him listed, even if he gave his right name? And how much if he gave an assumed name, as he would if he had any sense? And supposing, as often happens, that he comes from another part of the country, and gives neither his name nor his residence, a very frequent case, how then would the *Blue Book*, granting that the monster existed, be of service? This would be a greater wonder than the one which it is sought to explain away. But there seems to be no difficulty in believing wonders, if only congenial ones can be selected. There is nothing funnier than the extreme credulity of some of the flouters of spirits. Another example of Clodd's avid belief in any sort of a statement which he thinks can make a point against the "occult," is his quoting with *empressement*, an allegation "in a paper called *Health*, that above one thousand houses in London are tenantless because they are believed to be haunted." Does he really believe that the upwards of 7,000,000 people of London have that list of one thousand houses memorized, so that none of these can get a tenant? Let any one think, if he were walking through the streets of New York looking for an apartment, what likelihood there would be of his knowing whether any particular house where a sign " To Let " is displayed has a " haunt " story attached to it, and whether he would ask ere renting, " Is this house haunted? " And yet there are upwards of a thousand houses in London that cannot get a tenant on such account! Rubbish!

I have often marveled at that assurance of editors, surely depending upon an afflatus from high heaven or—somewhere, since mere mortal man could not attain such wisdom, which enables them, even in the hot haste of their daily scribbling, to pass upon the protracted labors of any specialist on earth, and to show where he is right and where he is wrong by a few twirls of the pen. And I marvel at the like assurance of Mr. Clodd. The Rt. Hon. Gerald Balfour,[56] not inferior in intellect to Mr. Clodd, as perhaps Mr. Clodd himself would admit, made certain statements about the lack of communication between Mrs. Verrall and Mrs. Willett, the automatists in the " Ear of Dionysius " case. Balfour was in a position to know something about the matter, Clodd was not, and yet the latter feels qualified to express dissent, saying that this is " a statement hard to reconcile with what is known of the relations between two people eager to solve a conundrum and sharing a common belief." What is the matter with the man, that he cannot imagine how any one interested in what he is pleased to call a conundrum, can patiently pursue the only methods by which it can possibly get a trustworthy answer? And on what sort of meat has he fed that he should have the face, after skimming a report, to place his dictum over against the verdict of Professor Sidgwick, F. W. H. Myers, Frank Podmore, Alice Johnson and Mrs. Sidgwick, which they formulated after long and patient analysis? They show why the figures warrant the verdict, he simply says that the figures do not warrant it, since the census was not big enough. If it had been bigger they might have added more emphasis to their very cautious opinion.

I will admit that the report on the " Census of Hallucinations "[57] is not primer reading throughout, but there was the privilege of letting it alone. It was not a duty that devolved upon Mr. Clodd to fall on the report, on the contrary, it would better have become him to have avoided it if it was too involved for him to follow. There is no excuse for saying that of those who reported their experiences, " 322 affirmed that they had seen apparitions of the human figure," when the report states that 352 reported having seen apparitions of living persons, 163 of dead persons, and 315 of unrecognized persons. And the state-

---

[56] Now Earl of Balfour. [57] *Proceedings* S. P. R., X.

ment that "32 reported death coincidences" is also untrue. The report said that 62 persons reported death coincidences. For one reason and another the committee scaled these down to a selected list of 32, but the fact remains that 62 were reported.

Many examples of childish logic could be given. After asserting that mediumship, apart from fraud, is the result of "an unstable nervous system, with resulting weakness of control of the higher brain centers," an allegation evidently cribbed from some vaporing psychologist who knows in his bones, and in no other way, that it must be so, Clodd goes on to say that "age would appear to count in impairment of mediumistic power," and to instance Mr. Home and Mrs. Piper, who lost their power to a large degree (both being under fifty). It would seem that practice in "instability" ought to produce increasing "weakness of control of the higher brain centers" instead of working a cure. The fact that Home's general health was breaking when his mediumistic abilities began to diminish would, in the absence of prejudice, be taken to denote that such abilities are *not* pathological.

Clodd, after relating "a modern instance," usually skips back two thousand years or so to show that something like it was alleged then. Contrary to those who believe that almost anything could have happened before the close of the "apostolic period," though now quite prohibited by "science," he seems to take it for granted that any ancient claim must be false, since those were "unenlightened days," and that therefore any modern resembling case is discredited by its likeness to the ancient one. Whereas, if there are genuine and widely diffused phenomena in our times, it would logically be expected that there would have been such phenomena in former periods and among many races. Of course he picks and chooses, and may make his ancient exhibits as ridiculous as he pleases.

Out of a wealth of instances I select two utterances of pure prejudice. The writer actually makes the fact that at the Crawford experiments prayer is offered by some member of the Goligher family, a presumption of fraud! "These pietistic preliminaries . . . lend an air of suspicion." Of course the prayers are not evidential of genuineness, but that their employment by persons of religious proclivities in conjunction with what is to them sacred should be presumptive of guile is a mystery to any but a jaundiced mind. And only a pen dipped in prejudice could write about "the thin lips, hard expression of feature, and calculating looks as if to take the measure of their sitter's credulity" of Mrs. Piper and Mrs. Wriedt. I have not seen the portrait of Mrs. Wriedt, but Mrs. Piper surely deserves the derogatory description

no more than a million other American women. In one portrait before
me she looks a little constrained from the knowledge that she is having
her picture taken, and in another not even that, and in both she is the
very picture of a refined, reserved gentlewoman. Some psychics have
thick lips, some thin, and others lips that are " betwixt and between,"
without any discoverable bearings of their labial measurements upon
their character or abilities.

We might go on indefinitely quoting passages which enforce the
conclusion that Mr. Clodd's book is a study in prejudice and the art
of special pleading, but these must suffice.

JOSEPH McCABE

In 1920, Joseph McCabe issued a book called *Spiritualism: A
Popular History from 1847*. It is designed to be popular, but a history it is not. It is a diatribe based on selective attention, and is composed of sketches of fraudulent cases, together with a few burlesques
on cases of a higher character, replete with blunder and innuendo.
Space is accorded for but one specimen, but it is quoted entire.

"In 1907 also occurred what is known as the 'Hope, Star, and
Browning incident,' which is regarded as very impressive. Mrs. Piper,
in America, gave (supposedly from Myers) a reference to 'Hope,
Star, and Browning.' This was on February 11. It was then found
that in the written records of Mrs. Verrall there were curious references to stars, to hope, and to Browning's poetry on January 23 and
28. The weakness is that Mrs. Verrall's record was already in America
on February 11, and had been seen by the sitter, Mr. Piddington;
because Hyslop tells us that he went straight from the sitting with
Mrs. Piper to search Mrs. Verrall's script. He adds that, later, Mrs.
Verrall, who 'had not been told what was happening,' received further
references to the matter. But as Hyslop gives no date for this, it is
useless. Indeed, unlike many of his colleagues, Dr. Hyslop concludes
that in this case, 'the evidence for cross-correspondence is not the
best'; and the reader will probably agree."

Woe to the amateur who relies confidingly on Mr. McCabe for his
facts, since he was under the spell of the enchanted boundary as he
wrote. (1) Mrs. Piper was not in America, and on the very page of
Dr. Hyslop's *Contact with the Other World*, where the material which
Mr. McCabe consulted begins, is the plain statement, " Mrs. Piper was
in London." (2) Mrs. Verrall's record was not in America on February 11, or at any time. (3) Mr. Piddington was not in America, as is

intimated. (4) Mr. Piddington's going from the Piper sitting to search Mrs. Verrall's script does not prove that he had previously seen it. But if he had (since he was one of the committee whose business it was to compare the scripts produced by the mediums involved in the tests), the fact is irrelevant, unless it is meant to suggest that Mrs. Piper may have looked into his mind by that telepathy which Mr. McCabe frowns upon elsewhere in his book. (5) The " further references " in the script of Mrs. Verrall were not rendered " useless " by Hyslop's not mentioning the date of them, since he had nothing to do with the experiments. Why did not McCabe seek the dates in the original record published by the S. P. R. instead of discounting an incident because of what an after commentator did not mention? (6) To stop with " Dr. Hyslop concluded that in this case ' the evidence for cross-correspondence is not the best,' " and not to add that, nevertheless, he regarded it good enough to prove cross-correspondence, is to mislead the reader. Besides, the faulty construction of sentences is liable to cause the reader to suppose that it was Dr. Hyslop who went straight from a sitting, and that he went with Mrs. Piper.

Dr. E. J. Dingwall comments, in part:

" We confess that we have thoroughly enjoyed this book. It is not a history, but a racy narrative, written by a man who, it seems, does not believe that the ' supernormal ' has any existence in fact, and who has put together his work in the hope that his readers may be left with the same impression. A short unbiased history of the spiritualistic movement was wanted, but Mr. McCabe has not fulfilled the want. A history, in order to be worth anything, ought to consist in the presentation of an ordered array of facts and events untinged by the author's own special predilections. Mr. McCabe's prejudices, on the contrary, do not permit him to marshal a mere chronicle of events supplemented by a dispassionate criticism. He delights in fraud and fraud hunting, and if a medium has ever been detected in such practices, he or she is promptly dismissed with some caustic comments. When certain mediumistic phenomena do not admit of so easy a treatment, Mr. McCabe resorts to the ' mirrors or wires ' theory of the youth at a conjuring entertainment, or deliberately omits to mention mediums whose manifestations are both beyond his own explanation and also that of his advisers."

PROFESSOR MARGARET F. WASHBURN

Margaret F. Washburn is a psychologist of excellent standing, being a professor in Vassar College and co-editor of the *American*

Journal of Psychology. In the summer of 1920 she had an article in a periodical entitled *The Chronicle,* with the heading " Psychology and Spiritism." Learned as she is and high as is the reputation she enjoys in relation to her specialty, when she crossed the enchanted boundary she met the usual fate. I replied in the October issue of the same magazine.

" How little knowledge the writer shows of the approved methods, common to both the British and the American Society, is evinced by the following astonishing excerpt. ' The record of a sitting with a medium, to be really of scientific value, should contain not only what the medium and the communicating spirits said, but every word said by the sitter or by any person present. This precaution has been almost uniformly neglected.' This is tantamount to a confession that the writer is wholly unfamiliar with the most important literature of the subject with which she is dealing, namely, the *Proceedings* and *Journals* of the two Societies for Psychical Research. For what she asserts ' has been almost uniformly neglected ' has been their procedure for many years, as witnessed by many volumes. Dr. Hyslop's practice was to go farther and record every slip of the pencil, every fall and resumption of it, every significant movement, as well as ' every word said by the sitter or by any person present.' He has been criticized and almost cursed by many of his readers for recording and printing *everything;* yet at this late day there comes along a learned lady, insistent on scientific caution, and proud of the skill of psychologists in its exercise, and ventures such statements as those quoted!

" One would suppose, also, that psychical researchers did not take into account the resources and activities of the subliminal mind, or if the phrase better suits, the ' dissociated consciousness.' Yet the very word ' subliminal ' was coined by a psychical researcher who believed in spirit communication, F. W. H. Myers, and psychical researchers, Myers, Hodgson, Hyslop and many besides, have discussed subconscious functions ' and developed personalities,' in all phases and manifestations. Whenever the subconscious (or dissociated consciousness) can possibly be the source of the material evoked, it is provisionally assumed to be responsible for it, whatever the fact may be. And all sorts of subliminal warpings and colorings are regarded as possible. But—nothing can be evoked from the subconscious which was not first precipitated into it, if not from experience then from some *other* source. If there are records which exhibit statements of facts provably unknown at any time to the medium, in such a ratio and of such characteristic quality that they make the explanation of chance ridiculous, and if all the sources of error are eliminated, then there is no help from the doctrine of the subliminal or dissociated consciousness. And there are such records, which no cocksure psychologist has ever yet even attempted to discuss and explain.

"The subconscious mind is very suggestible—in fact suggestibility consists in the susceptibility of the subconscious mind to take hints. Professor Washburn's way of saying it is that 'dissociated consciousnesses are as a rule extremely suggestible,' and I consider it a very faulty way, though a number of psychologists share it with her. . . .

"The subliminal mind is suggestible; it is like a sensitized photographic plate which will take impressions from the light of the sun or from artificial light. Those of us who are convinced that spirits of the dead succeed in imprinting impressions upon the sensitized plate of the medium's mind are not so deluded as to suppose that her mind, with all its subliminal suggestibility, can take impressions from no other source. If messages come from the dead, they come through the subliminal mind of the medium in consequence of a passivity which is very unstable, and demands that the experimenter keep his hands off. To the examples of how President Hall by falsifications led the subliminal of Mrs. Piper through all sorts of vagaries, I retort that of course he did. I can do that sort of thing at any time and thereby prove two things; first, that the subconscious is suggestible, which everybody knew already, and second, that I am a stupid blunderer if I experiment for the supernormal and first proceed to fog the plate.

"I knew of a physician whose son began to have visions of being in strange places. The doctor, who had been very skeptical but who toppled with a 'sickening thud' when the matter came home to his own circle, as sometimes happens to psychologists, would say when the boy announced that he was in a village in France, 'Well, go to the priest's house. . . . Ring the bell . . . say to the priest. . . . Now find the schoolhouse. . . . Go in and ask the schoolmaster . . .'—and the boy never failed to find and do according to directions. I—a poor, simple psychical researcher—had to tell him that whatever chance there was of his getting anything supernormal was being spoiled by his method. He was simply painting on the canvas of the boy's mind instead of waiting to see what came spontaneously. Dr. Hall's brilliant feats with Mrs. Piper are precisely on a par with testing a man in hypnosis for hyperæsthesia and at the same time telling him that he feels or hears nothing. The results which might have been obtained would be completely overlaid and obscured by the insistent suggestion. This was the method of a psychologist, it never could be that of a competent psychical researcher. . . .

"Not only is there the curious assumption that the professional mind must work like an automaton, that a physicist's mind can never transcend its professional boundary and study mental facts intelligently, and that only psychologists in a technical sense are fitted to

THE ENCHANTED BOUNDARY 61

pursue investigations in the field of psychical research, but we also read that 'psychologists know,' 'psychologists have learned,' etc., as if psychologists all told the same story and had reached exactly the same conclusions. Yet it seems to me that I have heard that F. W. H. Myers, who wrote *Human Personality and Its Survival of Bodily Death*, was something of a psychologist, and he was a psychical researcher who experimented with mediums and reported what he considered supernormal incidents. There was a William James reputed to be a psychologist, and he experimented with mediums, and was strongly inclined to posit a supernormal quality in some of the results he reported. F. C. S. Schiller, of Oxford, is also considered something of a psychologist, and it is not difficult to ascertain his stand. And J. H. Hyslop was learned in psychology and taught psychology in college.

" Psychologists, we are informed, are the proper persons to investigate in the field we are discussing.[58] Well, those who have done so most laboriously have not come to the conclusions reached by psychologists whose investigations have been of the dilettante order, so much so that they cannot make elementary general remarks about psychical research, its methods and literature, without falling into errors.

" What strikes me as most droll in Professor Washburn's argument is her skepticism of the power of the human intellect to keep cool in the discussion of evidence of spirit communication. 'We may doubt whether any amount of scientific training can ever make our reason trustworthy in any realm where the deep pull of instinct is so strong.' Well, then, why does she attempt to argue the subject? Or does she think that one can preserve his balance up to the point where he begins to see that there is evidence for spirit communication, but that precisely at this point his intellect goes to pieces from emotion? Has any scientific psychical researcher ever had to make so humiliating a confession as did the late Professor Muensterberg, when he wrote, ' But while the psychologist rejects . . . the explanation through spirits as superfluous, he ought to be willing to confess that behind the mere argument of reason stands more powerfully still the argument of emotion; his whole being abhors . . .,' etc.?

"Any one would suppose, from reading Professor Washburn's remarks, that most human beings, including the most learned, are on a level with a negro revival meeting in their interest in a future life. Yet where is the evidence of it? Professor Leuba, another psychologist, has been showing us by statistics that a large percentage of college professors, including psychologists, care nothing for a future existence. And here comes one and implies that they are probably

---

[58] And yet Professor Muensterberg, in *Atlantic Monthly*, January, 1899, declared that he, by *virtue of being a psychologist*, would " be the last man to see through the scheme and discover the trick " in a case of fraud!

all so subject to a 'pull' that their reason refuses to function properly in relation to this one matter!

"They may reason soundly on politics, love, their salaries, and various subjects which exert a 'pull,' but once a purported 'communication,' containing sundry statements corresponding with facts unknown to the ostensible writer, is placed before them as a simple problem for the reason to act upon, the reason becomes hysterical and unreliable unless it takes the anti-spiritistic side! And it must assume the skeptical position instinctively and at once or it is lost. For 'it is safe to say that everyone who undertakes to investigate in this field does so with a deep and powerful bias.' The writer of this is brought into a dilemma by her curious statement; either she bases her argument upon investigations made under a deep emotional bias which has vitiated her reasoning based thereon, or else she is giving forth opinions based upon no investigation of the subject which she is talking about.

"The sentence which follows fascinates me. 'If he were really guided only by a perfectly impartial scientific curiosity, he would probably be willing to wait until the end of his life for the solution of that puzzle,' etc. That is, a 'perfectly impartial scientific *curiosity*' would do nothing whatever for its own satisfaction. Scientific curiosity —and we do not pause in other matters to ask whether it is perfectly impartial, but only ask to inspect the proofs it brings forth—may investigate bugs and rocks, and the composition of the stars, and every other subject under heaven, but cannot inspect documents dealing with the subject of survival unless it suffers from a pathological bias! Possibly Peary did not have a 'perfectly impartial scientific curiosity' when he was searching for the Pole, but nevertheless he found it, though perhaps if he had been well balanced he would have waited until he was dead, in which case he might have bumped upon the Pole without trying. It is quite certain that from the day that Darwin was struck by his great conception of the origin of species, his scientific curiosity was partial to his theory, nevertheless his reason continued to function and he brought forth a multitude of proofs, and this is all that counts. All that can be required of those who hold to the spiritistic hypothesis is that they present proofs, and though *odium spiriticum*—to employ a barbarism—may prevent some intellects from reacting soundly on the documentary evidences, I am confident that other minds, regarding these simply as logical problems, will react as calmly and soundly as on any others.

"I have sadly been compelled to express the opinion that Professor Washburn has little acquaintance with the best records on the subject she is discussing. One illustration is her statement that 'as a matter of fact there is nowhere, so far as I know, on record a case where the communicating spirit exhibits traits of character which the communicating medium could not easily conjecture him to have possessed in life.' Really the records are not responsible for any one's lack of acquaintance with them. One case, and I refer to the same one of less than seventy-five pages which I keep recommending out of tender consideration for the valuable time of psychologists,[59] contains a detailed and lifelike portraiture of true characteristics, and since the medium was an entire stranger she could not 'easily conjecture' anything about them.

"Finally Professor Washburn proposes 'one last chance' for the spirits to prove themselves other than 'bits of the medium's mind,' and that is to examine the records and see if they can furnish 'facts on the earth plane' which the medium could not have known. This sounds fair enough, though she says, 'it is very hard to deal satisfactorily, from a scientific point of view,' with the alleged instances. At least the reader feels sure that she will proceed in a scientific spirit, so far as she goes. It would not be scientific nor even intelligent if Darwin's *Origin of Species* were in dispute, to pick out from thousands of data set down by Darwin, just two, and those facts on which he placed no emphasis or even regarded as not constituting intelligible proofs at all. But out of Dr. Hyslop's voluminous Report of 649 pages in fine print, with its many hundred incidents, she has culled just two, both expressly stated by Dr. Hyslop to be faulty. And her version of one of these is erroneous by statement, and her versions of both are erroneous by omission.

"1. Reference to a visit.

"*Professor Washburn's version.* 'The latter [Robert Hyslop] referred to a visit that he paid his son just before he died; Dr. Hyslop considers this a reference to a visit that occurred some years before his father's death.'

"*The facts of record.*[60] 'And do you remember the visit I paid to you . . . you? (When was it?) I cannot tell the date, but it was just before I came here. [If this had been "the visit you paid me" it would have been nearer right and pertinent. J. H. H.]'

"[61] 'I do not refer to these facts to show the pertinence of my father's statement [to a visit paid to the father some years before his death].'

"So then, Dr. Hyslop did not 'consider this a reference to a visit that occurred some years before his father's death,' but inclined to think that the reference was to his own visit shortly before the death. He points to the spontaneous correction from 'my last visit' to 'your last visit' on page 474. Indeed, it is not unlikely that if in the first

---

[59] See *Proceedings* A. S. P. R., X, index references to "Mrs. Fischer; communications," or preferably "The Mother of Doris," *ibid.*, XVII.
[60] *Proceedings* S. P. R., XVI, 440.   [61] *Ib.*, 508; note by Dr. Hyslop.

instance Dr. Hyslop had not interrupted after ' I paid to you . . . you,' there might have been written ' you paid to me.' But he nowhere lays any stress upon this incident, or regards so much of it as evidential. There was much that was evidential in the whole incident, for the father went on to give the subjects upon which they had conversed, ' hypnotism,' ' a young woman who had experiences and dreams,' etc., and to state his son's attitude, ' You were doubtful about life after so-called death,' all of which was correct. *It is precisely the evidential features and the only ones so regarded by Dr. Hyslop, that Professor Washburn omits.*

" 2. The Dog Peter.
" *Miss Washburn's version.*

" ' The supposed spirit of Dr. Hyslop's cousin asks, " Do you remember Peter who was or belonged to Nanie ? " After investigation, Dr. Hyslop finds that this cousin, when between two and four years old, had a dog named Peter, but no Nanie seems to have been involved.'
" *The facts of record.*[62]

" ' And do you remember Peter who was . . . or belonged to Nanie ? [I can detect no meaning to the name of " Peter " and " Nanie " in this connection. J. H. H.] (I do not recall Peter now.)'
"[63] ' What is meant by Peter ? [No meaning. J. H. H.] Was it the dog George had ? (I do not remember this.)'

" Dr. Hyslop thought that ' George ' referred to a brother of his when he answered, ' I do not remember.' But afterward [64] he learned that the communicator's son George had owned a dog named Peter when a small child. Dr. Hyslop was never in a position to have known this. And the communicator did have a sister named Nannie. Who shall say that there was no association between her and the dog, forgotten by the living? Yet Dr. Hyslop does not suggest this, and lays no stress upon the coincidences. But there are scores of better indications in the Report. Why does Professor Washburn select these comparatively weak ones, why does she mangle even these, and is this the treatment to be recommended from ' a scientific point of view ' and as an example of the superior acumen of the psychologist ?

" The report on ' Observations of Certain Phenomena of Trance '[65] by Myers, Lodge, Leaf and James, filling 223 pages, is annihilated by the supposed dissection of one minor incident.

" *Professor Washburn's version.*

" ' Sir Oliver Lodge's Uncle Jerry, communicating through Mrs. Piper, states that his brother Bob killed a cat in Smith's field, and tied it to a fence; it is found that his brother Charles once killed a cat, but not in Smith's field, nor did he tie it to a fence.'

---

[62] *Ib.,* 428-429.   [63] *Ib.,* 452.   [64] *Ib.,* 515.   [65] *Ib.,* VI.

"The point which Sir Oliver stresses is that there proved to have been a 'Smith's field' in the home region of his uncle, a fact which he never knew. And how did Mrs. Piper, going to England a stranger and carefully guarded afterwards, know that there was an 'Uncle Jerry,' a 'Bob,' etc.?

"And it is far from 'scientific' to allege that the statement about killing a cat was in error. Provisionally, we treat it as incorrect, and yet no one is in a position to assert that as a fact. A well known university professor wrote to Mr. Chauncey M. Depew, asking if the newspaper interview alleging that he had a certain remarkable vision afterwards fulfilled was true, and received the reply that it was. Yet eighteen years later the professor had not the slightest recollection of the vision or the correspondence, now in the files of the American S. P. R. Would it have been remarkable if two brothers met in the flesh and one failed to remember a cat-killing incident related by the other? The living brother in the alleged incident did not deny the truth of it, but said he did not remember that it took place.

"I confess surprise that Professor Washburn has been won over to the polemical methods of Dr. Amy E. Tanner!

"*Raymond*, although it contains some good pieces of evidence, by no means ranks so high in that respect, as do certain other experimental records. But, mainly because certain sentences coming through the psychic lend themselves to pointless ridicule, certain psychologists have centered their attacks upon it to the neglect of the more formidable cases,[65a] aside from a few carefully selected passages and sundry misquotations and bizarre blunders.

"This is not idly said. I have been for some time specifically calling the attention of objectors, principally psychologists, to a particular case, covering less than seventy-five pages, and asking them to face and discuss it, and to explain by any 'normal' postulates the facts therein. I will furnish the materials and all facilities for the examination. If any one will give an intelligent explanation on any other basis than a 'supernormal' one, I will accept that explanation like a shot. So long as psychologists are so sure of their ground, and have time for articles filled with sweeping assertions and particular observations which reveal nothing so much as lack of exact knowledge of the literature of psychical research, it would seem that they might find opportunity to read seventy-five pages, and analyze the contents, and clear up the problem of their production.

"The experiments embodied in the brief record to which I refer were conducted by one of the most exact and cautious of investigators, a man of sphynx-like demeanor; every word uttered is set down and

---

[65a] The best of all, in my judgment, is the remarkable episode of the peacock. See my discussion of it in *Journal* A. S. P. R., XVI, 94-8.

even every fall of the automatist's pencil. Fraud is excluded by the conditions set forth. 'Fishing' and information given by the persons present can be exposed if either is there. The subconscious mind of the psychic surely could not have poured forth a flood of correct statements of fact of which she was never aware. The chances of attaining by guess the results set down can be shown to be less than one to the population of billions of worlds like this.

"But we are told that 'in no case of alleged supernatural [supernormal] communication through a medium are the conditions known to have been such as to rule out other explanations.' Very well, I submit that there are many such cases, and I especially instance one because of its compactness and brevity, and challenge Professor Washburn to meet the issue which she had made. Short of accusing Dr. Hyslop, the sitter and myself of a conspiracy and a forged record, I am skeptical of her ability to do it with success. If she makes even a plausible showing, I shall be the first to congratulate her for doing what her psychologist colleagues have thus far been too shy to attempt. She may choose her own periodical, provided that in fairness the periodical will give me an equal place in the arena. Or I will throw open to her the pages of the *Journal* of the Society which I represent. The gauntlet is at her feet. Will she take it up?"

She did not. There followed a silence like that of the grave.

DR. MILLAIS CULPIN

Dr. Culpin is the author of an amateurish book called *Spiritualism and the New Psychology*, and Professor **LEONARD HILL** wrote an introduction for it. The evidences for enchantment in both I have analyzed at length.[66] Professor Hill was so ignorant of the recorded evidence for telepathy that he supposed it covered by this explanation: "It is to be expected that the sensory stimuli received from a given environmental condition will often arouse the same train of thought in two or more people, standing together, especially in those who habitually associate. Such coincidences of thought, which astonish the ignorant, are due to natural law."

To him it is all of a piece with a family sitting at dinner, and all having the thought that the beef is excellent. What was there in relationship or environment or proximity which can account for the following:[67]

---

[66] *Journal* A. S. P. R., XVI, 74-98.

[67] Illustrative material to confute Professor Hill could be drawn from many sources, but I choose to select from a noteworthy report published by Mr. Upton Sinclair in 1930, under the title of *Mental Radio*, and dealing at length with experiments indicating telepathic powers on the part of his wife. The particular experi-

First Experiment by Craig and Bob, forty miles apart

What Bob did and drew

1. While deciding what to draw he sat facing the sideboard, on which were silver candlesticks.
2. He sat at the dining-room table.
3. He sat at the northeast corner of the table.
4. He made his drawing on a half sheet of green paper.

5. HE DREW A CHAIR WITH SOLID LEGS with horizontal strips across the back and wrote the word "chair" in capital letters, beneath the drawing.

6. After he had drawn the chair, he lay down on the bed, gazing through the foot of the bed at the chair he had taken as a model. The bed-foot has vertical bars.

What Craig drew and wrote

1. "I saw Bob take something from the sideboard—think it was the glass candlestick."
2. "I saw Bob sitting at dining-room table—a dish or some small object before him."
3. "(on N. E. corner table)."
4. "I try to see object on table—see something white at last. I can't decide what it is, so I concentrate on seeing his drawing on a green paper."
5. "I try hard to see what he has drawn—try to see paper with a drawing on it and see a straight chair."

    HERE SHE DREW A CHAIR WITH SOLID LEGS, with horizontal lines across the back.
6. Here she made a second drawing, seeming to represent a chair, but with the lines at the back now running vertically, and three short lines representing the legs. She also wrote:

    "Am not sure of the second drawing. It does not seem to be on paper. It may be his bed-foot. I distinctly see a chair like first [drawing] on his paper."

At the second experiment, the following day, Bob drew a watch. Craig's drawing was a partial success hard to describe without the cuts

---

ments which I shall briefly describe were of a set planned by Mrs. Sinclair and her brother, and carried out sitting at the same hour when they were forty miles apart. "Craig" is Mrs. Sinclair, "Bob" her brother. Craig would not only draw but also, in some cases, write out her impressions. The conditions of the experiments seem to be well authenticated. The drawings are shown in the book.

of both drawings. At the third experiment, the next day, Bob drew a pair of scissors, and again Craig's impression, although it can hardly be represented by words, showed significant approximation. At an experiment three days later, July 13, Bob drew a table fork; Craig drew nothing, but simply wrote: "See a table fork. Nothing else." But the experiment of July 11 deserves special mention.

What Bob drew and experienced

1. With a compass making a hole in a sheet of paper he drew a large circle around it.
2. Then he discovered that he had a hemorrhoid " and couldn't put my mind on anything else than the thought, 'My God, my lungs—my kidneys—and now this!'" (And a hemorrhoid naturally suggests the likelihood of hemorrhage.)

What Craig drew and wrote

1. She drew several concentric circles around a black point.
2. After making the drawing she seemed to see a dark spot overspreading the paper, felt intense depression, tried to draw the spot, and wrote alongside of it: "All this dark like a stain—feel it is blood; that Bob is ill—more than usual."

There are four witnesses, two for each end of the experiments, as well as the original drawings and writing.

Dr. Culpin apparently is profoundly ignorant of Sir William Barrett's lengthy report on dowsing, but thinks he has solved the whole business by explaining that the movement of the diviner's twig is due to subconscious muscular action, which no intelligent person doubts, and to guess-work, judging by the mass of cases with which he is acquainted, three in number, and one of these from a newspaper, and a second told him in conversation. He annihilates an old recorded apparitional case by a process of imagining the facts quite otherwise than all the witnesses stated—a process which, as it had no warrant but prejudice, could be applied to any human testimony whatever. He makes Sir Oliver Lodge's very impressive incident of "Mr. Jackson," the peacock, ridiculous by quoting only the first lines of it for the purpose of showing that Lodge tried to help the medium, and very carefully stops at the point where Lodge tried to mislead the medium, who, nevertheless, poured out a lot of particulars which were by no means implied in anything that the sitter had admitted. And he pauses amidst his tilting at windmills to warn us gravely against "logic-tight compartments," and indulging in "pseudo-reasoning"!

Now let us note the caution with which a physiologist, the proper

THE ENCHANTED BOUNDARY

judge of such matters, analyzes an old case.[68] One Mr. Lett related that about six weeks after his wife's father's death, Mrs. Lett and a Miss " Britton " [this should be Berthon] entered a room and saw an apparition of the dead man, half-figure but life-size, as it were reflected upon the polished surface of the wardrobe, clad in his familiar gray flannel jacket, so vivid that they first thought it was the reflection of a portrait, but there was none. " While they were looking and wondering, my wife's sister, Miss Towns, came into the room, and before either of the others had time to speak she exclaimed, ' Good gracious! Do you see Papa?' One of the housemaids happened to be passing downstairs at the moment, and she was called in and asked if she saw anything, and her reply was, ' O Miss; the master.' Graham—Captain Towns' old body-servant—was then called for, and he also exclaimed, ' Oh, Lord save us! Mrs. Lett, it's the Captain!' The butler was called, and then Mrs. Crane, my wife's nurse, and they both said what they saw. Finally Mrs. Towns was sent for, and, seeing the apparition, she advanced toward it. . . . As she passed her hand over the panel of the wardrobe the figure gradually faded away, and never again appeared.

" These are the facts of the case, and they admit of no deceit; no kind of intimation was given to any of the witnesses; the same question was put to each one as they came into the room, and the reply was given without hesitation by each."

Mrs. Lett is positive that the recognition of the appearance on the part of each of the later witnesses was independent, and not due to any suggestion from the persons already in the room.

If Dr. Culpin had limited himself to objecting that in the lapse of twelve years between the phenomenon and the written recital errors of memory *might* have crept in he would have been on safe ground. But when he says that " we know what happens under such conditions," implying that the story was certain to have become distorted and exaggerated, he states what simply is not true. I know by actual tests that with some persons such a story after the lapse of many years simply loses some of its details, while the main structure remains essentially unaltered.

But the critic continues, "*As the tale is given* (my italics), however, it reveals more than the narrator thinks it does." Now comes in the fine work of the physiologist. Words to which special attention is

---

[68] *Phantasms of the Living*, by Gurney, Myers and Podmore, II, 213-14.

called will be put in small capitals and my comments italicized, within square brackets. Let us see what the tale reveals, as it is given.

Picture Miss Towns coming into the room whilst the first two were "looking and wondering" (and not in silence WE MAY BE SURE, in spite of the words "before either of the others had time to speak," which ARE INTERPOLATED TO STRENGTHEN THE STORY) [*This is not what " the tale reveals, as it is given," it is contradicting the tale and ascribing a purpose to strengthen the story contrary to the facts. Is it not possible for people to be silent, or not to have time to speak before something else happens? Well, then, only a determination at all costs to break down the story can make us* SURE *that anything was said. And if we are resolved to hew away every obstacle to our purpose, because the story cannot be true anyhow, why not make the process shorter and simply say with the countryman when he first saw the giraffe, " There ain't no such animal," and dismiss the story as a lie?*]; she straightway experiences the same emotion and sees what they see. [*These witnesses declare that no intimations were given; suppose the first two ladies did* NOT *describe to the third what they saw, would simple emotion infallibly indicate that the apparition of Captain Towns had been seen?*] Now we have three EMOTIONAL PEOPLE [*There is not a shred of evidence for this statement; for all the critic knows they may have been particularly cool and calm people, for even such might " look " and " wonder," be " surprised " and even " half-alarmed " at such an unusual experience*], and as each new witness is brought along the emotion increases till it would require a very self-possessed and skeptical person to resist its influence [*an admission that such a person might resist the influence, but coupled with an assumption, without an atom of knowledge of the facts, that not one of the eight persons was that sort of a person. Yet a single such person, if as voluble as it is again assumed, in contradiction of the testimony, that the witnesses were, might have broken the power of suggestion for all who subsequently came in. Is it likely that out of the eight, not one was a cool, incredulous one, proof against subtle suggestion to the extent that he or she could not be caused to see an apparition of a particular dead person?*] The butler and nurse simply HAD TO SEE the ghost [*Even if we agree that they had to see something, it does not follow that they had to see the same thing—the apparition of Captain Towns*] though the account is a little ambiguous at this point. [*Verbally it is, but there can be no doubt what is meant. And why are the housemaid and body-servant, with their explicit statements, and why is Mrs. Towns, with the explicit statement as to what she saw, left out of account, if not for the reason that there is less opportunity to cavil at the testimony related to them?*]

"The same question was put to each one as they came into the room," but is it likely that under such a condition of excitement enough self-control was left to every individual to insure that the same question, *and nothing else*, was put to each newcomer? [*In the first place the degree of " excitement " which it is supposed must prevail on such an occasion, is exaggerated. I have been present at two or three scenes which theoretically would have frightened and excited the participants, and they remained calm, though interested and surprised. Many instances are known to me. I have been myself surprised, though by no means thrown into a state of uncontrollable emotion about it, that* USUALLY *people take such things as apparitions so coolly. But again the critic, after promising that he was going to show what " the tale as given " revealed, contradicts the solemn statements of two witnesses and that of a third person (Mr. Lett) who had an opportunity to question all immediately afterward.*] Such a thing COULD ONLY HAPPEN BY CAREFUL PREARRANGEMENT [*Is this true? Could not a single person be intelligent enough to warn the others in turn, even by the gesture of a finger to the lips, before the next came into the room, to be silent? Surely Dr. Culpin would have had the sense to see the importance of such a precaution. It would certainly have been my instinctive course, and I venture to contradict and say that there* COULD *have been such a person, say Mrs. Lett or Miss Towns, who first entered, in this group with the no excessive quantity of sense requisite to adopt the same procedure. Both Mr. Lett, who talked with all the witnesses directly afterward, and Mrs. Lett, who was a witness, as the narrative is* GIVEN, *assure us that no intimations were given what had been seen. But this very assurance is made the ground for a subtle objection.*] which was lacking here, and the writer's insistence SHOWS THAT SOMEWHERE IN HIS MIND WAS PRESENT THE SUSPICION THAT SUGGESTION HAD A HAND in the production of the unanimous evidence. [*Take this in connection with what follows.*] Mrs. Lett is equally insistent that the recognition was not due to any suggestion from the persons already in the room, but SHE WAS UNAWARE THAT SUGGESTION CAN OCCUR WITHOUT INTENT and that the most powerful suggestion is that which is unintentional. [*How does Dr. Culpin know that she was unaware of this? I will agree to invalidate any story which he may tell if I am at liberty to contradict any of his statements according to my notion of what is likely or conceivable, and to ascribe* to him without any ascertained data whatever psychological make-up is convenient for my purpose. If he had said that perhaps Mrs. Lett was unaware, etc., or even that she probably was, I would not object, but no physiologist or other man has a right to affirm positively what he does not know is true. But especially note another proof of his determination to make all grist for his mill. He invalidates the testimony because Mrs. Lett does not signify that she understands about the power of indirect suggestion, and he earlier invalidates it because the witnesses signify that they do understand what direct suggestion can do. " The writer's insistence (as well as his wife's), that no ' intimation ' or ' suggestion ' had been made, shows that somewhere in his mind was present the suspicion that suggestion had a hand in the production of the unanimous evidence!" What is a poor witness to do?

"You are damned if you do,
You are damned if you don't."

One is reminded of the procedure for trying if a woman was a witch by throwing her into the water—if she floated, execution followed; if she drowned, it was much the same.] Can we suppose that there were no signs of wonder and awe on the faces of those present, no excited exclamations, no glances towards the wardrobe, no pointing of hands, only a few calm and self-possessed people asking each newcomer if he or she saw anything? [Nowhere does Dr. Culpin charge or intimate that any one described what he saw to the person next entering, his whole argument at this point is that the efficacious suggestions were unintended and indirect. And he does not see the logical hiatus that he has created. Allow that the witnesses were in a state of excitement bordering on frenzy, so that each particular hair stood on end like quills on the fretful porcupine, granted that they uttered ejaculations such as "Oh!" and "My!" and "Heaven help us!," grant that they all glared at the wardrobe and pointed all their fingers at it, how could all these signs infallibly indicate the same thing, that an apparition was to be seen, and that the apparition was to be that of Captain Towns? I grant that Captain Towns had recently died, though the passage of six weeks would not suggest that his ghost was to be expected. But why need every mind have gravitated at once to an apparition? Why might not this one have thought of an infernal machine and have looked to see if one was visible? And another that perhaps a burglar was shut up in the wardrobe and that he was being *called on to see a trembling movement of that article of furniture? Is it credible that out of six who came in subsequently to the first two, not one, when asked if he or she saw anything, would have looked in great perplexity and have made some such answer as, " No, I don't see a thing. What is the matter with all of you? What do you see? " If there was something unusual apparently reflected on the wardrobe, it might well be that suggestion would cause some of the eight to think it looked like Captain Towns, though it is hard to believe that not one would say something like, " Yes, I see a peculiar appearance on the wardrobe, it must be the reflection of some object." But if there really was some peculiar appearance on the wardrobe in the bright gaslight, what became of it? Why did it gradually disappear and why could none of the excited and highly-suggestible group get any renewal of the impression?*] The minute account of the apparition, given by someone who was not present [*It does not appear to be convenient to quote Mr. Lett's statement: "I was in the house at the time, but did not hear when I was called," for this would have revealed that he had opportunity to hear the testimony of all eight witnesses within the hour—a very different situation from that when a man tells a story years after the facts which happened at a distance, and the auditor, who never has talked with any other witness, afterward rehearses the story*] and told as if it were the result of the immediate observations of the first two witnesses [*I can see no possible justification for this statement. Furthermore, it seems not quite ingenuous to set down such a sentence and to ignore the signed declaration of Mrs. Lett and her sister which makes Mr. Lett's account their own: "We, the undersigned, having read the above statement, certify that it is strictly accurate, as we were both witnesses of the apparition." And it seems to a misguided psychical researcher to be of importance that these witnesses " never experienced a hallucination of the senses on any other occasion " as bearing upon the extreme suggestibility credited to them, as well as the remaining six witnesses, by the physiologist, on no evidence whatever.*] HAS BEEN influenced by discussion after the incident [*Verily, the man must be omniscient!*] and IS itself another product of suggestion [*First the apparition was the eight-fold product of suggestion and now the whole narrative about it is the product of suggestion. Some people use that word to conjure with, to paralyze any fact, statement or evidence which they do not fancy. And this good doctor, though doubtless an expert physiologist, really seems to use the word " suggestion " as recklessly as his profession used to use calomel. Here is a story guaranteed by two witnesses and written by a man who* had conversed with six more, and it is resolved into " a product of suggestion." I can imagine the doctor called as an expert witness. " The story which that man has just told is the product of suggestion," he declares. The cross-examiner takes him in hand. " You heard two persons declare that they were eye-witnesses, and all that he says is true; you have heard that six other persons were present at the time and that all testified to the same thing; how, then, can the account be the product of suggestion? " " Don't you see," says Dr. Culpin, " the actual witnesses might have forgotten what really took place, and various circumstances might have suggested what they now tell." " But," replies the lawyer, " they declare there was no suggestion about it, that they have always adhered to the same story." "Ah, but that might be part of the product of suggestion; it might, and I affirm that it was." " Not so fast," says counsel, " we want to learn how you know it was." " Because the story is so improbable." "And that is your ground for stating that the story is the product of suggestion? " " Yes, and that I don't like such stories at all." And the lawyer wearily says, "As we are not here to determine whether the testimony is to your liking or whether it is probable, but whether it is true, you may step down."] The narrator has overshot his mark in his protest against the possibility of suggestion [*We have already attended to this beautiful specimen of* petitio principii], and has produced a story in which the apparition is not the only improbable feature. [*Earlier, the apparition was so probable a feature as to be certain in the given circumstances*—" the butler and the nurse simply HAD to see the ghost " —*but now it has become improbable. Presto, change! We must inform Dr. Culpin that apparitions as subjective facts are not questioned by any well-informed persons. If he meant to say that the objectivity of the apparition is improbable, that is another thing, and he should really learn to express his meaning more accurately.*]

Finally we read, " I have given this analysis because the story is quoted repeatedly by writers on the spiritualist side, and until one examines it critically [*as one would examine a watch with a claw-hammer*] it appears convincing."

And *I* have given this analysis of the analysis because it is a type of the sort of thing in which many professional gentlemen who have the loathing-for-psychical-research complex but who are tyros in the field of psychical research, feel it is fitting to indulge, and until one examines it critically it might appear convincing. It is convincing to a great many people to whom anything, no matter how full of misapprehensions and misstatements, suppression and distortion of evidence, lame logic and sounding generalities, so long as it favors their prejudices and is proclaimed with Olympic assurance by academics and professionals, is sweet and juicy meat. But incorrect statement and poor logic are incorrect statement and poor logic no matter by whom uttered nor by how many. Dirty water may in Asia become fit for use, provided a sufficiently large tank is filled with it, but nowhere else. We respect any painstaking, learned and intelligent argument against the alleged supernormal, and will combat it respectfully or agree with it, as the case may be, but practically all that is served out by the intellectuals is of a grade that they would not dare to employ upon another subject. It seems as though some enchantment seizes upon men of ability in their respective fields the moment they pass the boundary line of psychical research with deadly intent. Even though psychical research were a windmill, there would otherwise seem to be no reason why they should tilt against it with wooden lances and on rickety Rosinantes.

DR. C. B. FARRAR

Dr. Farrar, a Canadian psychiatrist, had an article entitled " The Revival of Spiritism " in the American *Archives of Neurology and Psychiatry* for June, 1921, which is analyzed in the *Journal* of the A. S. P. R. for October, 1922. It is characterized by all the tokens of enchantment which we catalogued at the beginning of this paper, including the misspelling of proper names familiar to psychical researchers. Farrar's main thesis is that no man ever reaches conviction that there are spirits through evidence, but that it is always achieved by " an act of faith temperamentally determined," which dogma pleasantly relieves Farrar of the trouble of paying the purported evidence any attention. His main argument in support of the dogma is that such men could not have become convinced by *evidence* (he puts the word between scornful quotation marks, since he is sure without examination that it would not be evidence to him), because they have been studying this evidence a long while! Sir William Barrett began his investigations " upwards of forty years ago." " Hodgson devoted years of his life to the subject." Others have " grown old in their quest." As there appears to be no reason why this logic should not be of universal application, the conclusion seems to be that the only way to reach a rational conviction upon a subject is to refrain from studying it.

" The earliest antecedents," we are told, of the " spiritistic " movement are to be found in the period of the Old Testament and that of

Greece and Rome, and this is said as though it implied a reproach. It appears to me that if purported supernormal phenomena had never appeared before the nineteenth century this would have been claimed as a damning fact. "Why," it would have been demanded, "have such things never happened before in the long history of the race, if they happen now?" Contrariwise, if such phenomena are fundamental to human nature, we should expect to find them in the ages of the Old Testament and of Greece and Rome.

But as by the magic of the pen a sinister aspect is given to the fact that "modern phenomena have their prototype and pattern in the early days of our race," so in the next paragraph "Modern Spiritism" is twitted for being so young. It dates back, we are told, only to the Hydesville rappings of 1848. "Modern Spiritism dates from 1848,"—and if by "modern spiritism" we are to understand a particular cult, the statement is correct. But if it means phenomena such as are alleged to happen now and more or less widespread interest therein, it is far from correct.

Andrew Jackson Davis was already known as the "Seer" in 1843. From 1838 to 1848 phenomena ascribed to spirits swept through all the Shaker communities in this country. It is said that spiritistic sittings were being held in San Bernardino, California, before 1840. On the other side of the sea, as early as 1824 the "Seeress of Prevorst" was seeing and talking with apparitions, manifesting psychometrical, clairvoyant and previsionary powers, in trance states, which prevailed for many years. The case was widely known. Forty years earlier, Jung-Stilling, whose experiences so much interested Goethe, was seeing apparitions, having premonitions, making predictions and collecting with moderately critical care accounts by his contemporaries of all sorts of phenomena such as are alleged today, including raps that were accustomed to sound when deaths occurred, premonitory dreams, messages, and even the feeling of a "cold wind," which accounts were published in his "Pneumatology." In 1743 began the "clairvoyant" visions of the great engineer, Swedenborg, which impressed Kant, the talks with spirits and angels, the dreams and other experiences which he related. In 1716 came the raps, groans and poltergeist performances in the house of John Wesley's father which made John a believer in spirit manifestations all his life. We go back to George Fox, who, born in 1624, heard voices and saw visions, made predictions said to have been fulfilled, wrought cures and banished obsessing spirits. Back of this, in the sixteenth century, the "Tremblers of the Cevennes" largely overran Germany, and these had visions, believed that

THE ENCHANTED BOUNDARY

they communicated with good and evil spirits, and performed psychical cures. Jacob Böhme, the noted mystic, born in 1575, had a range of experiences, did automatic writing, saw and conversed with what he appeared to regard as an unearthly visitor, heard music inaudible to others, and claimed to have seen different spheres of the supernal world. Martin Luther, a little earlier, heard raps, bangs and terrific noises in his room at Wartburg Castle, as he had earlier heard inexplicable sounds in his monastic cell at Wittenberg. He saw apparitions which his prepossessions identified as the devil, exorcised and made cures. And everyone knows, or ought to know, the story of Joan of Arc in the thirteenth century.

The point is not that all of this list of instances, which might be indefinitely extended, were correctly interpreted at the time, and for present purposes it is immaterial whether they were or not. The point is that if one cares to travel back through the generations, he keeps running upon alleged phenomena of types similar to those asserted to occur in our own times. Thus it is quite erroneous to say that "modern spiritism dates from 1848." A certain religious cult may be said to date from 1848, but that is a very different thing.

If I should write an article criticizing several eminent members of Dr. Farrar's profession and should spell their names Janey, Sydis, Morton Printz, Ossler, he would be warranted in presuming that I had never been familiarly acquainted with either these men or their works, else the true form of their names would have been a part of the records of my brain. And if I had no other evidence of his unfamiliarity with the literature of psychical research I would find it in his spellings, " Meyers," " Edmunds," " Seibert," and in the mixing of the initials of F. W. H. Myers ("F. H. W. Myers"). Even physical science cannot be very familiar, else he would hardly have written " Tindall."

Dr. Farrar entertains the theory that, so far as religion is concerned, personal attitudes "are not arrived at by processes of deliberation, logic and judgment, but are, first and last, questions of temperament, to change which lies not within the power of the individual." This he admits applies at both ends of the scale, so that religious skepticism as a psychological attitude is no more rational than is religious faith. Of course this generalization flies in the face of the testimony of millions that they were irreligious, if not opposed at least indifferent to religion, until well on in life, when *something occurred* to cause an inward revolution. And it flies in the face of the evidence furnished by the visible lives of millions. Furthermore, multitudes of people went through the process of "deliberation, logic and judgment" before arriving at settled conclusions on religion, as printed biographies show, and they did not believe and never would have admitted that this process was without force or meaning. That is, the dogma that men are mere automata so far as religion is concerned, is contradicted by both consciousness and external observation. Whence, then, does Dr. Farrar draw assurance that his dogma is true? If we point out a man—and there are hosts of such cases—who has been a materialist, and so far as he or any one else could see, was satisfied in his materialism, until the age of fifty or sixty, when he somehow made a right-about-face, Dr. Farrar says that all the while the man was a predestined believer in religion. Byron wrote that

"When Bishop Berkeley said there was no matter,
And proved it—'twas no matter what he said."

I should say that when a man, in the face of all the evidence which the nature of the case admits of puts forward a generalization which he can support only by barren assertion, it is of interest only as swelling the list of curious and rickety psychological speculations. If religious attitudes "are first and last questions of temperament" I would like to know what temperament was doing all of sixty years before a man of that age finally changed his views. · It reminds me how a phrenologist, when I was a youth, declared my organ of "form" to be the largest in the whole nest, which would imply that I was wonderfully keen in remembering faces. I told the phrenologist that my memory for faces was very poor, and he said that the faculty was large in me, but "latent." But I cannot understand what is meant by a strong faculty which remains latent, as that one has in me to this day. Nor can I understand an innate disposition which works in a contrary direction for half a lifetime and then suddenly begins to work as it would be expected to do.

All this is relevant because our writer advances a step and says that the belief in spirits is also "an act of faith temperamentally determined." And I do not see why the doctrine is not every whit as applicable to all human beliefs and convictions, just as easy to assert, just as unlikely, just as impossible to prove. Thus we should be landed in the midst of a universal skepticism of reason, and be spared the examination of any facts hitherto supposed to support this or that belief, or any mental effort at all aside from a languid interest in those fatalities of birth which gave us fixed beliefs as it gave us fixed complexions. But I do note that in advancing his " temperament " theory so as to include views on spiritism, the good doctor forgets to let it work both ways, as he did in the case of religion. That is, he maintains that " belief in spirits is an act of faith temperamentally determined," but he does not, and he should, add that disbelief in spirits is also not reached by any process of reasoning about it, but is temperamentally determined. To have done so would have destroyed any utility in his article, for what could be the use of arguing against spiritism in a world of beings hopelessly sewed up in their individual bags of reason-proof temperament? Besides, the doctrine that " belief " in spirits is never really based on reasoning from facts, enables one to disregard the facts and arguments of psychical researchers as irrelevant, while the implication that disbelief in spirits is, must be, and ever shall be the result of intelligent processes makes golden coin out of many a criticism of psychical research which is otherwise counterfeit as to fact and to logic.

What nonsense! There is no subject upon which a sound and candid mind is not capable of acting according to the " processes of deliberation, logic and judgment "! There are no subjects in relation to which the reason of all men is paralyzed. To hold that there are is manifestly to be superstitious on those subjects, for they would have to be regarded as possessing a resistless fateful power of inhibiting human reasoning unless it happens to take an adverse direction. There is no other subject, politics, medicine, psychology, biology, art, literature, on which human beings cannot hold differing views without either side laying down a doctrine that the logical processes of the other are in absolute abeyance. To be sure, this is a convenient dictum, for it avoids the necessity of attending to the troublesome evidence and argument of the adversary; it is sufficient to ascribe to him on purely imaginary and theoretical grounds a certain psychological make-up and then to illustrate it with carefully selected quotations wrenched from their connections.

Does Dr. Farrar entertain such a skepticism of his own mental capacities as to believe that if he had a visual or an auditory hallucination he could not record it at the time, as he could record in his diary the bodily visit of a friend? That if the apparition made a prediction he could not as easily watch, report, and prove the fulfilment of the prediction as its failure? That, if after living in twenty-six houses without a thing happening that did not readily answer to normal explanations, he should take up residence in the twenty-seventh, where (I have in mind an actual case) raps sounded in various parts of the house, beds shook and a variety of singular things occurred, he could not investigate the raps and other facts as coolly as he would investigate cockroaches or defective drains? That if automatic writing rehearsed a variety of facts regarding a deceased friend, which the psychic provably did not know, he could not reach a rational conclusion, at least tentatively, whether or not the correspondences were too many and too particular to be ascribed to chance? Unless he made haste to deny the facts, must he worship them and be drawn into a whirlpool of unreasoning credulity? He discourses as though there were no objective facts on record, but only delirious fantasies. But there happens to be on record a great body of facts, and a great many witnesses whose testimony in regard to other types of facts would be regarded with respect. I am not here defending any particular interpretation of the facts, but only maintaining that since, if any of them took place in the vicinity of Dr. Farrar, he could keep his head and observe, call in other witnesses to observe, truthfully report and attest by corroborative testimony, and afterward calmly set down arguments *pro* and *con*, others can do the same. Or will he admit that he could not do it? Does he think that "hereditary and developmental neuropsychical attitudes, tendencies and inclinations" *create facts* external to the possessor of the assumed characteristics? If not, how in the name of common sense can the vexed question of "spiritism" be settled solely by inventing psychological theories about the observers?

I pass over the claim that Sir William Osler, in his *Science and Immortality*, teaches the same doctrine of temperamental determinism, with the remark that to read the little book to the end is to refute the claim. Osler does indeed classify temperaments, and of course they exist, but he emphatically does not hold that these are chains which cannot be broken. Otherwise there would be no sense in his words, "Some of you will wander through all phases, to come at last, I trust, to the opinion of Cicero, who had rather be mistaken with Plato than be right with those who deny altogether the life after death." The temperament is not a mold but a current which may have its course shaped.

But let us see how the psychiatrist proves his contention that spiritists of the type of Hodgson, Lodge, Hyslop and Barrett were not moved by facts, but by the irresistible tendency of a native temperament. His main argument is that such men could not have been persuaded by "evidence" in quotation marks, because they have been studying this evidence a long while! Sir William Barrett began his investigations "upwards of forty years ago." "Hodgson devoted years of his life to the subject, and made it practically his whole occupation." Doyle, "for more than thirty years has devoted most of his spare time to psychical research." Others have "grown old in their quest." Therefore they did not really, rationally investigate, therefore their "evidence" was not evidence, therefore they were simply trotting round and round in the circle of their temperamental prison-cell, without adding an iota to the stock of facts worthy of attention.

If this is logic, it should be mercilessly applied. We need not pay attention to Darwin's evidence, it will suffice to put the word in derisive quotation marks, for Darwin spent nearly twenty years of his life on the subject of Natural Selection and made it practically his whole occupation prior to the publication of his exposition. Almost from boyhood Peary was engrossed with desire (and desire is the great provocative of imaginary wish-fulfilment) to reach the North Pole; it was his study and passion for many years (probably "largely a matter of endocrine glands," etc.), he tried again and again ("this is the factor of habit"), and as "there is another factor in the psychological metamorphosis of conviction, the striving, if one may so express it, of every thought process to arrive at a definite *goal*," he at length believed he had found his! Why consume valuable time examining and accepting or else controverting his "evidence" when psychology, without leaving its cloister, can so easily explain the delusion? Semmelweiss was another of that infatuated set who "have practically devoted their lives" to a particular subject, his subject being the investigation and promulgation of the art of asepsis. He was one of those who "dedicated themselves to [an] inquiry . . . which, assuming for them more and more importance as the years passed, eventually became a veritable obsession." Perhaps because they divined his "natural constitutional bent" the great majority of his medical contemporaries refused to examine his "evidence," though they contemptuously repudiated it, and he at length contributed to their psychological theory by going mad over the matter. Oddly they are all following in his footsteps now in regard to asepsis. Alas! if it should be discovered that Dr. Farrar himself long ago devoted himself to the subject of psychiatry, and has spent many years in study and investigation preëminently in this field, for we should then be assured that whatever he considers to be "evidence" within that field is probably only the buzzing of a neuropsychic center in his brain, and should be compelled to request him to discuss some topic which neither of us had given any particular attention to, in order that our reason might be released from remorseless bias.

Let us see how the account stands between the psychical researcher and the psychiatrist, each of whom thinks he has found something worth while in his respective field. We will choose usual and typical cases:

Psychical Researcher	Psychiatrist
1. Pursues general courses of study in psychology or physical science with view to a profession.	1. Pursues medical studies with view to become a physician.
2. Continues his profession for years, uninterested in and skeptical to psychical research.	2. Interested in psychiatry—confides in it on *authority*—early in his medical studies.
3. His attention is attracted by some fact hard to explain on " normal " grounds.	3. His attention is still more attracted by psychiatry as promising a career.
4. Although his colleagues, who can give no explanation, make light of it—	4. Especially as his instructors speak well of it—
5. And he knows he may lose caste and injure his professional and financial prospects if he does not leave such matters alone.	5. And there is good money in it.
6. He pursues independent investigations, and reads the records of other investigators.	6. He listens to cut-and-dried lectures, faithfully takes notes, and believes all he hears.
7. He spends much of his *spare* time continuing his investigations, although they are regarded askance and are not lucrative.	7. At length he spends *all* his time studying and practising psychiatry as a gainful and well-reputed profession.
8. He publishes a *complete* record of a series of experiments containing incidents which he regards as weak or unevidential, also incidents carefully guarded and corroborated, which he regards as evidential, discusses the whole matter thoroughly, and asks that another than a supernormal explanation of the incidents on	8. Without any knowledge whatever of the psychical researcher except that the latter has studied his subject a long time, he invents, on purely theoretical grounds, a neuropsychic determinism for him, and disposes of both the evidence and the argument by the innuendo of quotation marks, or else picks out the incidents

Psychical Researcher	*Psychiatrist*
which he places emphasis be brought forward.	for annihilation which had expressly been designated as unevidential, and ignores those to which attention had specifically been called.

The above comparison is intended and believed to be perfectly fair. And I boldly affirm that I know of no doctor, psychologist, physicist, or other man of scientific pretensions in America who, since the day when Hodgson landed on these shores more than thirty years ago, has attempted or purported to confute the results of such psychical researchers as those of Hodgson himself and Hyslop, and whose success has surpassed what is described in the eighth section above. If there is a single, solitary instance where the parts of an automatic record upon which a scientific psychical researcher places emphasis, have been fairly met and an attempt made, by the kind of logic employed in other fields, to deprive them of supernormal significance, let it be pointed out.

DRS. SANDS AND BLANCHARD

It is a matter of history that in the course of the last fifty years many persons who had earned reputations for intellectual rigor, became convinced of the " supernormal " character of certain phenomena, and not a few went so far as to favor the theory that discarnate intelligences have been able to give tokens of their existence. At first the favorite explanation was that the prominent men were not trained scientists, and a call went forth for a man like Crookes. Crookes and other physicists were convinced, and it was said that they were beguiled in consequence of being out of their own bailiwick, and that, after all, the psychologist was the proper man to investigate. Myers, James and certain other psychologists became either convinced or benevolent, and lately it has been stated that the physiologist is the better fitted to judge. But the fact is painfully apparent that a number of well-known physiologists have become also convinced or been made favorable, and pretty generally resource has been found in a dogma, unaccompanied by proof, that all cases of conversion to supernormal facts of any kind, particularly spirit communication, or even respectful consideration of the problems, is due to a psychoneurotic tendency, to an innate predisposition or " will to believe " that is bound to find its goal. Dr. C. B. Farrar, as we have seen, is one of the most confident exponents of this theory, for which no proof but mere assertion is offered by him or any one else. And now come along two other psychiatrists, Drs. Irving J. Sands and Phyllis Blanchard, Ph.D., with a theory to account for at least a part of the mournful catalogue of cases, a theory which looks as though it were at war with the theory of Dr. Farrar and others. We quote from the book by Drs. Sands and Blanchard, *Abnormal Behavior: Pitfalls of Our Minds*.

"Arteriosclerotics are apt to become intolerant of opinions of others. They find difficulty in adapting themselves to new customs and habits of life. They often become cranks and faddists. By virtue of their recognized authority in their various callings, they are apt to gather new followers and disciples in various movements which they may undertake. Thus several prominent men who have in their later years become actively engaged in such movements as spiritualism have done so because of impaired judgment due to cerebral arteriosclerosis, and have gathered many disciples because of the prominence which they have achieved in some field of human endeavor during their prime of life."

In the cases referred to, at least, then, interest in "spiritualism" was not due to an innate psychoneurotic tendency impossible to resist, but to impaired judgment owing to a morbid condition of arteries in the brain, with the presumption that if this physiological condition had not come about the obnoxious opinions would never have been embraced.

The authors are not very precise. After asserting that the tendency from impaired arteries "often" operates, they come down to "several cases" which they say exist. They do not tell who the several men are. But the accompanying description makes it nearly certain that such men as Lodge, Hyslop, Hodgson, Myers, Crookes, Wallace, and Conan Doyle are referred to.

The majority of the men just named, as well as other men of the class described, came to their opinions before their "later years," and it is improbable that the confident writers can show that these men were ever proved to be afflicted with cerebral arteriosclerosis or that there are any indications that they had it. Some of them died before much was known about the malady. It is difficult to see how anything more than a mere guess can support the proposition so oracularly affirmed.

If the examples are collected from a lower range of prominence, then the "several" are the pick of a much larger number of cases than if drawn from the first rank, and the " several " are so much the less convincing.

Will the authors say that the " several " were subjected to examination which determined that the physical condition named existed, and that as a matter of fact they are not simply dogmatizing? Even if they know of three such actual cases (for three cases would be " several ") of prominent men who in their later years embraced " spiritualism " and acquired followings of " disciples," how are we to be sure that *post hoc* is not mistaken for *propter hoc?* If of twenty-five prominent cerebral arteriosclerotics, twenty-two remain by their prejudices and three depart from them, may not the malady be a blessing in disguise? We have known persons so hidebound that almost any change would be welcome. More seriously, if of twenty-five or thirty persons who come to adopt opinions which somebody doesn't like, I find that three, or " several," adopted them at an age when that somebody thinks they were old enough to have arteriosclerosis, isn't that slender material for an indictment of the opinions?

Later in the book it is admitted that spiritualistic belief may sometimes be quite useful in preventing the " development of a frank psychosis." However,

" One must not lose sight of the unscientific and false attitudes of the spiritualists, or be deceived by the statements of these deluded sufferers. We have seen many frank psychoses precipitated by lectures delivered by well-known spiritualists who have recently toured this country. Thus one case of Dementia Præcox in a state of remission, who was able to lead a fairly satisfactory life, was again thrown into active excitement after listening to one of the lectures. He there and then again began to see his sweetheart who had died several years before. It was necessary to have this patient committed to a state hospital because of his excitement."

It appears to us that the statement just quoted falls far short of proving the point aimed at, even granting that the " many psychoses " were all real ones and not the false diagnoses of prejudice, and that they became overt and recognized after the lectures. Many psychoses are first called to the attention of psychiatrists after they have centered around some such object as wireless telegraphy or aeroplanes, following some thrilling article on that subject in a newspaper or magazine. Dementia præcox and paranoia must fix upon some subject or subjects, and some event or other must immediately precede their becoming recognized, or their resumption after temporary recovery.

It is not fair to pick out one subject sometimes thus superficially connected, and to let the others go scot free.

The danger in psychical experimentation has been monstrously exaggerated. There is no logical reason why utter absorption in such matters to the neglect of others should not be dangerous, and it is, as the same type of undue absorption in religious exercises, politics, science or art in the cases of persons whose cerebro-neural or mental constitution contains a factor of instability. People become insane following troubles in business and love, but this is not urged as a reason why everyone should shun business and courtship.

Again, it is very common for a person who is beginning to become insane to fix his attention upon something of a recondite nature, around which his imagination can play, and which satisfies the demand of his disordered intellect for a cause to which he can ascribe his hallucinations.

The paranoiac hears voices and believes that they come from phonographs concealed in the walls to annoy him. Or he is persecuted by some telepathist who, wherever located, can read his every thought. Or some one once stared at him, and he has been under hypnotic influence ever since. Or the notions buzzing in his brain are charged upon wireless telegraphy. Or it is spirits who are doing the mischief or conferring supernal favors. Many more cases come to my notice where the fixed ideas are concerned with phonographs, telepathy, hypnotism and wireless telegraphy, than where they relate to spirits, yet the same persons who confidently claim that spiritism or interest in psychical research has caused the insanity in certain cases would never think of blaming phonographs, wireless telegraphy, etc., in the more numerous cases. That is to say, it is infrequent to get trustworthy data on cases where interest in psychical phenomena has been followed by insanity due to that interest, but frequent to hear of cases where minds whose disorder has already begun gravitates to spiritism or concealed phonographs, wireless telegraphy, telepathy, radium, X-rays, *et al.*

We can agree with whatever any one may say about the theoretical dangers of too great absorption in any of these subjects, but have come upon very little evidence of their causing mischief to a person of sound mentality who conducts himself with common prudence.

Nor can we, nor ought we, stop all investigation and progress in relation to subjects upon which people may apparently, or really, go insane. To do so would stop not only all investigation and discovery, but the human race itself, for there is no matter which is so frequently connected with insanity as love between the sexes. Yet none thinks of framing a fearful indictment against loving by saying, what would be perfectly true, that thousands of frank psychoses have been precipitated by incidents in connection with falling in love, and that we have known of relapses in consequence of meeting an old sweetheart, or hearing that she or he has married or died.

It is time that it were understood that the truth or falsity of any matter is not determined in any degree by the reactions of the insane toward it. This is already recognized in relation to every subject but one.[69]

If only to see how, in one generation as another, prejudice makes writers shun reality, or recreate facts to suit their fancy, we go back a quarter of a century to

---

[69] Mr. H. J. Osborne, a scholarly Spiritualist, furnished an article from *Reason* from which the following extracts are taken. A fuller selection may be found in *Journal* A. S. P. R., XVI, 226-27.

"A year or so ago I put the subject to the test of close and definite research. I put under contribution, in evidence, the medical superintendents of most of the great lunatic asylums of England and Wales; and I ransacked, over a series of years, the government reports on statistics on lunacy.

"The replies of the asylum doctors were, uniformly, that these asylums did not contain any inmates whose insanity has been certified as caused by Spiritualism; and in the rare cases where it enters at all as a causation, it is shown to be only contributory, if that, because of the presence in the case of heredity or other leading cause.

"The government figures are uniformly against the slander. The asylums of England and Wales contain few over 100,000 lunatics, of all types and conditions; none are certified as due to Spiritualism; and so far from this being a cause the real causes are shown to be in the heaviest proportions—alcohol, heredity, privation and syphilis. These, and some others, are preventable causes, and the slanderers of Spiritualism would be better employed in trying to secure better laws and better application to these subjects.

"It became obvious, from a study of the official figures, that if Spiritualism be a cause of insanity, its incidence must be sought in one line—that dealing with sudden mental stress. Under that heading in the official records are included all cases of religious mania, so certified.

"I carefully examined a table covering five years—the latest—and found that this phase of mental stress, standing alone, gave only—males, 1.4; females, 2.3. That is about one and a half hundred—the totals, as well as the percentage, being negligible. It is evident, then, that Spiritualism as a factor in the causation of insanity is, practically, a minus quantity.

"I found it, however, an interesting diversion, after proving that Spiritualists do not become insane, further to inquire where the preachers and the doctors—our chief slanderers—stand as regards insanity.

"From the same government figures I found, according to the latest report, which showed the incidence of insanity in respect of 'all occupations' the proportion of insane per 10,000 is 4.94. But the clergy of the Church of England average 10.3—more than double the general average; and that *one* cleric is certified insane every week!

"Of the doctors, three are certified insane every five weeks, and the average is 14.3—nearly three times as many as the general average."

E. W. SCRIPTURE, PH.D.

In a book entitled *The New Psychology* (1897), by E. W. Scripture, Ph.D., then Director of the Yale Psychological Laboratory, seven pages are devoted to psychic research. I borrow from Dr. Hyslop's review.[70]

" Professor Scripture's mode of attack consists in a comparison of what he regards as the slipshod method of psychical research and the more scientific procedure of Hansen and Lehmann in their criticism of the Sidgwick experiments. How much he knows about the Society's work is shown by the single fact that there is not the slightest evidence of his ever having seen the Society's Reports. The first instance of this negligence is found in the reference to some experiments alleged to have been made by Dr. Ochorovicz, and ridiculed here with a persiflage that is wholly unscientific. The character of the experiments I do not defend. They may be anything you please. But we are entitled to know where they were published and how much weight was given them by Ochorovicz himself. Not a reference is given, while it would seem from the very language that Ochorovicz attached no value to them. The record of them is not found in any of the publications of the Society, nor can I find any trace of them in Ochorovicz's book on *Mental Suggestion*. A few of his experiments were mentioned in *Phantasms of the Living*,[71] but not a word in them refers to the instances criticized by Professor Scripture. If psychical research is to be held responsible in this way for matter to which it has never given its imprimatur, what is to be said of the author's boasted scientific method? . . . The example of scientific method here recommended for imitation is that of the two Danish students, Hansen and Lehmann. The value and suggestiveness of their experiments I shall not question, but recognize with unstinted praise. But Professor Scripture shows no knowledge of either Professor Sidgwick's original experiments or his reply [72] to Hansen and Lehmann."

If Professor Scripture had been animated by any fair spirit toward psychic research, he would surely have wished to see what Professor Sidgwick had to say in reply. And he would have looked at the many reproductions of results of telepathic experiments published by the S. P. R. and found for himself how impossible it is to explain a part of them, such as irregular figures which have no name, on the theory of "involuntary whispering." And he would also have found instances where the original drawing could be named, but where the drawing of

---

[70] *Proceedings* S. P. R., XIV, 144.   [71] II, 660 ff.   [72] *Proceedings* S. P. R., XII, 298-314.

the "percipient," while too like the original for chance, is not what it would have been had there been, on the part of the "agent," successful involuntary whispering of the name. Take the complicated original drawing on page 95 of Volume I of the *Proceedings*. One part of it is a well-drawn profile of a man's head, the face turned to the left. Two attempts at reproduction show to the right the curved line corresponding to the back of the head in the original figure, and to the left a jiggling perpendicular roughly corresponding, suggesting the line of features in the original, but not revealing the slightest consciousness of a human head and face. But surely, any involuntary whispering would have contained the word "head" or "face," and the result would have been a distinctly recognizable head or face.

We turn again to Dr. Hyslop's criticism:

" Further, Professor Scripture says:—' Hysterical or hypnotized persons are the most frequent percipients in such experiments.' But what evidence is produced for this statement? None. Professor Scripture lays great emphasis on quantitative measurements, and surely here is a statement that is capable of statistical method! The statement, indeed, is a pure assumption entirely without foundation. But what if it were true? What difference would that fact make in careful experiments of the kind under review, viz., drawings? The percipients could just as well be insane. It matters not who or what the percipient may be, if the precautions are sufficient to prevent fraud. If we should prove telepathy, and assume or prove that the percipients were abnormal, the fact might require us to abandon the materialistic theory of insanity."

And, finally, Dr. Hyslop shows that Professor Scripture attempts to criticize experiments and calculations by the S. P. R., while he is in ignorance of the nature of those experiments, and misrepresents them.

" His words are: ' We might, like the psychical researchers, proceed to calculations of probability, *e. g.*, if a counter be drawn by chance from the total of 90 counters, the probability of drawing any particular one is 1-90, and likewise the probability of recording at random any particular one of 90 possible figures is 1-90. Now, the probability that the two agree by chance is equal to the product of the separate probabilities, or 1-8100. Only once out of 8100 times ought an experiment to succeed.' The probability that Professor Scripture describes is the probability that the number drawn and the number recorded will *both agree with a previously designated number*. But this is not the question. For example, to take one of the instances quoted by Professor Scripture, the problem is not the determination of the chance, prior to the experiment, that the agent would draw the particular number 33, and the percipient also guess 33. The problem is the determination of the chance, that after the agent has drawn one of the numbers, no matter which, the percipient should guess the same number. The agent having drawn 33, this number is already settled, and is calculated as a certainty. It is one of 90 numbers, any one of which the percipient may choose, and the chance that he will guess right is obviously 1 in 90. I do not blame Professor Scripture merely for being ignorant of the very simplest application of the laws of probability, but I do blame him for being ignorant and at the same time attempting, in a professedly scientific work, to deal with a subject where some elementary knowledge of these laws is absolutely essential for even a superficial judgment."

Here is a specialist in experimental psychology who takes pride in the exactitude of his methods, and yet who breaks into the field of psychic research with the blundering violence of a bull in a china-closet. How shall we explain the phenomenon, if not by the magic of the enchanted boundary?

JOSEPH JASTROW

Joseph Jastrow, Professor of Psychology in the University of Wisconsin, evidently has a Saul of Tarsus complex on the subject of spiritism, telepathy, and everything that savors of the supernormal, since for years he emitted a stream of articles, lectures and interviews in opposition. He evinces no experimental acquaintance with the disputed phenomena, only superficial first-hand knowledge of the records, and openly avows that " there is no real obligation to consider minutely all the circumstances " attending any claim,[73] since it is sufficient to rely on certain scientific maxims, the " will to believe " of those who have reported affirmative evidence, and the " temper " under which it was accumulated. He reproaches the Research Officer of the A. S P. R. for failing to be governed by dogmas which beg the very issues for which the Society exists to try, and which, if assented to in advance would automatically put it out of business. And, so powerful is the spell of the enchanted boundary, that he fails to perceive his comical position as an Advisory Scientific Counselor of that same Society. He relies with touching confidence upon such writers as Clodd and Mercier and, to crown all, refers with unqualified approval in a syndicat

---

[73] See his article in *Journal* A. S. P. R., January, 1923.

article of the public press to the work of Amy Tanner, the greatest atrocity of misrepresentation that ever was issued on the subject. Personally a charming gentleman, and no doubt an authority on psychology, he seemingly cannot lift his pen to write a paragraph on psychical research without an error of fact or a solecism in logic falling from it.

Some psychologists seem to think that modern science is a steel-riveted structure into whose rigid framework no facts radically new and unexpected can be introduced without wrecking it. Professor Jastrow writes that "obviously if the alleged facts of psychical research were genuine and real, the labors of science would be futile and blind," that what psychical researchers "fail to remember is the solid integration of science without which modern life and rational thinking in the environment which it has slowly created would be impossible." [74] An anthology of similar passages could be compiled from his writings. It happens that I am largely in agreement with Professor Jastrow's estimate of the particular book and case which furnished his texts for the remarks quoted, but the remarks themselves are not the less unsound. It is well that they were answered by a scientist, Edwin C. Kemble, Professor of Physics in Harvard University, who, whether or not he feels any particular interest in psychic research, cannot share in Dr. Jastrow's touching confidence in the immutability of present-day science, and responded as follows:[75]

"The central point of Professor Jastrow's contention is his belief that the phenomena reported by the psychical research investigators are logically inconsistent with the general body of modern science. This inconsistency is so obvious to Professor Jastrow that he is content with reiteration unaccompanied by elucidation.

"In a final slightly arrogant passage, he remarks that 'what the revival of the belief in occultism proves is the weak hold which principle and logic have gained upon minds otherwise of fine quality and more than ordinary caliber.'

"Your correspondent, a physicist, is reminded of a story told him years ago of a gentleman who, returning to his laboratory after a vacation, had great difficulty in getting his quadrant electrometer to behave properly. The deflections of the delicate little instrument were irregular, and it showed an unaccountable tendency to 'kick,' when by all the laws of science it should have remained steady. Finally, in anger, he took the instrument apart and found to his disgust that during his absence a spider had woven its web about the top of the

---

[74] *Weekly Review*, July 14, 1920. [75] *Ib.*, July 28, 1920.

suspension. Perhaps Professor Jastrow will find a flaw in the analogy, but it does seem to your correspondent that the assertion, 'if the alleged facts of psychical research were genuine and real, the labors of science would be futile and blind,' is at least very nearly on a par with denying the laws of physics because of the discovery of a spider.

"I venture to suggest two reasons for believing that the statement last quoted above is wrong.

"(1) Let me, in the first place, call attention to the fact that practical science is merely a detailed description of Nature's ordinary *modus operandi*. It is absurd to suppose that any psychic discovery, however true, will alter that *modus operandi*, and therefore it is absurd to suppose that any such discovery can affect the body of practical science. The acceptance of the Einstein theory of relativity has brought with it an entirely new science of mechanics. Does this send Galileo, Newton, and Poincaré to the scrap heap? Must we teach beginners the theory of relativity before we can explain to them how to calculate the torque required to accelerate a fly-wheel at a given rate? By no means. The classical mechanics remains the mechanics of engineers and of ordinary life. Within a certain limited field it gives an essentially correct and very much simpler account of the facts than does the more exact theory of Einstein. The discovery of new phenomena may add to the field of scientific inquiry, may modify old theories, and alter our philosophical interpretation of well-known facts, but nothing short of a revolution in the order cf Nature itself can relegate established practical science to the scrap heap.

"(2) In the second place, I would observe that there is no present reason to allege that the supernormal phenomena reported by the scientific spiritualists, if true, constitute a break in the reign of law any more serious than that involved in the behavior of any small boy. The laws governing the spiritistic phenomena have not yet been formulated, and the origin of the forces behind them is as yet mysterious, but, despite all the work which has been done on child psychology, who would be so bold as to say that the laws governing small-boy nature have been formulated, or that small boys have lost all elements of mystery? And be it remembered that small boys are much more common and more easily investigated than the alleged phenomena of spiritism.

"If there is any true logical inconsistency involved in the belief in the reality of the phenomena reported by the psychical research investigators, Professor Jastrow and his fellow critics will do all the world a service by pointing it out. If they cannot do this in a clean-cut manner, their strictures on the mental housekeeping of those who maintain an open mind with regard to these phenomena may recoil on their own heads.

"Behind a very large part of the opposition to psychical research from both popular and scientific sources seems to lie the superb confidence which nearly every man seems to have in his theory of the universe. His mind is a semi-orderly place where, rightly or wrongly, things are tagged and pigeon-holed. The gaps in his knowledge are unconsciously filled with the works of his own imagination as some maps of the ancients were extended beyond the regions of actual exploration. He is at home, and more or less at ease, in his mental world and meets any attempt to upset its order with an opposition nearly as violent as that which he bestows on those who would undertake to undermine the social structure.

"Perhaps no antidote for this attitude would be better (if it were possible for the average man) than a study of the progress of the science of physics in the last two decades. The period in question has been marked by an extraordinary double revolution which has recklessly overturned many of the basic principles which in 1900 seemed established beyond question. The public is more or less familiar with the Einstein relativity theory, which in its primary limited form is meeting at present with well-nigh universal acceptance from those who have studied it. The public is much less familiar with the even more subversive and more powerfully illuminating 'quantum' theory, the discussion of which has for some years filled the pages of the journals of physics the world over. The fundamental ideas of these theories did as great violence to the preconceptions of the physicist of fifteen and twenty years ago as do the alleged phenomena of spiritism now. And they met with violent opposition. Today, in spite of the fact that they bring with them great unsolved problems, they are proving the key to a thousand mysteries, and we begin to see how little we knew in 1900. If the basic ideas in the highly developed and relatively simple science of physics could undergo such a complete revolution at the beginning of the twentieth century, are we to believe that the fundamental hypotheses of modern biology and psychology are so firmly established as to make it possible to ridicule those who report phenomena which seem to conflict with them?"

Extracts from an article with which I closed a brief debate between myself and Professor Jastrow still further describe the peculiarities of his dialectical technique, when dealing with psychic research.[76]

"Professor Jastrow has much to say about logic, but his own is peculiar. He finds in the fact that most persons who seriously pursue psychical research become convinced that the 'supernormal' exists, evidence that they are wrong and that those who won't study are right.

---

[76] *Forum*, March, 1924, 401-02.

He thinks that since some psychical researchers are less cautious than others and some who call themselves such are charlatans, they are all fools together, though this logic would annihilate his science of psychology, whose advocates are divided into exactly the same classes. After complimenting my critical abilities of which he has had 'convincing evidence,' he supposes me capable of uncritical blundering and credulity. Because I rule out testimony which is 'spurious or too feebly evidential'—which is exactly what every judicial tribunal does—he thinks a presumption established that all the testimony is of the same quality, which logic would not only stop the proceedings of every court but would also produce the grim corollary that Professor Jastrow is in the same class with the psychological quacks whom he occasionally denounces. A large fraction of his 'reply' attacks alleged facts which I did not mention and which he knows that I do not advocate. As well might I oppose some psychological contention of his by a diatribe against Christian Science and Yogism.

"He makes me say that every advocate of an unusual claim is entitled to be met on his own ground, as if I thought that claimants that the earth is flat, and that the stars influence human affairs, were so entitled. What I say is that *after* a supposed 'law of nature' is questioned by leaders in natural science, and a body of data in justification of their doubt is on record, *then* all persons who will not examine the alleged facts and meet the specific arguments should keep still. Resort to the dogma that opponents are possessed by a 'will to believe' is hysterical and irrelevant. Darwin probably had a will to believe, but his facts and his arguments were not answered by alleging it. Professor Jastrow desires it to be understood that whenever I report laborious investigations and the reasons for affirmative conclusions, I am dominated by a will to believe, and that his own persistent evasion of the facts and the arguments of his opponents is not evidence of a will to disbelieve. He promised to 'explore the evidences of Mr. Prince's mental processes,' and then simply paints an imaginary portrait of the man whom he had pronounced critical and qualified, as one suddenly become uncritical and blundering.

"My article was entirely devoted to cases, two telepathy groups and one of purported spirit communication. My adversary answers these, respectively, in fifteen, sixteen, and thirty lines.

"He meets my assertions in the West telepathy case with counter guesses which have exactly as much warrant as there would be for my guessing, if that could help me out of a difficulty, that he once stole a sheep. And he—or any other man—would not find it easy to prove that he had never done so. He meets my solemn declaration that not even my wife and daughter had been told the title of a poem, by the sage remark that '*we* exaggerate the "privacy" of much that we regard as known to no one but ourselves.' Perhaps the professor does, but it is my business not to do so. Does he not see that any assertion of individual experience and observation which he could make might be discredited by the same process? He saw a particular man on such a date? But sometimes *we* undergo subjective experiences known as visual hallucinations. He can bring the man to prove it? So can I bring my wife and daughter to prove my assertion. . . .

"Any factious objection which is made to a particular case for which I stand can be met by other cases. Many investigators of 'the highly critical group' are at work by methods more exact than are usually in vogue in the psychological laboratory, and the tendency of such critical first-hand study, as the professor admits, is toward conviction that the 'supernormal' exists. And here and there stands a critic moved by some emotional complex to vocal disgust, who, while he will not experiment for himself nor fairly meet the evidence and arguments of those who do, yet expects his guesses to be accepted as 'logic,' and his nightmare fancies as to the mentality and methods of his opponents to be accepted as solutions of the problems involved."

Dr. Jastrow, in his books and articles, not infrequently gets his missiles from the psychic researchers themselves—their studies of sources of error, their criticism of spurious or doubtful cases, etc.—and, without thanks or decent acknowledgment, fires them back upon the psychic research camp.

In an article by him in the *Popular Science Monthly* of April, 1889, he told a story of the confession of a medium regarding his fraudulent *modus operandi* in the production of "materializations," and said it was D. D. Home who confessed. Someone must have called his attention to this perversion of the facts, for the latter statement does not appear when the story is repeated in his *Fact and Fable in Psychology* (1900). But he gives no source and no authority. The truth is that Home told the story in his *Lights and Shadows of Spiritualism*, not naming the medium, but saying that he copied the tale from "an American newspaper," not even specifying what newspaper it was. In the first place, it was careless reading which caused Dr. Jastrow to represent that the medium was Home himself. In the second place, what would he think of a psychic researcher who printed as evidence of the supernormal a story which he said he saw in a newspaper, and regarding which he had no other information whatever? But any unsponsored floating yarn is good enough if to the discredit of mediums, although he could have procured plenty of authenticated exposures of pretended mediums had he applied to a society for psychic research.

Any one who desires to read an extended analysis of Dr. Jastrow's peculiar logic may find ten pages of it from the pen of Mr. F. N. Hales, in the S. P. R. *Proceedings*, XVII. We content ourselves here with two extracts, both of which reveal that, while supposing himself very scientific, the attitude and spirit of Jastrow are the reverse of that. Mr. Hales is reviewing *Fact and Fable in Psychology*.

" ' The present collection of essays is offered as a contribution towards the realization of a sounder interest in, and a more important appreciation of, certain problems upon which psychology has an authoritative charge to make to the public jury. These essays take their stand distinctively upon one side of certain issues, and, as determinately as the situation seems to warrant, antagonize contrary positions; they aim to oppose certain tendencies and to support others; to show that the sound and profitable interest in mental life is in the usual and the normal. . . .' In other words, Professor Jastrow claims the right and assumes the responsibility of making a number of *ex cathedra* statements upon a variety of subjects, some of which he conceives have dangerously engrossed the public interest to the detriment of others. He wishes to educate the interest of the public in psychological matters. He conceives that a science cannot prosper if the public take no interest in it, cannot thrive if it be misunderstood by the layman. It is difficult to see what the layman's opinion can possibly matter on a question of pure science, or why the layman should be allowed any voice whatever. To the public, science is revealed religion, and the *savant* its prophet. The layman believes on authority, that is his privilege. But in what sense can he be supposed to form part of a jury? "

And Mr. Hales is emphatically right. It is quite proper to enlighten the public (although mere *ex cathedra* ejaculations are poor materials for enlightenment), but no scientific man thinks of appealing to laymen as a jury, or can be influenced with regard to his own findings one tiny particle if every shopman in seven cities ridicules them.

Also, according to Jastrow, psychology cannot be expected to investigate any psychical claims.

" The psychological problem [with Jastrow] in all these cases is a quite different one: ' It takes up the inquiry as to how such marvelous pretensions came to be believed, by what influences conviction is formed and doctrines spread.' Such is the fundamental difference of principle between psychologist and psychical researcher, according to our author—that while the psychologist knows there is 'nothing in it,' without the tedium of a special inquiry, the psychical researcher takes the trouble to collect evidence in order to have some special proof whether there is 'anything in it' or not.

"We protest, in the interests of psychology, against this caricature of psychological ideals, and in fairness to psychical research we protest no less strongly against the charge of occultism insinuated by Professor Jastrow's phrase 'something in it.' It is a mood which he thus characterizes, not a definite logical position; it is a mood which we detest quite as much as he does; it is a mood which every scientist detests, because it denies the rationality of his pursuit. And we gladly abandon to any one's satire the idly curious layman who, by a kind of *Schadenfreude* rejoices whenever some outhouse of science collapses on the heads of the masons within. Such a mood has nothing, however, to do with logic. The scientific conservatism upheld by Professor Jastrow is no less a mood, and no less foreign to logic. Is psychology, then, so perfect a science that we need not trouble to investigate phenomena which at first sight seem difficult to explain by the theories current in any one year? Is the basis of our science, then, so secure that it is mere waste of time to study facts which at first sight do not harmonize as perfectly as we might wish with facts already investigated? Does not the very essence of research consist in finding out whether there be or be not 'something in' a certain fact at present obscure; in finding out whether this fact makes for one theory or for another?"

DR. IVOR L. TUCKETT

This gentleman in 1911 published a book entitled *The Evidence for the Supernatural*, and of all books known to me which attempt to discount the evidence for the supernormal, including telepathy, this makes the best superficial appearance of being a rigorous frontal attack. The uninformed reader who takes no pains to compare statements in the book with the original records and to compare what its author says with what the actual experimenter said, would certainly think that the former had made an onslaught all along the line and had inflicted an irretrievable defeat. This appearance is very deceptive, but thoroughly to demonstrate that this is the case would require the marshaling of citations and the comparison of statements with facts to the compass of fifty pages. I am confident that, avoiding all the passages from the records which Dr. Tuckett chooses, I could construct at least as plausible an argument to account normally for all of Mrs. Piper's phenomena, and could then answer, exposing my fallacies and inconsistencies of logic, and the insufficiency of all my explanatory suggestions, partly gleaned from the admissions of the critical original experimenters or reviewers, and partly the products of my ingenuity in guessing that facts and conditions were other than reported, to explain the totality of the automatic material. And, with the same amount and quality of study devoted to *The Origin of Species* as Dr. Tuckett devoted to records of Mrs. Piper, those for cross-correspondences, etc., and employing the same methods, I could to the uninformed and hasty reader produce an effect fully as annihilating. Such in fact were the methods employed by some clerical amateurs in the third quarter of the nineteenth century, regarded by themselves and by many readers as quite devastating.

The author tells us on his title-page that he is " M.A., M.D. (Cantab.), M.R.C.S., L.R.C.P., formerly Fellow of Trinity College, Cambridge, and Senior Demonstrator of Physiology in Cambridge University." It was perhaps not quite cricket for Dr. Hyslop to be sarcastic in referring to this array of dignities,[77] seeing that his own title-pages announce his degrees and former academic position. Very likely both men yielded to the wishes of their publishers. I quote the portentous list only to emphasize the fact that no amount of learning and official standing can save a man from crossing the enchanted boundary insufficiently prepared.

The author's amateur quality is betrayed in the very title of the book. Writing in criticism of psychic research, he is apparently unaware that its exponents from the first had repudiated the notion that anything can actually exist and be above or outside of the system of " nature." Or else he would crowd this concept down the throats of psychic researchers despite their protest. He quotes with approval [78] Huxley's words: " The world of psychical [mental] phenomena appears to me to be just as much a part of ' Nature ' as the world of physical phenomena," and every sensible psychic researcher is of the same opinion. The sub-title: "A critical study made with ' uncommon sense ' " should not be mentioned without regard to his explanation that he has in mind the fact that many people are betrayed by what they esteem " common sense," but it is fair to conclude that the writer thought he had accomplished a very successful undertaking, and that the sense he had displayed was very superior to that of Myers, Gurney, the Sidgwicks, Hodgson, Lodge, Hyslop, Piddington and a long list of persons who had studied the subject matter at first hand and at the expenditure of vastly more time, labor and pains. On what meat do

---

[77] *Journal* A. S. P. R., VI, 567. [78] *Evidence for the Supernatural*, 6.

men feed that they feel themselves competent almost offhand to contradict and outlawyer men who have been at infinite pains?

On the very first page begins an astounding sentence, seeing that it was penned in 1911. "In the following pages I do not profess to have written much that can be described, even vaguely, as original, seeing that it is largely a reproduction of ideas much better expressed by philosophers like Herbert Spencer and G. H. Lewes, by experts in natural science like Tyndall and Huxley, by a student of psychical phenomena like Mr. Frank Podmore." To be sure, 130 pages of the book are devoted to such themes as Prayer, Miracles and the Soul, but there remain 269 relating to psychic research, and these are not excluded from the general statement that what he has written has been expressed much better, by a man who died before there ever was a society for psychical research, by two men whose only interest was expressed in brief utterances of contempt for psychic research, and by Frank Podmore. Therefore, according to his own confession, his ideas derogatory to such supposed evidence of the "supernatural" as are included in the limits of psychic research have been already better expressed by Podmore. Here he is perfectly correct; then why not have left the exposition to Podmore? And while he depends with all the fidelity of a disciple upon Podmore up to the borderline of telepathy, at that line Podmore is no longer, in his judgment, a reliable guide, being in all the region beyond quite demoralized by "bias."

This sentence confronts us: "We know . . . that the S. P. R. was founded in order to establish the existence of telepathy. Therefore it is fair to consider that those early members of the S. P. R. were biased in favor of telepathy." But surely the place to find what the S. P. R. was organized for is in its own official publications. And in the earliest draft of its Constitution its chief object is thus stated: "To unite students and inquirers in an organized body, with the view of promoting the investigation of certain obscure phenomena, including those commonly known as Psychical, Mesmeric, or Spiritualistic; and of giving publicity to the results of such research." Telepathy is not even specifically named, though of course it was included among the purported phenomena in view, and there is not a hint at a wish to "establish" anything. Special committees, as we learn from the first *Proceedings*,[79] were assigned to investigate five named subjects, one of which was "An examination of the nature and extent of any influence which may be exerted by one mind upon another, apart from any gen-

---

[79] I, 3.

erally recognized mode of perception." "May be," mark you, not is. At the very start it is evident that Tuckett needs to be watched or he will slip in some counterfeit change.

He thinks that one of the ways of accounting for Mrs. Piper is muscle-reading. Was it " uncommon sense " to assume because he saw in a report of 1889 that she sometimes held a hand of the sitter that this practice had continued during all the years up to 1911? Ignorance is no excuse to the man who appoints himself a judge, yet will not read the facts of record.

Dr. Hyslop had stated that all that was mentioned about John McClellan in the county history was that he had been an ensign in the War of 1812. It was not quite fair in Podmore to say " to whom reference was made in a county " history, as though an explanation of other true particulars given in the Piper trance might be in that direction. Dr. Tuckett does no original thinking on the matter, but depends wholly on Podmore, giving exactly his references to pages.[80]

Dr. Tuckett says he proposes to give a specimen of Mrs. Piper's "*wonderful* [italics of sarcasm] skill in medical diagnosis—where her success was not surprising, seeing that Phinuit first said there was something wrong with the throat, then altered the statement by saying it was a stammering kind of speech and all the time the sitter was assenting and leading him on." Referring to the father of the sitter (Miss Alice Johnson), the control said:

" 'Ah (feeling her cheek and jaw), there is a sort of numbness here. What is it? Is he paralyzed?' *A. J.:* ' No—oh, no—he is not paralyzed.' [Then she began to feel my face and under my chin, finally coming to the angle between the chin and throat.] *Phin.:* ' This is the place. There is a peculiar condition here.' *A. J.:* ' Do you mean in the throat, or further up in the mouth?' *Phin.:* ' Here (touching me quite at the top of the throat). Not quite in the throat—at the root of the tongue. [She wavered a little in the exact localization of the part affected.] There is something curious about him in the top of his throat—when he talks it catches in his throat—at roots of tongue. Sometimes when he goes to say a thing he can't—then again, he can talk again as well as any one. Speech seems to be cut off for a moment—he stammers a little (she cleared her throat to illustrate how he did it). Sometimes this troubles him much—then he is not troubled at all.' [This description seemed to me, and to all of my family, including my father, to whom I repeated it, to be remarkably good and accurate. During the description of my father's throat, I at first

---

[80] *Evidence for the Supernatural,* 137.

answered, ' Oh,' in a doubtful way, thinking of something else suggested to me by her first words and gestures. Then I saw this did not fit, and thought of the other thing, which she was really describing. I probably assented to her description at various points.]" [80a]

Now let us see. The trance consciousness of Mrs. Piper somehow gets an idea that there is something peculiar in relation to the throat of Miss Johnson's father, which was true. Where was the " leading " in that direction? It is certainly desirable that no question should be asked the sitter, but it is not certainly a sign of trickiness, any more than if I met an old friend for the first time in years and in the course of conversation said, " Let's see, your sister married a man named Brown?," when the name was really Browning. There is one stern rule to be adopted when the medium puts a particular in an interrogative way and that is to regard it as one would an affirmation. So to this point the medium has correctly announced that there is something peculiar connected with the father's throat, but has not yet correctly stated what was wrong, and was told so by the sitter. Presently the medium succeeds in relating what is wrong, that " there is something curious about him in the top of his throat—when he talks it catches in his throat—at roots of tongue. Sometimes when he goes to say a thing he can't—then again, he can talk as well as any one. Speech seems to be cut off for a moment—he stammers a little (she cleared her throat to illustrate how he did it). Sometimes this troubles him much —then he is not troubled at all." It will be noted that this is rather a precise description, it is not a case of stammering alone, but a peculiar form of stammering. The description seemed to the sitter, all the family, and the father himself, " to be remarkably good and accurate." Very well, but Dr. Tuckett says that Miss Johnson was all the while " assenting and leading him on." Let us study how she did it. The first thing she said was, " Oh, " in a doubtful way. If Mrs. Piper was being guided, the doubtful tone should have stopped her, but she went on. Miss Johnson said: " Do you mean in the throat or farther up the mouth? " Will someone inform me what data that question afforded for the description of peculiar symptoms associated with stammering, and their intermittancy? And several times, as the description went on, she assented. How in heaven's name can saying " yes " after one particular has been correctly stated, give a hint for a further particular?

One is reminded of the horse which, having broken through the ice

---

[80a] *Ib.*, 332.

in winter at a particular spot and cut its leg, ever after refused to go over that spot in summertime. For a great many years expert psychical researchers have been showing how unskilful sitters may, quite without intention, supply information and "lead" mediums by their own responses. And they have furnished or analyzed many illustrative instances. If, following the words "an old lady with white hair, who wears glasses," the sitter weeps and says, "Oh, mother! Are you happy?" there has certainly been leading—the medium can infer that, so far, the description fits the sitter's mother, and that she is dead. If the "message" should continue, "Your mother wants to send a message to another of her children," and the sitter impulsively says: "I will take it to her," two more facts have been furnished gratuitously, one that the deceased has but two living children, and secondly, that the other child is a daughter. But such critics as Dr. Tuckett, having learned principally from the psychic researchers themselves the lesson that "leading" vitiates some mediumistic results, proceed to apply it unintelligently. They become credulous, almost superstitious, in their hazy imagining that a medium can draw secure inferences where they themselves could draw none, and where they would be quite powerless to explain how on earth the medium could have done so. How would Dr. Tuckett go to work to show that Miss Johnson's query whether the "condition" was "in the throat or farther up in the mouth" would *lead* the medium to reply that it was—not in the mouth or exactly in the throat, but—"at the root of the tongue"? If, after the medium said "when he talks it catches in his throat," Miss Johnson assented, how could her "yes" lead to the statement that the stammering was not constant but intermittent, or that he "stammers a little," instead of very badly? Remember that all the family, including the father himself, recognized the description as *remarkably good and accurate*.[81]

In an article entitled "A Sceptical Sitter"[82] I analyzed the report of a lady who had read much critical discussion by expert researchers, and had learned, parrot-fashion, the necessity for caution in regard to "leading," but who, like the horse, shied not only at thin ice but at a patch of hard ground. According to her own record she had some unusually evidential results, but she made an appearance of voiding the most of it by a series of misapplied explanatory suggestions. For instance, Mrs. McLeod said that when she handed a cardboard box to the

---

[81] Miss Alice Johnson was a woman of very keen mentality, who afterward served the S. P. R. as Editor, and also for a time as Research Officer.
[82] *Journal* A. S. P. R., XII, 356-74.

medium the latter said: "I see S written all over the box. S - u - e." Mrs. McLeod testifies: "No one but Mr. McLeod [who was supposed to be communicating] ever called me Sue." But, she says: "I was surprised when she gave S, and my expression may have been tell-tale. I probably was sufficiently alert to let her see that she was on the right track." Yes, surely she could see from Mrs. McLeod's *expression* that the name was not Sarah, not Stella, nor Sophie, nor Sylvia, nor Selma, nor Sophronia,[83] but Susan, and furthermore, that the form of the name employed by the sitter's late husband was *Sue!* How plain that is, when we remember that the medium's "long experience has taught her to enlarge very cleverly on the slight supernormal impressions she may receive"! Having received the slight supernormal impression that S is the initial letter, she is not further informed from the source of that supernormal impression, but proceeds to study her sitter's face. A certain "expression" would make it clear that her name is Sarah, another expression and there would be no doubt that her name is Stella, but in fact she had an expression of the Susan species, variety Sue!

Let us look at another specimen of Dr. Tuckett's "uncommon sense," exhibited under the sub-heading, "*Knowledge obtained (from hints) during the sitting.*" He says:[84]

"Other interesting extracts from the sitting are:—

"'. . . Messages were then given from Miss C.'s father and mother of the same import as those told to the other sitters.'

"'. . . Dr. Myers spoke of Miss C. as Mrs. Robinson, a name which Phinuit indignantly repudiated. "That lady's name is Emily. She is not Mrs."'"

We go to the record [85] and find that a Miss C. was for the first time taken to a sitting with Mrs. Piper, and was introduced as "Mrs. Robinson." Dr. A. J. Myers, well-grounded in science and elected a few years later a Fellow of the Royal College of Physicians, was the note-taker. He was a brother of F. W. H. Myers and was thoroughly versed in the methodology of precaution. In accordance with the necessity for precaution, when Dr. Myers had occasion during the

---

[83] Limiting inspection to family stocks seemingly from Great Britain and Ireland, since Mrs. McLeod appeared to be of such origin, the first 200 of feminine names beginning with S found in Boston telephone directory brought the following result: Sarah, 88; Sara, 16; Sadie, 19; Sallie, 2; (Total, 125). Susan, 30; Susie, 10; Sue, 4; Susanne, 1; (Total 45). Stella, 6; Sophie, 4; Sophia, 2; Selma, 6; Sylvia, 3; Sybil, 2; Sibyl, 2; Sigrid, 2. Sophronia, Sabina, Selwyn, Selda, Selena, 1 each.
[84] *Evidence for the Supernatural*, p. 336. [85] *Proceedings* S. P. R., VI, 635-6.

sitting to refer to Miss C. he called her, of course, Mrs. Robinson. And Dr. Myers records as a noteworthy fact that " Dr. Phinuit (the ' control ') indignantly repudiated the name, said the lady was named Emily and was not Mrs." And Dr. Tuckett triumphantly remarks: " This last sentence shows that Mrs. Piper was quite alive to the fact that sitters were introduced under pseudonyms, which did not deceive her." And he puts the incident under the heading: " Knowledge obtained (from hints) during the sitting." This is sheer insolence. There is no hint anywhere in the record of the sitting. Dr. Myers says he gave an assumed name to the lady and kept up the use of it. Of course Mrs. Piper knew that sitters were frequently introduced under pseudonyms, but, assuming that it were so in this case, how could that fact inform her that the lady was not a Mrs. and that her name was Emily? And the name Emily was applied to her " immediately " after the sitting commenced, a fact which Tuckett acknowledges was in the record. Does the immediate application to the sitter, never before seen, of her Christian name show that Mrs. Piper *must* have known it previously? When not only it was asserted that Mrs. Spencer did not tell a medium a set of odd pet names applied to her by her deceased husband, and that they were known to her alone, but it was also shown to be beyond any intelligent suspicion that she *could* have told them,[86] Professor Jastrow's reply was that the medium evidently knew them, just the same. So we find Dr. Tuckett here and in many other places, not dealing fairly with testimony and evidence, but assassinating it.

Under the heading: " *Knowledge acquired in the interval between two, or more, sittings,*" we find this proof: " Thus, in the sixth volume of the S. P. R. *Proceedings* I find that on at least *fourteen* occasions she [Mrs. Piper] gave information at a second or subsequent sitting, which she had not succeeded in giving at the first sitting." It quite takes one's breath away that Dr. Tuckett should find that fact either a strong indication that the medium picked up information in the intervals between sittings, or that in itself it is even in the slightest degree suspicious. If a psychic shows knowledge not normally obtainable in her first sitting with a stranger, why, even were she locked up in the interim, should she not state other facts gained in the same way at the next experiment? But Tuckett has formulated a law that any true statements made subsequent to a first sitting must be regarded, *ipso facto*, as derived by surreptitious effort between sittings.

Dr. Tuckett obtains a considerable share of his criticisms from

---

[86] *Journal* A. S. P. R., XVI, 635-45.

statements by the experimenters themselves that they made mistakes or that for other reasons certain details given in the trance were evidentially impaired. It is curious, after they have done this so frankly and have made due deductions accordingly, to enter these very instances in the indictment, as though they had *not* been laid aside. For instance, we read that when " Phinuit " said " She's very near to you, a good mother to you," Professor Lodge said: "(stupidly indicating the fact of decease), Yes, she was." How does the critic know that Lodge " stupidly " did this? Because this is the language of Lodge himself.

The critic is quite confident that Mrs. Piper must have obtained information between sittings, since, as he shows at some length, later sittings would disclose facts not stated in earlier ones! He throws out hints that while in Professor Lodge's house she managed to pick up a great deal of information about relatives long dead and a variety of little facts regarding them which surely no one would have talked about in her hearing unless intentionally coaching her. When I remember that Mrs. Soule told a variety of things which happened half a century ago in my family and which she could not have learned had she read every book, letter and manuscript in my house (which she has never entered) I doubt if Mrs. Piper could have extracted all her information had she ransacked everything in his house. But at any rate it is an audacious thing to indulge in such speculations and disregard entirely two very important considerations. First that Mrs. Piper had been watched by many keen investigators, including the eagle-eyed Hodgson, and had never, so far as is known, been detected in any suspicious course of conduct. Secondly, that Lodge himself discussed at considerable length all possible theories of her normal acquirement of facts and was convinced that none or all of them in combination could explain the results.[87] To that discussion Tuckett pays not the passing glance of a single sentence. He does not note that Lodge, although convinced that any information gained by Mrs. Piper normally was a bagatelle, yet was willing constructively to grant to the critic that she saw everything in his house, in which case his verdict would not have differed. No one in contact with her saw any appearance of indirection, caught her in any suspicious situation or act, although her baggage was examined, and her movements watched, but a man who never saw her has " no reason for doubting that Mrs. Piper had observed the place where Mrs. T. was in the habit of keeping her paint-box," [88] and

---

[87] *Proceedings* S. P. R., VI, 446-449.   [88] *Evidence for the Supernatural*, 347.

whenever any pinch comes finds relief in imagining the medium as prowling and peeking around.

He feels competent to dispute the witness point blank, when nothing else will do. Thus Lodge reported [89] that in broad daylight the medium was handed several papers among which was a letter; with but one hand free she put the set on top of her head, flicked away the blank papers one by one, then told a number of particulars which were in the letter. Lodge says: "*She did not inspect them.*" But Tuckett says: "The only explanation is the *exceedingly probable* surmise that the words given by Phinuit had caught Mrs. Piper's eye." The italics are mine and I think are warranted. I would very much like to see the trained conjurer who could take a group of papers among which was a folded letter, and with one hand so lift them and so manipulate them on his head that he could read parts of the letter without my being aware of anything of the sort. Here, however, is Mrs. Piper, who, whatever she is, certainly is not a conjurer, and it is *exceedingly probable* that in broad daylight, with one hand and with the eyes of Professor Lodge upon her, she did exactly this. I am quite aware that Lodge and myself and any other man is liable to illusions in the midst of the conditions surrounding some phenomena in entire or near darkness, but the feat ascribed to Mrs. Piper and the blindness accredited to Professor Lodge does not belong to that category. Perhaps this Boston gentlewoman did perform a feat which would make a magician turn pale to attempt under the same conditions; the contemplation of that possibility is not nearly so enthralling as the complacent remark that the feat was exceedingly probable.

Everyone who is not exactly of Dr. Tuckett's way of thinking is, in his view, biased. Myers,[90] James,[91] Hodgson,[92] Lodge,[93] Leaf,[94] Hyslop,[95] Piddington,[96] with all their varying shades of opinion, are biased more or less when brought to the norm of Tuckett. Podmore is unbiased in regard to spiritism—like Tuckett, he was not an advocate of that doctrine, but in regard to telepathy he was biased[97]— for, unlike Tuckett, he was convinced by the evidence for it. Dr. Bramwell "cannot be accused of bias"[98]—he did not believe in telepathy, and "has before now put his powers at the service of the S. P. R." But the fact that the condemned had rendered manifold service to the S. P. R. does not help them—it is rather an indication of bias. Professor Alexander and Darwin were "impartial," because

---

[89] *Ib.*, 340. [90] *Ib.*, 353 seq. [91] *Ib.*, 355 seq. [92] *Ib.*, 388. [93] *Ib.*, 357. [94] *Ib.*, 358.
[95] *Ib.*, 357. [96] *Ib.*, 359. [97] *Ib.*, 359. [98] *Ib.*, 397.

on the basis of exactly two experiments each they drew unfavorable conclusions, which the S. P. R. duly printed.[99]

One of the evidences of Dr. Leaf's bias, we are told, is that he sometimes speaks of an "unsatisfactory sitting," whereas to an investigator anxious only to get at the truth, "all phenomena carefully recorded are interesting." This is a foul blow, and only by the confession of ignorance can Tuckett claim that he did not deal it wilfully. One, and a common, sense of the word "satisfy" is *convince,* and that Leaf meant that the sitting was unconvincing is shown by his remark directly following that the unsatisfactory sitting led to "justifiable incredulity on the part of the sitter."

One other example of Leaf's bias is given, consisting in his opinion "that telepathy is more probable than muscle-reading" to explain the results of a certain experiment. And how is it contrived to present an appearance of bias? By carefully cutting out the intelligent reasons given by Leaf for his opinion.

As Dr. Leaf's use of the word "unsatisfactory" was unjustifiably misrepresented, so the only evidence presented for bias on the part of Mr. Piddington consists of an unwarranted construction of an unfortunately selected word. After Piddington had given considerable attention to certain "cross-correspondence" material, to quote his own words: "Before, then, the next reference to the Latin Message was made in the trance, on February 19, I had become impressed, I may even say obsessed, with the idea that there was perceptible an intelligent effort in the scripts of one automatist to make connections with those of another." Podmore unfairly says that this shows "the state of mind in which he *approached* [my italics] the séances," when in fact it shows the state of mind produced by their study. Of course Piddington did not mean to imply by the word "obsessed" that he became the victim of either a *dæmon* or a pathological fixation, but that he became, because of what he found in the scripts, not only impressed but very much impressed.

These very instances of strain by Dr. Tuckett to show bias on the part of others go far to demonstrate his own bias. And the fact that he could change Piddington's language from "I had become impressed, I may even say obsessed" to "I had become possessed, I may even say obsessed," as though to rub in the notion of pathological victimship, is probably evidence for his own assertion that bias "is essentially a subconscious, emotional factor."[100] When a man is really strongly

---

[99] *Ib.,* 365. [100] *Ib.,* 354.

biased, that is swayed by a feeling, whether of prepossession or prejudice, to a degree that the working of his reasoning powers is embarrassed, he is apt to search so hard for what he wants to find that he at times quite fails to notice what he does not want to find. Tuckett makes much of leading questions or remarks by sitters. And on page 358 he points to what he says is " an excellent example." The control " Phinuit " had spoken of cancer. The sitter did indeed ask a very leading question: " Was it a relation of my mother's—her sister? " And the answer was, " No, a relation of your father's," the fact being that the sitter's stepmother died of cancer. Yes, the question was a very leading one, and Tuckett saw that, but he took no notice of the very interesting fact that it did not lead, that it was contradicted. Had the control said " Yes, it was your mother's sister," we should as in other cases have heard the doctor's merry ha-ha.

The whole of Appendix R, of three and a half pages, is an exhibit alone sufficient to convict the author of fatal bias. Out of all the series of experiments for thought-transference reported by the S. P. R. in its *Proceedings*, just one, that with Messrs. Smith and Blackburn, is chosen for the reader's benefit, and this because Blackburn, thirty years later, claimed that he and Smith systematically cheated in it by the use of a code.

The statement that " these thirty-one experiments were considered to establish satisfactorily a case for telepathy," is not correct. The original report,[101] referring to the " possibility of a code " expressly said that it would " be an exaggeration to affirm that the possibility of such signals was absolutely excluded." It was doubtless on this account that the Smith-Blackburn series was not reprinted, as were other series, in *Phantasms of the Living*, issued three years later, long before Blackburn's " confession." Why, then, did Tuckett choose it, and it alone? Not because it was the best, not because it was considered a conclusive test, but surely because of the Blackburn story. We need go no farther to infer bias, since this is no fair method of dealing with a mass of evidence.

We are told that Blackburn told the story thirty years after, but we are not told that by his own statement he waited until he thought that all the participants in the experiments were dead.[102] But Professor Barrett and Mr. Smith happened to be still living. We are told that Smith indignantly contradicted Blackburn's statement, saying it

---

[101] *Proceedings* S. P. R., I, 161-216.
[102] *Daily News* (London), Sept. 1, 1911: " I am the sole survivor of that group of experimentalists."

was "a tissue of errors from end to end, and that there was no trickery," but we are left to suppose that Blackburn's account was just as respectable as that of Smith, and several sentences slyly hint that Smith probably lied.[103]

It is held that since slate-writing mediums frequently confuse their clients, "there is nothing essentially improbable about Mr. Blackburn's statement that there was little difficulty in deceiving Messrs. Gurney and Myers." This ignores the great gulf between the two species of experiments. A slate-writing medium talks and acts at will, shuffles slates, takes them up and puts them down, puts them under the table, twitches, directs his sitters to do this and that. But the committee of the Smith-Blackburn series, Messrs. Gurney, Myers, Barrett and Podmore, made their own conditions, and established their own procedure. Blackburn would be taken out of the room and a drawing would be held before his eyes a few moments. He was then led back into the room to a spot facing the blindfolded Smith's back, where he sat or stood at about two feet distance. All preserved silence and members of the committee who, as Tuckett admits, "were well aware of the possibilities and dangers of collusion, deception and malobservation," watched Blackburn, near enough to detect any sound from or motion of his lips. The situation was radically different from that in a slate-writing performance, and while, as the committee themselves said, signaling was not absolutely excluded as a possibility (even though they declare that anything unusual in the way of shuffling feet, coughing or breathing inevitably would have been noticed), it is very difficult to understand how it could have been carried on.

There is not a whisper from Tuckett of anything suspicious in Blackburn's belated "confession," yet it is full of questionable sentences. He claimed to have detected the secret of W. I. Bishop's pretended thought-reading; Smith challenges him to produce any record of proof that he did so. He claimed that "two youths, with a week's preparation" began a series of successful fooling of the committee and advanced so rapidly that shortly after the first experiment they performed a feat which "to this day no conjurer has succeeded in approaching"; a statement which includes magicians who had practiced their art for forty years, and Zancig, the supreme master of codesignaling. Supposing Smith was dead, he declared that the latter had been "the most ingenious conjurer I have met outside of the profession"; Smith turned up to say, "I am the worst conjurer in the

---

[103] *Ib.*, issue of Sept. 4. Subsequent letters by Blackburn and Smith Sept. 5 and Sept. 6.

world," an expression he would hardly have dared to employ had any one known him as an even passably good conjurer. He says that the signals were at first " produced by the jingling of pince-nez, sleeve-links, long and short breathings, and even blowing "; the committee had distinctly reported that anything unusual in his breathing " must inevitably have been noticed," and it is incredible that either on his nose or taken off and held in his hand he could have jingled a pair of eyeglasses loud enough to have been heard by Smith and never have attracted the attention of two or three watching observers of the caliber of the persons composing the committee. He says that the code was " developed " further, but does not tell us how. I am acquainted with the nature of many codes and do not believe that in the positions of Blackburn and Smith relatively to each other and the watchers any code was ever devised which could direct so close a reproduction of such peculiar and irregular drawing as, for instance, No. 8.[104] Examine the reproduction in this case and test it by Blackburn's statement that " irregular drawings completely snuffed out the psychic power which, according to Mr. Smith, I possessed." He says that in the case of " a grotesque irregular figure," " the result was always a failure "; Nos. 2, 3 and 7 of Report II [105] and Nos. 5, 8, 20 and 22 of Report III [106] refute him. The reproductions were not perfect, but they too strongly resemble the originals to be chance products. Try substituting any of the reproductions for another, and see if there is then any impressive resemblance to the original drawing.

But in the case of No. 22, says Blackburn, a different process was employed, that of conveying to Smith a copy of the drawing, which he imitated. This was the experiment in which Smith's ears were stopped with putty, a bandage tied around his eyes and ears (this particular weighs little), a bolster-case fastened over his head, and his entire head and trunk enveloped in a blanket. Blackburn says that Myers showed him the drawing in the same room, that he took it, and for perhaps ten minutes paced the room, repeatedly redrawing the figure under the pretense of fixing it on his brain, that one of the copies was made on cigarette paper and tucked into the brass protector of his pencil, that he gave the signal for " ready " by stumbling, that thereupon Smith called for a pencil and was given the one conveying the drawing, and that by the light of a luminous slate Smith, under cover of the blanket, having pushed up the bandage over his eyes (which of course he could have done), " copied the figure with extraordinary accuracy." Mr.

---

[104] *Proceedings* S. P. R., I, 187.   [105] *Ib.*, I, 85, 87, 95.   [106] *Ib.*, I, 187, 191, 211, 215.

Smith declared all this a tissue of misstatements, and challenged Blackburn to repeat his alleged success, or to arrange any code by which under like conditions to convey knowledge sufficient for the essential reproduction of irregular drawings like some in the S. P. R.'s series, a challenge which the latter seems not to have taken up.

But we need not rest on Smith's statement. The committee, reporting that experiment, had said, "*Figure 22 was now drawn by one of us and shown outside the room to Mr. Blackburn, who on his return sat behind Mr. Smith, and in no contact with him whatever, and as perfectly still as it is possible for a human being to sit who is not concentrating his attention on keeping motionless to the exclusion of every other object. In a few minutes Mr. Smith took up the pencil and gave the successive reproductions shown below.*"

Note that the committee reporting at the time, said that the drawing was shown outside the room; Blackburn, thirty years afterward, said this was done in the room. Tuckett ignorantly judges that the committee could have been deceived as sitters are in regard to small but important movements in the midst of the many non-significant movements of a slate-writing medium. But it has never been supposed that a sitter in a slate-writing séance could be confused to the extent of *thinking he had gone outside a room when in fact he had never done so.* And it has never been supposed by the most skeptical that in broad daylight two or three unusually intelligent and well-informed men could be hallucinated into thinking that a man sat almost perfectly still when in fact he was on his feet pacing up and down a room for ten minutes making drawings, and performing other acts. The elaborate precautions taken in respect to Smith (acknowledged by Blackburn) presuppose that the regular program of locating and keeping Blackburn back of Smith would not be relaxed in this crucial experiment. That the committee did fully realize the importance of this precaution is indicated by the emphasis of the assertion that Blackburn "on his return sat behind Mr. Smith . . . and as perfectly still as it is possible for a human being to sit who is not concentrating on keeping motionless to the exclusion of every other object." The idea that in the most critical experiment of all, what the committee declare was the *modus operandi* of the experiments was repeatedly violated—that instead of showing the Blackburn drawing outside the room they showed it in the same room with Smith; instead of being "held before him for a few seconds," it was now put into his hands and he was allowed to retain it throughout; that instead of locating him at one point he was allowed to trot about at will, multiplying the chances of signaling which they were guarding against; instead of concentrating on the memory-image he was allowed repeatedly to redraw the figure—all this is extremely unlikely in itself, and no one can intelligently credit it in face of the committee's statement and that of Smith.

But this is not all. Blackburn knows of only one attempt at reproduction; Smith made four attempts before he emerged from the blanket. The first and second are very imperfect, as though only part of the original were sensed, and a different part in each case. The third is sufficiently like to be incredible as a chance result. The fourth is not quite so good. One feature of the original, the serrate basal termination, is not reproduced at all, but is replaced by a curved line without the saw-teeth. Even had Smith judged it best not to copy perfectly the drawing alleged to have been in his possession, how could he have resisted the temptation in one of the four drawings to have given some hint of this feature? But Blackburn says he did copy the figure "with extraordinary accuracy." Yet there in the *Proceedings*, published twenty-nine years previously, is the refutation of this allegation. Strikingly alike as the fourth attempt was, considered as the result of thought-transference, a child of five could have made a better copy with the drawing before him. And there in the *Proceedings* is the drawing, said by Blackburn to have been "a tangle of heavy black lines, interlaced, some curved, some straight," etc., but which shows no tangle and no interlacing whatever.

All these facts were open to Dr. Tuckett—the misrepresentations of Blackburn, the categorical statements of the committee admitted to be "well aware of the possibilities and dangers of collusion, deception and malobservation," their exclusion of the series from the best evidences for thought-transference exhibited in *Phantasms of the Living*. Yet he prefers to credit the patent misrepresentations, quotes not a line by the experimenters, and upon this one series rests his argument against experimental thought-transference.

So far as Dr. Tuckett has convincingly pointed out weak spots in evidence they had been for the most part those already designated by the original reporters and investigators; but he announces them with the air of a discoverer. He also largely borrows weapons from Podmore's armory, but dulls them by rejecting the telepathic theory which Podmore carried to the greatest lengths in order to explain otherwise puzzling phenomena. His own contributions to the negative argument on psychic research are not formidable, although they might appear to the uninformed reader to be so, and he probably honestly thought they were so. One gets the impression that he is an earnest soul, without malice, and meaning well. But out of the innocence of his amateur quality and out of that other quality, which if noted in another he would call bias, and which at all events causes him to flit and dip as selectively over a field of evidence as a bumble bee over a field of flowers, he derives, paradoxically, his superficial appearance of effectiveness.

PSYCHOANALYSTS

Psychoanalysts are for the most part silent on the subject of psychical research, but when they do speak, it is to fall into the traps already mentioned, and also one peculiar to themselves. We find A. A. BRILL, translator of Freud, inventing a biography for Sir Oliver Lodge (in a newspaper article), encouraged, no doubt, by the inability of the dead to resent psychoanalytical imaginings regarding them. He forgets that Sir Oliver is not dead, and can refute the reckless statements that his convictions are due to the wish of an old man to continue his own existence, and to his desire to meet his son Raymond, by showing what everyone is supposed to know, namely, that his convictions were reached before he was an old man and long before his son's death.

WILFRED LAY, PH.D.

A special trap that psychoanalysts fall into is well illustrated by the book, *Man's Unconscious Spirit*. I quote from Dr. Dingwall's review.[107]

" I do not remember any book purporting to be written by a psychologist which contains so many absurdities in so small a compass. We are told that ' Psychical research is striving to prove that the laws of the material universe are not the same as those of the world of mind and spirit, and this without adequately showing what is the relation of mind or spirit to matter, and even incidentally what mind or spirit really is.' Imagine *research* trying to *prove* anything! Some researchers might try and prove something, and this is I suppose what Dr. Lay is trying to say, but the passage is typical of the book, nouns, adjectives and verbs all jumbled up and used in their wrong senses till the reader is left in a whirl of hopeless confusion. That is to say, if he does not see through Dr. Lay. For what is the matter with this book, as with so many others on psychical research, is that the author has very little idea of the subject with which he is attempting to deal.

---

[107] *Journal* A. S. P. R., XV, 249-50.

Listen to this paragraph on supernormal information imparted through the agency of trance mediums:

" 'And here it may be remarked that the familiar argument that the so-called supernormal information is due to mere chance is far more potent when we have taken the unconscious into account than it has ever been before. It is the commonest argument of the psychical researcher, that the information which is gained by telepathy, or by any form of spirit communication is much more remarkable than could possibly be subjectively guessed on the theory of probabilities. This information, he says, could not possibly have been guessed or divined or otherwise subjectively evolved by the person into whose consciousness it comes. This impossibility would mean that all the combinations and permutations of all former experiences, sensations, perceptions, etc., on my part would never give me the material to make the combinations of ideas constituting the message in question. Possibly not, if we take into account only those mental states of which we have been conscious from the date of our birth onward. But when we consider the innumerable perceptions, external and internal, we have had during our entire lives of which we have not been conscious, but which yet remain in the almost infinite storehouse of our individual unconscious, we shall clearly see that from the merely mathematical point of view of the theory of probabilities alone, the chances are at least tenfold greater that the message is but a message from our own unconscious to our conscious life, and that until this chance is absolutely removed by means of laboratory methods comprising the strictest scientific control, we shall not have fulfilled the most rigorous requirements of science.'

" This explanation of the 'supernormal' element in trance communications is certainly the most remarkable that I have ever encountered during a fairly extensive acquaintance with these matters. Let us analyze it and get some idea of what Dr. Lay means. He begins by confusing the word *information* with the word *message*, a confusion which is necessary for his argument. Supposing that a medium had a sitting with a person X, whom she had never seen before. Supposing also that the sitter was told that he (or she) had previously had a nurse called Susan Potts, who possessed a peculiar trinket shaped rather like a scarab. Suppose thirdly that all these things happened to be true. Dr. Lay thinks that all this can be explained and that the 'material' might certainly have formed part of 'the innumerable perceptions, external and internal, we have had during our entire lives.' Of course it might! The medium knows the name Susan; she has perhaps heard the surname Potts; she is aware that trinkets exist and that some are shaped like scarabs. What is supernormal is not the material but the *relation the information in the message bears to the sitter.* This relation Dr. Lay ignores, and the whole paragraph above quoted is so much beating of empty air. No combinations and permutations of personal experiences will account for the relation which certain statements bear to certain sitters, not in one case but in dozens of cases."

I have talked with psychoanalysts and tried to make them see the point in the above paragraph, and have indeed reduced them to a feeble pawing of the air, but never, I think, have quite rid them of the queer conviction born of the " will to believe " in their own particular complex.

I spoke in the preface of writers using a logic when they wandered into the alien field of psychic research which they would never employ in their own fields. But an exception must be made of certain psychoanalysts, who employ in their own field a logic which they would recognize as ridiculously lame if the like were indulged in by psychic researchers.

Thus Dr. Lay, in another book, *Man's Unconscious Conflict,* pages 98-9, tells us that if I receive a letter from a man who owes me money, I naturally think that maybe the man is enclosing a check, but " I tear open the envelope and I read that the wretch is going to be married to a girl whom I know quite well and think very highly of. *There was no chance that this idea should ever have come into my mind!* " [My italics.] Suppose a psychic researcher had made this statement, and added that the thought did arise, nevertheless, implying that it had a supernormal source. Dr. Lay quickly and properly would have responded that the combination of a dozen facts previously seen and heard regarding this man and girl, or any one of them, in quite normal fashion might have suggested the thought. But what psychic researcher would ever have made so bald a statement!

Dr. Lay immediately follows with the incident of a man who feels horror when he sees a horse apparently step on another man, who thereupon gets up uninjured, and he declares that the witness unconsciously desired to see the man hurt. To be sure, from the point of view at which the spectator stood it really looked as though the horse's hoof was on the man, in that case the man would be hurt, and humane sympathy would seem sufficiently to account for the horror. But humane feeling, sympathy, compassion, seems to have no place in the psychoanalyst's concept of a human being, so some secret motive must be sought. And what is the proof that the right one is found? This, that a crowd immediately gathers around when there is any accident.

Suppose a psychic researcher claimed that crowds gather in such a case because victims of accidents telepathically attract the crowds, would he not be reminded that crowds also collect to see a man frying flapjacks in a shop window? People gather to see anything unusual, but this is far from demonstrating that they wish the unusual to result in blood and death.

The mother who says she doesn't want Willie to go out in a rowboat with a couple of other small boys, and explains, " Oh, I'm afraid he might get drowned," would seem to be quite justified by the number of accounts we read in the newspapers of little boys who get drowned when out together in rowboats. But no, says Dr. Lay, for the great majority of boys in boats do not get drowned. We are led to infer that a sensible mother would take a betting chance. Really, he tells us, what prompts the mother is a subconscious wish that Willie shall get into trouble, since " her own importance, her size in Willie's world, so to speak, is greatly enlarged by any mishap that can occur to him." It is hard to understand how her importance in Willie's world would be increased after he is drowned. But the doctor's " unconscious " subtly alters the terms; " If he only gets a fishhook in his foot, he and she both go backward, maybe several years, to the time when he was wholly dependent on her for life and sustenance." Since now it appears that Willie has advanced, " maybe " only several years beyond infancy, one would think that her reluctance to have him go out rowing on the bay with two other little boys was sufficiently accounted for by the wish to keep her son alive, unless love and common-sense are nonentities.

One more gem from this treasury of logic. Dr. Lay informs us [108] that when " a person sits down to write a letter that he does not very much want to write and begins by biting the end of the penholder, he shows in that act the working of the unconscious on his actions. The biting of the end of the penholder is a return to the nutritional level." Suppose a psychic researcher were absurd enough to claim that the true reason for the act is that the union of wood and saliva (the latter increased by the act of biting) generates vibrations which reach to the brain and stimulate thinking. Even so quaint a psychic researcher would stutter, when called on to explain why, then, the act of biting penholder is not more general with those who do not want very much to write—why some instead scratch their heads, others tap with the pen on the desk, and still others walk the floor. Not that the psycho

---

[108] Page 187.

THE ENCHANTED BOUNDARY 117

analyst need be at loss for an answer. Walking the floor is a return to the toddling level of infancy, scratching his head a return to the level of the clutching movements of infancy, while tapping on the desk might be explained, since one is but very distantly related to the woodpecker, as a biological return to the club-fighting habits of remote ancestors!

On pages 47-8, Dr. Lay recounts an old alleged incident and proceeds to state what it "shows clearly." Psychoanalysts of greater fame have related this same incident without any visible scruples, and have used it as valuable material for psychological inferences. Personally, because of its content, I think it is probably true, at least to some extent. But the acceptation of it as certainly and entirely true shows that some noted psychologists might do well to take lessons from psychical research, whose standards would not permit the story to pass as first-class evidence.

Suppose that Dr. Dingwall, from whom I have quoted, should print a story

1. Traceable only to the pen of a man who, as is well known:
   (a) All his life was characterized by a dreamy and imaginative mentality,
   (b) Had been, at the date when he told the story, for fifteen years a victim of the opium habit, often consuming from two to three quarts of laudanum a week,
   (c) Besides being addicted to the use of alcohol;
   (d) Fifteen years before the story was told, as a biographer expresses it, began to show "diminished power to distinguish fact from fiction,"
   (e) And wrote to his correspondents "fabrications adapted to the taste of each correspondent."

2. Suppose this man declares that the incident
   (f) Took place some sixteen or seventeen years earlier,
   (g) In a German town which he does not name and to which he gives no clue,
   (h) And concerns an unnamed servant-girl
   (i) Of an unnamed clergyman,
   (j) And was investigated by a physician of whose name and whereabouts we are given no information or slightest clue,
   (k) Who made remarkable discoveries which it would certainly have been expected that he would report to some learned society or publish in some professional journal, yet no word from him has ever been discovered.

Suppose further that the narrator does not say
(l) That he ever saw the maid,
(m) That he got the story directly from the physician,
(n) Or that he ever saw or met any direct witness in the case.

And suppose, finally, that the incident as related contains many particulars and that its importance largely depends upon the accuracy of a number of these particulars in combination.

Then, I ask the reader, at the same time asking Dr. Dingwall's pardon, what would he think, what would Dr. Lay think, if Dr. Dingwall printed that story without any slightest question of its entire authenticity, and proceeded to say what it " shows "?

Yet this is precisely what Dr. Lay and a number of psychologists have done with the famous story told by Samuel Taylor Coleridge in his *Biographical Literaria* about the servant-girl who, in fever, uttered sentences in Latin, *and* Greek, *and* Hebrew, of which whole sheets were written out; the phenomenon being investigated by *a* physician, who found that when nine years old she used to hear *an* old pastor " read to himself in a loud voice out of his books," some of which in Latin, *and* Greek *and* rabbinical Hebrew were found, and in which many of the servant-girl's glossolalic ravings were identified.

The frequent retelling of this story launched by the poor victim of opium whose mind, constitutionally unstable and imaginative, had so degenerated under the influence of the drug that the boundary between fact and fiction had become hazy indeed, seems to imply that no more recent and well-authenticated one of exactly the same sort and of the same excellence for pedagogic purposes is at hand. In that case my doubts whether there was ever anything more than slight foundation for Coleridge's story are much increased. Psychical incidents which are authenticated, at any rate, though they may be sporadic, yet do not wait a hundred and forty years to reproduce their like.

There remains to pay attention to some clerical classes of hostile adventurers into the psychical field. Most of these believe that all sorts of supernormal occurrences took place two and three thousand years ago, but that they ceased at about the close of the apostolic age, without any intelligible reason for so believing. Some admit that they probably occur now, but are inimical to them, since they hold, again for no intelligible reasons, that any external intelligence which may be connected with them must be diabolic. The most vocal and emphatic of these clerical classes are Roman Catholics and certain sects calling

THE ENCHANTED BOUNDARY 119

themselves Adventists. Almost without exception these fall into the same pitfalls which have been named, except the psychoanalytical one.

REV. C. M. DE HEREDIA

Father de Heredia has written a book entitled *Spiritism and Common Sense*. He differs from the most of his Catholic colleagues in thinking that diabolism has played comparatively a small part in the " witchcraft, black magic, satanic societies, and the like " of history, which for the most part were based upon " the inventions of ingenious, shrewd, imaginative men and women, to mystify their followers." This is probably a concession to " common sense," though it is not quite common sense to make the phenomena at the same time the work of imagination and of invention for a calculated purpose. But when we consider the many bulls of pontiffs which recognize and affirm the reality of witchcraft (especially the bull *Summis Desiderantis* of Eugene IV., and that of Innocent IV. which directed authorities to leave no means untried to detect sorcerers, and especially those who by evil weather destroy vineyards, gardens, meadows and growing crops), the *Malleus Maleficarum* or handbook of the Inquisition for the detection and prosecution of witches, and the dire results upon the thousands who were condemned as wizards and witches, and then turn to Father de Heredia's assertion that there was seldom any " origin of fact " to correspond, and, still again, our eye falls on his warning counsel that the judgment of the Church is to be followed on all such matters, it seems to us that he has involved himself in a bull of unpontifical character.

Father de Heredia cites one case which he thinks is one of real devil possession. A little girl in Natal did things which have much the appearance of hysteria, sometimes understood and talked Latin (but whether more than she could have picked up from her ecclesiastical superiors is not stated), and had her dress and bed set on fire (but whether when any one was looking does not appear). By holy water, relics, and the like, a devil was presumably expelled. It seems singular that recourse should have been made to this lonely case in Africa, when the churchly literature is so rich in cases of more dramatic character, such as those of Nicole Aubry at Vervins in 1566, Madeleine de la Palud de Mandolx and Gafridy at Aix in 1609, of the nuns of St. Brigitte at Lille in 1613, of the Ursulines and Urbain Grandier at Loudun in 1634–1637. Not even when the exorcizing priests became themselves possessed and their devils stubbornly and victoriously resisted all the sacred objects and ceremonies, as in the cases of the noted Fathers Lactance, Tranquille and Surin, did they doubt their diagnoses and remedies. And here comes Father de Heredia and tells us that there was seldom any " origin in fact " to correspond, and yet that " The Church is our mother. Her maternal eyes are keen to detect danger even afar off," and that the judgment of the Church should be followed in all these matters.

The author is obliged to acknowledge that " the argument that offers the testimony of the ' spirits ' that they are Satan or his servants is a two-bladed one, for if such testimony is to be considered, one must also put credence in the testimony of the other ' spirits ' who insist that they are the souls of the dead." That is quite true, and one must add that neither can the fact of diabolical possession be proved by holy water, relics or exorcisms, for all these fail too often, and profane suggestions too often seem to work as well. For example, in the famous case of the Ursulines of Loudun, a skeptic, the Count of Lude, brought to the exorcists a box of relics which he desired them to test on Jeanne de Belfiel, a possessed nun. The exorcists applied the relics to the body of the nun, who at once began to cry out and make frightful contortions as if she suffered horribly. They were taken away and she became quiet again. When opened, the box was found to contain feathers and hair of quadrupeds. The only sequel was a good scolding for the doubting Thomas, and renewed use of relics of a better odor of sanctity.

Father de Heredia is fortunate that it is in this age that he does his rationalizing, instead of the age wherein the Jesuit Delrio harried Cornelius Loos, Professor at Treves, for just such liberal ideas, and Dietrich Flade, Rector of the same university, met his hard fate. Nevertheless, he is to be congratulated for his courage and progress.

After relating how the impostor Taxil, at that time a member of the Roman Church, successfully fooled its dignitaries and secured the blessing of Leo XIII., the author rather inconsequently remarks, " We must be very careful not to take the word of non-Catholics, however pretentious is the scientific authority that pronounces it, when that word touches on matters that have to do with faith and endeavors to declare what we should or should not believe." Dr. Hyslop is classed as a " pseudoscientist," on the strength of the fact that a study of his books (seven are said in the appendix to have been consulted) reveals one chronological error, which the Father charitably pronounces a " falsification " with a motive.[109]

---

[109] See review in *Journal* A. S. P. R., XVII, 390-92, written by myself but mostly on the basis of facts furnished by " F. L.," an erudite man who did not wish his name to appear.

THE ENCHANTED BOUNDARY 121

Another logical difficulty is encountered when clerics write books denying that there can be communications and apparitions of a beneficent nature, although their Church has issued a whole library of stories narrating the beneficent apparitions and communications granted to the very choicest Saints of the calendar. And when Herbert Thurston, S.J., says that although the faithful must not have dealings with mediums, yet the Church does not condemn psychical research, which must necessarily deal with mediums, it would seem that all the faithful of inquiring turn of mind need to do is to call their dealings by the title "psychical research," and go to it.

Much of de Heredia's book is made up of descriptions of fraud, which are so trite that one is reminded of the reason which King Kalakaua gave for not attending a horse race, "Everyone knows that one horse can run faster than another."

PROFESSOR RINE

Adventists cannot view any evidence for survival with clear vision, since they wear the colored spectacles of a dogma, to the effect that when a man is dead he is absolutely dead, and remains so until he is resurrected at the Day of Judgment. Ask them a question which you think will be embarrassing, and it proves not to be so in the least, for they at once construct an epicycle to take care of it. An Adventist orator was asked about the apparition of Moses and Elijah on the Mount and replied that they were specially resurrected for the occasion, but was quite certain that no one else can be resurrected for any occasion prior to the general resurrection, when the constituent particles of all human bodies, miraculously preserved distinct, will be reassembled.

Considering their small numbers, the Adventists are diligent in issuing books and pamphlets against theories which psychical research must consider. One of these was written by a Professor Rine. It confounds Washington I. Bishop, the "mind reader," with Washington Irving, and actually calls him "the eminent author." It calls Professor Charles Richet "the great authority on *medicine* in France." It declares that "after more than a quarter of a century of painstaking, scientific investigation of all sorts of occult phenomena the Society [meaning the S. P. R.] unanimously reports that the reality of telepathy, clairvoyance, clairaudience, telekinesis, materialization, prevision, and automatic writing and speaking, has been definitely proved." It refers to Hamlin Garland, an American novelist, as the "eminent Polish scholar," when he is neither a Pole nor erudite in the

Polish language. It refers to the predictions in Mrs. Piper's script, and adds, " all of which actually took place." Then, having authenticated so much that " ain't so," it ascribes all the marvels to the devil and his imps. But the most staggering proof that Mr. Rine's intelligence was obfuscated by the influence of the enchanted boundary is found in his assertions that " Professor Wundt, of Germany, and Professor Carpenter, of England, and Professors James and Ladd, of America, succeeded in completely discrediting the old traditional psychology based upon the assumption that all mental life was simply the expression of the various energies of an indestructible, ethereal principle within man, named the soul "; that " they proved incontestably that all mental phenomena are manifestations of nerve or brain energy, and that therefore, without brain there can be no intellect "; and that " this momentous achievement has naturally dealt an irreparable blow to the immortality hypothesis." Rine could not have fallen upon worse selections in support of his views. It is well known that Wundt turned entirely away from his earlier materialism, and insisted on " independent psychical causality, which is related at all points to physical causality and can never come into contradiction with it, but is . . . different from this physical causality." Carpenter said that " the view here taken does not in the least militate against the idea that mind may have an existence altogether independent of the body which serves as its instrument," and much else to the same effect. Ladd said that physiological psychology " shows no decisive reason against the belief that such a non-material and real ' unit being ' as the mind is should exist in other relations than those of its present admitted dependence upon the structure and functions of the body." James's interest in the question of survival alone is a refutation of the reference to him.

As though to prove how far enchantment can go, Rine makes John Fiske a supporter of his dogma, by quoting a sentence which Fiske puts into the mouth of an opponent and then proceeds to refute at length, and this in a book whose very title, *Life Everlasting*, would seem to have been warning enough to a mind not under a spell.

REV. CHARLES REYNOLDS BROWN

Let us now glance at the state of knowledge relating to psychical research exhibited, and the arguments resorted to, by the Rev. Mr. Brown, Dean of Yale Divinity School, in a very respectable book of its class, *Living Again* (1920).

The author pays respect to psychical research, and thinks that its product should be attended to with an open mind. But, says he, "I am frank to say that in my own investigation of these claims, I have never seen with my own eyes or heard with my own ears what other men claim to have seen and heard." We are not told how extensive his personal investigations have been, and the statement, though it may be weighty to him, has little value for others. Has he ever seen a case of multiple personality? Has he ever heard the African Pygmies sing? " I am reluctant to credit the full report which some of them make." This sentence does not weigh much, either, for any person of sense would say the same.

He does not believe that his mother, if she communicated with him, " would seek out some dark, dingy room in the back parlor [sic] of a professional medium." Well, if there is such a thing as communication from the dead, she would not, unless he frequented only such places, have to come in a " room in the back parlor," or a dark room, or a dingy room, or to a professional.

He thinks his mother, if she came to him, would come in " church " or in his " study." This demand ignores the whole theory, forced by the appearance of things, that some persons are so constituted as to be conductors of communications, while others are not. Supposing that she, when on earth, had desired to send him a telegram to let him know that she had survived a railway wreck; would she have declined to do so because the available telegraph office was dark and dingy, and she had to pay the operator?

As Professor Brown carefully picks his medium and her surroundings to make an unpleasing appearance, so he as unnecessarily chooses his sample " message " with the view that it shall be banal. And he declares that nothing of permanent value on religion has been received. If this is true, he should, considering that many " messages " teach the ethics of the pulpit with an equal fervor and mellifluence of diction, make his indictment broader in application. If he means that nothing *new* in religion is said, we are forced to remark that some of his colleagues complain that novelties are taught, and to ask if he really makes it a condition that there should be a new revelation. One of the very sentences which he quotes as " trivial and commonplace," namely, " Be good and love Jesus and he will bring you here "—is it the Dean of a Divinity School who declares its teaching not of " permanent value "? What of his own essay, which contains not a thought, not an affirmation, which has not been expressed repeatedly before? For the arguments adduced in favor of " living again " are the old familiar deductive ones. That most people want to live again, is one; that survival is demanded by the moral nature of man, is another. The dean believes that he will survive death because he believes in God, and because Jesus said so.* This is all, except for some picturesque and moving stories.

We are told that much which seemed to spiritualists proof of communication has been explained by psychology. Yes, and psychical research has done the most to explain these particular factors, and yet the problems which psychology has not explained, and shows no indication of explaining, loom up as before.

MORRIS H. TURK

The author of *They Live and Are Not Far Away* [110] is a clerical, or at least a theological writer. He declares (p. 31) that "immortality can never be adequately proved by physical or psychical phenomena. Proofs of any kind are of little use in gaining a conviction of eternal life." It is difficult to see how a man who so reveres the New Testament, and is presumably familiar with it, could be unaware that this flatly contradicts its plainest teaching. If ever there was a religion founded on the claim that a fact had been proved, it is Christianity. And that alleged fact is a psychical fact, the survival of Jesus after his crucifixion. If "proofs of any kind are of little use in gaining a conviction of eternal life," what did Jesus mean when he said: "Because I live, ye shall live also" (John 14:19)? Why, after the surviving Jesus had said, "Ye shall be witnesses unto me," and the apostles determined to elect a man in the place of Judas, did they require one qualified "to be a witness with us of his resurrection" (Acts 1:22), if the psychical fact of that resurrection was of little value as proof of continuing life? Why did the first preaching proclaim the survival of Jesus and allege by way of proof that "all we are witnesses" (Acts 2:32; 3:15; 10:39-42; 13:30-31), if it is of little use to offer proof? If the survival of Jesus was of "little use in gaining a conviction of eternal life," then the whole of St. Paul's magnificent argument comprised in the fifty-eight verses of the fifteenth chapter of I Corinthians is persiflage.

Mr. Turk repudiates any value in psychical research. He will not entertain even the possibility that any of its evidence points to surviving intelligences. Then on what does he base his confident affirmation —"They live and are not far away"? On feeling, the power to visualize, and "perhaps." He quotes with approval the Rev. Dr. G. A.

---

[110] A. B. Barnes & Co., 1923. The book sold so well that a second printing followed the first in but two months.

Gordon's expressions of scorn for psychical research, and the reason of his assurance that his father was still living and conscious of earthly affairs—"As I thought of him and his blessed state I began to *feel* distinctly that he was near." What looks to the psychologist extremely like auto-suggestion, the subjective realization of a wish, was sufficient for Dr. Gordon, who distinctly affirms that he wants and would value no further proof (89-96). Carlyle, we are told, wrote "*Perhaps* my father, all that essentially was my father, is even now near me, with me" (87-8). Mr. Turk evidently thinks that a "perhaps" from so great a man as Carlyle lends considerable support to his thesis—"They live and are not far away." But *perhaps*, after all, the father was then dancing a Highland fling before Henry VIII. Now the author gives his own grounds for assurance that *his* father's spirit survives. "We may *visualize* the faces of our Immortals. So I see my dear father now in his spiritual body. I picture him in the height of his powers, in the strength and beauty of his ideal manhood. . . . He is as real to me now as when I saw him in the flesh" (86-7). Oddly, this passage comes only four pages after another, wherein the author speaks of "the uncritical but persistent habit of thinking in pictures. We are forever trying to imagine how a thing appears"!

Mr. Turk unintentionally often comes into conflict with the Bible which he reveres, and even with himself. He says: (83) "No one has a soul; he is a soul. A better word is person. Soul, spirit, person— these words mean one and the same thing." Then I wonder how the "dividing asunder of soul and spirit (Heb. 4:12) is managed, and why Jesus said, "My soul is exceeding sorrowful" (Mark 14:34). And how came Mr. Turk himself to say "he commits his soul" (25), "in his soul" (47), "the soul of man" (52), "his soul" (61) and "souls of men" (64, 148)? The fact is, of course, that *soul*, as well as *spirit*, is a word used in different senses, and it is too late to attempt confining it to one.

One gets the impression that the author of *They Live and Are Not Far Away* is a pleasant gentleman, and rather dislikes to add to selected specimens of enchanted logic, examples of bewitched dealing with facts.

It is hard sometimes to determine what he means by his frequent word "spiritualism." If the doctrine that spirits survive, are conscious of happenings on earth, and come into helpful relations with their surviving friends, then he himself is a most fervent exponent of it, although he spurns any attempt to find if it is supported by evidence, resting his assurance contentedly on religious ratiocination and ability to visualize. Generally he must refer to a certain religious cult, and consequently is in error in his intimation that such an organization as the Society for Psychical Research has been of aid in building up that cult (37). On the whole, it may have encouraged spiritualism, but Spiritualism it certainly has not. It has never taken an attitude of opposition, but as a historical fact has generally been criticized, frowned upon and bitterly opposed by the cult.

The statement that " following the Civil War in America, spiritualism held the attention of many eager persons for several years " (34) is faulty in several ways. There has never been a year in the last eighty of which the same could not correctly be said. Neither during any one of the several years following the Civil War nor any year since, so far as I can glean from histories or files of Spiritualist publications, was there, in America, such a furor of popular and largely indiscriminating interest as during the last years *before* the Civil War. Mrs. Emma Hardinge Britten did make the claim in 1870 that there were 11,000,000 Spiritualist adherents in the country, but the sole foundation for this ridiculous claim was a declaration to the same effect made by an alarmed bishop in a Roman Catholic convention held in Baltimore in or about 1860. It may be that there was a slight impetus received from the War, but between the years 1860 to 1870 Spiritualism was increasing in England without any Civil War, and if after 1870 there was a decline in America, there also was in England.[111] In 1855, according to the *North American Review*, there were twelve or fourteen Spiritualist periodicals in the country; in 1877, Mrs. Britten, the Spiritualist historian, knew of only eight.[112] It was for the period 1850–1855, rather than for the several years following the Civil War, that she made exultant claims, such as that in Auburn, New York, circles were being held in every other house.

Our author also declares that "the origin of Spiritualism," by which he means the Rochester rappings and other events connected with the Fox sisters, "was utterly non-religious. Its development was equally innocent of any religious content or quality " (39). Now I hold no brief for the Fox sisters, and am convinced by handwriting tests, for instance, that the messages supposed to have been written by a baby under spirit influence, were written by his mother, Kate Fox Jencken. Nor do I think that any alleged phenomena are validated by a religious accompaniment. But I believe that every writer should be careful not to set down statements which are not true. Mr. Turk,

---

[111] Podmore's *Modern Spiritualism*, II, 354. [112] *Nineteenth Century Miracles*, 451.

as well as myself, is dependent upon the testimony of the Fox sisters and their friends. According to them, in the very first period of modern Spiritualism, the "spirits" were exhorting the witnesses to "Go forth and do your duty and good will come of it," promising the protection and rewards of God, declaring that their duty was to "proclaim these truths to the world," and that "You have been chosen to go before the world to convince the skeptical of the great truth of immortality," etc.[113] Mrs. Underhill, referring to 1849, says, "We were truly converted, and as the dear old Methodists used to say, 'born again.' We could then realize that we had something to live for, something to hope for, in that sacred hour when each one in our humble group 'lay at the feet of Jesus,' willing to be guided and directed in the paths of truth and duty." If all this is true—and no one is in a position to say it is not, it looks very much like "religious content and quality."

I select one more specimen illustrating the easy confidence with which well-meaning men venture to make assertions regarding a subject of which they have little knowledge, providing that subject is psychical research. Speaking of the records of experiments with psychics such as are contained in the reports of the S. P. R. and those issued by Dr. Hyslop, he says (40-41): "Not one item of knowledge above that which any average intelligence could easily imagine, has been transmitted from the supposed spirits. . . . To every item of information so far reported the question might well be in kindest sincerity, 'What of it?'" After forty years of publication of records which have baffled the efforts of the keenest investigators to explain by normal processes the knowledge displayed in automatic deliverances, after the failure of every critic who has attacked these records to do so other than by unfair selection, malpractice or quibbling, and with all this carefully compiled official literature of documents facing him like a sphynx demanding reply, Mr. Turk, who perhaps has never taken pains to lift a single cover of this literature, calmly says that it contains "not one item of knowledge above that which any average intelligence could easily *imagine*," and asks "in kindest sincerity, 'What of it?'"!

REV. I. M. HALDEMAN, D.D.

Referring to *Can the Dead Communicate with the Living*, published

---

[113] *The Missing Link in Modern Spiritualism*, by Mrs. A. Leah Fox Underhill, 22, 25, 26, 48, 49, 58.

in 1920, Dr. E. J. Dingwall, who has never been suspected of favoring the spiritistic hypothesis, wrote:[114]

" This book, by a writer who has been called ' the greatest prophet of the Lord now standing in any pulpit in this country,' aims at showing that the so-called phenomena of modern spiritualism are due to the agency of evil spirits. Psychical researchers are always willing to listen to anybody who presents theories which have some evidence to support them. Dr. Haldeman presents no evidence, and this is not really surprising. The devil theory is often held by persons of the clerical persuasion who naturally see in the religious aspect of spiritualism a menace to their own profession. Dr. Haldeman imagines that by pointing to the Bible he can put these subjects beyond the range of discussion. Anybody who can read at all knows that any sect or any school of religious thought can quote the Bible to advantage, and in this respect the spiritualists themselves are often singularly successful. The Rev. Walter Wynn, for example, an English pastor, and curiously enough also a ' prophet,' is now touring South Africa demonstrating the essential unity of Biblical and spiritualistic teaching. The author of this book claims to answer these questions:—Where are they? What are they? and Are they? yet his ignorance of psychical literature is such that he writes calmly of the ' case of Howe caught by Browning,' [115] and of ' Euspasia Palladino.' Further comment on this production is unnecessary."

A FEW MORE WRITERS

GUSTAV SPILLER in 1902 published a book entitled *The Mind of Man,* in which he pays some little incidental attention to the subject-matter of psychic research, which he regards as all humbug. Mr. N. W. Thomas informs us in his brief review [116] that Mr. Spiller also has no good opinion of psychologists either, so it is odd that he picks out psychologists as best fitted to investigate Spiritism, especially as he thinks that " competent persons " should investigate the subject, which he is sure is not worth any attention. An extract from the book reads:

" There is no science of spiritism . . . after the short experimental stage came undiluted dogma and reckless speculation. Professors Wallace, Crookes, Lodge and James illustrate what I am saying. Only

---

[114] *Journal* A. S. P. R., XVI, 584.
[115] He meant Home, and Home was never caught by Browning.
[116] *Proceedings* S. P. R., XVII, 426.

the last of these is a psychologist, and he has never written anything bulky."

I have heard this kind of logic before, but the particular test to be applied to a man, whether or not he has written anything bulky, in order to ascertain his standing, is new to me. If the scientific world of the present generation had borne it in mind they would not have been so impressed by the theories of Einstein, who embodied them, not in anything that was bulky, but in the compass of but a few pages.

The Rev. A. V. MILLER, O.S.C. (Roman Catholic), in his *Sermons on Modern Spiritualism* (1909), shows that he has not been so negligent in research as some of the representatives of science, and accordingly he admits that there are supernormal phenomena. But he is sure that the object of all these is to destroy the True Church, hence the resemblance of some cases to instances in the Bible is for him evidence that the former have been fabricated by the great deceiver of humanity. Why, then, may not the devil have brought about the Scriptural examples? Of course the proof that they could not have been is to be found in the very fact that they *are* in the Bible, which is good clerical logic of a sort.

DR. GUISEPPE LAPPONI in 1906 printed an enlarged edition of his *Ipnotismo e Spiritismo—Studio medico-critico*. The book has anticipatory interest because it was written not only by a physician but also by the physician who for years was charged with the chief responsibility of guarding the health of that remarkable pope, Leo XIII. But it might almost have been written in 1870, for all the acquaintance with psychic research manifested therein. It deals with crude spiritualism. It admits the genuineness of some mediumistic phenomena, but hints that the devil is the prime cause thereof. It makes the definite charge that all purported messages are nonsensical and stupid. Now this broad statement, although it has been echoed by writers who, if resolved to go into the matter at all ought to have better informed themselves, simply is not and was not, in 1906, true. Heaven knows a great deal purporting to be from spirits has been banal, vapid, foolish, ignorant. But those epithets emphatically do not apply to the " Patience Worth" utterances. They do not apply to the two books of Mary McEvilly. They do not apply to *Spirit Teachings* of Stainton Moses, which antedates 1906. But no scientific psychic researcher would ascribe evidential weight to *Spirit Teachings* on account of its clear thinking, excellent diction and lofty ethics, since the automatist was a learned clergyman.[117]

By the same logic and for the same reasons incoherences, apparent stupidities, etc., could not with certainty be credited to the spirit, granting that a spirit was concerned at all, as the subconsciousness of the "medium" could mix in to mar as well as to improve. Dr. Lapponi knows nothing of all this, but writes almost as remotely from the times in which he lives as if he were the physician of Pio Nono.

FATHER A. M. LEPICIER, O.S.M., Professor of Divinity in the College of Propaganda, Rome, wrote, in or about 1909, a book entitled *The Unseen World*. It deals with the subject in an almost exclusively dogmatic and oracular fashion, not attempting to give any proof of its declarations which would be acceptable to any one not disposed to bow to ecclesiastical authority. Thus Father Lépicier dwells upon the alleged evil effects of spiritism, physical, mental and moral, but brings forward no evidence that his assertions are true. In view of all which is related in the purported biographies of canonized saints, he wisely does not deny that there may occasionally be a case of communion between the living and good spirits. Referring to spiritistic phenomena he says:

"What the Church condemns in them is their abuse, not their right and lawful use, if such a thing can be said respecting some of them. It approves of these practices so long as they do not require entering into any kind of compact with the spirits of the unseen world, and provided their result can be turned to a useful and laudable purpose."

This leaves us in the dark whether psychic research, as such, is permissible according to the Church (although Father Thurston says it is). Certainly it does not make a practice of "entering into any kind of compact" with purported spirits, but is the ascertainment of facts, *per se*, a "useful and laudable purpose?" There was a time when William James said that he knew no practical use whatever of psychology. Much of the investigation of pure science is directed to objects for what there is, for the time being, no known *use*. It is doubtful if any psychic researcher expects that telepathic faculty will be developed to the point of being dependable, for example, as a guide

---

[117] We have a more difficult problem when we try to account for the output of "Patience Worth," since it manifests a number of qualities and abilities far transcending anything ever normally shown by the automatist in that case.

for dealings in the stock market. I suspect that "the useful and laudable purpose" which the Church which Father Lépicier represents is the making of saints. But if psychical practices had to wait until sainthood was officially determined, the Church would today be lacking many of its saints. Despite the grudging admissions of some of its theologians, the Roman Catholic Church in our day generally views with a suspicious and chilly countenance the curious phenomena which are plentiful in its hagiology.

One F. B. STOCKDALE in 1921 issued a book entitled *The Future Life: Facts and Fancies*. "The fallacy of ouija boards, and mediums, . . . critical, convincing, constructive," the publisher's announcement assures us.

It is simply a piece of ignorant effrontery, and its critical and convincing quality may be tested by a single quotation from its page 104:

"Now suppose that you could dissect a bird. . . . If your knife were sharp enough and your sight keen enough, you would find inside the body a disposition. We call it the migratory instinct."

Think of a man who talks about dissecting out a *disposition* and having eyes keen enough to see an *instinct*, and who pretends to tell his readers what's what in psychic research!

An article by one JAMES BLACK, in the *Scientific American* for September, 1922, was so full of misstatements as to call forth a chorus of protests in which one of the editors joined, in the December issue. No less than eleven proper names were misspelled, historical facts were outrageously misstated, and a document, the only source of information, was falsified in order to make out a case. As the writer was certain to be convicted, he could not have intended all these errancies, therefore they must have been due to the enchantment of the boundary.

The same remark applies to DR. A. T. SCHOFIELD, who wrote a book called *Modern Spiritism* (1920). We call attention to fourteen lines on page 20, wherein he speaks of "W. Stainton Moses, B.A.," "a college master at University College," and of "a D. D. Home," and then of "their advent and, at the same time, the wonderful talents of the Rev. Henry Irving, the founder of the Latter Day Saints, or so-called Holy Apostolic Church," which "combined to interest all society." This is all correct except that it is the initials M. A. rather than " B.A." which have a somewhat noted connection with the name of Moses, he was not a " college master," he was a master in University College School, and not in " University College," Irving and the popular vogue of his movement were not " at the same time," but both were dead before Moses was born or Home was two years old, *this* Irving's name was not " Henry " but Edward, he had and claimed to have no occult talents as is implied, his followers were never called " Latter Day Saints," which is the title appropriated by the Mormons, and the official title of his sect is not " Holy Apostolic Church," but Catholic Apostolic Church.

Many such errors appear. Daniel Dunglas Home becomes " Douglas D. Home "; the founding of the Society for Psychical Research is put at 1891 instead of 1882; it is incorrectly stated that Mrs. Piper " denied she ever had any communications with the departed "; the " opportune conversion " of Sir Oliver Lodge is falsely said to have taken place during the Great War; it is declared that Mrs. Piper was " exposed in fraudulent practices," which is untrue; Richard Hodgson receives the title of " Professor," which was never his; Professor Newbold, of Pennsylvania, becomes " Professor Newbolt "; and so on. It is said that spiritism is " the child of theosophy," that is, the child was born before its mother. On page 101 readers are informed that " Professor Hyslop " died some years ago, early enough for William James to pass upon the validity of messages claiming to be from his spirit! [118] And on page 32 they are gravely told that belief in communication from the dead " mainly rests on this work of one medium, Mrs. Piper," while belief in genuine " physical manifestations " (levitation, sounds, lights, etc.) being real and not fraudulent, rests on the work of Eusapia Palladino!

There is considerable good material in the book, but one must tread with wary step amidst the not infrequent erroneous statements of fact, misleading arrangements of material, and contradictory reasonings.

It has not been my purpose in these sketches to champion any particular opinion on the subject matter of psychical research, but only to sketch a strange and seemingly irresistible tendency on the part of those who enter its field with hostile intent. No man wants to make a laughing-stock of himself. Then what induces these writers to shun real acquaintance with the matters which they discuss, to misquote or reverse the meaning of sentences before their eyes, to misspell familiar

---

[118] Hyslop died in 1920, James in 1910.

names, to rely without misgiving on secondary and unreliable sources, to misstate facts easy of reference, to employ schoolboy logic, to yield to emotion and boast of it, to parrot materialistic dogmas instead of discussing evidence, and to parrot dogmas regarding their opponents' intellects instead of meeting their arguments. Surely my hypothesis of the enchanted boundary is the most charitable one, and it is quite sufficient to explain the phenomena.

III. SOME SAMPLE EXPLANATIONS

AN ATTEMPT TO EXPLAIN AWAY TELEPATHY

A book called *Aberglauben und Zauberei*, by Dr. Alf. Lehmann, Director of the psychological laboratory in the University of Copenhagen, was issued in 1898. Dr. Lehmann and Dr. Hansen were the gentlemen who, on the basis of their own experiments, attempted, with a large degree of unsuccess as it seems to me, to explain away the S. P. R. experiments for telepathy. Dr. F. C. S. Schiller reviewed the book,[1] and the most of what is said here is quoted or summarized from his remarks.

Probably as the direct consequence of Dr. Lehmann's having deigned to experiment for himself in the field of psychic research, he is not animated by a spirit of entire condemnation and scorn toward it. But yet he is somewhat dogmatic and oracular, and accordingly we find, as we might expect, some of the defects with which we have now become so well acquainted.

Dr. Schiller says:

" Owing either to his early training or to a cautious deference to popular and scientific prejudice, Dr. Lehmann occasionally lapses into crudities of judgment for which the bulk of his narrative and his admissions elsewhere hardly prepare the reader.

" To give a few flagrant examples. In his historical survey of ancient sorcery the Jews receive a ' favored nation ' treatment which it would be hard to justify on scientific grounds. *Per contra* in his preface Dr. Lehmann takes up quite a comic and Canute-like attitude of one stemming the rising tide of superstition. Yet in the rest of his book he is largely occupied in showing, with great skill and success, how most or all of these superstitions arose as well-meant, though erroneous, attempts at a scientific explanation of phenomena. Again, in his final paragraph, he warns us that the modern ' occultists ' (among whom he seems for the moment to include the S. P. R., although he ordinarily makes much and appreciative use of its work) have burdened their consciences with a terrible responsibility for the new superstitions, to which he fears the new conceptions of telepathy,

---

[1] *Proceedings* S. P. R., XV, 437.

SOME SAMPLE EXPLANATIONS

subliminal consciousness, etc., will lead. Yet in the body of his work he found these new conceptions useful and even indispensable. He admits that there is no intrinsic absurdity in the assumption of telepathic forces, and, on his own showing their assertion has at least enriched science by the discovery (made by himself) of 'involuntary whispering.' As for the subliminal, he is constantly compelled to have recourse to it or its equivalents in explaining hypnotic phenomena, automatisms, etc. Not that he likes it: indeed he has to explain that he prefers to use the term '*unconscious*' in such cases just because unconscious ideas or states of consciousness are sheer *nonsense* (!), while '*subliminal*' and '*subconscious*' (though intrinsically preferable, *cf.* p. 431) imply theories. Are we to infer from this that it is scientific to adopt a nonsensical, and superstitious to adopt a workable formula?"

Dr. Lehmann attempts to show that Sir William Crookes's two accounts of the phenomena of Home, one in the *Quarterly Journal of Science*, the other in the S. P. R. *Proceedings* (VI) are marked by such discrepancies as to justify the conclusion that Crookes imagined what he wrote, and either did not think the circumstances omitted from the first account of importance or else was guilty of intentional deception. But Dr. Schiller says:

"I own that it passes my comprehension how Dr. Lehmann should have arrived at conclusions of such gravity from premises so flimsy as those which he adduces. For the two accounts correspond so completely in all essentials that it seems to me a gross exaggeration to speak even of discrepancies between them, and the only legitimate inference would seem to be the very obvious and harmless one that the first account was a highly condensed, and not a *verbatim*, account of what occurred."

Lehmann says that the account by Crookes was lacking in many details which we would like to know (which criticism I think just, but Crookes wrote at a period when it was not yet apparent that any psychical experiment must be reported with more particularity than any other type of experiment), but Dr. Schiller reminds him that "he himself is unwittingly sitting in the same glass house," for his report of the "involuntary whispering experiments" are very far from being as complete as they should be for our satisfaction. And the adjective "involuntary" is exceedingly questionable. Professor Sidgwick had already given his opinion that, in the nature of things, whispering could have been at most only "semi-involuntary," and now Dr. Schiller is unable to credit that it was involuntary at all.

"It seems to me a strange abuse of language to describe the whispering as 'involuntary,' and I do not wonder that when Professor Sidgwick tried to repeat Dr. Lehmann's experiments he could not attain to the 'involuntariness.' The fact is that Dr. Lehmann's whisperings, as is practically admitted by Dr. Hansen, were quite voluntary and conscious. The agent was perfectly aware of what he was about and could regulate the loudness and distinctness of his whispers to a nicety. I am surprised only at the moderation of the experimenters in limiting the percentage of their successes to 33 per cent. They might just as well have made it 100 per cent! I suppose they stopped where they did in order to 'mimic' better the telepathic series of the S. P. R. But the analogy between Messrs. Lehmann and Hansen's experiments and *bona fide* telepathy seems to me wholly illusory."

And I, too, doubt the practicability of consciously experimenting to see what can be accomplished by involuntary whispering, and at the same time keeping certain that no volition enters in. On psychological grounds I do not think the thing can be done.

In 1930 we can judge what a rash statement was made by Dr. Lehmann when he said that in consequence of catching Eusapia Palladino in tricky conduct, "spiritism has ceased to exist as a scientific problem."

"Altogether he is not quite fair to the spiritist theory. He tends to regard it as intrinsically superstitious and *a priori* inadmissible, in a way in which 'occultism,' *i. e.*, the assumption of unknown forces, is not. He is consequently puzzled to understand why both 'spiritism' and 'occultism' have so often been held together. But surely a moment's reflection would have shown him that if there is room in the universe for undiscovered forces, 'spirits' may be among them, while if a spirit world interacts with ours, the forces whereby this occurs are practically unknown. In point of fact, the spiritist hypothesis is intrinsically as good as any other, and has certain well-marked advantages, *if it is treated in a scientific manner.* It must therefore be repeated as often as is needful that superstition consists, not in holding any particular theory, but in the way in which it is held."

Finally, while Dr. Lehmann pays no slightest attention to the modern evidence relating to "haunted houses," much of which is very formidable, he can credit on a poor state of evidence certain fakir feats. "Verily," says his critic, "Dr. Lehmann also is sometimes capable of the feat of swallowing a camel!"

It would seem that while there is much which is admirable in the book, it manifests here and there dogmatism and prejudice, and that the factor of blunder and faulty logic is directly proportioned thereto.

"MESSAGE" MEDIUMSHIP EXPLAINED (?)

In 1920, Lieutenant E. H. Jones, a British officer of the Great War, published a book called *The Road to Endor*. For the purpose of putting amateur experimenters in the field of psychic research on their guard it merits high praise. I have not seen it, but have read a long and able review of it by Mr. W. H. Salter,[2] to whom I am indebted for a part of what follows:

Lieutenant Jones and several other British officers were together for many months in a Turkish prison camp, and to beguile the tedium began to practice on a ouija-board. Presently he conceived the idea of attempting to fool his companions, and the book is a history of his success. Fortunately for him, his companions included no person abreast with the methodology of modern psychic research nor, it would appear, was a single one of them at all familiar with its critical literature, or anything other than a rank amateur, else it is highly probable that the book would have ended at an early chapter. Mr. Salter says:

"Dogmatism is the great blemish on Lieutenant Jones's book. He is, of course, too logical and cautious to assert in so many words that, because he 'faked' psychical phenomena so as to deceive his companions, therefore no genuine psychical phenomena exist. He doubtless reflected that he would have exposed himself to the retort, 'In that case, because you and Lieutenant Hill simulated madness so as to deceive the mental experts, do you say that there is no such thing as real madness?' What he does suggest is that he produced phenomena as remarkable and varied as those produced by any medium, under conditions at least as rigorous as those to which mediums are ever subjected, and that therefore fraud, which was certainly the cause in his own case, cannot be eliminated as a possible explanation of the others. It is no doubt due to the paucity of psychical literature at Yozgad prison camp that Lieutenant Jones has committed himself to this untenable position."

His companions blindfolded him, and were amazed that the pointer still indicated the letters and spelled out sentences. But if a single up-to-date investigator had been present, he would have known that one can nearly always, with the muscles of his forehead, lift an ordi-

---

[2] *Proceedings* S. P. R., XXXI, 229-40.

nary bandage sufficiently to see out from beneath it, would have taken pains to improve the method of blindfolding, and if it still offered means of peeking would have detected the fact by observing that Jones held his head at a particular angle. They then turned the blackboard upside down, but an experienced investigator would not have failed to observe the nicks on the edge by which Jones assisted his unusual visual memory. What further means were employed to complicate the task were extremely faulty, and no experienced psychic researcher of the critical type would have chosen them.

Lieutenant Jones also amazed the men by the knowledge, real or apparent, of them and their past lives and associations which came in the form of messages. But the conditions under which these "messages" came were antipodal to those of the best experiments in psychic research. I quote again from Mr. Salter:

"But in point of fact Lieutenant Jones was working under conditions far more favorable to fraud than the average medium enjoys. He was one of a small group of men shut up together for months and even years: to relieve the tedium of captivity they freely told each other all sorts of details of their past lives, both before and during the War, and then forgot they had ever told them: they shared with each other news from the outside world: and finally, as the book clearly shows, they none of them had the slightest idea of the precautions necessary to exclude fraud.

"Very different is the lot of a professional medium. Any member of the public may obtain a sitting with him. Many of his sitters will no doubt be as guileless as Lieutenant Jones's victims, allowing themselves to be 'pumped,' or of their own accord giving away vital information without knowing that they have done so. But not all will be of this class: from time to time the medium will be confronted with sitters he has never seen before, to whose identity and previous history he has not the slightest clue, who say little (if anything), and keep a careful note of what they say to him and he says to them. If they have more than one sitting, they carefully check anything said by the medium at the later sittings, to see whether he is working on any statement made or hint given at a previous sitting. Nor is the possibility of the medium making inquiries between the sittings overlooked. Private detectives have even been employed to discover whether anything of this kind has been done." [3]

Many of Mrs. Soule's most surprising results have come in connection with sitters brought from hundreds or thousands of miles and

---

[3] *Ib.*, VI, 438; XXX, 343, etc.

SOME SAMPLE EXPLANATIONS

whom she was not allowed to see or, in some instances, to hear utter a word.

Since Lieutenant Jones gives what purport to be verbatim accounts of certain sittings, it is in order to ask if such word-for-word records were actually made at the time. The reviewer does not inform us. But it is next to absolutely certain that they could not have been. Surely Lieutenant Jones, while operating the board, could not also have been making a record. And it is not likely that any one would put down such details as, "Tony ran his hands through his hair." Nor would any of the believers have put down in the notes, "There was a sharpness about his questioning that showed he was hooked." No, what looks like a record was written afterwards, probably long afterwards, and must be regarded with misgivings. Not that there is any reason to doubt the slips made by the sitters which appear in the account given, and which afforded much guidance to Jones. But I doubt whether Jones had not more information given him than he acknowledges, more, probably, than he remembered when he came to write. It is indeed probable that when, sometime before, Tony had talked in a sentimental fashion about a road in Egypt that looked so "spiffing by moonlight," Jones guessed that there was a girl mixed up with it. But when it comes to granting that Jones quite accidentally in the sitting hit upon Louise as the name of the girl, one may be permitted to doubt, considering the long time that the two men had been together, that Tony had not tenderly mentioned the name Louise.

But let that pass, and grant that at the sittings or before no more was divulged by sitters than appears from Lieutenant Jones's account. That the account, then, represents the carelessness of many clients of professional mediums, there can be no question. But it does not represent the quality of the best work done with, for example, Mrs. Soule, or with Mrs. Leonard. Take the purported utterances of the Mother of Doris.[4] The sitter was not allowed to speak and was not even seen. She was brought unheralded and unknown from across the continent. The only person besides Mrs. Soule to speak was Dr. Hyslop, and very seldom could he have given away anything had he desired, for there was very little he knew. All he said appears literally in the report.

This is the point, that the leading societies for psychic research have reported many experiments with mediums to whom the sitters have been unknown, and have reported every word written or uttered

---

[4] *Proceedings* A. S. P. R., XI, and particularly XVII.

in the room by any one present. If any of them have printed records of experiments the sitter wherein had been the daily, almost hourly, associate of the psychic for many months, and if in the records it appears that the sitter gave much added information, as where Tony exclaimed, " Yes, I know; Egypt—Cairo," then Lieutenant Jones has satisfactorily explained them.

As I study the purported record of a part of a sitting reproduced by Mr. Salter, the more I see reason for suspecting that it was written long after the actual sitting, and that constructive imagination has supplemented defects of memory. For while it claims to explain how Jones hit upon the facts, in part it quite fails to explain, and would almost force one to conclude, assuming the excerpt is a fair sample, and is a verbatim report, that he was psychically endowed, after all. Exactly as we find Sherlock Holmes gravely inferring as certain something whose certainty the premises do not warrant, we find in the excerpt referred to several instances where Jones assumes to explain how he was certain of a fact, when to no ordinary mortal would there have existed any certainty.

1. Tony had, a month or so before, talked rapturously about a moonlight scene in Egypt. Jones, as purported medium, ventures the name " Louise," and when Tony gives " a little start " correctly infers that this was the name of the girl who witnessed the moonlight scene with Tony. I submit that Tony might have given a little start had Louise been his sister or his mother, or his favorite maiden aunt, or a lady whom he had that lovely dance with in Paris, or another lady, say at Nice, with whom he had corresponded.

2. Jones makes the board ask, " Why did you leave me? " and explains: " Tony must have left her, because he had come to Yozgad without her." But here is a big logical hiatus. Louise could easily have left him and gone away somewhere before ever he started for Yozgad. But, exactly like Sherlock Holmes, we are told that he must have left her, because he appeared elsewhere without her. And, like Holmes, he hits the bull's-eye.

3. " You told me to go," answered Tony; " I wanted to help." And Jones adds: " which showed he hadn't." But it showed no such thing, although that would be more likely. It is quite conceivable that a situation existed in which Tony could help her by going elsewhere on some errand for her sake.

4. Tony asked, " Have you gone ba—" he checked himself. But, says Jones, " He had already, without knowing it, answered his own question." So the board answers, " I *told* you I was going back. I

went back." But he had not, with certainty, answered his own question. He might have been intending to say, " Have you gone back on me? " He might not have known whether or not she went back, and have thought it better for some reason to ask the question in the form which he immediately substituted, " Where are you now? " And certainly his question in no degree betrayed that she had *told* him that she was going back. For aught I can see she was as likely not to have told him, and yet Jones again hits upon the fact.

5. There is another example of what we are expected to accept as a sure inference. Probably Tony had handsome hair, which would explain the message, " I did love so your hair." We are told that this pleased Tony, who again asked, " Where are you now? " and Jones adds that he " was thinking, *no doubt* [my italics], of her soft hands on his hair." Now surely there have been many instances of girls who took a moonlight walk with a young man yet did not paw his hair. Why Tony might not have been pleased simply to learn that Louise admired his hair I have not the intellect to fathom; yet probably Jones could have put the hair-patting in a message and again have rung the bell.

Lieutenant Jones purports to explain how his answers were guided, and for half of them in the excerpt before me he has really given no adequate explanation. That he could have guessed correctly in all four instances on the very insufficient data is unlikely. I do not doubt that he received many hints, on the contrary I suspect that he received more than he thinks or remembers. Attempting, long after, to recover the substance of what was said and done, he has pictured himself uncannily shrewd, and I think that constructive imagination has often, in his narrative, helped out memory.

While the book utterly fails as a key to many stenographically recorded and carefully guarded cases which have been reported, it serves as a useful lesson to the learner in psychic research, who will, however, probably be disappointed if he expects to find such marvelous powers of normal inference displayed by mediums.

It is one thing to deal with experimenters who are utterly green both in practice and pertinent reading, and with whom one has intimately associated for months, and long after to attempt to reconstruct what took place, with all the pleasing glamor that fancy under the stimulus of self-appreciation casts over memory. It would have been quite another thing had Lieutenant Jones attempted to show what he could do with a sitter utterly unknown to him, an experimenter who because of experience and reading knew how to conduct the experiment, and with a stenographer who contemporaneously recorded every word which was uttered.

THAT EXPLANATORY BLUE BOOK

In several publications there have been references to a mysterious Blue Book which is privately printed for the benefit of mediums. There was a short-lived attempt to furnish mediums with mimeographed sheets containing data about persons in particular towns who had attracted attention to themselves by their zeal in visiting mediums. There may be, although I doubt it, some remnant of the practice still. But a "blue book" is local, not general. On the other hand, it is regarded as etiquette when a fraudulent medium visits a place for mediums of his ilk to supply him information, " give him a load," as the argot has it. What a big tome a Blue Book would need to be, to serve such a psychic as Mrs. Soule, who has experimenters come to her from distant States! It would have to contain many millions of names and data in connection with each, to be of use. And since in many of these experiments the name is not disclosed, it would also be necessary to have millions of photographs and to require some days' notice after making an inventory of a stranger's points, before giving the initial sitting, in order to have some chance of hunting the right photograph. It is well not to be credulous, and it is well, also, not to be credulous in one's incredulity.

Another instance of inverted credulity was displayed in one of the late popular magazines.[5] The writer was showing how easily some mediums perform their marvels, which he could have succeeded in doing, if he had carefully selected his instances. But he brought forward the case of a medium who told a friend of his, whose first initials were "E. E.," that he was born in 1861, that his father was a Union man, etc. Now, remarked the astute journalist, these were easy facts to guess, since almost every man who appears to be in the neighborhood of sixty years old and has the initials "E. E." was named after Elmer Ellsworth, the first Union man to be killed in the Civil War, and consequently of course he would have been born in 1861, his father would have been a Union man, etc.

Well, that explanation is satisfactory, providing that nearly every man who is somewhere in the neighborhood of sixty years, and who boasts the initials "E. E.," *was* named after Elmer Ellsworth. It reminds one of an alleged remark by General Longstreet, lately quoted

---

[5] This was written in 1921.

SOME SAMPLE EXPLANATIONS 143

by James M. Beck in a *Saturday Post* article. Longstreet is supposed to have learned that the average age of Union generals was much less than that of Confederate generals, and to have made a remark indicating despair of the Southern cause, since " gray-beards " were pitted against " invincible youth." But a fresh examination of the ages of the first thirty Union generals whose names came to mind, including all the leading ones, and of a corresponding number of Confederate chiefs, revealed that while the former averaged 40 years and 7 — months, the latter averaged 41 years and 9 + months, hardly enough difference to constitute the former " invincible youth " and the latter " graybeards." [6] Doubtless the remark attributed to Longstreet belongs in the same category with " Ring, Grandpa, Ring," " The Old Guard dies, it never surrenders," and " Shoot, if you must, this old gray head."

But this is wandering from our subject, which is " E. E." It occurred to me that a good many men were named after Everett, who was a famous statesman and orator, but to whom the particular date, 1861, is not so relevant as it is to Ellsworth. And an examination of the first ninety " E. E.'s " observed in the telephone directory of New York, showed that the men named after Edward Everett outnumber those named after Elmer Ellsworth, about three to one, and that the " E. E.'s," whose first names are Edgar, Edwin, Emil, etc., are about as many as the Elmer E.'s. No doubt many a reader of this shrewd " explanation " at once " told the world " that the journalist juvenile was smart, and had shown up those psychic research fellows well. For readers of magazines and newspapers are shown by the cartoonist that the psychical researcher is mainly engaged in sitting opposite a greasy, fat fortune-teller, with his hands on a planchette and his eyes raised devoutly to the skies. How beautiful upon the mountains is any slick and ingenious piece of plausibility that can be " put across "! Why should a magazine writer spend time in the dry business of testing his own statements when he can get just as much a line without that annoyance?

---

[6] Any one who has misgivings may look up for himself the dates of birth of the following generals, and gauge by the date of the first battle of the Civil War.
Union Generals: Grant, Sherman, Sheridan, Meade, Thomas, McClellan, Hancock, Hooker, Schofield, Rosecrans, Slocum, Hunter, McPherson, McDowell, Halleck, Smith, Wallace, Buell, Burnside, Canby, Reynolds, Howard, Pope, McClernand, Butler, Garfield, Sigel, Lyon, Fremont, Porter.
Confederate Generals: R. E. Lee, J. E. Johnston, Jackson, A. S. Johnston, Beauregard, A. P. Hill, D. H. Hill, Longstreet, Stuart, Early, Ewell, Bragg, Hardee, Price, Pickett, Smith, Forrest, Morgan, Gordon, F. Lee, Polk, Wheeler, Van Dorn, Breckinridge, Buckner, Magruder, Pillow, Cobb, Hood, Pemberton.

IV. HOUDINI AND DOYLE

Houdini himself administered an antidote for that almost superstitious estimation which many intelligent people put on the astuteness of magicians, as such, seeming to think that these can infallibly detect the false, and infallibly guide to the true. He says,[1] "I want to call attention at the same time to the incompetence of the opinion of the ordinary magician with a knowledge of two or three experiments in Spiritualism who stands up and claims that he can duplicate the experiments of any medium who ever lived. My personal opinion is that notwithstanding the fact that innumerable exposures have been successfully made, such fact is no proof that any investigator, legerdemain artist or otherwise, is fully capable of fathoming each and every effect produced."

He knows that magicians, like Maskelyne, Kellar and Hoffmann have been hocussed to the point of acknowledging the supernormal character of tricks, which they afterward learned to execute themselves. The magician Dunton staked his reputation on the genuineness of Alfred James's flower-apports, the trick of which was unriddled by a layman a few weeks later.[2]

On the other hand, many persons are awed by the confidence with which many magicians assert that there are no supernormal phenomena. Yet very few of the latter have any expert knowledge of the field of mental phenomena, beyond the fact that there are many mercenary professional mediums abroad who, to give their money's worth, employ various species of trickery. And that every intelligent person is supposed to know.

Sometimes the magician informs his audience not only that there are no supernormal phenomena, but also that he can present as satisfactory an appearance of any alleged type as can any so-called psychical person. I think that the magician on a platform before an audience must be distinguished from the same magician, off the stage and talking in private. A magician's profession is to deceive people. There is nothing reprehensible in this; they know he is doing it, and it is what they have paid to see. But it is necessary to employ language

---

[1] *A Magician Among the Spirits*, 1924. [2] *Bulletin* XII, B. S. P. R., 84-5.

in connection with tricks which is deceptive also. The more wonderful he is the more he attracts, and the bigger the claims he makes, the more wonderful he appears. Thus it is easy, on the platform, to slip into the habit of claiming that he can duplicate anything alleged to be supernormal. I have heard a magician make such a sweeping claim on the stage when he had already told me in conversation that he did not know much about mental phenomena.

Once Houdini and I had a friendly public debate in New York City. I briefly described the vain efforts I had made to trace to a normal source raps that sounded in a former residence, upon my dressing-table, upon a stand by my bed in a room where I slept alone, in all sorts of places in the house and under various conditions. He said that he could go to my house and make raps. I replied that I had no doubt he could rig up a rapping contrivance; but, said I, "Give me the same liberty of examination that I had and exercised in my house, and I will root out your method within two hours at most. If you think otherwise, I invite you to come over and try it." He did not come. On another occasion he rose after I had told about the amazing results of Mrs. King's "psychometric" impressions from a letter held between the palms of her hands, and said that she probably, by sleight-of-hand, got a chance to peep into the letter. I responded that for the most of the 34 tested affirmations, of which 33 were literally and 1 partly correct, she would have received not a hint had she read the whole letter. But I would waive that and allege that she could not have peeped into the letter, for it was folded with only white outside, and remained unmoved between her hands. "You cannot juggle without making movements." He reminded me that there have been witnesses who swore that writing appeared between slates while they were all the time within sight, and yet it was afterward shown that they were mistaken. I replied that this was a very familiar fact, and one which was easily explained. "Their attention was wearied by the time consumed, and distracted by a great variety of movements, and the tricky acts were slipped in by such means, exactly as in the work of magicians. I repeat that this woman used no conjuring movements, held the folded paper quietly between her palms, sat directly before me in the light of day,[3] waited but a few moments before she slowly began to speak, and every sentence was taken down at once. You know me and my experience in the detection of fraud. Do you think I can be so easily de-

---

[3] But I again remind the reader that we would be very far from explaining the results, even if she had deceived me, since the contents of the letter would give hints for only a few of her amazing remarks.

ceived? If you do, please come to me some day and try it. If, holding between your palms a letter with writing folded inside you can tell a single significant word in it, or if under such conditions you can move your hands and I not be aware of it, I will publish it to the world. You are a great magician, she is a humble private person. You should be able to do it if she did. Please demonstrate that my observation can be thus deluded." He did not say he would demonstrate. In private he had shown me physical tricks, but neither he nor any other magician has ever offered to duplicate or equal any of the incidents which I have reported as being, in my judgment, of supernormal character, and none has ever made any serious attempt to throw light upon them.

I would not have it supposed that I am condemning or deriding magicians, even while remarking that one must not take too seriously anything they say in a professional capacity, on the platform. In general they are good fellows, and I felt honored when they invited me to become a member of the S. A. M.[4] Least of all would I have it supposed that I did not respect and admire, in many ways, Houdini. I have no belief whatever that he ever did or would play a mean trick to convict a medium, as he was charged with doing. In the same connection a great many statements without foundation, or twisted out of semblance to the real facts, affecting myself, were put in print. Few of them have I publicly noticed, since it is to me extremely distasteful to be involved in controversy which in its very beginning takes the form of unscrupulous misrepresentation. Some of the attacks launched against Houdini, to my personal knowledge were without foundation, and I am deeply skeptical of certain others.

Houdini was a remarkable man, one of the most dynamic of personalities. I knew him well, and the world seemed poorer when his big heart and eager brain were stilled. He always remained something of a boy, enthusiastic, boisterous, vain, apt to think that he only had preserved from scrapes and blunders any group to which he belonged, but in the genial sunshine of his presence one hardly minded these little peculiarities. His biographer has told us that at times he would fly into a fit of temporary rage, but I never saw anything of the kind, although I have seen him when engaged in sharp oral controversy. I once rebuked him when it seemed to me that he was refusing credit due to his colleagues, and he said nothing—only looked at me with an " et tu, Brute " expression which made me feel guilty. Poverty and

---

[4] Society of American Magicians.

chance turned his attention to magic when he was a boy, and he became great in it, greater perhaps in his consummate showmanship even than in the feats he performed. But there is no question in my mind that if he had had opportunity, and if his attention had early been turned in the direction of scholarship, he would have achieved fame as a scholar and an investigator. He had the instinct, and it came to expression more and more as time went on. He haunted bookshops, pored over catalogues, and collected books, pamphlets, manuscripts, etc., relating to magic, Spiritualism and psychical research, many of them old and rare. He got to know considerable about the history of these subjects, but the two latter in an uncertain and scrappy way. His highest point of authorship was reached in *The Unmasking of Robert Houdin*, a book of real value, the fruit of much research in the history of the magical art, and largely compiled from original sources comprised in his own large collection of materials. It is not specially to his discredit if a "ghost" assisted in getting up his books, seeing that many eminent men have utilized the same intervention. Robert Houdin himself had his memoirs composed by a gentleman more accustomed to the art of literary composition than a magician is expected to be, although he really ought not to have placed upon the title-page—" Written by Himself." I should say that *A Magician Among the Spirits* was really, in the first instance, composed by Houdini, for I recognize some of his characteristic expressions, though it was probably smoothed over somewhat by another hand. *The Unmasking of Robert Houdin*, I have no doubt, was written entirely by another person.[5]

But it was certainly Houdini himself who sought everywhere for rare and curious materials to add to his collection. Not long before his death I saw quantities of boxes of such materials yet unpacked in the basement of his house. I witnessed his enthusiastic zeal in searching out and purchasing old books, pamphlets and papers related to his favorite subjects, at his last visit to Boston. And I have no doubt that the writing of the *Unmasking* was on the foundation of Houdini's own discoveries in relation to Robert Houdin and of his study of the relics of other magicians.

I see no signs of haste, slap-dash judgment, or one-sided selection

---

[5] The style of the *Unmasking* is far superior to that of the other book. Another curious proof of disparate authorship is found by comparing the length of sentences in the two works. The Introduction to *A Magician Among the Spirits* is made up of sixty-one sentences, of an average length of 37 words. The first sixty-one sentences of the Introduction to the *Unmasking* average 23 words in length. The former shows 15 sentences of fifty or more words, the latter but 2. The longest sentence in the former is of 142 words, of the other 58.

of materials in this book, which, as said, was his masterpiece. He sets himself to a task and attacks it in front and all along the line—one does not feel at the close that large aspects of the matter have been avoided, and that, even granting the particular instances which he brings forward, yet one is not forced to agree to his sweeping conclusions. One feels that Robert Houdin has indeed been cornered, hemmed in on every side, proved a charming liar, and a purloiner of the credit due to other men.

But *A Magician Among the Spirits* has not escaped the influence of " the enchanted boundary." First we note that instead of the meticulous care shown in the other book to fix and found every statement of fact, this book is strewn with blunders. He says that Margaret Fox was but eight years old and Kate six and a half when the " Rochester rappings " began in 1848.[6] They were somewhere about 15 and 11 respectively.[7] He says that Leah Fox was 23 years older than " little Margaret," [8] whereas we have in hand no evidence to dispute her own statement [9] that she was but 19 in 1848. The statement that Leah immediately began to exploit her sisters and began in Rochester, " publicly exhibiting their feats to great crowds for money " [10] is against such evidence as we have. They did not go next to New York City, as stated, but first to Albany and then to Troy. Thus far he is putting confidence in what Margaret said during her short period of confession. But she was then a wreck through drink, and what she said was a mixture of truth and falsehood. She was even capable of alleging " Nobody has ever suspected anything from the start in 1848 until the present day as to any trickery in our methods." [11] Thousands suspected them. And in 1851 three professors of the University of Buffalo published their detection of the method of producing raps by joint-snapping, exactly the method which Margaret afterward confessed. A Mrs. Culver made a sworn statement in the same year that Margaret had told her how the tricks were done.[12] Other and later investigations came to the same conclusion, as Houdini is aware.[13]

We meet the assertion that the reader will find " many such cases," *i. e.*, of " proofs of fraud by Home," " reported by Mr. Frank Podmore in *Modern Spiritualism*, London, 1902, and *Newer Spiritualism*, London, 1910," accompanied by the astounding statement that " Mr

---

[6] *A Magician Among the Spirits*, 1.
[7] Podmore says they were 15 and 12; Doyle that they were 14 and 11; Holm that they were 15 and 11.
[8] *A Magician Among the Spirits*, 2. [9] *The Missing Link*, 30-31, 252.
[10] *A Magician Among the Spirits*, 3. [11] *Ib.*, 8.
[12] *Modern Spiritualism*, Podmore, 184–86. [13] *A Magician Among the Spirits*, 9

Podmore was a Spiritualist."[14] But the reader will search the named volumes in vain for the proofs. Podmore discusses three claims or rumors of detection, but concludes: "Home was never publicly exposed as an impostor; there is no evidence of any weight that he was even privately detected in trickery"[15]—this in spite of Podmore's opinion that probably Home did employ trickery. The story that Browning caught Home's bare foot posing as the head of a baby was repudiated by Browning himself.[16] The story quoted by Houdini from Stuart Cumberland to the discredit of Home,[17] with its guarantees "a famous diplomat assured me," and "so the story came to me," etc., cannot seriously be considered evidence. If we may not accept anonymous testimony at second-hand in favor of a medium, it is worth no more when against him.

As Houdini tells it, Carrington, Feilding and Baggally had their sittings with Palladino in 1895, then brought her to London, where Dr. Hodgson joined them and caught her cheating.[18] The latter event did take place in 1895, but the three persons first named had their experiments in 1908, after Hodgson's death. Nor did they bring her to London.

How far the assiduous collector of materials on Spiritualism and psychic research was from knowing the history of either movement may be judged by the fact that he actually says that the famous Committee of the Dialectical Society never published any report, and that all the information he could find about it was in garbled form in Spiritualist publications of 1877.[19] The committee, of course, printed its report in book form, in 1871. The fourth thousand was issued in 1873. There is no evidence for the assertion that "a large majority of that committee were full-fledged Spiritualists," and the committee itself declared the contrary. It is not true that the reports of the sub-committees were "based on hearsay evidence." In large part they were based on their own experiments.

He makes Mrs. Deane and Mr. Vearncombe, the spirit-photographers, members of the Crewe group,[20] which they were not. There never was a "New York branch of the Society for Psychical Research."[21] Mrs. Margaret Deland never wrote the paragraph attributed to her.[22] The statement that "there are over 30,000 lunatics in England alone who lost their minds through this modern necromancy,"[23] is an ancient preposterous one whose falsity has long been

---

[14] Ib., 41. [15] Modern Spiritualism, Podmore, II, 230. [16] Ib., II, 230.
[17] A Magician Among the Spirits, 43-4. [18] Ib., 52. [19] Ib., 160, 201.
[20] Ib., 123. [21] Ib., 53. [22] Ib., 206. [23] Ib., 165.

demonstrated.[24] W. S. Davis never was a "practicing medium"[25] in the sense that would be conveyed by that term; although for a time he held mock séances to demonstrate that he could convince sitters as well as professional mediums of physical phenomena. "Poor old Professor Zoellner"[26] was 48 when he died. I agree that he probably was fooled by Slade, but not that he was a doddering ancient. The first pages of Mrs. Home were read very carelessly to exchange the respective homes of the Home's aunt and mother, in Norwich and Waterford, and to allow the statement that at the death of his mother, when he was seventeen, he went to his aunt, with whom he had really lived since his ninth year. But I cannot spare more space to illustrate the influence of the enchanted boundary upon Houdini in the matter of blunders, and entirely pass by the long list of misspelled proper names.

Doyle[27] correctly says that Houdini "stuffed so many errors into his book," and "has shown extraordinary bias on the whole question." But the errors which stare you in the face were not wilful ones, since few of them were of any advantage to the argument. And bias is less reprehensible in a book which professes from the beginning to the end to be an assault than it would be in what professes to be a history.

Sir Arthur Conan Doyle deservedly gained a great reputation, first as a writer of fiction perhaps not entitled to be called "great," but certainly very charming and clever. His invention of Sherlock Holmes, the man who could trace the solution of all mysterious crimes from "clues," caused a multitude of unreflective readers to suppose that the author was himself a man of superior ability of the kind that a successful detective possesses, and that therefore his judgment in matters relating to psychic research must be peculiarly valuable. The inference is quite unwarranted. Doubtless the tales were plotted backward. For example, suppose a man who commits murder has lived twenty years in India, is left-handed, and favors a particular brand of tobacco, etc., etc. It does not show detective ability to interpret clues when one knows all about the murderer in advance, since he has constructed him, and when he can plant all the clues of which he knows in advance the interpretation. Does the murderer use oil on his hair? Then let him rest his head a while against the wallpaper. Is he an old man? Then let him carefully leave behind a gray hair. The ability of the author is displayed in the thinking up of facts about the murderer

---

[24] *E. g.*, in *Journal* A. S. P. R., May, 1922. [25] *A Magician Among the Spirits*, 11.
[26] *Ib.*, 80.   [27] *History of Spiritualism*, I, 228.

and his crime, providing clues to balance, and picturing a super-intellect capable of proceeding with infallible certainty from the clues to the facts, as the author has gone from the facts to the clues. But while clues are of great value to a flesh-and-blood detective, he knows well that many of them are ambiguous and may have any one of several significations. With an invented detective they may, and in the Sherlock Holmes tales do, always point infallibly in the right direction. A particular complexion means to Sherlock Holmes that the man has long lived in India, and the author sees to it that he has lived in India, whereas in fact that same complexion might have been produced by a sojourn in some other hot country. A cigar-ash means to Doyle's detective that the murderer was addicted to a particular quality of tobacco, and it is even so, but in real life the murderer may have been given the cigar by another man. A pipe is found charred on a particular side of it—therefore the owner was left-handed, but a right-handed man may have an idiosyncrasy in regard to his method of lighting a pipe. Every clue leads back to some particular cause, and it is necessarily assumed that all men act in the same fashion, whereas different causes may produce similar effects, and men are not automata, but have differentiating peculiarities. A woman in the story commits suicide with a pistol to which she has tied a cord leading to a weight beyond the rail of a bridge, so that when she falls the pistol is drawn over the rail and into the water. As the pistol strikes the stonework of the bridge in passage it nicks off a chip of the stone. Sherlock Holmes sees the little chip and at once visualizes the whole scene. But the chip could have been broken off in any one of numerous ways. There is no foreordained size and shape for a chip knocked off by the impact of a pistol—much might depend upon the peculiarities of the stone at the particular spot struck, much would depend upon the particular angle which the flying pistol took, and this on whether it dropped from the woman's hand or was convulsively flung this or that way as the bullet entered her body. Much would depend on the particular weight of the object attached at the further end of the cord. But not so with the detective of the story. He takes a pistol, arranges it with a string, weights the string and fires the pistol and drops it. Thanks to the author, the pistol strikes the stone balustrade and knocks off another chip exactly like the first. Were the experiment really tried, this probably would not be the case once in fifty trials. No, the Sherlock Holmes stories are proofs of facility in imaginative construction, not of skill in the interpretation of indicia.

Sir Arthur was big-hearted, zealous, sincere, and " an earnest godly man," [28] but these qualities, admirable as they are, do not define an astute psychic researcher. And however excellent the cases may have been which first brought about his conviction, as the years went on he surely showed himself lacking in the power or will to analyze calmly and dispassionately, and to discriminate between the certainly or probably authentic and the certainly or probably spurious, without fear or favor, solely from the evidence.

The persistency and ingenuity with which he argued in favor of some of the most suspicious mediums of our day or the most discredited ones of an earlier day has conferred no benefit upon the sober business of psychic research.

Sir Arthur Conan Doyle and Harry Houdini, who seemed personally to like, even though they belabored, each other, resembled one another in several respects. With each, propaganda in relation to Spiritualism partook of a religious nature, and perhaps with each it was a substitute for the religion of his youth. Doyle was reared a Roman Catholic, which religion he forsook. When he became a Spiritualist, he avowedly adopted Spiritualism as his religion. Houdini was reared in the Hebrew religion and was the son of a rabbi and descendant of a line of rabbis. He gave up Judaism, but the fervor with which he carried on his anti-Spiritualistic propaganda, not publicly only but in earnest private conversation, was to me so striking, that I once told him that the preaching-zeal of his fathers had descended to him, only it was turned in another direction. It was his religion. Both men carried on their propaganda with apostolic zeal, one to preach the gospel of Spiritualism, the other to banish the superstition of Spiritualism.

Each felt that his personal work was vastly important to mankind. If Houdini showed plainly that he felt no one else understood the subject so well as himself, or could test claims as well as himself, if he felt that no old-time faker was quite exposed until *he* administered a finishing stroke, so also Doyle felt entitled to say: " With all modesty I am inclined to ask, is there any man on this globe who is doing as much psychic research as I." [29] Each favored pictorial illustrations containing his own portrait. Houdini, in *A Magician Among the Spirits*, does not afford us solely views of Doyle, Mrs. Houdini, Davenport, Martin and Kellar, but of himself in company with these persons in turn; besides one of himself alone. Doyle, in *Our Second American Adventure*, gives us gratifying views of himself in the company of the Rev.

---

[28] The Rev. F. Edwards in *Journal* A. S. P. R., Vol. XVII, 273.
[29] Letter to *Journal* A. S. P. R., XVII, 266.

Vale Owen, himself in company with Mary Pickford and Douglas Fairbanks, himself with a group of prominent Spiritualists, and, over the caption " Oil-Bearing Ground, Ventura, California," himself holding out what may possibly be mud on the end of a stick. These innocent evidences of a sense of one's own importance I do not find in the least offensive, and only remark that both manifest in the same way.

It would have been strange if the university man and trained physician had committed so many perfectly obvious blunders of fact and citation as we have noted in the book written by the man who had to launch out and earn his own living when he was a mere boy. But Sir Arthur was not by any means so immune from palpable misstatements as he on several occasions intimated to the public was the case. Yet on careful comparison, one is impressed by one peculiar difference—the mistakes of Houdini very frequently do not help his argument—that is, if he had got the facts straight they would have served his type of propaganda just as much, while Sir Arthur's blunders nearly always work to the favor of his argument. It is not to be understood that the latter deliberately misrepresented the facts, but that his intense zeal in behalf of a cause, his burning wish that " phenomena " should be vindicated, colored his mental vision and disturbed his judgment to the point that he did not always mentally grasp sentences actually before him in print, or appreciate the overwhelming preponderance of evidence. Thus, in 1923,[30] he published a letter in which he claimed that in thousands of statements made by him relative to psychic research only one error had been discovered, and that a venial one, and went on to criticize the report on Mrs. Stewart's case, printed in the *Scientific American*. I had already discovered errors of his concerning which I had remained silent, but now I assisted Mr. Bird in making plain that in this very letter he had made twelve misstatements of fact, in face of the report before his eyes, upon which he had to depend.[31] Nothing ever quite so significantly defined the type of research which he represented as the fact that he soon afterward reversed the position he had so emphatically taken upon the Stewart case, and held that the conclusion of the committee of the *Scientific American* was entirely justified, simply because he learned that in *another* investigation, *eighteen years earlier*, the lady had been found guilty of fraud, by a committee of *Spiritualists!*[32] This, and this alone, was the specific reason he gave for his sudden reversal of judgment.

---

[30] *Light*, Dec. 22, 1923.   [31] *Journal* A. S. P. R., June, 1924.   [32] *Light*, Feb. 2, 1924.

In his first lecture in New York on one of his American tours, Sir Arthur showed a certain picture which, although he acknowledged he did not know its history and therefore could not vouch for it, yet so resembled the celebrated •Cenotaph picture that he was strongly inclined to think it a spirit photograph. The picture showed the faces of a number of firemen on the background of the smoke of the fire in which they had perished. The next day I communicated to him the information that this picture was made by a Chicago photographer to show Dr. Hodgson that he " could make as good a spirit photograph as any one else," and offered to show him the original correspondence. I did this so that he would not repeat this careless and credulous act of exhibiting that trick picture all over the country, and perhaps be brought unnecessarily to confusion. It was not until some years later, when no lectures were in jeopardy, that, because Sir Arthur was then bitterly attacking certain investigators for over-caution, I made this illuminating incident public.

In *The History of Spiritualism* [33] we are told that Lincoln was persuaded to issue the Emancipation Proclamation through a trance-address by a medium, Nettie Colburn, and that " the facts are beyond dispute." Yet the story rests upon the sole testimony of one Colonel Kase, an old time Spiritualist of the most credulous type, who told it years after the war, whose memory was so fuddled that he recollected a woman of at least twenty-two years who had been lecturing for six years as " a little girl," and the last discouraging months of 1862 as a period of uninterrupted Union victory. A little research would have shown the historian that, while the medium's own story which he quotes dates her address in December, 1862, the preliminary proclamation which it is supposed to have inspired was issued in September, and was first read to the Cabinet in July.

Certainly Houdini was biased in one direction, and Doyle was equally biased on the other. Houdini's bias shows itself by his paying attention almost exclusively to physical mediums, some of whom he paints blacker than the evidence really warrants, and by the impression which he conveys to the reader that he has, nevertheless, sounded the depths of all purported psychical phenomena, and found all wanting. In vain will you look for Mrs. Piper, Mrs. Leonard, Mrs. Chenoweth [33a] or many another name in the index. So far as I recollect no single person whose psychic work has been reported with respect in the *Proceedings* of the S. P. R. is so much as mentioned. He knows

---

[33] I, 144-6. [33a] Mrs. " Chenoweth " is Mrs. Soule.

nothing about them. He knows nothing about Hyslop's reports or my own.

Doyle's bias shows itself particularly by the ingenuity of the devices through which he persuades himself that mediums of extremely doubtful character are or were genuine.

In the book *The Missing Link*, by one of the Fox sisters, printed in 1885, she told how the spirit message to the effect that a pedlar had been murdered and buried ten (!) feet under ground in the cellar of the Fox house was verified by digging, in 1848, and finding some "human hair and bones." It is curious, as Frank Podmore found it,[34] that Capron and Barron, who in 1850 printed an entirely sympathetic narrative of the Hydesville phenomena, did not even mention the finding of the remains. Five years later Capron wrote a book in which he does mention it, but says "it is not generally known." No statements were obtained from any of the alleged participants of the digging outside of the Fox family. This has a very suspicious appearance. Why was an event of such importance not mentioned by the book of 1850 which professes to give the whole history? How came it not to be generally known in 1855, though the world had been ringing with the story of the "Rochester" rappings? But in 1904 "almost" an entire human skeleton was found "between the earth and the crumbling cellar walls." This seems like an embarrassment of riches—remains below ground and remains above ground under a crumbling wall. But Doyle says in his history[35] that the later discovery "proved beyond all doubt that someone had really been buried in the cellar of the Fox house," and "These discoveries settle the question forever and prove conclusively that there *was* a crime in the house."

If the stories were not so pleasing to him, it is probable that the genial author would have asked a few questions before becoming so sure. First, have we any sufficient guarantee that the first story was true? It is simply incomprehensible why, in that case, Capron and Barron did not know of it in 1850, and that it should not have been generally known in 1855. Secondly, what guarantee have we that, if any bones were found, they were human ones? Again, what proof have we that the second story was true? Doyle knows none except that it was in a newspaper. If true, how do we know that the skeleton under the "crumbling wall" was not "planted" there, perhaps for a joke, perhaps for the propagation of the faith, as the ancient monks forged scriptures? It may be that putting the

---

[34] *Modern Spiritualism*, I, 182. [35] I, 73.

skeleton there is why the wall was found "crumbling." Have there never been hoaxes?

But the stories are demonstration to Doyle, and he reconciles them by supposing that the criminal thought that many feet under ground was not a safe place, so, leaving a part of the bones and (if the Fox story was true) other evidences there, he dug the rest of the skeleton up and deposited it on top of the ground under the wall. Would not Sherlock Holmes have objected that a criminal would not leave *two* places in the cellar where the bottom showed signs of disturbance, and would not have been so careless as to leave bones in two places?

The evidence that Henry Slade, the first of the slate-writers, committed fraud, is abundant. He was caught again and again, at least twice by Spiritualists, and by others. One exposure, in Canada, was so overwhelming that the *Banner of Light*, even, could not defend him, and mourned that for some mysterious reason he had resorted to such means. Doyle himself refers to an instance where Slade's tricks were seen through an aperture and Spiritualists denounced him, but inclines to think that what they saw were "ectoplasmic limbs"![36] And if Slade confessed to Truesdell after being caught, as the latter testified, Doyle explains that this "may probably be accounted for by a burst of ill-timed levity on his part in seeking to fool a certain type of investigator by giving him exactly what he was seeking for!" Long ago exposures of fakery were explained on the basis that spirits give naughty skeptics exactly what they are looking for, but it has remained to the historian of Spiritualism to explain a medium's abject confession in the same way. This method of voiding the force of testimony is capable of wide extension. It is not necessary to deny the story of Remigius Weiss, the magician, that he also caught Slade and forced him to sign a written confession; this too was probably just Slade's fun! If we are at liberty to assume, without evidence, that a man does not mean what he says, then we might say that Doyle's explanation of Slade's confession was probably written in a spirit of ill-timed levity.

We are told that "usually" investigating committees "create such intolerable vibrations," and "surround themselves with so negative an atmosphere, that these outside forces, which are governed by very definite laws, are unable to penetrate it."[37] These hypothetical "intolerable vibrations" are set up by caution and suspicion on the part of committee members. We are also told that while the materializer

---

[36] *Ib.*, I, 296-7.   [37] *Ib.*, I, 306.

Monck certainly did sometimes cheat, bringing in paraphernalia to assist him in impersonating a spirit, " we must not argue that because a man once forges, therefore he has never signed an honest cheque in his life." [38] But with the knowledge that he has forged is it possible for any sensible person to feel confidence that he will never forge again, and should he repress such a thought lest he set up intolerable vibrations which will cause the man to forge again? Note what a dilemma the assumed psychic law forces upon the investigator. Knowing that a medium has committed clever frauds, it is a psychological impossibility for him to help thinking that the medium may attempt fraud again in a given experiment, but if he does have that thought, it is likely to set up vibrations which may inhibit phenomena or actually induce phenomena of a fraudulent character! The investigator must not think caution lest he produce mischievous consequences, and if he does not think caution, a shrewd trickster can surely deceive him.

The portrait of President Wilson exhibited by Eva C.[39] with a big moustache imposed upon it, Doyle explains as probably one of " thought-forms from the brain of Eva taking visible form." [40] It is odd that Eva thought of Wilson thus decorated and disguised, but some reason must be found.

The evidence against Charles Bailey, the apport specialist, in the Grenoble case, was so overwhelming that even his patron and promoter, Willy Reichel, who had been convinced by some of the most shady of American professionals, turned against him. But Sir Arthur not only defends Bailey even in the Grenoble incident but, when it was proved that the tablets claimed to be taken by spirits from ancient mounds in Mesopotamia were really forgeries, he frames the theory that " the forgery, steeped in recent human magnetism, is more capable of being handled than the original taken from a mound." [41] It seems of no account to him that this hypothesis, framed to fit the emergency, convicts the " control " of lying, and he does not notice that the " human magnetism," recent or remote, would not seem to be indispensable, if, as he credits, the spirits also brought a nest with eggs from a tree or bush in India.

The foregoing instances sufficiently illustrate the tenuous apologetics, arising from sincere but too fervent prepossession, so prevalent in *The History of Spiritualism.*

Sir Arthur says that Houdini writes under the influence of bias. Of course he does, and so does Sir Arthur—a bias in the opposite

---

[38] *Ib.,* I, 305.   [39] Schrenck-Notzing's *Phenomena of Materialization,* Fig. 196.
[40] *History of Spiritualism,* II, 110.   [41] *Ib.,* II, 217.

direction. The proof of this assertion is of similar character for both persons, and in part consists in unjudicial selection and rejection of material.

Houdini, for example, telling about the trial of the spirit photographer Mumler, mentions that photographers testified against him,[42] but says nothing about testimony of photographers in his favor. Doyle tells of the testimony in favor,[43] but not a word about that opposed. Doyle says, " The evidence of professional photographers who were not Spiritualists was strongly in Mumler's favor." This is strictly true if he means that the testimony of *some* photographers was strongly in his favor, but not if he means, as readers would understand him to mean, that the testimony of photographers was either totally or overwhelmingly for him. Houdini could have made his statement stronger, and still strictly adhered to the truth, by disclosing that certain of the photographers, though amateurs in deception, themselves produced trick pictures which witnesses, including photographers, found it as hard to explain as the photographs of Mumler. But he should have mentioned the testimony in favor, also.

Houdini shows his bias especially by the selection, for the most part, of mediums and phenomena long regarded, by most careful researchers in America and England, as either spurious or very dubious, and by silence concerning psychics and phenomena generally treated with respect by such persons. Doyle shows his bias by the ingenuity of his defense of some of the most doubtful characters of the past and by his oversight of unpleasant particulars.

He speaks of David Duguid, " the well-known medium for automatic writing and painting," [44] but does not mention the fact that Duguid's method of producing the mysterious " spirit " paintings was discovered by a Spiritualist, in a sitting of Spiritualists, and the details laid bare in the Spiritualist paper *Light*. He says that the magician Kellar admitted that Eglinton's work was genuine,[45] (not strictly correct—Kellar's words were, " If my senses can be relied upon "), but fails to inform readers that Kellar soon retracted the statement, learned to produce similar phenomena himself; and afterwards baffled the Seybert Commission by his slate-writing performance, although the committee had detected the methods of the slate-writer Slade, and had reduced Mrs. Patterson to impotence.[46] Pride is taken in the fact that the account about the Cushman " spirit " photograph appeared in the *Journal* of the A. S. P. R., but silence preserved about the reasons

---

[42] *A Magician Among the Spirits,* 119.   [43] *History of Spiritualism,* II, 133.
[44] *Ib.,* II, 142.   [45] *Ib.,* II, 54.   [46] *Report of Seybert Commission.*

given in a later issue by the editor of that publication for doubting that the photograph represented Miss Cushman.[47] We are told that a picture taken in Africa showed a figure of a " dark spirit " with a " mantilla effect " over the head, but we are not told that the " dark spirit " fitted perfectly in every way into a group of Negroes, and that what appeared over her head and hanging down was the exact replica, at least, of a sort of scarf worn by the women of that tribe.[48]

To these illustrations of selective attention, which might be multiplied indefinitely, I will add two or three of trustful naïvete. We are told that E. A. Brackett " saw with the medium Helen Berry in the United States in 1885 ' a small, white, cloud-like substance ' which expanded until it was four or five feet high ' when suddenly from it the full, round, sylph-like form of Bertha stepped forward.' "[49] Mr. Brackett, good, simple man of 1885, may be excused, but how shall we explain the phenomenon of an educated man, writing in 1926 a history of Spiritualism, who makes this old trick, so many times explained, once common with materializers but now abandoned except by a very few survivors of the old school, one of his proofs for ectoplasm? I have seen this charming illusion, and know exactly how it is produced. The author also tells us that " there was no possibility of deception " in " a streak of material six inches long, not unlike a section of the umbilical cord, embedded in the cloth of the dress " of Eva C. Why so sure it was not a deceptive device? Because " the author was permitted to squeeze it between his fingers, when it gave the impression of a living substance, thrilling and shrinking under his touch."[50] Yet a piece of rubber tubing, closed at one end, passing through the clothing and connected with a bulb pressed by thighs or under the arm, will produce exactly the sensations specified. Again, in his eagerness to find early instances of ectoplasm he identifies as such what Swedenborg himself said was *vision*—the first of all his myriad visions—of " a watery vapor " issuing from his body and falling upon the carpet, where it then changed to worms, which vision the seer understood to signify that he must not eat so much.[51]

The more I reflect on what I knew of Houdini and what I have heard of Doyle,[52] the more it seems that the two men resembled each

---

[47] *History of Spiritualism*, II, 147.
[48] *Ib.*, II, 151. For further particulars see my article in *Scientific American*, December, 1925.
[49] *History of Spiritualism*, II, 97.   [50] *Ib.*, II, 122-3.
[51] *Ib.*, I, 16; *Spiritual Diary* of Swedenborg, Section 397.
[52] My only real meeting with Doyle was in 1927, when I entered his psychic bookshop in London and, seeing him seated at a desk, advanced and said: " You probably do not remember me, Sir Arthur. I am Prince, from America." He rose and

other. Each was a fascinating companion, each big-hearted and generous, yet each was capable of bitter and emotional denunciation, each was devoted to his home and family, each felt himself an apostle of good to men, the one to rid them of certain beliefs, the other to inculcate in them those beliefs; and each urged his views as a lawyer or preacher might, but not in the manner of a dispassionate judge or a painstaking historian.

Frank Podmore, *when he wrote as a historian,* to sift and weigh facts, was as remote from either Houdini or Doyle, as Chief Justice Hughes is from a police-court shyster lawyer. He looked at facts in the light of day, the others respectively through green and red glasses. Take the incident, for example, of the accusation made by Professor Lankester and Dr. Donkin against Slade. Slade often notified sitters when the writing by spirits on the slates was supposed to have begun, and they usually were able to hear the purported writing. One day, Lankester, Donkin being present, snatched the slate from the medium's hands before any sound of writing was heard, and found a message on the slate.

Now to Houdini there is no possible question that Slade was detected by Lankester, and that the incident so thoroughly proved fraud that everybody should so conclude. And in his account [53] he gives only the statements of the accusers and does not hint that anything could be urged against the conclusion.

Doyle, on the same body of facts, comes to the opposite conviction, that Slade was certainly innocent. Doyle properly points out that the fact that Slade sometimes knew in advance that writing was coming did not prove that he must always know it in advance (although this was not Slade's reply).[54] But Doyle did not tell all the story, and part of it was Lankester's testimony that he saw the muscles of Slade's wrist working. That fact, once revealed, would make the medium's innocence very doubtful.

Neither Houdini nor Doyle was capable of writing such sentences as the following by Podmore:[55]

"No doubt to an observer in Professor Lankester's position the demonstration of fraud left nothing to be desired. He had seen

---

said, "Oh, yes; we have had one or two spats, but no hard feelings." "None whatever," I responded. After a few moments' conversation I paid my sixpence to go into the basement, and Sir Arthur accompanied me and remained until he was called away by an engagement, while I looked over the museum of apports, spirit photographs, automatic drawings, and other curious and interesting objects.

[53] *A Magician Among the Spirits,* 80-82. [54] *History of Spiritualism,* I, 284-87.
[55] *Modern Spiritualism,* II, 89-90.

HOUDINI AND DOYLE   161

the movements of Slade's arm in the act of writing, and had found the writing so produced, where and when no writing should have been. But the Spiritualists were perhaps justified in not accepting the incident as conclusive. Slade defended himself by asserting that, immediately before the slate was snatched from his hand, he had heard the spirit writing, and had said so, but that his words were lost in the confusion which followed. If we grant that Slade's testimony was as good as Professor Lankester's or Dr. Donkin's, it was difficult summarily to dismiss that plea."

This was written by a man who in other parts of his book [56] records more satisfactory exposures of Slade, and who undoubtedly was of the opinion that Slade practiced fraud in the instance under discussion, but who nevertheless took cognizance of evidence *pro* and *con*, assigning each piece to the pan of the balance where it belonged. Neither Houdini nor Doyle could do this, and it is indeed difficult for any one who writes in the spirit of a plumed knight rescuing a fair lady, to pay attention to anything but the knocks which he administers to what is to him the dragon.

I once knew a man who in behalf of a cause dear to him got out all by himself an occasional little paper in which he expounded his views. In order to impress the reader he employed all sorts of conspicuous type to emphasize his sentences, to pound his thoughts into the reader. The paper was so thickly strewn with these marks of emphasis that their very purpose was defeated, sense was dulled by the frequency and common-sense disgusted by the eccentricity of the capitalized words.

So a writer who pontifically assumes to tell the world that there is nothing worth while in the subject-matter of psychic research, but who manifests a hasty zeal betrayed by frequent errors of fact, exaggerations, selective attacks upon cases already notoriously vulnerable, and entire neglect of cases and types of material in the forefront of a cautious researcher's interest, cannot long impress thinking men that he is an authority, but in the end will beget distrust even when his statements are historically correct. And a writer whose zeal is so excessive in the contrary direction that he habitually employs tortuously ingenious arguments to defeat preponderant evidence relating to questionable characters of the past and present, seems incapable of crediting contrary testimony unless it is that of Spiritualists,[57] is

---

[56] *Ib.*, II, 195, 216.
[57] See page 153 in this book and *History of Spiritualism*, I, 305; II, 137, etc. Persons not convinced by mediums, whose cause Doyle espouses, if they are non-

capable of summoning witnesses of notoriously unreliable character,[58] omits even to mention masses of evidence which cannot justly be left out of account,[59] and brings forward as proof matters which a little dispassionate and patient examination would have shown to be forged, irrelevant or illusionary [60]—that writer weakens the cause for which he is fighting, and by all except those already partisans at length comes to be distrusted even where his position is historically unassailable.

Spiritualists, are frequently scorned by him as malignant persons, and called "traducers" and the like. See II, 219-20, for an example.

[58] Fifteen pages of proof that the materializations of the Eddy family were genuine depend, except for one paragraph, entirely upon the testimony of Colonel H. S. Olcott. The rehabilitation of the still more shady Holmeses again is made up mostly of pages from Olcott's book. And still again Olcott is drawn upon principally in support of a wonder by Mrs. Compton (I, 254-79).

One would think it important first to establish that Olcott was not only a truthful but also a competent witness. But Dr. Richard Hodgson, who Doyle says had a "first-class brain" (II, 82) and whose testimony, wherever it favors Doyle's views, is quoted as reliable and important, had said in a report not unknown to Doyle (II, 72): "The testimony of Colonel Olcott himself I found to be fundamentally at variance with fact in so many important points that it became impossible for me to place the slightest value upon the evidence he had offered," and the committee which sponsored his report, including F. W. H. Myers, referred to the proofs laid before them of "Olcott's extraordinary credulity and inaccuracy in observation and inference" (*Proceedings* S. P. R., III, 210, 205).

[59] With all that is said about Kathleen Goligher, there is not a word about D'Albe's experiments, begun in hope and ended in disappointment and disbelief. We read (II, 115) of the many savants who believed that Guzik's phenomena were genuine, but not a word of his many exposures. There is a paragraph endorsing the veteran slate-medium P. L. O. A. Keeler, but not a lisp about the mass of evidence by which I so demolished his claims that no one has since attempted a word of reply (*Proceedings* A. S. P. R., XV, 315-494). The testimony of Dennis Bradley in favor of Valiantine is given full weight, but the definite proof by the *Scientific American* Committee that every single time any one was touched by a "spirit" or a "spirit" voice sounded in the darkness at what would otherwise have been a puzzling distance from his chair, Valiantine was out of it from three to fifteen seconds, is thus dismissed: "He was examined by the committee of the *Scientific American* and turned down on the excuse that an electric apparatus showed that he left his chair whenever the voice sounded."

[60] "Forged," as the claim that Nettie Colburn brought about the Emancipation; "irrelevant," as the fact that a woman in a group of negroes in Africa was shown in a photograph to be wearing an article of dress common among women of her tribe; "illusionary," as the instances of "spirits" seeming to develop from a small spot of light on the floor.

V. OLD DOGMA AND LATER STATISTICS

About the year 1820 [1] there was printed in Edinburgh and London a book entitled *An Essay on Capacity and Genius, also an Enquiry into the Nature of Ghosts*. The author's name does not appear, and is probably quite unknown, but he was evidently a scholarly person, and his books reveal considerable research, not of facts but in other books. Only the second half of his treatise concerns us. This is by no means contemptible, and indeed it contains many statements which are acute and just, and a few well in advance of his time. He is not guilty of repeating Macaulay's errors in regard to Samuel Johnson. He correctly points out the commonplaces of our time that some apparitions are morbid hallucinations and that some are the product of illusion. That we should be slow to accept stories which come down from a remote and unscientific generation, or which have been passed on from mouth to mouth, is as true when he said so as when we say the same. He had some inkling of the possibilities of subconscious observation and recollection, although his thoughts, and hence his words, on the subject were obscure.[2]

He was as filled with disgust for "ghosts" and the rest of the flock as any scholar a century to come, and he was as dogmatic and assured as many of them are without much knowledge except what they too have gotten by dipping into poorly selected books or glancing at better ones while safely armored with the determination to destroy. But none of the latter venture out into so deep water, none

---

[1] The book itself is undated, but a study of citations, typography, etc., led me to fix on 1820 as the approximate date of publication. Subsequently I find that the catalogue of the S. P. R. Library (*Proceedings*, Part 104) tentatively gives the same date.

[2] "I remember hearing it said, that a lady inquired one morning if there was such a place or country as Madagascar, for she had dreamt of it, but had never heard of it before. The fact is this: the recollection of particular transactions, and of things which have formerly happened to us, is frequently taken from us in our dreams, and after we have awakened, by a method as singular as that by which we often dream that we recollect facts and circumstances which, on waking, we are convinced never did in reality occur to us. The mind, it is likewise well known, seizes upon circumstances, and lays them into its store, without its own knowledge, so that it often presents to itself, as new, what was procured from some other place by its own power of reception."

of them so patiently spin out, spider-like, a dialectical system of propositions. It will be of interest then, to read some of these propositions and affirmations, and then to see how they stand the application of statistics gathered from actual cases sixty or more years later.

The statistical basis for the comparison is found in 200 reports of apparitional experiences. These are not selected in reference to their content, though a few in the collections consulted were passed over because in them the data needed for comparison was too scanty or doubtful, or because there was not time to translate them from a foreign language, or from mere inadvertence in doing the work as rapidly as possible.[3] I will not guarantee that the figures to come are flawless, but they are certainly approximately correct.

The scholar of 1820 begins by quoting with approval a series of affirmations regarding "ghosts" from Mr. Grose, and by enlarging them:

"A ghost is supposed to be the spirit of a person deceased, who is either commissioned to return for some especial errand, such as the discovery of a murder; to procure restitution of lands or money unjustly withheld from an orphan or widow; or, having committed some injustice whilst living, cannot rest till that is redressed. Sometimes the occasion of spirits revisiting this world, is to inform their heir in what secret place or private drawer in an old trunk they had hid the title deeds of the estate; or where in troublesome times they had buried the money and plate. Some ghosts of murdered persons, whose bodies have been secretly buried, cannot be at ease till their bones have been taken up and deposited in consecrated ground, with all the rites of Christian burial. There are some more important purposes, however, to which these beings are subservient. They have appeared to foretell approaching dissolution, and to warn and convince the unbelieving sinner of a state of existence beyond the present. They have sometimes shewn themselves, to give notice of misfortunes of a tem-

---

[3] They are as follows, the figures standing for pages: *Phantasms of the Living, volume I*: 194, 204, 207, 209, 210, 212, 214, 216, 218, 239, 264, 267, 414, 415, 417, 417, 418, 419, 420, 424, 425, 426, 428, 429, 430, 431, 431, 433, 434, 435, 436, 437, 439, 440, 441, 443, 444, 445, 447, 448, 449, 451, 453. *Ib., volume II*: 30, 31, 34, 35, 37, 40, 41, 42, 44, 45, 46, 47, 49, 50, 51, 51, 52, 54, 55, 57, 59, 59, 61, 63, 66, 67, 68, 69, 70, 71, 72, 74, 141, 143, 146, 149, 156, 162, 176, 178, 179, 181, 182, 199, 200, 202, 204, 205, 208, 209, 210, 509, 510, 511, 511, 512, 513, 513, 514, 516, 516, 517, 519, 520, 520, 520, 521, 522, 523, 523, 524, 525, 526, 527, 528, 529, 529, 530, 532, 533, 533, 534, 536, 537, 539, 540, 541, 542, 543, 543, 544, 545, 545, 546, 547, 548, 550, 551, 552, 553, 554, 555, 556, 557, 603, 604, 606, 607, 609, 610, 610, 611, 612, 613, 613, 615, 616, 617, 617, 619,, 622. Flammarion's *"Death and Its Mystery"*: 49, 52, 54, 59, 64, 67, 69, 127, 133, 137, 146, 147, 151, 152, 153, 168, 169, 170, 182, 182, 183. *Journal A. S. P. R., volume V*: 109, 139, 481. *Ib., v. VI*: 440. *Ib., v. VII*: 124, 362, 474. *Ib., v. VIII*: 480. *Ib., v. IX*: 344, 346. *Ib., v. XI*: 556. *Ib., v. XII*: 578. *Ib., v. XIII*: 656. *Ib., v. XIV*: 260, 276.

porary nature, in order that they might be avoided. But, by far the greater number have appeared for no other cause but that of terrifying rustics, of killing old women, and weakening the intellects of children." (337-9)

"The generality of ghosts are seen by persons who are alone. . . . Their standard hour is midnight." (343)

We will now test these statements and others to come, in the order which is most convenient.

I. "*Their standard hour is midnight.*" (343)

How far does our list of 200 apparitions (really more, since a few were double cases) vindicate the statement that "their standard hour is midnight," a statement reiterated by Prof. Persifor Frazer as late as 1875 (in a lecture before the Social Science Association of Philadelphia): "*Midnight is the hour of appearance, because this period is farthest from the day, a period when the bright illumination of objects leaves nothing to the fancy*"? It is worth while to give the facts so far as they are stated by the original narratives, *in extenso*.

No indication of hour, night or day, 4; night, hour not given, 43; night, hour not given, but certainly not midnight, 5; "towards morning" (probably dark), 1; "early morning," 1; day, hour not given, 15; morning, 19; forenoon, 4; afternoon, 11; evening, 20.

A.M. *7*, 1; *7* to *8*, 1; *8*, 2; *10*, 2; *10* to *11*, 1; *11*, 3; *11* to *12*, 1; *12* noon, 5.

P.M. *1*, 3; *1* to *2*, 1; *2*, 3; *3*, 3; *4*, 1; *4* to *5*, 2; *5*, 1; *5* to *6*, 2; *6* to *7*, 2; *7*, 3; *7* to *8*, 2; *8* to *9*, 3; *9*, 5; *9* to *10*, 2; *10*, 7; *10* to *11*, 1; *11*, 6; *11* to *12*, 3; *12*, midnight, presumably, 2 ("about midnight," and "in the middle of the night").

A.M. *12* to *1*, 5; *1*, 2; *1* to *2*, 1; *2*, 2; *2* to *3*, 1; *4*, 2; *5*, 2; *5* to *6*, 1; *6*, 1; *6* to *7*, 2.[4]

The statistics absolutely destroy the validity of the declaration so confidently made by the unknown writer more than a century ago and by Prof. Frazer nearly a half century ago. Midnight is *not* the "standard hour," is not "*the* hour of appearance." Midnight is specified as the hour in the cases of only 2 out of 210 apparitions. I am wrong: in neither of these is it declared that the moment was precisely at midnight. "About midnight" may stand for anything from 11 P. M. to 1 A. M. "In the middle of the night" ditto. Let us

---

[4] The totals in the several lists to be presented must differ according to the subject-matter. Here the total is 210, since in 6 cases two or more persons saw the apparition in different places.

assume that there are two declared cases when the hour was midnight. But there were 163 declared cases where it was not. Regarding the remaining 47 we know nothing, except that 43 of them were in the night. If we knew the hours in these 43 instances, doubtless the figures for midnight would be increased, but so also would those for other hours of the night. Doubting, as I do, whether all the 5 "noon" cases were precisely at noon, and expecting, as I would, that a number would say "at midnight," meaning that so far as they could judge their experiences came about in the middle of the night, I am surprised to find the latter tendency exhibited not at all in these statistics.

But even though a philosophical scholar of about 1820, who dedicates his book "to the immortal memory of John Locke," and shows himself to have been familiar with many learned writers, and even if an eminent "geologist, chemist and bibliote" of a half century later, could be so far mistaken in declaring that midnight is "the standard hour" for apparitions, and that "midnight is the hour for appearances," the reader would think that before venturing such guesses they had collected enough data to be sure that all or nearly all apparitions are at least seen at night. But what do our statistics show? Assume that "evening" in narratives means after dark, and that "morning" means after dawn (the exceptions would probably about balance each other). Also assume that darkness on the average through the year, begins at 7 P. M., and ends at 7 A. M. inclusively. Then 121 of the apparitions were seen in period of the dark hours, and 84, or 40 percent of the whole number (omitting the 5 of which we know nothing), in the hours of sunlight. There is, therefore, in fact no such rule as that apparitions appear only in the night—far from it. If not true that midnight is "the hour of appearance," and since it seems that about two out of five of such experiences occur in the daytime, what becomes of Prof. Frazer's *explanation*, that midnight "is farthest from the day, a period when the bright illumination of objects leaves nothing to the fancy"?

The fact that of more than 200 persons who witness to apparitions only two said that they were at approximately the stroke of twelve midnight is somewhat surprising in view of the many tales of fiction which most of them must have read, in which the "ghost" appeared exactly at that hour. It tends to indicate that those who stated the hour or division of the day were uninfluenced by suggestion, and depended upon their memory and judgment.

But Prof. Frazer is still farther from the facts, and therefore his

OLD DOGMA AND LATER STATISTICS 167

reason for the assumed fact is still more empty, than we have yet seen. "Midnight," he told us, is the hour of appearance, because this period is farthest from the day, " a period when *the bright illumination of objects leaves nothing to the fancy.*" We have found that out of our random long list of apparitions 40 percent occurred during the day. But artificial light and even bright moonlight may as effectually leave nothing to the fancy. And 34 apparitions of our more than 200, although they appeared during the night hours, appeared in spite of illumination. Omitting 7 of these cases in which the light may have been poor, we have the following 27:[5]

(I, 207) "As the apparition " passed between my bed and the lamp I had full view of it; it was unmistakable; (I, 415) " saw by light burning in the room"; (I, 420) " bright moonlight"; (I, 445) " bright moonlight . . . and all objects in the room and outside the windows were plainly visible"; (II, 34) " moon shining brightly into the room"; (II, 37) " in a concert hall " (of course there was bright light); (II, 46) " in a theatre " (must have been well-lighted); (II, 54) " was reading " (so there must have been light); (II, 70) " under lamp . . . had a very good view"; (II, 141) " large duplex lamp . . . so it was quite light"; (II, 200) " room . . . was brilliantly lighted"; (II, 208) " room was lighted by a powerful gas light in the roof and by candles on the table"; (II, 511) " the gas was full on "; (II, 529) " was reading, soft facing light, apparition near sofa "; (II, 532) " busily occupied with her needle "; (II, 524) " still quite light "; (II, 544) " with a company of ladies in drawing room, playing piano "; (II, 548) at a concert; (II, 613) " at a dance "; (II, 616) *a:* a light in the room for one person was writing a letter; *b:* same figure seen by his two boys the same evening, as they were " watching the bright moonlight "; (II, 617) " bright moonlight pouring in "; (F, 69) " a bright fire shone in the room and there was a lighted candle "; (F, 127) " was reading " (so there must have been light); (F, 133) " I saw the moon . . .; its bright beams lighted up my room "; (F, 168) Apparition seen " under the lighted gas-jet "; (J. V, 481) " bright moonlight "; (J. VI, 440) a " lamp illuminated the passage."

So our statistics seem to show that 111 of the apparitions were seen in the daytime or in the night by excellent or fairly good light,

---

[5] Throughout this chapter I in parentheses will signify volume I of *Phantasms of the Living.* II will mean volume II of the same. F will refer to Flammarion's *After Death,* and J to *Journal* of A. S. P. R. Pages given are those on which the incidents *begin;* the actual reference may be on the page following.

only 94 in darkness or perhaps poor light. We cannot be sure that these figures are exactly correct, but they cannot be far wrong.

II. "*A ghost is supposed to be the spirit of a person deceased, who is either commissioned to return for some special errand, such as* [a] *the discovery of a murder* ";

(a) There are just 2 alleged cases in our list of 200, which have this appearance, both in Flammarion. In one (170) a man's murder is said to have been seen in visions (not at the same time) by his mother and his widow, and his hallucinatory voice to have been heard giving an unusual mark of the murderer's description, the same unknown to the percipients. In the other (138) a girl, before the murdered body of her mother was found, in a vision saw her mother, who correctly pointed to the location of her wounds.

(b) " *to procure restitution of lands or money unjustly withheld from an orphan or widow* ";

The list of 200 actual cases includes not one of this character.

(c) " *or, having committed some injustice while living, cannot rest until it is redressed.*"

Not one case in the 200 gives evidence of anything of this sort.

(d) " *Sometimes the occasion of spirits revisiting this world is to inform their heir in what secret place or private drawer in an old trunk they had hid the title deeds of the estate; or where in troublesome times they had buried the money and plate.*"

Not one case in the 200 shows any evidence of a desire to show the location of any object whatsoever.

III. " *Some ghosts of murdered persons, whose bodies have been secretly buried, cannot be at ease until their bones are taken up and deposited in holy ground, with all the rites of Christian burial.*"

There is not one case as above described among the 200, though in one, mentioned above (F, 137) the apparition says: " Dig a grave for me."

IV. (a) " *They have appeared to foretell approaching dissolution* "

If I mistake not, with one exception (F, 49), in none of our 200 cases does a " ghost " either tell of the approaching death of any one or does anything about the vision plausibly suggest that meaning.

(b) " *and to warn and convince the unbelieving sinner of a state of existence beyond the present.*"

The case last cited (F, 49) is the only one in our list of 200 in which anything of this sort is intimated. Here the " ghost gave assurance that all that was said of the other life was true, that he [the percipient] should change his way of life; that he would soon die." Flammarion is rightly doubtful if this case has not been embellished.

V. "*They have sometimes shewn themselves to give notice of misfortune of a temporary sort of a nature, in order that they might be avoided.*"

Not one single case out of the 200 gives evidence of any such intention or desire.

VI. "*But by far the greater number have appeared for no other cause but that of (a) terrifying rustics,*"

So far as can be ascertained—and the data is nearly always sufficient to judge safely—among the whole list of 201 percipients [6] apparently more than sixteen years old, there were but 5 rustics—3 men and 2 women. Including the servant class there were 22 altogether.

(b) "*of killing old women,*" [7]

It is not possible to tell how many of the female percipients were "old women." However, none of them were killed, were in any danger of death, and only three, or, so far as appears, even suffered illness afterward from the shock, whatever the age or the sex.

(c) "*and weakening the intellects of children.*" There appears to have been about 27 percipients sixteen years old and younger, a few more girls than boys. There is no intimation that any intellects were weakened, either of children or older people.

So far as concerns the insinuation that rustics and children are specially addicted to seeing ghosts it is sufficient to report that about 79 percent of the percipients were not rustics, servants, nor children. Among them were 4 Generals, 4 Colonels, 3 Majors, 1 Sergeant Major, 1 Captain, 1 Lieutenant, 1 Sea Captain, 1 Naval

---

[6] Sometimes there were two or more percipients of the same apparition and in two or three instances it is not made certain how many of the group actually saw it. Here I make the number of chief percipients 228. Close scrutiny shows that about a dozen other persons were present and saw, but they play no part in the stories beyond casual mention.

[7] Disregarding the actual number of percipients and counting a case as one which produced fright if one percipient only was frightened, we find that no one was terrified in 56 cases, according to declaration; in 21 it is highly improbable that any one was: total 77. In 19 one or all percipients were frightened according to declaration; in 9 one probably was: total 28. In 17 cases a percipient says he was "startled," in 4 one probably was: total 21. The "surprised" and "astonished" were 6, the "agitated," "excited" and "disturbed" 6, the "awed" 1, the "unnerved" 1, the "shocked and bewildered" 1. In 58 cases we are left quite in the dark. It seems to me conservative to estimate that probably in a majority of instances, the man or woman who sees an apparition is not at all frightened. But there cannot from so imperfect statistics be any certainty that this is the case.

Lieutenant, 15 Clergymen, 5 Physicians, 1 Judge, 1 Lawyer, 3 Schoolmasters, 1 Lady Principal, 2 Legislators, 1 Chemist, 2 noted Writers, 1 Traveler and Writer, 1 noted Sculptor, 8 persons of title, 2 Gentleman Farmers, etc., etc. A respectable crowd, with the military men rivaling the clergy!

VII. (a) "*Either the stories of these ghosts* [coincidental with death of person represented] *have grown marvelous by coming through a number of hands*" (360)

In the whole list of 200 cases there are only 3 (all in Flammarion) where the story may possibly have come "through a number of hands," although this is by no means certain.

(b) "*or, if not far from the original seer, he is dead, abroad, or some circumstance prevents him from appearing to testify to the truth of the relation.*"

All that the philosopher of 1820 is willing to grant is that there are *some* cases which did not come through many, but only a few hands. He appears to be certain that the original witness is never present to testify. But what do we find when we analyze the list of 200 reported cases? That in 125 of them the story is told by one or more persons who actually saw the apparition, and in 36 by persons who were present at the time or who were otherwise in a position to have immediate proof at the time. In 1 case we have what purports to be a copy of the original statement by the percipient. In 20 cases the story was told by a person in close touch, as a member of the family who had heard it many times, or someone who carefully interrogated the percipient. In 18 cases the story is second-hand without such close touch, as where it passed down two generations, or was heard on "good authority." The most of these 18 are not found in the S. P. R. list.

So much for the set of cases in general. But our author's statement refers to apparitions said to have coincided, in point of time, more or less closely with the deaths of the persons they represented. So we must inspect this class of the list of 200. There appear to be 165 of the 200 which involve this species of coincidence. We find that out of the 156 narrations, 94 were written by the seers themselves. Others were taken down by investigators from the lips of the actual seers.[8] Something like 110 out of 156 cases contradict the dictum

---

[8] It must not be supposed that a narrative not written or dictated by the original seer, is necessarily unauthenticated. The most of the remaining cases were told by witnesses present at the time, or in other ways well accredited.

that the percipient of an alleged death-coincidental apparition is always dead, abroad, or for some other reason silent.

Of course our 200 are to a large extent picked cases, with view to their being authentic and at the same time coincidental with something, if only the fact of being seen at the same time by another person. But that does not hinder that they contradict the proposition so confidently laid down. Also, while it is no doubt true that there are "ghost" stories which have "grown marvelous by coming through a number of hands" there can be found no evidence of this from the list of 200 cases. None of the 18 which have come through two or more hands is any more "marvelous" than some which are told by the original witness or witnesses.

VIII. (a) [Referring to apparitions said to] "*have been seen at the precise period of the death of those whom they represented*" [there is] "*one general rule in relations of this kind, viz.: that they are not made public till after the death has been known to have taken place, and till every fact can be reconciled in order to add to the stories' credibility. The appearance is not much regarded till the ghost seer hears of the death of some person whom he knew,* (b) *and then his imagination, suppressing every difference and exaggerating every resemblance, forces upon him the belief that he saw the deceased precisely as at the time of his death, and dressed exactly in the same manner.*"

(a) Again let us refer to the 200 cases. Of these about 156 involve death coincidences.[9] In some 135 of these 156 cases it is claimed that the apparition was recognized at the moment of its appearance. If one had no more data, he might well hesitate before disputing the testimony of many witnesses of intelligence and standing who declare in positive terms that they "distinctly recognized" the figure at the moment of its appearance, some that they recognized the clothing or called out the apparition's name and by various modes of expression make it plain that they never had doubt as to the identity, before or after the news of death reached them. This would require the more assurance since a large percentage of the apparitions represented parents, brothers, sisters, and other near relatives whom the percipients really ought to have been able to recognize. The fact that in 13 of the 156 cases the apparition was not identified before the news came and only inferentially or uncertainly afterward, is proof that

---

[9] The rest are coincidences with near loss of life, accidents, illnesses, and other peculiar periods of stress, together with a number of apparitions seen by two or more persons, without any known coinciding relevant event.

not all persons, even after the death news arrives, reconcile the facts, to employ the phrase quoted above, " in order to add to the stories' credibility."

When he says that there is one general rule, and that is that ghost stories are not made " public " until it has been discovered that someone died, to whom the apparition could be adapted, presumably the author means that it cannot be shown, as a rule, that the description was told before the event, as it could hardly be expected that one would print the experience in a newspaper or proclaim it upon the highway before news of the corresponding event. But of the 135 cases where it is claimed that the apparition was clearly recognized at the moment it was seen, in 98 it is also alleged that prior to the arrival of news of the death, the identity of the apparition was unequivocally declared to one or more other persons.[10] In 2 other cases a note of the event was made prior to the reception of intelligence, in 3 other cases a letter was written inquiring about the person seen, and in 4 other cases the percipient made a journey purposely to ascertain if anything had happened to the person seen. Such acts being as affirmative of prior certainty of identity as telling another person, they properly may be counted in, so we have out of 135 cases of death coincidence where it was declared that the " ghost " was clearly recognized at the moment, 107 where the percipient in some way expressed his or her conviction prior to knowledge of the actual death.[11] And I leave out of the account cases such as that where the percipient thought the apparition was her mother, whereas it proved that her mother's strikingly resembling sister was the one who died.

So again a proposition very confidently asserted by the writer of 1820 falls to the ground; it is very far from being " a general rule " in well authenticated and sponsored apparitional cases that the identity of the apparition was not clearly recognized and declared to others prior to information as to a death.

(b) One would suppose from the last sentence quoted, and its writer evidently was strongly of the opinion, that another general rule is that the narrators of such experiences come finally to believe and declare that they saw the person " precisely as at the time of his death, and dressed exactly in the same manner." But this is not true either

---

[10] These 98 include instances where two or more persons were percipients and, as would be expected, told each other.

[11] Those familiar with the sources will not need to be told that not all the " death coincidences " fell within the hour when the apparition was seen, though very many did. But all were near enough to be sufficiently striking.

OLD DOGMA AND LATER STATISTICS 173

in the set of cases we are consulting or in death-coincidence cases in general. Very few of them make any such claim. In fact comparatively few, regrettably, describe the dress, and those who do more frequently say that the apparition was in the " usual " or " customary " dress of the person, or it appears (as in the case where the person seen was a military man or a seaman) that the dress described *was* the customary one although the narrator may not say so. On the other hand there appears to have been no apparition, throughout the whole list of 200 cases which was seen in a night-garment and the actual person recognized was not certainly or in all probability so dressed,—no single case where the actual person was proved to have been at the time up and about, and the apparition was seen in a bed-garment. Besides, there are several cases (I am now including all cases, and not referring only to those coincidental with death) where the actual person had some unusual feature of dress unknown to the percipient and the apparition corresponded. But so far as there is any " general rule," it is that narrations of apparitional experiences which correspond with the death of the person recognized, do not claim to have seen " precisely as at the time of his death " or " dressed exactly in the same manner."

In the face of the array of actual records who would dare to say today: " *The identity of the ghost with the person, and the coincidence in time, are not discovered till it is found that about the period of the appearance some person expired, and then the seer exclaims with astonishment, ' I saw his ghost ' "?* (361) Of course, however, the coincidence in time could not be established until news of the death is received.

IX. " *The generality of ghosts are seen by persons who are alone.*"

A survey of our trial list of cases reveals that the percipient at the moment of the apparition was with one or more persons in slightly more than 30 percent of them.

X. " *These stories generally, when traced to their origin, depend upon the veracity or credulity of one person.*" (361)

" These stories generally " is a phrase which does not confine us to stories of apparitions coinciding with the death of the person seen. We are at liberty to include coincidence with accident, sudden illness, etc., and apparitions seen by two or more persons although with no known relevant coincidence. We find that in the 200 cases, out of the 95 alleged to have been told by the single percipient before the coinciding event, 33 are corroborated by statements of other persons in proof that they were told. Of 27 cases seen by two or more persons when together, plus 6 cases of the same apparition seen by persons separately, accounts are given by two seers in 10 cases. Most of the remaining cases have strengthening features of one kind or another, aside from the standing and reputation of many of the narrators, but which would require too much space to set forth. Enough has been said to indicate that such stories do not " generally " depend upon the veracity or credulity of one person.

XI. "*As far back as we can trace, we have accounts of persons appearing either at the moment of their death or soon after, but through all time we have scarcely one relation indisputably proved.*" (361.)

This sentence may have been true when it was written but, thanks to psychic research, it is true no longer, as the foregoing statistics indicate and as the records abundantly prove.

XII. " *It is by no means uncommon to hear of apparitions appearing just after a light has been extinguished. It will plainly appear that these are generally produced from the strong spectrum left of the light, greatly assisted by fancy.*" (354)

On the contrary, it is very uncommon to hear this; the percentage of apparitions seen just after a light is extinguished must be exceedingly small. And the spectrum or after image of the light takes a definite form, appears wherever one turns his eyes, may change in color or disappear to return, but otherwise changes only to decrease and fade out. None of the numerous apparitions described as distinctly dressed, clearly seen, standing, walking, etc., every whit as real looking as a living body, could be so caused.

XIII. " *It is observed that in nocturnal visitations of the ghost kind, the candle generally burns blue, as a kind of announcement of the apparition.*"

There is not a single report of a candle burning blue in all the 200 cases. To be sure many of these were of apparitions seen in the daytime or in the moonlight or in the darkness, and to be sure where the nature of the artificial light is not stated it would be rather unlikely today that it would be that of a candle. But candles are not infrequently used even now in England, as a light to go to bed by, besides some of the cases in the list go back to the fifties. It is noteworthy therefore that the blue-burning candle is not once mentioned. And why not a blue-burning lamp or gas-light? But nothing of the sort do I remember to have read of in any authenticated record.

OLD DOGMA AND LATER STATISTICS

XIV. (a) *"But how happens it that apparitions take the shapes they bear? It is evidently the mind itself that occasions any peculiarity in the shape of apparitions. Thus, they always appear in garbs which are well-known to the person who sees them;—because the mind could not conjure up things of which it knew nothing; (b) they generally agree in every respect with the seer's idea of apparitions, from reasons already stated; (c) and as the mind is more subject to melancholy or to terror at the time, so there is more melancholy or terror in the circumstances of the appearance. I will venture to say, that apparitions of the dead would never appear in the present circumstances; if instead of lamenting over a deceased person, a jovial banquet were held at his interment."* (354-5)

(a) Why should it be a criterion of an apparition causally related to the death of a person that it should appear in some kind of a garb which human beings of the race do not wear? Besides, it *is* possible for the mind to " conjure up " a garb such as it has never seen, made, let us say, of codfishes or wasp-nests. But apparitions have been seen dressed or otherwise marked in a singular fashion which the percipient had never seen in relation to the person identified. Thus there is a well-sponsored story (F, 52) of a woman who saw her friend in " a sort of cape with a hood, which my aunt had never seen her wear," worn over her dress, and it proved that she was so dressed in the coffin. A man (II, 530) saw the apparition of a friend who had been in distant parts for nearly two years and whom he had no reason to expect to see soon again, " wearing a necktie of striking pattern " and having " a kind of excrescence on the cheek," both novel features. About twelve hours later this man called, and he was " exactly as he appeared in the vision." In another detailed account (J. V, 481) which has every appearance of truth, an old lady saw the apparition of a man whom she had been accustomed to see shockingly ill-dressed and unkempt, but the apparition had on a black suit and white shirt, with his hair and beard trimmed, and she described the vision before news came that he had been found dressed as seen, a suicide that very night.

(b) How the author knew or thought he knew that apparitions " generally agree in every respect with the seer's idea of apparitions " is a mystery. Then in I, 204, the woman's ideas of an apparition were that it should wear a dirty white garment, a dirty night-cap, and have a bloody bandage about the head! And the facts were sufficiently accommodating to have the head of the person seen split open the same hour with the apparition, while he was similarly dressed. And in I, 214, the woman's ideas of an apparition were to have her husband run away with by two horses, although he had told her that he was going in a (one-horse) dogcart, and again the actual facts accommodated themselves so to provide that the man changed his mind and went in a carriage drawn by two horses, which ran away at approximately the moment of the vision. A certain clergyman's ideas of an apparition, II, 199, must have been that of an old white-bearded man in dark-blue overcoat and flat-topped felt hat, for he saw such a one pass the window of the room he himself was sitting in, and no such man passed the window, since a physician, who adds his testimony to that of the clergyman, would have seen him, for he also passed the window a moment later. Nor could it have been the doctor, for he had on a brown top-coat, a silk hat and no beard. And the doctor's ideas of a phantom must have agreed with those of the clergyman for, just before he rang the bell he saw through the window in the room with the clergyman an old man of exactly the same description, only that he did not have on a hat! Examples could be multiplied, where the facts agree in peculiar detail with the phantoms, but how it is deduced that the " seer's ideas of apparitions " corresponded, or what explanatory assistance that correspondence would furnish in view of the external coincidences, is a mystery.

(c) When we take up the actual analysis of cases it is found impossible to correlate moods of percipients, whether of a melancholy character or any other, with the character of the apparitions they see. Of course all we have to go by is the testimony of the witnesses, and usually they say nothing of their thoughts and feelings just previous to seeing the vision. We cannot safely depend upon occupation at the time, for in spite of the fact that one is " at a concert," " quietly reading," and the like, his thoughts might be of a melancholy character. But we have distinct affirmations, as in the following cases.

(I, 194) " I was reading geometry as I walked along, a subject little likely to produce fancies or morbid phenomena of any kind." Saw his mother lying on the floor, to all appearances dead.

(I, 218) "A deep melancholy was oppressing me." About 20 minutes after making a remark to that effect, he saw an apparition, but not of a melancholy or frightening character, simply of a lady dressed as if to go out walking, and thought her real.

(I, 431) Was " far from well." The apparition was not affected by that fact, but looked just as the living person customarily looked.

(II, 149) A man was " in a perfectly cheerful, healthy frame of mind " when he saw the phantom of his friend, of whose sudden illness he had not heard. The phantom's eyes " glared into mine, with a look so intense and deeply earnest that I fairly recoiled from the spot and started backwards."

(II, 513) A young girl in the midst of " frolicksomeness " saw a tall, slight figure in white.

(J. V, 109) A woman " worn out with loss of sleep and anxiety " on account of the illness of her child, saw her husband standing looking at her. He was really drowned at about if not exactly the same time, but the point here is that the woman's state of mind did not make the apparition look disturbed or anything other than his real self, for she thought him flesh and blood, and merely said that she would rise and get him something to eat.

(J. XIV, 260) When her " heart was very sad," a woman saw the apparition of her dead daughter, and " on her face was transcendental joy."

Even where the percipient is melancholy just before an apparition appears, if the melancholy mood has seized him suddenly, there is reason to suspect that, causally, the apparition preceded the mood, already being present in the subconscious before it became consciously objectified. One man (II, 63), for no reason that he could discover, was " seized with a fit of deep melancholy, a thing very unusual with me, who enjoy great serenity of mind," and in order to prevent bursting out crying he rushed out of the house into the strong wind and pouring rain, and there saw the apparition of his brother. But even then the apparition presented no appearance corresponding with the mood, for it looked as usual, and was " stepping leisurely along . . . as if the weather were fair and calm."

Of course there are cases where the percipient had been feeling " melancholy " and where the ensuing apparition was of a melancholy appearance. And there have been other cases where both the apparition and the previous mood of the percipient were calm and placid. This would be so on chance. But there is no discoverable causal relation, and many cases contradict the supposed rule.

Even if such a relation did exist, while it would explain the emotional tone of the apparition, it would not explain the identity of the person seen and the temporal coincidence of his actual death or accident. Nor would it furnish the least clue to an apparition seen, identically the same, by two or more persons, independently.

XV. *" If, however, a ghost appears neither for any purpose nor to any but one person, though others are present when it is seen, what is there that can prove it to be anything but the effect of a disordered mind? "*

We can still agree that an apparition *per se* seen by only one of several persons present, could not be proof of anything but the effect of what may be called, or may be really, a disordered mind. And the quoted sentence must have appeared very sound and sensible in 1820. But it is so no longer, now that psychic research has gathered so many authentic cases of recognized apparitions seen at the hour when the persons they represented were dying or undergoing accident, and even cases which pictured the very details of the death or accident. And the sentence contains two notions which are now quite *passé*.

1. The notion that an apparition must, if the valid effect of an external cause, have been planned and intended, is now a *non sequitur* because of psychic research. When, for example (I, 443), General Richardson's wife experienced the hallucination of seeing her husband carried off the field wounded, and of hearing him say, " Take this ring off my finger and send it to my wife," which the General's corroborating statement asserts is exactly what took place at that hour, it was not because he was *trying* to produce an apparition of himself in his wife's mind, or to make her cognizant of his words. The effect seems to have been a telepathic one, operating by laws of mental mechanics not yet understood.

2. We now realize that the inability of any but one of a group to experience an apparition fails to prove that it had no cause outside of that one person's mind. As well might two partially deaf persons reason that the sound of a violin, heard by a third person of sharp ears playing in an adjoining room, must be the effect of a disordered mind. There have been many instances where two persons did simultaneously and independently see an apparition. Wherever other persons were present and saw nothing, it simply argues that they lacked in their make-up a something which the percipients possessed.

XVI. " *If such callings and apparitions as we continually hear of did really exist beyond the mind, it is necessary to imagine that they existed by some law or general providential arrangement, that they should only appear in particular circumstances, and should always appear in like situations; i. e., if one man had made an agreement with a friend to appear to him after death, and had afterwards appeared another person who had made the like agreement should do the same; if a voice should inform one person that a relation was dead or dying a voice should be heard by another person telling him of a relation under similar circumstances. This is no more than the usual regularity of nature, but amongst ghosts and* SUPERNATURAL *voices there is no regularity, and therefore I assert, they have no real existence.*" (368-9)

OLD DOGMA AND LATER STATISTICS 179

Now as the author discards the notion of the supernatural,[12] his argument should equally apply to apparitions that do *not* " really exist beyond the mind," and to the actions of living people. The " regularity of nature " does not provide that what one person does under given circumstances, another will certainly do. One promises to keep an appointment and does so; another promises and does not fulfil the promise, afterward explaining that he forgot it, was too busy, was unavoidably prevented by circumstances. Assuming that a person survives bodily dissolution, we still would be in no position to assume that he never forgets, and is able to do everything that another spirit can, or to overcome all obstacles. It might be that he did keep his compact but the living person was incapable of recognizing the fact. There would be many analogies, despite all the " regularity of nature,"—for there are persons who are color-blind, others who are tone-deaf, others who are quite blind or quite deaf, etc. After a half century of psychic research, however scanty their reading of its literature, probably there are few intelligent minds to which so little of its logic has seeped that they would be capable of making such an argument.

We now go forward some 55 years to Professor Persifor Frazer, who delivered an address to the Social Science Association of Philadelphia, printed in 1875, in the course of which he says:

XVII. (a) " *The fact that the ghostly uniform is usually white suggests as reasons, first,* (b) *that this is likely to be the color which most attracts the eye in feeble light; and, secondly,* (c) *custom teaches us to expect more dead men than any other class of visitants, because this can prove no alibi, and the robes of the dead are generally white.*" (9)

(a) Prof. Frazer first lays down what he assumes is a fact, namely, that ghosts are usually dressed in white. He does not think it worth while to give any evidence of the alleged fact, but appears to think that his auditors and readers will readily agree, so far.

Let us re-examine our same set of 200 cases. There is to be found no description of the dress of 126 of the apparitions, though in many instances the language is such as makes it highly probable that the " ghosts " appeared in ordinary, familiar clothing. Five of the

---

[12] In a note he says: " If there were any such word, an apparition ought to be called *supercommon*." This word has exactly the sense of Henry Holt's choice, *superusual*. The S. P. R. fixed for psychic research the word *supernormal*. However, the term *supernormal* includes apparitions conceived as having some kind of objective validity, while such an apparition (the existence of which he denies) would by our author be regarded as *supernatural*.

"ghosts" were seen within a halo or cloud of light or developed out of it, or were luminous, but such a halo or cloud or luminosity is not clothing. Of the remaining 79 apparitions, but 9 are definitely said to have been clothed in white, including one which was "dirty white," and a "soiled or somewhat worn bridal dress." The "shroud" was probably white, so add that case. Eight more were dressed in a "night-dress" or a "night-shirt." Such garments are not always white, but assume that all were. Also include the garment which was "grey, darker in the middle," and that which was "ash-grey," though these are not strictly white. Now we have 20 white or constructively white "uniforms," or a little more than one-quarter of the 79 about which we have data.

Thirty-five of the 79 are either distinctly said to have appeared in their ordinary day-clothing or almost certainly did so appear, since they were supposed at the time to be the persons themselves in the flesh. And when we consider that out of more than 200 apparitions, 172 were distinctly recognized at the time of appearance, 5 less certainly, and 4 seemingly identified by description, it seems very unlikely that any large proportion of them, except where so stated, appeared in the spectral white garments to which fiction has accustomed us. Where there is anything unusual in the apparent clothing, the witness would be likely to mention it. It is very uncommon for a man to wear a white suit of clothes, and of the 205 apparitions involved whose sex was determinable, 132 or 64 + percent were males. Where the apparition was that of a woman dressed as the percipient had been accustomed to see her, it would be of no significance if the dress were white. But even such cases must have been comparatively few.

Some of the particular descriptions follow: "Black clothes," "tweed suit," "dark figure," "sailor uniform with a monkey jacket," "wide-awake hat with a rather oddly-cut Inverness cape," "black silk with a muslin 'cloud' over the head and shoulders," "in black," "dark-blue overcoat" and "felt hat," "black cloak and hood," "drab overcoat," "big black poke bonnet and a checked black-and-white shawl," "his usual shell-jacket, mess-dress, with my rose in his button-hole," "a dark blue pelisse, buttoned, and the ribbon on her bonnet," "a rough brown shawl," "a wide-brimmed hat, and a veil," "in a buff jacket and boots," "colonial helmet on his head," "a black suit."

So Prof. Frazer was wrong, "ghosts" are not "usually" clothed in white. And his principal explanation of the fact is as spurious as the fact itself, for whereas he attributes apparitions to white objects dimly seen in "feeble light," we have already discovered that more

OLD DOGMA AND LATER STATISTICS

than half of the apparitions were experienced in daylight, bright moonlight or good artificial light.

A more detailed exhibit of the 20 cases of white or constructively white (for we have been very accommodating; very likely half of the night garments seen were of other colors) will be worth study.

(I, 204) Male apparition seen in "dirty white garment." Seen at night. The man died at same time, in such a garment, other features of vision corresponding.

(I, 434) Male apparition "in his night-shirt." Seen at night. The man was then in bed (presumably in his night-shirt) in a state of coma.

(I, 437) Male apparition "in his night-dress." Seen at dawn. The youth died of illness at that hour. (Was in bed, so undoubtedly in a night garment.)

(II, 41) Female apparition "in her night-dress." Seen at 2 P. M. The lady died at the same hour, after an illness (hence almost certainly so dressed).

(II, 49) Female apparition "in white." Seen at night; 10 P. M. The lady had been "almost bedridden for long." Said to have died same night at 7 P. M. (So probably in bed with night-dress on.)

(II, 179) Female apparition "in her night-dress." Seen in the night. The lady died of an illness "in the middle of the [same] night" (so was almost certainly in her night-dress).

(II, 181) Female apparition "in a long night-dress." Seen in the night, "before light." Hour of the lady's death not known, but within a day of the vision. (However, the death was from "suppressed smallpox," so she was presumably in her night-dress.)

(II, 208) Female apparition "in what appeared a soiled or somewhat worn bridal-dress" (so presumably white). Seen by several officers at evening, in a fully lighted room. Resembled a bridal-dress (presumably white) photograph of the deceased wife of a man lying ill in the same building who died within two days afterward.

(II, 513) Female apparition "in white," resembling seer's mother, though features not visible. Seen at night. The mother died about the same time (so probably was in white).

(II, 520) Male apparition "in his night-shirt." Seen in night, while seer was walking with a candle. About the same moment the man died. (He was very ill, so probably in bed, and very likely in a white garment.)

(II, 521) A boy apparition "in a white night-dress," and lilies in his hand, seen at about 6 P. M. by a person awake and about the house.

The boy, known by seer to be dying of an illness, had died about two hours previously, while holding lilies. (He was in a white night-dress.)

(II, 522) Female apparition "dressed in white." Seen at night. The woman died the same night after illness. (So was probably in a night-dress, more likely white.)

(II, 525) Female apparition "in her night-dress, and her head bound up as in a turban." Seen at night. Seer within a half hour reached the lady (his mother) and found her in bed just as he had seen her.

(II, 539) Female apparition "dressed in white," not stated when seen. The woman died "at that time," but no further particulars are given.

(II, 606) Female apparition "in her usual white dressing-gown." Seen at night. The woman died "about" that time, but no further particulars are given.

(II, 612) Male apparition "in his night gown." Seen at night. Man died the same hour "of an epidemic disorder" (so was probably in bed, very likely in a white night-gown).

(II, 616) Female apparition in "a cap with a frill under her chin, and a dressing-gown of the appearance of white flannel." Seen by two persons at night. Grandmother of seers (her daughter also saw and recognized her the same night, but it is not stated how she saw her dressed) died the same evening. (No further particulars, but the dress seems appropriate to an old lady.)

(F, 151) Male apparition "in a shroud and no longer had his characteristic mustache." Seen in the morning. The man had just died, and seer "went that very morning," and found that his mouth and mustache had been covered with a cloth. (Whether or not a shroud had been put on not stated.)

Now let us add the two cases where the apparition was not dressed in exactly white.

(II, 205) Unrecognized apparition, sex apparently not distinguished, "grey, darker and thicker in the middle." No assignable sequence or meaning.

(II, 512) Female apparition "covered over with a loose glistening robe or sheet of an ash-grey color." The lady died about almost exactly at the same absolute time, in consequence of childbirth several days before. (So she was almost certainly in bed in a night-gown, whether of that shade not stated.)

In one of the 20 cases of white, nearly white and possibly white clothing the apparition was not recognized and [perhaps consequently] no corresponding event was traced. In four, we are not given particulars how the person was or probably was actually dressed at the time his or her apparition was seen, so we must set them aside. But in 5 instances the person seen in white seems to have actually been in white at the time, and in 9 more the probability that this was the case is high. In the one remaining case, that of the apparition in a bridal-dress, the only correspondence was that a dying man in the house had a portrait of his deceased wife in a bridal-dress.

Several more apparitions, not in white, were dressed as they actually were at the time of death or accident, and without the knowledge of the percipients that they were or had been so dressed.

Consider all the facts given in this section and then whether it is not probable that the absence in most narratives of any description of dress is because there was nothing unusual in the clothing. Thus will emerge the general rule, subject of course to exceptions, that apparitions, seen at or near the time when the person represented dies, has an accident, etc., appear either (1) dressed as the seer has seen the actual person dressed, or (2) dressed as the person was dressed at or near the moment of the vision.[13]

Having assumed as a fact that which is not so, the professor proceeds to explain the fact which is not so. (b) First, because white " is likely to be the color which most attracts the eye in feeble light." Evidently he supposed that apparitions are nearly always illusions produced by looking at light-colored objects in near darkness. But the fact assumed in this explanation is as erroneous as the supposed major fact, for, as we have seen, in about 40 percent of 210 cases the apparition was seen in the daytime, and in a majority of cases either in daylight or by what is declared to have been good moonlight or artificial light. Besides, an illusion occasioned by an object would generally be stationary, whereas, as we shall see, in a large percentage of cases the apparition moves.

(c) But again, he explains, " custom teaches us to expect more dead men than any other class of visitants, because this can prove no

---

[13] As psychologists are so fond of ascribing apparitions of sane people to imagination, emotion, suggestion, etc., it ought to seem very singular to them that not one of these more than 200 apparitions appeared as in the standard form of an " angel." Hardly a person but has seen pictures of angels a thousand times from infancy onwards. These winged shapes have been depicted by a host of artists, the greatest to the least; they are in the galleries and in books and on religious cards; they walk, they stand, they wing their way upward, or they come down feet upmost. Yet not in this set is there a single instance where an apparition had wings, not one where the figure appeared to be either soaring into the heavens or emerging thence, even in those cases where the percipient knew or believed the person was dying, or knew he was actually dead.

alibi." I have puzzled much over this sentence and am not yet certain what it is supposed to mean. It certainly sounds as though most people expect to see apparitions but expect to see more apparitions of dead than of living people. Judging from the statements of people who have seen apparitions, it is doubtful whether one in fifty had previously expected to see one either of the living or the dead. But let this pass. The sentence ends: " and the robes of the dead are generally white." But they frequently were not, even so far back as 1875. Besides, if the ghost were an illusion from seeing a white object in near darkness, the additional reason for the color is redundant. And finally, if the " ghostly uniform " is suggested by the knowledge that the robes of the dead are usually white, then suggestion should not only prescribe the color but also the actual shape of robes of the dead, and there are not more than two or three cases out of the 200, where the dress is a shroud or any kind of grave-clothes. The statistics of psychic research, gathered since Prof. Frazer's time, show that his fact is unfounded and his reasons fallacious.

XVIII. We have already attended to Prof. Frazer's agreement with the writer of 1820 in the unfounded opinion that, as the former put it, " Midnight is the hour of appearance." He goes on:

(a) "*It is not improbable that the origin of the idea that these objects glide* (b) *without noise, may be partly due to the fact* (c) *that to be far off to be indistinct* (d) *they must be too far to be clearly heard; or else it may be connected* (e) *with the gradual passage across the eye of an imaginary picture, as in the case of dreams.*" (9-10)

Here again there is assumed to be a fact too well known to need proof, namely, that " these objects " (*i. e.*, apparitions), always or as a rule " glide without noise."

(a) We resort to the same list of 200 cases to see if it is a fact that apparitions always, or generally, glide. It is to be understood that in a few of these cases two apparitions were seen, and in a few two or more persons saw the apparition at different times. The following figures are intended to cover these facts also.

Standing, 68; same + walking, 5	73
Walking, 54; same + standing, 1; same + lying, 1	56
Sitting, 9; lying, 8; being carried, 2	19
Kneeling, 1; leaning down to or in window, 2	3
Run away with by horses, 1; riding horse, 1	2
Falling into water	2
Only head, face, or upper part of body seen	13
Instantaneous, no apparent impression of movement	3

OLD DOGMA AND LATER STATISTICS

No details regarding movement..................... 35
Gliding movement, declared or implied.............. 10

Total................................216

There very possibly were other cases where the apparition "glided," but probably silence nearly always means that there either was no movement or that the figure moved as living persons do. At any rate, there is no evidence that in this set more than one out of 20 apparitions glided.

(b) There are, it is true, but five cases where the sound of footsteps, etc., is reported in connection with the experiencing of an apparition. But there are these, and in two cases the sound came before the apparition. But a further number of cases were not soundless. In 19 cases the apparition spoke or seemed to speak, the sound having the effect of being quite external. This is not exactly what one would expect, even when a sane and healthy person takes a white object seen in near darkness for a ghost. In several of these instances the percipient received information about what was then happening at a distance or what had happened, and we should still less expect that. We may instance Mrs. M. A. Richardson (I, 443), who says that one evening she distinctly saw her husband, Gen. Richardson, then 150 miles distant, carried off the field seriously wounded, and heard him say: "Take this ring off my finger, and send it to my wife," and all the next day could not get the sight or the voice out of her mind. It was not until sometime after that Major Lloyd told her that he helped carry the General and that the request was actually made to him at that hour. We also have the testimony of Gen. Richardson himself to the same effect. It may be added, in view of what Prof. Frazer says later, that we hardly expect such things of "the gradual passage across the eyes of an imaginary picture."

Voice Cases

(I, 417) Seer awake in morning. Person seen died that night. Did not know he was more than ordinarily ill.

(I, 440) Seer awake in bed. Person seen then fatally ill, fact not known. Died two days later.

(I, 443) Seer dozing. "Saw" and "heard" actual incident, nearly or quite contemporaneous.

(I, 444) Seer wakened. Person seen, illness not known, died same hour.

(I, 447) Seer wakened. Person seen, illness not known, died near same hour.

(I, 449) Seer awake in bed. Person seen drowned same night.
(II, 141) Seer up and awake. Person seen nearly drowned ten hours before apparition.
(II, 143) Seer up and at work. Person seen, illness not known, died same evening.
(II, 146) Seer up and at work. Person seen, illness not known, died about same time.
(II, 523) Seer out walking. Voice gave information of injury. Person seen physically assaulted same hour.
(F, 49) Seer rose from bed, and apparition pointed to wound, etc. Person seen killed in battle; not known how close the coincidence.
(F, 67) Seer writing a letter. Person seen, illness not known, died about same hour.
(F, 137) Seer ? Apparition correctly pointed to wounds. Person seen killed same night.
(F, 169) Seer up and at work. Person seen killed by accident twenty-four hours earlier; fact not known.
(F, 170) Seer ? Apparition described murderer. Person seen killed, fact not known, the day before.
(J. V, 109) Seer wakened. Person seen drowned within the hour.
(J. V, 139) Seer wakened. Death of person seen already known.
(J. VII, 124) Seer up, holding baby. Apparition correctly told when he died, etc. Person seen, illness unknown, died at or near same time.
(J. VII, 363) Seer had not gone to sleep. Person seen, illness known but case thought favorable, died fifteen minutes later, of hemorrhage.

It cannot then be laid down as a rule that "ghosts" are unaccompanied by sound. In about one out of every eight in our 200 cases, there was an auditory hallucination also, of voice, or some other sound. But it is not the voice as such which is to be emphasized, but first, as in other cases, the more or less close coincidence with the death, accident, etc., of the person seen, and, secondly, the assertions that in 6 of the 19 voice cases information was given of facts hitherto unknown to the percipient.

(c) Prof. Frazer next takes it for granted that "ghosts" are as a rule seen indistinctly. This notion is consistent with the Professor's theory that apparitions are usually illusions, caused by real objects viewed in near darkness. But we found that they are seen in daylight, good artificial light and bright moonlight more frequently than in the night time with poor light. And careful inspection of our 200 cases shows that they are more generally than not distinct. Our only

OLD DOGMA AND LATER STATISTICS

possible way of judging is by the testimony of the seers. Counting only cases where the seers declare in one way or another that they saw the apparitions distinctly, recognized them without a doubt or had no doubt that they were seeing real and recognized persons, the figures are 111, or more than half. In less than 20 cases are terms used which aver or from which we can reasonably infer that the apparitions were indistinctly seen.

(d) In order to explain why " ghosts " usually glide (which is not the case), the Professor tells us that to be far off to be indistinct (which is more frequently not the case) they must be too far to be clearly heard. In many instances they seem to have been very clearly heard, but let that pass. It is evident that the Professor thought that " ghosts," when seen, are generally at a considerable distance from the percipient.

One is puzzled to decide at what distance it is supposed to be sufficiently " far off to be indistinct." It is possible to speak so faintly as hardly to be heard at a distance of three feet, and it is possible to speak so loudly and clearly as to be understood at the distance of a hundred feet or more. Probably it will be agreed that twelve feet or less is not either far off or far enough off to hear indistinctly unless the speaker murmurs softly or speaks very thickly. Let us go to our 200 cases again. We are not informed in regard to 52 of the phantasms in these cases. Out of the 164 which remain we find them, relatively to the percipient:

At bedside, 20; at foot of bed, 18; " near " the bed, 2; on the bed, 2; bent over the bed, 3 45
In the same room or in its door, 62; probably the number within 12 feet were not less than half of this, say 31
Expressly stated to have been less than 12 feet....... 7
Close, 22; very near, 3; near, 8; " a few feet," 1 34
———
117

Over against these we assume that one-half of the apparitions seen in the same room were more than 12 feet away................................ 31
By statement distant (180 feet), 1; probably distant, 1   2
Doubtful (" a few yards," " opposite side of the street," " a few steps," etc.): assume all exceeded 12 feet .. 14
———
47

By fair construction of terms and calculation we show that the Professor is as mistaken in supposing that apparitions usually seem distant to the seers, as he is in all his other confident assertions regarding " ghosts."

(e) Or, if his hearers are not satisfied with his first explanation of what isn't so, the good Professor will try again, exchanging his theory of illusion for that of hallucination. The " idea that these objects " [*i. e.*, " ghosts "] " glide without noise " may, after all, " be connected with the dual passage across the eye of an imaginary picture, as in the case of dreams." This sentence causes one to ponder and to ask many questions. It is true that in a dream a picture is drawn across the eye? If an imaginary picture is drawn across the eye in dreams, in what sense is it a " dual passage "? Does he mean it is drawn across *both* eyes? Or does he mean that, besides the visual imagery, the *sounds* which one seems to hear in a dream are drawn across his eye? Did the Professor really think that when one imagines, say a landscape, a picture is drawn across the eye? If a " ghost " is drawn across one's eye, what draws the ghost? I think that he thought that any sort of thinking was good enough for ghosts.

A little later than the *Enquiry into the Nature of Ghosts*, that is to say in 1824, there was printed in Edinburgh and London, *Sketches of the Philosophy of Apparitions, or an Attempt to Trace Such Illusions to Their Physical Causes*, by Samuel Hibbert, M.D., F.R.S.E., and member of several learned societies. It is a book of 460 pages, on which the author spent a great deal of mental labor and ingenuity, but with a lamentable paucity of material, in the way of authenticated actual reports of apparitions. He has to go back to mythology, to legends of antiquity, and to narrations of the fifteenth, sixteenth and seventeenth centuries for the most part, aside from the visual hallucinations experienced in shoals by persons suffering from delirium tremens, paranoiacs and victims of other forms of neural and mental disease. Poetry is frequently cited by way of illustration [14] and at least one as proof,[15] a means of enforcing one's conclusions which would meet little favor with scientific men of today. Pages 243-341 are occupied by an elaborate attempted analysis of mental states, waking and sleeping, which would furnish quaint reading to a psychologist of our own times if one could be found sufficiently curious and patient to read it. Even if it were the very psychological gospel,

---

[14] On 74 of the 460 pages. [15] 298.

it would not in the least shed light on the problem of coincidental apparitions which now confronts us.

Schizophrenia, or disjunction of thinking, is exhibited not infrequently by scientific and professional writers of our generation, when they attack psychic research, but not in the way illustrated by the following sentence of Hibbert:

"As we are not warranted, for many reasons, which may be defended on scriptural grounds, to suppose that any direct converse with good or evil spirits, connected with either the Jewish or Christian dispensation, has extended beyond the Apostolic age, there will be no hesitation on my part to proceed on the hypothesis, that all subsequent visitations of this nature which have been recorded, deserve a medical rather than a theological investigation." 87-8.

And, it later appears, only apparitions experienced by Jews, not those of Greeks or Romans or any other people prior to the close of the Apostolic period, are to be credited as supernormal, nor even any incident from Jewish sources, unless it is to be found in the Bible. Having made this special reservation in favor of scriptural apparitions, the author avoids any further reference to them, as though his intellectual conscience were a little uneasy, after all. The thought, quickly suppressed, must have flitted across his consciousness that it was odd that the supreme ruler of the universe whom he acknowledges should have issued a fiat that certain manifestations from the supernal world which had been permitted for some centuries should on a particular year, some decades after the beginning of the new and supposedly more spiritual and free " Dispensation," utterly and forever cease, without notice given. When did the "Apostolic age" come to an end? Presumably the year when the last of the Apostles died, exactly as the "Augustan age" closed in the year 14 A. D., when Augustus Cæsar died. No one knows when the last of the Apostles died, but let us suppose the year 80 A. D.

If Dr. Hibbert had allowed himself to think, he might have imagined an incident like this. In the year 81, one Joab, a Christian living in Jerusalem, says to a friend:

"Last night, at the third hour, before I had gone to sleep I saw a vision of my father, who lives in Bethlehem.[16] I saw him just as clearly as I see you. He walked into the door and stood looking at me, then suddenly disappeared. I fear that he is dead, although he seemed to be in perfect health when I saw him last."

---

[16] Six miles from Jerusalem.

"Oh," replies the friend placidly, "I wouldn't trouble myself about that. There was probably something wrong about your stomach."

"Why do you talk that way? You yourself heard our great brother Paul tell how he had a vision from the Lord of a man who said to him, 'Come over into Macedonia and help us.' I never heard you say that you thought there was something the matter with his stomach."

"But that happened to an Apostle."

"What of that? Did not Cornelius see a spirit who instructed him to send for Simon Peter? And Cornelius was no Apostle, nor even a Jew."

"But Simon Peter was an Apostle, which explains what happened to Cornelius."

"I don't follow your reasons—they seem to be drifting away into clouds. But I call you to witness that only last year Nadab of Bethel told us that he had seen an angel, which gave him great joy. Nothing happened in consequence, and Nadab had no proof that it was an angel, since it appeared like an ordinary man. Yet you believed it was, and never once suggested that Nadab was not digesting properly. What has changed you?"

"But at that time last year the Apostle John was still living. He, the last of the Apostles, died two months later. The Apostolic age has ended; the Lord will send no more visions or spirits of the departed; henceforth any experience of that kind, although it may seem precisely like those of last year or a century ago, will be the effect of some diseased condition."

Can Joab be blamed if here he breaks out: "In the name of all the saints at once, how did you find that out? And what is the *sense* of it—why should the Lord change His ways and withdraw His mercies since John is dead?"

Just then comes in a messenger and informs Joab that his father had suddenly died during the night. After a decent interval for the expression of grief, Joab asks the messenger, "At what hour did he die?" and the messenger answers, "At the third hour." Joab turns to his friend and inquires, with emphasis, "And what do you say to that?"

The friend, being a remarkable forerunner of a class of schizophreniacs yet to come, calmly answers: "It was probably an accidental coincidence."

And Joab, despite the shadow of death which has fallen upon him, quite loses his patience, and ejaculates, "I never in my life before saw the form of a man actually not in the flesh before me. Last night I saw a vision of my father, in the same hour he died, and you argue that, since it is this year and not last year, my only vision merely chanced to occur just when the man I saw died, and that the explanation is that I ate something which did not agree with me. Go, fellow of muddled brain, before I cast a stone at thee."

Dr. Hibbert declares: " I believe that no apparitions of profane history [17] were ever seen under any such circumstances [those of " perfect health "]; but that they have universally arisen from morbific causes." How men come to conclusions on a large subject, so positively that they are willing to print them, before ever there has been made any survey of the subject, any considerable collection of authentic instances and actual analysis of them, is mysterious and wonderful. Yet Dr. Hibbert had no difficulty in coming to a general conclusion before ever there had been any collecting and survey of cases, worthy of the name. But worse is what we sometimes see now— men who announce various dogmas since such surveys have been made, and in defiance of them.

It is true that even yet collections of cases have not gone into the matter of health so closely and systematically as is desirable, but the indications agree with the many cases of percipients of apparitions whom I have questioned, and fail to disclose any such general rule relating to pathological states. Far from it. On the contrary, many of the witnesses expressly declare that they were in excellent health and good spirits when the experience came to them. Whether estimated by their own feelings and convictions or by their appearance and the vigor of their activities, most persons who have experienced evidential apparitions seem to be or to have been sound and healthy persons.

Three excerpts comprise Hibbert's theory of apparitions.

"All the subordinate incidents connected with phantasms might be explained on the following general principle:

" In every undue excitement of our feelings . . . the operations of the intellectual faculty of mind sustain corresponding modifications, by which the efforts of the judgment are rendered proportionally incorrect." iv.

"An adequate cause of spectral illusions may arise from an undue vividness in the recollected images of the mind." 19.

---

[17] There it is again; any apparitions recorded in the Old or New Testaments, or any among Christians up to the year when the last Apostle died, could have been and probably were, supernormal and unrelated to ill health, but any subsequent ones are from " morbific " causes.

"Apparitions are nothing more than morbid symptoms, which are indicative of an intense excitement of the renovated feelings of the mind." [Capitalized in the book.] 342.

It is not easy, even with all the context, to discover just what the man is driving at, but as best it can be determined, I will try to put his meaning in clearer language.

I understand him to mean that an apparition is simply a symptom of a pathological condition. A state of excitement roused by some " morbific " cause, raises a memory image to that degree that it seems external and at the same time so disturbs the intellect as to deprive the victim of the power to distinguish it from reality.

But with the advantage of our large collections of attested cases, see how utterly this formula fails to fit the generality of the facts.

In the first place, in many instances the apparition occurred when the person was pleasantly occupied and in a state, so far as he or she knew, of mental calm. Here are a few cases.

(I, 194) " I was reading geometry as I walked along, a subject little likely to produce fancies or morbid phenomena of any kind, when, in a moment "—she experienced a coincidental and evidential apparition.

(I, 415) " He was in perfect health at the time [says a friend of the percipient in a death-coincidence case, present when the apparition was seen], and of a thoroughly practical nature; not at all given to sentimentality."

(I, 417) It is John Addington Symonds who says: " I woke about dawn, and felt for my books upon a chair "—when he felt impelled to turn his head, and saw a death-coincidental apparition.

(I, 448) Harriet Hosmer says she " retired to rest in good health and in a quiet frame of mind," and woke from sound sleep with a feeling that some one was in the room, then saw the death-coincidental apparition.

(II, 37) Percipient saw the death-coincidental apparition while enjoying herself at a concert.

(II, 40) Percipient was knitting and listening to the reading of a story by Dickens when she dropped her work and uttered an exclamation, as that moment she experienced a death-coincidental apparition.

(II, 41) A General testifies that his clerk was reading some documents to him when he saw the death-coinciding apparition of his sister.

(II, 45) Lieut.-Gen. Fytche was dressing in the morning when he saw a friend walk in, and greeted him warmly, not doubting his substantiality. The death occurred the same morning.

(II, 54) Percipient was "reading, when on looking up from my book"—she saw the death-coincidental apparition of a friend. She thought her real and felt "horror" only when she disappeared.

(II, 149) Percipient "in a perfectly cheerful, healthy frame of mind, no surroundings of any kind to excite the imagination," "suddenly" experienced a death-coinciding apparition.

(II, 199) Three persons are "chatting" when suddenly all see the same apparition.

(II, 200) Percipient was playing the flute, and intent on the music, which was hard to read, when he felt as though some one were approaching, and then saw a face dimly. Another person present saw the figure approach the flute-player.

(II, 513) Percipient, a young girl, saw a death-coincidental apparition in the midst of "frolicsome" conduct with other girls.

(II, 514) Percipient was practising the piano, when she saw the death-coinciding apparition of her grandmother.

(II, 519) Percipient, a boy of about two years, was playing when he called out, "Papa, papa, come to me." The father is alleged to have been killed the same day.

(II, 530) Percipient had been "listening to some fine music" and, afterwards, while "in good health and spirits" saw the apparition of a friend supposed to be on the other side of the North American Continent, where he had been for nearly two years. The next morning the friend called, having the same necktie and excrescence on the cheek, which were new to the percipient, who noted them in the phantom.

(II, 555) Percipient, a little girl, was playing with young companions, when she screamed and pointed to what she said was her "papa lying on the ground, and the blood running from a big wound," which vision corresponded with the violent death of her father at or near that hour.

(II, 609) Two percipients, young girls, were "chattering and laughing" when the apparition appeared to both, coincidental with the person seen being in mortal danger.

It is impossible to conjure out of such narrations, which could be multiplied, a "morbific" appearance. And what of the cases where there were two or three percipients, who independently of any suggestion, saw the same apparition? Is it to be supposed that morbific symptoms would reach their climax in two or three persons at the same moment, and not only that, but reproduce the same "recollected image of the mind"?

Secondly, the seeing of apparitions is frequently accompanied by excitement, it is true, but Hibbert has the cart before the horse.

A dog yelps when a stone hits him, but the stone does not hit the dog because he yelps—at least not then. Far more frequently than otherwise, it appears, there is nothing uncommon in the state and environment of a person at the moment he experiences an apparition. He is engaged at some ordinary task, or is dressing, or reading, or listening to music, or chatting, or just wakened from a calm sleep, and the like, when suddenly the apparition is before him. Sometimes he does get excited afterward, not by any means always.

Thirdly, the "judgment," in nearly every case cannot be regarded as having anything to do with the formation of an apparition. Nearly always the figure appears suddenly and entire, before the judgment has any time to act. It is not as with many a "spirit photograph" which gradually, as one gazes at it, seems to grow in resemblance to someone, but nearly always, unless we are to contradict testimony, recognition, if there is recognition, is immediate.

Dr. Hibbert pays almost no attention to coincidences of external facts with apparitions seen. And if there were at our command as few cases as he seems to have known, and those of so low a grade, we should be as little impressed by them. He cites three (351-356). In one, the person whose death more or less corresponded in time with the time of the apparition, was known to be exposed to danger from a plague raging in London. In the second, where a man had a vision of his absent wife with a dead child in her arms, and the child was somewhere about that time born dead, of course he knew that the confinement was imminent, and he likewise knew that she was ill. No sensible person would give weight to such a coincidence. The third is a case of the fifteenth century related by a man of the sixteenth.

We cannot criticize a writer of 1824 for publishing such opinions, as we should be compelled to do if he issued them a century later, disregarding the mass of material which had by that time accumulated. But he did know that, aside from the swarming visual hallucinations of delirium and of mentally diseased persons, he had made no examination of contemporaneous and authenticated apparitional instances. And he really should not have been so cock-sure in proclaiming his theory.

Sir Walter Scott's book, entitled *Lectures on Demonology and Witchcraft*, hardly manifests consciousness of any knowledge that many apparitions are seen at or near the hour when the persons they represent died, or at the time when some accident or other critical or emotional event happened to them (sometimes picturing the actual scene). He knows that dreams are said often thus to correspond, but

OLD DOGMA AND LATER STATISTICS 195

argues that, since we have so many dreams this might easily happen through chance coincidence.

But as a rule those who experience an apparition coinciding as stated, have not been subject to such experiences, and with the great majority of them, there has never been another. Were Scott living, it would be interesting to ask him what he thought of the following sample cases.

(I, 214) Two hours before the maid, Helen, who had accompanied her mistress, Lady Waldegrave, to a place where she was a stranger, Frances Reddell, maid of the hostess, saw the figure of a stout old woman carrying a candlestick, and wearing a red shawl and a petticoat with a hole in the front. This figure she "instantly felt to be the mother of the sick woman." *She told her mistress, Mrs. Pole-Carew, about an hour after Helen's death, saying, " her mother came last night," and describing the apparition.* We have Mrs. Pole-Carew's signed statement as well as Reddell's. Two days after, the dead maid's parents and sister arrived and the mother was at once recognized by Reddell, and also, owing to the description, which extended even to the facial expression, by the mistress. Then Helen's sister was questioned, and it was learned that *the mother's appearance, including the hole in the petticoat and the candlestick as described, was exactly what it probably would have been, had she been roused at night.* Furthermore, not having received any letter from Helen for several days, the mother had said as she went up to bed on the night of the apparition, "I am sure Helen is very ill." It is fairly certain, then, that she was then anxious about her daughter.

(I, 443) It is common for women to worry about their husbands absent in military service, and the mere coincidence, under those conditions, of an apparition with death or wounds, would be much discounted. But Mrs. Richardson testifies that she saw a vision of her husband being carried off the field seriously wounded and heard his voice saying, "Take this ring off my finger and send it to my wife," and all the next day "could not get the sight or the voice out of my mind." Also that she afterward learned from Major Lloyd, the man who helped carry *Gen. Richardson at or near that hour, that the latter used just those words.* And the General himself testifies that *this is what happened, wound, being carried off, and the utterance of the sentence.*

(II, 35) Mr. Searle, a barrister, testifies that at about 2 P. M., he saw, as if in a window-pane, the head and face of his wife, "in a reclining position, with the eyes closed and the face quite white and bloodless, as if she were dead." When he returned home he found that *his wife, at about 2 P. M., had fainted.* Observe two additional facts, first, that " this is *the only occasion on which I have known my wife to have a fainting-fit*," and, secondly, that this was the *only time that the lawyer had ever experienced a hallucination.*

(II, 45) Lieut.-Gen. Fytche saw a friend whom he had not met for years enter his room, and had no doubt of his reality. At " about the very time " the friend died some 600 miles away. The General had had no news of his illness, and did not learn of his death until a fortnight later, *nor had he himself ever had any similar experience.*

(II, 182) *A man and his sister, more than 1,000 miles apart, the same night experienced the apparition of another sister,* who within the same day rather suddenly died, there being no reason on the part of either seer to expect such an event. The man, at least, had never before had a subjective hallucination.

(II, 199) A clergyman and two ladies, sitting in a room, saw an old man in dark blue overcoat, flat-topped hat, and having a white beard, pass the window just outside. A few moments later a doctor rang the bell and entered. A lady said, " But where is the old man with the white beard? " and the doctor replied, " Yes; where is he? " and related that he had seen an old man, of exactly the same description except that he wore no hat, sitting in the room, as he himself passed the window. *Neither clergyman nor physician had been subject to hallucinations.* We have the testimonies of both.

(II, 204) A man *who had never had any former experience of the kind* sees a figure of a crouching old woman, enveloped in a black cloak and hood, which slowly goes from the bedroom door to a wardrobe and then disappears. He so testifies. His wife declares that *she woke to see her husband leaning on his elbow and that she saw an old woman crouching by the wardrobe,* which she supposed to be a real person, but it suddenly disappeared. Also, it was learned that in another room, the same night, no one having been told of the above story, their child, three years old, cried out to the nurse: " Clara, Clara, *there is an old woman in the room.*"

(F, 133) The Rev. Charles Tweedale tells us that his grandmother died at 12:15 midnight, that he, living in another place, saw an apparition of her in the neighborhood of 2 A. M. that night; that his father, in another room of the same house, saw her apparition at 2 P. M.; and that his aunt, living some thirty miles distant, saw her apparition the same night, at some time later than that of the death.

Would Sir Walter have said that these sample cases, even taken by

OLD DOGMA AND LATER STATISTICS

themselves, to say nothing of the numerous other cases and the careful mathematical calculation of chances made by the S. P. R. committee,[18] presented no problem to his mind, but seemed quite likely to happen through chance coincidence?

Selecting the phenomenon of apparitions, I have exhibited the views of four writers ranging from 1820 to 1875, one a philosopher, another a physician, the third writing as a historian, and the fourth a college professor—views as to the nature of the facts and their underlying causes. We have seen that these writers err as to the facts and that their theories to account for the facts are in part negatived by the facts themselves and in part fail to meet the real issues as these present themselves today. And no wonder, since not one of them evinces any first-hand study of actual cases, or acquaintance with any even moderately considerable number of authenticated records. Probably no one since the beginning of the world has been able to frame a correct descriptive summary of widely-scattered and perennial phenomena, and to spin from his brain a theory which would hold water, upon data which, so far as his knowledge extends, are scanty and hazy.

We have traveled a long way since 1820 or 1875. Great numbers of apparitional cases have been collected, authenticated, analyzed, appraised and submitted to mathematical calculation of chance probability. Hardly a cultivated person of today is so little aware of these researches as to repeat certain of the quoted allegations so confidently uttered, even but fifty-five years ago. But still the *voces reclamantes* betray insufficient acquaintance with the facts, and logic vitiated in consequence. The lessons we have found in these older writers might well be heeded today.

---

[18] See *Phantasms of the Living*, ch. XIII.

VI. PSYCHICAL VERSUS VISCERAL HALLUCINATIONS

It is very easy for a person who has had considerable experience with patients in a pronounced pathological condition, and with the hallucinations to which certain classes of these are subject, to fancy that the hallucinations reported by psychic research, and which reveal a surprising percentage of coincidences with external events such as deaths, accidents and other events of strongly emotional character, are really of the same order and species, and that the persons experiencing them are really in a pathological condition at the time, even though none of the usual pathological symptoms appear. This is, apparently, the opinion of most psychiatrists who have not given much attention to the instances reported by psychic research. It is very unsafe, however, to make a generalization, unless one has familiarized himself with every part of the field which the generalization covers.

Are the hallucinations of psychic research, in fact, generally of the same nature as those which occur as the result of disease? Then they should exhibit, in general, the same characteristics.

Now it happens that this matter has been tested, at least in relation to certain diseases, in a very important paper by Mr. J. G. Piddington,[1] which has not, I think, received the attention that it deserves.

In 1901, Dr. Henry Head published a short work entitled *Certain Mental Changes That Accompany Visceral Disease*. It was founded on studies extending over seven years in London hospitals, embracing the cases of 192 men and women suffering from visceral disease, chiefly pulmonary, cardiac or abdominal; and who were subject to various hallucinations, visual, auditory, olfactory, etc. He had noted and lays down many characteristics of these hallucinations.

In its *Proceedings* of 1894,[2] the Society for Psychical Research published a "Report on the Census of Hallucinations." The committee which had the Census in charge, Professor Henry Sidgwick, F. W. H. Myers, Miss Alice Johnson, Frank Podmore and Mrs. Sidgwick, so far as possible excluded all pathological subjects. It might be objected that a number may have passed unsuspected, whom a

---

[1] *Proceedings* S. P. R., XIX, 267-341. [2] X, 25-422.

medical specialist after personal and thorough inspection would have found diseased. If, nevertheless, the Census hallucinations should be found to present with but few exceptions characteristics in striking contrast to those which Dr. Head assigns to his hospital cases, the logical deduction would be that (1) the Census embraced but few cases of visceral disease, (2) the hallucinations of the Census people in general were of another species than those of the people who certainly suffered from visceral complaints, and (3) that while there is a causal connection between the visceral diseases of the hospital patients and their hallucinations, hallucinations such as are reported in the "Census of Hallucinations" and elsewhere are not the product of such diseases.

Following, put in smallest compass, are some of the comparisons which Mr. Piddington presents. We select only those relating to hallucinations of a visual character.

Sentences enclosed in quotation marks and prefaced by the letter V are from Dr. Head's pamphlet, and refer to Visceral hallucinations.

Sentences printed in italics, enclosed between quotation marks and prefaced by the letter P are from the S. P. R. Census Report and refer to what purport to be Psychical hallucinations.

Sentences enclosed between quotation marks, prefaced by the letter P, but not printed in italics, are in the language of Mr. Piddington.

Sentences not enclosed between quotation marks are based upon facts stated by Mr. Piddington.

We start with the datum that both V and P visual hallucinations represent human beings.

(I, a). V. "Neither arms nor legs are seen."
V. "The limbs are never visible."

P. "*When they* [the phantoms] *move . . . the movement is almost always such as we are accustomed to see. The phantom stands on the ground and appears to walk along the ground.*"

P. "There can be no doubt that the majority of Psychical Percipients either saw the legs of the figures or failed to notice their absence. Skirts and trousers are mentioned specifically, and though skirts and trousers are not legs, still as they cover the places where legs ought to be, it would be unfair not to infer that they hid spectral legs from view."

[Until the late change in the dress of women it was seldom that one met a living man or woman and saw deeper than trousers and skirts.] Also, very frequently one sees a flesh-and-blood man or woman and afterward is unable to remember having noticed his or her lower extremities.

(I, b). V. "The figure appears to be draped and not clothed. Patients are unanimous that the figure is unlike anything that they have ever seen and they are peculiarly definite in describing it as 'draped,' 'wrapped in a shawl,' 'wrapped in a sheet' . . . The head may be covered."

P. So far as the reports as to dress enable us to judge, phantoms, both recognized and unrecognized, generally appear in ordinary modern dress. The great majority of hallucinations are like the sights we are accustomed to see.

(I, c). V. "The face is frequently misty."
V. "The face is frequently not visible."

P. "Any one who will take no more trouble than to scan either the Census Report or the S. P. R. *Proceedings* or *Journal, passim*, will readily discover that mistiness of the face is emphatically not a trait of S. P. R. apparitions, and that Psychical Percipients again and again insist on the distinctness of the features of the hallucinatory figure."

There are a few instances where the face was not seen, some of them because it was turned away.

(I, d). V. [The face] "when seen is always beardless."

P. The beard is seldom mentioned in the reports of Census apparitions, but since it is often stated that the resemblance to the real person was perfect, a beard must have appeared in many instances. The absence of a beard on a recognized person who in fact possessed one could hardly have escaped notice and mention. In one of the few instances where a beard is mentioned the person did not wear one to the knowledge of the percipient, but had in fact, since becoming ill, grown one, short and white, exactly as with the apparition.

(I, e^1). V. "Patients express great difficulty in deciding whether the figure was that of a man or a woman. The face is frequently not visible. When seen it is always beardless, which makes many say they think it must have been a woman."

P. "Out of 793 apparitions of human figures, reported at firsthand [in the Census Report], 673 were classed as 'realistic,' and if a figure is realistic, there can practically be no doubt as to the sex. Of the remaining 120, although classed as incompletely developed [cloudy, dimly seen, etc.], it must not be assumed that the sex was necessarily

PSYCHICAL VERSUS VISCERAL HALLUCINATIONS 201

open to doubt." In only three instances was doubt expressed by the narrator.

(I, e^2). V. " The complete flatness and absence of the usual undulations of a woman's figure suggest that it may have been a man."

P. " This point is met by the comments on e^1, unless, indeed, the cruel suggestion be advanced that all the female figures described [in the Census Report] as realistic, or recognized as those of female relatives or friends of Psychic Percipients, were wanting in the 'usual undulations.' "

(I, f). V. " If the figure was white, most say at once 'It was a corpse.' Curiously, not one of my patients spoke of the hallucination as a ghost, possibly owing to the almost entire ignorance shown by the London-bred population of ghost stories and fairy tales.[3]

P. "*Apparitions of the dead, like other apparitions, usually appear dressed like ordinary human beings, and without symbolic accompaniments, such as white robes or wings.*

"*In four cases it is specially mentioned that the phantom appeared in the clothes in which the dead person was buried. Usually the appearance in dress and otherwise is what the percipient was accustomed to associate with the person in life.*"

Not that the clothes in which the dead person was buried were always grave-clothes; in one case they were a black suit of evening dress, such as it subsequently appeared was the actual dress. It is not true of the seers of psychical phantoms that the most of them say, when the figure is dressed in white, " It was a corpse."

(I, g). V. " Whatever the form assumed, the figure or face is single. I have found no instance so far in the sane where more than one face or figure appeared if the patient's eyes were open."

P. " *In the great majority of realistic cases, the apparition represents a single figure only, though there are exceptions.*"

In one psychical instance of the Census, the percipient saw her own dead mother and two children, a little girl and a baby apparently lately born. The apparition informed her that their mother had just

---

[3] That the people of London are in this peculiar condition of virginity in regard to ghost stories I find it hard to credit. Passing over the S. P. R., " Light," newspaper accounts of materialized ghosts, and such collections of narratives, including ghost stories, as those of William Howitt and Catherine Crowe, published in London, are we to understand that the people of London did not read Dickens and Scott, that dozens of English novels containing ghost stories, that the weird narratives which had been for generations connected with certain old castles and residences were all to Londoners quite unknown? Mr. Piddington justly remarks that few people are willing, in relating the experience of an apparition, to call it a " ghost," as this term invites ridicule.

died. It was afterwards learned that her sister-in-law was dead, leaving a little girl of the age seen, and a baby three weeks old, of whom the percipient had not heard. In another case a wife and child were seen, in another a mother and child, in a fourth an old woman nursing a child, in a fifth an Indian nurse and child, and in the sixth an uncle and two other persons. These instances are few, but it cannot be said that they "never" occur.

(I, *h*). V. "In the majority of instances the figure remained stationary at the foot or on one side or the other of the bed. It may, however, pass in front of the bed, from left to right or from right to left, and is sometimes seen in the doorway."

P. "*In more than half the visual cases the figure is seen to move in various ways.*"

"*When they* [phantoms] *move, which . . . happens more often than not, the movement is almost always such as we are accustomed to see.*" [4]

(I, *i*). V. "Usually the patient wakes from sleep to see [the figure] standing near his bed."

P. "*In 38 percent of visual . . . cases the percipient was in bed.* [But] *the proportion that occurs immediately after waking* [is] *about 12 percent of visual hallucinations.*" [5]

(I, *m*[6]). V. "The figure did not speak [in any case]."

P. "In 106 out of 1,120 first-hand cases of visual hallucination in the Census collection the apparition seemed to speak articulately." [7]

---

[4] A glance through the Report reveals not only that the psychical phantoms are not limited to movements at the foot of the bed, from left to right and from right to left, but that they are to be found doing a variety of things in a variety of places. Walking in a room, or a corridor, or down or up stairs, or on a gravel path or on a street; walking from one room to another, sitting at a table writing, standing looking out of the window, coming into a room and going to a mirror and then taking down the hair, lying apparently ill with servants walking in the room and sighing, sitting by one in a railway carriage, thrown from a tricycle, entering a room with papers in hand, jumping into and sinking in the water, leaning over a Bible as if reading it, entering a room and sitting down in a chair,—these are samples. There is nothing stereotyped about the movements of psychical apparitions.

[5] Mr. Piddington could have made the contrast between "usually" and "12 percent" more impressive if he had remarked that a considerable proportion of the 12 percent who woke to see an apparition did not wake to see it "standing near his [the] bed." A hasty glance through the Report shows that the apparition was seen before the fire, lying beside the percipient, shaking her and then walking out of the room, coming into the room on hands and knees, passing from a window toward a door, in the right-hand corner of the room, etc.

[6] I have taken the liberty to change Mr. Piddington's order so as to bring the items about vocal sound and sound in general into conjunction with each other. But his letter-order—here m, not j—is retained for convenience of reference to the original paper in the *Proceedings.*

[7] In several instances giving information of an unknown event.

PSYCHICAL VERSUS VISCERAL HALLUCINATIONS 203

(I, j). V. "No sound accompanies the appearance of the hallucinatory vision in any case."

V. "When [the figure] moved no footsteps were heard."

P. "*There are 71 cases . . . in our collection where a non-vocal sound is heard accompanied by a visual hallucination, and in 56 of these the sound precedes the apparition.*" [8]

The cases of accompanying vocal and non-vocal sounds combined were 177 of the whole number of 1,120 visual hallucinations, or nearly 16 percent. But, while it is probable that practically all percipients who seemed to hear a voice reported the fact, it is very doubtful if in all cases non-vocal sounds were reported. If all had been interrogated on this point the percentage might have risen to 20 percent. But of the nearly 16 percent of contrast to the visceral set we are sure.

(I, k). V. "After a variable interval it [the figure] disappears without movement."

P. "*Appearance or disappearance by an unrealistic means is . . . rare. Even when a phantom is stationary, it does not usually either suddenly appear out of empty space, or similarly vanish before the percipient's eyes, but is generally seen by the percipient on turning his eyes that way, and vanishes, he does not know how, or when he is looking away. There are, however, instances of sudden appearance and disappearance in free space.*" [9]

(I, n). V. [The figure] "made no gestures, and the 'grimacing' occasionally mentioned probably refers rather to an unpleasant expression of the face than to any mobility of the features."

P. "Gesture is a common characteristic of S. P. R. apparitions; so common that it is unnecessary to quote examples. . . . On the whole, though there are hardly definite enough data from which to

---

[8] Mr. Piddington remarks that consequently in but 15 cases did the sound *accompany* the visual hallucination. But here I think he leans backward in meticulosity. To accompany is not necessarily to be precisely contemporaneous with. When "The Persian dames in sumptuous cars accompanied his march" they were probably not beside him. Surely Dr. Head meant that in no case was sound a part of the hallucinatory incident.

[9] Dr. Head did not say that in all cases the apparitions of his patients disappeared while they were being gazed at. And it is not entirely clear what the boundaries of "unrealistic means," as understood by the S. P. R. Committee, are. Is it "realistic" for a phantom to seem to pass through a closed door, for instance? But at any rate the rule of visceral apparitions that they disappear without movement, is contradicted by a very large percentage of psychical apparitions, which disappear while walking around a bed, while walking into another room, while approaching the percipient, by apparently walking behind the percipient, while walking down a garden path or a stairway, by apparently passing through a closed door, etc.

At this point I omit one of Mr. Piddington's comparisons(l), since the data are so scanty that it is doubtful if any inference can be drawn.

form an estimate, I am inclined to think that while mobility of feature is sometimes met with, immobility is much commoner."

But often the S. P. R. apparitions smile, whether or not in mobile fashion. "Grimacing is not mentioned, and an unpleasant expression is very rare indeed," while it appears not to be rare in visceral cases.

(II). Sometimes the visceral hallucination consisted of a face only, and 30 of the Census set consisted only of a face or head. In one only of the doctor's cases a hand and arm were seen, while in the Census collection there are 15 cases of hand or hand and arm only, and 3 of legs only.

(III). V. "These hallucinations in all cases are white, black or grey. They are never, so far as my experience goes, colored or even normally tinted. For if the face is white, even the lips are said to be colorless. . . . This forms a differentiating point between these hallucinations of the sane and the usual hallucinations of the insane."

P. "Color is a very common characteristic of psychical hallucinations. Specific reference is often made to the color of the clothes or the face of the apparition; and even where no such reference is made, there is usually little doubt about the vision having been colored." This seems to be the rule with fully developed apparitions. "The constantly reiterated and emphatic statements of numerous percipients as to the lifelike character of the features of the phantoms is evidence enough that the faces and lips are not pale and bloodless like those of the ghost of literary tradition."

(IV). V. "Hallucinations of vision do not occur in the bright light of day. . . . In other cases the hallucination appeared in the evening when the patient was sitting quietly in a dimly-lighted room."

P. Of what they regarded as genuine visual hallucinations (as distinguished from hypnagogic visualization, etc.) the S. P. R. Committee found in its Census 30 cases seen in the dark. In 17 of these the figure alone appeared illuminated, in 12 the room seemed illuminated, although it was really dark, and in one there was the hallucination of a figure with a light upon it proceeding from a particular spot. Dr. Head makes no mention of any figure seeming to emit light or of the room seeming to be illuminated.[10]

---

[10] Mr. Piddington cites several illustrative cases of apparitions seen in the daytime or by good artificial light, but I do not think that he has sufficiently emphasized such cases, which are very many in the Census. Unfortunately, it was not estimated how many of the apparitions were seen by daylight, although it appears that more than half were seen when the percipients were "up" or "out of doors." Several hundred must have been seen in the daytime, in strong contrast with the visceral apparitions,"" which do not occur in the broad light of day."

(V). V. "Almost every case felt frightened with the first hallucination of vision, and in many cases the fear was accompanied by sweating, heart beating, and 'goose-flesh.'"

P. The Census took no direct account of emotional states accompanying an apparition, and only where the report happens to mention the effect upon the percipient does it furnish this datum. "The large majority of cases of hallucination in the Census collection were unique experiences in the lives of the various percipients," and therefore instances of "first hallucination."

"Fright is often admitted, and even horror; yet it would be very far from the truth to say of S. P. R. cases that 'almost every case felt frightened.' Not only is fright often expressly denied, but composure or even pleasure is affirmed."

(VI). V. "The feeling-tone that accompanies the colorless white figure varies greatly, but the dark or black hallucinations are uniformly associated with fear or [11] its physical manifestations.

P. "Except possibly for a few examples among 'incompletely developed' cases, I doubt if the Census report contains any instances of dark or black hallucinations in the sense intended by Dr. Head."

(VIII).[12] V. "These hallucinations are not uncommonly accompanied by the depressed mood. . . . In such cases the patient is convinced that the appearance is a sign that some ill-fortune has happened, or is about to happen. He believes some near relative is dead or in trouble, and not infrequently says that the figure was that of some dead relative, e. g., 'my sister.' Asked if it resembled his sister he answered, 'Not in the least, but I know it must have been my sister, because she is the only one of my relations who is dead.'"

P. "The latter part of this statement might be paraphrased as follows: 'Recognition of the figure is inferential, not instinctive.'[13] The large number of unrecognized apparitions—315 first-hand cases out of 830 first-hand cases of realistic apparitions—as well as the large number of apparitions recognized as those of living persons—352 out of 830—show that there is little tendency among Psychical

---

[11] The "or" would literally imply that there were some cases which did not cause fear but in which the physical manifestations of fear were visible—which would be nonsense. Dr. Head probably meant that the patients either confessed fear or showed it by their actions.

[12] Mr. Piddington's No. VII is omitted, since it cannot be condensed into small compass. But it appears improbable that a majority of the psychical hallucinations were preceded by "depression," as Dr. Head says was always true of the hallucinations of his visceral patients.

[13] Or one might put it: "Recognition of the figure is an indirect inference, not an immediate conviction from resemblance."

Percipients to assume causelessly that apparitions represent dead or dying persons, or subsequently to identify an apparition which at the moment of its appearance was unrecognized. In other words, there is little tendency to inferential recognition."

Of the twenty propositions laid down by Dr. Head in regard to visceral visual hallucinations only one, No. II, is true in relation to psychical visual hallucinations. To every other one of his rules, the Census shows exceptions, frequently a majority, nearly always many. Further, where a Census case agrees with one characterization set down by Dr. Head, it disagrees with others. Mr. Piddington says: "I do not believe that there is a single case of hallucination [including those of an auditory character] printed or referred to in the Census Report which completely falls into line with the visceral type."

It follows then that the Census list of cases contains either no or very few visceral cases, and that there is something about the Census hallucinations and those generally to which critical psychic research calls attention which very markedly differentiates them from the hallucinations of visceral disease.

PART TWO

DISCUSSION EVOKED
BY A
QUESTIONNAIRE

I. A HYPOTHETICAL QUESTION
THE QUESTION

Suppose:

(a) That a woman (incidentally I will say that she was a private person discovered by my own experiments, the only one possessing what seemed to me demonstrated powers for this particular kind of experiment whom I have ever myself discovered) sits in the bright light of day, and there is put into her hands a letter written by a person living at some hundreds of miles distance (really a number of the details I give are not necessary to the question, as the question does not call for any opinion as to the accuracy of the facts), the letter folded so that not a word appears on the outside, the letter is held motionless between her palms, so that no conjuring is possible, whatever she says, and all that I say, is taken down verbatim, and she makes thirty-seven statements respecting an unnamed man, a church and its environs, and a journey (nearly all of which could not have been ascertained had she read the whole letter);

(b) That of these thirty-seven statements, nothing could be ascertained respecting three, so that they must be set aside; one proved true but exaggerated, and thirty-three were exactly true regarding the writer of the letter, the church of which he was pastor, and a journey made by him just before the letter was written;

(c) That a prominent mathematician, Alan S. Hawkesworth, F.R.S.A., was called in to pass upon the mathematical probabilities of the items, severally, being hit by chance guessing; he asked me also to estimate, and my estimates proved to favor chance much more than his;

(d) On the basis of my estimates for the items separately, the mathematician then calculated, by exact mathematical processes, the chance of the woman's getting all her results, the thirty-three items separately, one item say one-half right, and found that there was certainly not more than one chance in 5,000,000,000,000,000 of her doing all this by guesses:

Would you then (assuming that the facts are as stated, and that there actually was no possibility of normal leakage of the facts to this woman's consciousness), conclude that the notion that some process of gaining this knowledge, at present not isolated and explained by science, was involved, or would you regard that notion as irrational?

Names, in this and the following sections, with a few exceptions, are given when express permission was granted to print them.

PROFESSOR A. A., a Ph.D. and College President (Church of the Brethren), expressed himself with vigor:

"I am past fifty years of age and I have never yet seen anything that could by any stretch of the imagination be called mysterious. And neither has any one else. It is all due to a half-baked philosophy and to arm-chair science. Forget it and go to work on something that has at least the semblance of truth and reason."

Letter to the president, enclosing a copy of the above hypothetical question:

"I thank you for the interesting reply which you made to the questionnaire sent you. I could not help wondering, as I read that you had never yet seen anything that could by a stretch of the imagination be called mysterious, 'and neither has any one else,' whether you, as a member of the Church of the Brethren, consistently applying that same doctrine to all times as well as our own, would say that in the time of Christ and the apostles no one ever saw anything that could by a stretch of the imagination be called mysterious? And as I read your interesting opinion that 'it is all due to half-baked philosophy and to arm-chair science,' my mind reverted to my two journeys to Europe, to my journey to Mexico, another to Nova Scotia, one to Kansas, one to Missouri, innumerable shorter journeys, and very many hundreds of experiments, and meditated, a little humorously, on what constitutes 'arm-chair science.'

"A number of persons are being asked a certain hypothetical question which I am sending out and of which you will find a copy on a sheet enclosed. The question is purely a logical one, not requiring the least assent to the claims of facts set down therein. Those who answer it may regard those facts as fictitious, the experimenter an imbecile or anything he likes, and he may express himself to that effect. The only thing that is asked is to answer 'yes' or 'no,' on the *assumption* that the facts are true. I have no right to expect this of you, and yet I am not able to see any reason why any man should decline to do it."

A HYPOTHETICAL QUESTION

But the learned member of the ultra-fundamentalist Church of the Brethren did not answer " yes " or " no."

PROFESSOR A. B., PH.D., LL.D., who occupies a university chair in Philosophy, has written works not only on philosophy and psychology, but also on religion (probably of a type related to the Christian Scriptures). The use of his name was allowed, but advantage is not taken of the consent. He says:

" There are many phenomena the explanation of which is ' not apparent.' The question is whether the hypotheses offered by ' spiritism ' are acceptable, and my view is that they are not."

When the words " not apparent " were written in the question, it was fully understood that they were subject to criticism; they were chosen in order to stimulate greater variety and, perhaps, vehemence of expression, and also, guilefully, to bring in incidents which puzzled the learned reporters but for which an experienced psychical researcher might be able to suggest an easy explanation. It could not be expected to occur to the persons addressed that for *this* report bad cases might be wished even more than good ones.

Professor A. B. was reminded that the questionnaire papers did not contain the word " spiritism " and that there are purported psychical phenomena which have no plausible relation to the spiritistic theory.

The hypothetical question was sent him, but he did not reply to it.

MEDICAL DOCTOR A. C., university Professor of Bacteriology, kindly gave advice:

" You will find ' Pancrobilin[?] Pills, Plain,' Reed and Carnrick, a splendid ' antidote.' "

With thanks to the doctor for his prescription and promising to profit by it if there ever should be the least need, he was asked kindly to answer the hypothetical question. The doctor has brains. He saw the deadly two horns of the dilemma, and nimbly leaped the barrier:

" Having, unfortunately, qualified as a witness of fact I may not, under the rules of evidence, answer an hypothetical question."

And there is no such rule of evidence! Thousands of doctors have qualified and testified in court as witness to medical facts and afterwards have answered a hypothetical question related thereto.

DOCTOR OF PHILOSOPHY A. D., miscellaneous writer, Naval Officer, and World War hero (Deist), is (or should I, in view of what is to come, say was?) among those to whom the expression "psychic research" acts as a rubicund fragment of fabric upon a male bovine quadruped. He is willing to be quoted by name, and asseverates:

"By no means. I despise all totally unscientific stuff of this kind, founded on the silly hope of a personal survival in some other existence."

The annotator remarked:

"I thank you for your remarks upon the blank, which I found very interesting. I confess to not being able to appreciate the logic of them, since many alleged psychical phenomena have no apparent relation to the 'hope of a personal survival' and there are many psychical researchers who have no faith in a personal survival."

The hypothetical question was sent him, and he replied:

"I hope you did not find my remarks in any manner flippant, though I think such things should be left to a very few of the highly trained, practical psychologists, just as vivisection should be left to one or two especially qualified physiologists in each State. The danger of course is, that a horde of semi-wits will try to prove individual life of the so-called soul after death.

"I don't know what good any expression of mine would be in regard to your hypothetical question. I am, if anything, a pure agnostic, and do not pretend either to affirm or deny things which I cannot possibly understand. I believe, with Hamlet, that 'there are more things in heaven and earth than are dreamt of in thy philosophy.' Mind reading and many other things have, I take it, been demonstrated, with no wonder on my part. Why not much more wonderful things, since mankind has just begun to think and investigate?

"Therefore,—go to it! I'm with you. If it is worth anything to you, I will state that my impression is, that anything is possible in psychology except seeing into the future; I mean beyond what human experience enables us to prognosticate."

That is frank and manly, and an *amende honorable* for having spoken, as the Psalmist once did, too hastily.

A HYPOTHETICAL QUESTION 213

PROFESSOR A. E., a Ph.D., Psychologist and university teacher of Philosophy (Unitarian), was at first uncompromising enough. He thus expresses himself in liquid terms:

" I have come across a flood of such instances, but none that would seem to me more than the floating superstitions that come out of the wish-wash of sentimentality."

The hypothetical question was sent him. He did not dodge it.

" The case you mention of the woman making the thirty-seven statements picked up from a letter held in her hand, one must confess that that is a challenging instance. I believe I have never had any disposition to be insensitive to such cases. I should like to inquire, however, whether you who stood by were conscious of the contents of the letter. You see I am looking towards the possibility of a very subtle sort of thought transference. Since my student days I have tried to tinker in the direction of discovering evidences of a hypersensitivity of mind in its reaction on mind, and should not be surprised any day to find discoveries in that respect which run parallel to the new energies that physics and chemistry have been opening up of which we were quite innocent a while ago.

"As a working hypothesis, I hold rather strongly to the notion that whatever energies of that type are ever discovered they will move in the direction of thought transference only through some refined means of specific intercommunication. I would not want to swear that they might not happen even with the palm of the hand as interpreter of handwriting, though that staggers me to the point of just about bowling me over."

The professor is one of those men, unfortunately not very common, who, notwithstanding how strongly they have expressed themselves, do not pretend they cannot see facts presented to them and looming up like elephants. He wrote again:

" Thank you heartily for sending this fuller statement about the Baltimore woman. I confess it is challenging if not staggering the report you have made about her. I shall watch for a fuller report, which I dare say you will be writing up in one of the journals.

"As I confessed to you before, I belong to the tougher variety of the students of mental life, though I shall be very happy to have my shell of psychological assurance shattered."

He was informed that the case is to be found in detail in *Proceed-*

ings A. S. P. R. for 1924, pages 204-18, together with all the other experiments with Mrs. King, pages 178-244.

PROFESSOR A. F., a Ph.D., Zoologist and College President (Latter Day Saints), not unwilling that he should be quoted by name, was sent the hypothetical question. His reply consisted in underlining two lines in it, " conclude that the notion that some process of gaining this knowledge, at present not isolated and explained by science, was involved," and saying, " I should conclude the above."

And so should I, and so I do.

DOCTOR OF PHILOSOPHY A. G., Engineer and successful inventor (Presbyterian) says:

" No. Whenever I come into such a circle the operations cease. For many years I offered a substantial prize if any medium could tell me how many peas or beans, dumped into a pan in an adjoining dark room, there were. Quite a few tried, some succeeded. If ' spirits ' can't count a handful of peas or beans lying in one layer on a pan, I don't believe they can do much more."

How prone even scientific men are to read their prepossessions into documents which do not please them! The paper blank sent contained no reference to either " circles " or " spirits," but Dr. A. G. assumes these are what it chiefly concerned.

He was told:

" I thank you for the remarks which you entered upon the blank. I sympathize with you in your effect upon a ' circle,' since, so far as professionals of several alleged species of phenomena are concerned, the effect of my presence, when I am known and do not give a guarantee to keep ' mum,' often seems quite similar. But I do not know whether spirits ought to be expected to count beans in the dark or not. Personally, I am more accustomed to inquire whether certain phenomena which I have actually observed are of ' normal ' causation, than to make the criterion some stunt, which I am unable to be certain would have any bearing upon the situation. Of course, if in a particular ' circle ' the claim should be made that the ' spirit ' is able to go into a dark room, count a lot of small objects and report, your test was an excellent one."

Dr. A. G. is somewhat like the man of the parable who refused to

A HYPOTHETICAL QUESTION 215

go to the vineyard but later was found there, since, although one of the Noes, in reply to the letter, containing the hypothetical question, he says:

"We are all aware of the phenomena of thought transference and hypnotism. They cannot be denied or scientifically explained any more than can gravity, electricity,—we go into the realm of the unknown quickly when we begin to enumerate the many *effects* observed in daily life.

"I believe it possible for some persons accurately to read thought; and I know thoughts can be transmitted long distances. In other words, whatever is known to any living person can be revealed by a 'mind reader' who 'tunes in' on that person's thought emanations."

The writer of the above apparently does not know that to most psychologists, particularly (though there are brilliant exceptions), telepathy is as obnoxious as spiritism. He likewise does not know that telepathy is "supernormal," according to the definition of that provocative word by psychic research. He might justly be added to the list of Yeses.

It may be inferred that, although he does not directly say so, his belief in telepathy is his answer to the hypothetical question. But it ignores the stated fact that many of the facts declared by Mrs. King were not within my conscious knowledge, and some of them were never known to me.

The engineer narrates an experiment he had with Bert Reese which convinced him that this venerable genius was a mind-reader, but as there are reasons for thinking his observations faulty and his inferences erroneous, it is not worth while to print it here. He adds:

"I still contend that my late beloved father and son would, to please me, count beans in a dark room, if able to do so, and transmit to me the result."

Why not make the test a still more satisfactory one, and insist that his father's spirit should go out into a field and plant the beans, while committee men take notes and newspaper reporters crank motion pictures?

If able—most necessary proviso! Even if the father's spirit were able, occasionally, to get into such telepathic *rapport* with a psychic as to inject some of his memories into her consciousness and thus transmit them, it would not follow, as the night the day, that he must be able to go into a dark room, see a lot of beans in the darkness, paw them over, count them correctly, and report the result.

MEDICAL DOCTOR A. H., a Psychiatrist held in honor by his professional brethren, Superintendent of a hospital for the insane, and author (Unitarian), writes that while without personal experiences "which could not be satisfactorily explained as having a basis which would be understood and appreciated by all familiar with mental life and physical laws," he entertains no " prejudice against the investigation of facts which may seem supernormal to others, or even to myself " and has " read with keen interest accounts of many psychic phenomena."

His attitude was commendable, and it was desirable to learn how the hypothetical question would strike such a man. To this Dr. A. H. replied:

" Your letter of the 7th inst., together with mimeographed copy of 'A Hypothetical Question,' has been received. I am not one of those who would throw such a matter aside as being of no particular interest any more than I could accept one such exhibition as you describe, without being personally able to exclude the possibility of collusion or deceit on the part of the woman in question, nor should I be willing to accept beyond question the statement of any other person that there was no such possibility, unless I had full knowledge of all the details connected with the experiment.

" I should, however, take the attitude that if such a phenomenal feat could be done once by any individual, it could be repeated, and I should be actively and honestly interested in further experiments so carefully checked and guarded as to avoid any possibility of deception. Then, if the results were as convincing as they appear to be in the case you have reported, I should be convinced that something had been done, concerning the mechanism of which I knew nothing, that would satisfactorily account for the result of the experiments.

" I think it would be unfortunate if there were some investigators who did not approach these problems in an agnostic frame of mind, prepared as you have done, to check deceit and to further appreciate that not all the possibilities of the human mind have been, as yet, thoroughly catalogued."

If I correctly understand every sentence of the above, then every sentence is approved by me. If I had never personally had proofs from experimentation I certainly should not be convinced by an abstract of such a case, written and signed by Dr. A. H. If I read his full report, and it evidenced conditions and care taken to cover every possible opportunity of leakage, I should be impressed; and if I learned that the author has a reputation for doing careful scientific work, and for experience and skill in the discovery of fraud and the operation of normal causation, I should be still further impressed. I expect no more from any scientific man who himself has either not found or not embraced opportunities for successful experimentation of the kind; to this much I feel entitled.

The demand for repetition of a success is proper, and Mrs. King did have repeated successes. The others of course could not be as brilliant as the case selected because it *was* the best; but several were, as the printed report shows, successful to such a degree that to suggest they were achieved by guesswork is nothing short of being grotesque.

MR. A. I., a man of many adventures, and a writer, particularly about foreign countries, after expressing the opinion that I am " full of prunes," claimed that he was " unable to comprehend what you want to know or what you are driving at. Is it a ghost story you want? "

Somewhat doubting if his mind was quite in that virginal state of innocence regarding psychic research, I yet responded that certainly I would like a ghost story, especially if the narrator could give any evidence for the genuineness of the ghost. I also sent him the hypothetical question and, simply to see how his intellect would cope with the situation, asked what his explanation would be.

He responded by recounting a long dream about a ghost (probably invented for my discomfiture) and ending with an O. Henry climax, save that O. Henry would never have written anything unprintable. He did admit that " the example you present is altogether too deep for my shallow intelligence " (*homo frugi!*) but asked: " But now, really coming right down to plain, every day, common-sense talk, don't you think my example of psychic phenomena a darned sight better than the mathematical process of billions you send me? "

My friend balked at the inquiry addressed to his intellect, and turned to " common-sense talk," which means the tabloids and superficialities of the herd.

PROFESSOR YANDELL HENDERSON, PH.D., of the chair of Applied Physiology at Yale University, returned the observation:

"I have no patience with such superstitious nonsense."

The hypothetical question based on the Mrs. King experiment [1] was sent him. He responded in part:

"I am very glad to answer to the best of my ability the questions which you put to me regarding 'spirit photography,' 'ectoplasm,' 'spirit-slatewriting,' 'telekinesis,' and so on. The answer is that it is only a short time since even well educated people and the most intelligent members of the community believed in witchcraft and ghosts. In fact much of what the orthodox religion of today teaches, or at least expresses in the church services, is equally spiritualistic. All of this seems to be quite well presented in the book on witchcraft by Kittredge, which has just appeared. I enclose a review of this book from the New York *Times*.

"There are fashions in thought as in clothes. The general fashion of our time is to make everything 'scientific.' The particular fashion of this decade is to bring everything that can be under the head of 'psychology.' Following this fashion those instinctive forms of thought which two centuries ago were called witchcraft now appear under the form of the science of psychics, mind reading, telepathy, and so on.

"In regard to the hypothetical question which you put under heads, 'A,' 'B,' 'C,' and 'D,' I do not feel that a calculation of probability has any bearing whatever. It is exactly the same sort of calculation as that by which the theologians prove the necessity for recognizing the existence of God. That argument neither proved nor disproved His existence, nor did it afford the slightest evidence regarding the probability or improbability of His existence. The same sort of argument applies to the existence of life on the planet Mars. An excellent discussion of the worthlessness of calculations of probability, when facts are not available or pertinent, is contained in a book recently published by Fry, entitled *Probability and Its Engineering Uses*. I can report from my own experience a coincidence against which the probabilities can be estimated probably into the billion billions, yet it happened. It consisted in the fact that during just five minutes of my life I was in one place through a most improbable succession of events and that just at that very instant an old lady, a relative of mine, was brought to that spot because of an accident in which she had been wounded in a most unusual way."

The remainder of the professor's very pleasant letter was to the effect possibilities may exist where we do not suspect them, that the

---

[1] See page 209.

A HYPOTHETICAL QUESTION 219

mind is a function of the brain and he thinks purported telepathy is either clever faking or guessing.

Annotator's reply ran:

"Please regard this brief note as simply an expression of thanks for your kindness in taking time to answer my letter. I shall not attempt to controvert any of your opinions or arguments; I was interested, however, in getting your reactions.

"Allow me, however, to correct your intimation that I asked you questions regarding 'spirit photography,' 'ectoplasm,' 'spirit slate-writing,' 'telekinesis,' and so on, of a similar nature. My reference to these alleged phenomena was in connection with my having 'laid bare the methods of certain frauds of these species.' And I will add the remark that there is at least this difference between the case alleged in my hypothetical question and the argument for the existence of God, that the former was capable of being, and actually was, the result of inductive experiment, and susceptible of mathematical estimation within limits, whereas the latter is amenable to neither. Also I will indulge myself to remark that I have repeatedly, in print, remarked that among the almost infinite number of details in a human life it should be expected that sometimes there will occur a singular coincidental combination, and I have given historical instances. Between such a case and the production of thirty-three and one-half coincidental particulars with an error of only one-half by a stranger under circumstances which demonstrably permitted of no normal information (every word by the 'psychic' and by the experimenter being recorded) there exists but little likeness. When you are able to *select* the time and place of your coming upon your relative in connection with an accident, without any conjunctive cause and without actually pushing her under a trolley-car, we can compare the two cases."

Professor Henderson remembers one very unusual accidental coincidence in his lifetime. He gives such scanty data that we are unable to judge whether or not he has exaggerated the mathematical value of the coincidence. And confessedly, it is only a guess. But in the case furnished him from the record of an experiment it was possible to make a reasonable minimum estimate of probability in each of the thirty-three items, after which the one chance out of $5,000,000,000,000,000$ for the thirty-three in combination is easily figured out.[2] And all the steps of the process were laid before readers.

---

[2] Of course it is not meant that this valuation is exact, or anything like it. What is meant is that the separate items were estimated with such evident moderation that the total valuation CANNOT BE LESS THAN THE ENORMOUS FIGURE GIVEN. The margin of error is on the side of the true valuation being more, even very much more.

Now the events in one's lifetime, small and great, including all one's contacts with multitudes of people and events and things, tremendously outnumber all the items in the records of a psychical researcher's experiments with psychics. Hence there is vastly more likelihood of a remarkable coincidental combination occurring in one's miscellaneous and multitudinous affairs than there is of such a combination coming by chance in an experimental record. And yet, if in the course of my years of experimenting I only once got a combination obviously no more complex and unexpected than the coincidence of the professor's meeting his relative just as she had been brought to the spot by an accident, it would not for a moment impress me as being other than a remarkable product of chance. Consequently, there is no reason why I should be brought upon my haunches by the professor's incident.

Cannot it be made so very plain that every reader, be he a man of science or not, will understand? I and other exacting psychic researchers are impressed because in our experimental work we have met *so many* combinations enormously unlikely to come about by chance. Once, and I can think chance the probable explanation; twice, or three times and chance is possible; but I cannot stomach too many chances of prodigious improbability in the course of my experiments. Just so I could well credit that a tenderfoot, casually wandering about the mountains where many have searched in vain, chances to stumble upon a gold mine of immense productivity. It was initially a very unlikely thing to happen, but not at all an incredible one. In the whole history of the West it might happen that there was one instance of a tenderfoot discovering by accident two bonanzas, each in a region supposedly bare. But if this tenderfoot has that good fortune a third time, a fourth and a fifth, in the same circumstances, I cannot credit that all was chance,—posit any cause you please, any imaginable cause is better than to admit that it was all chance.

To put it another way, after the analogy of the many who searched and the one who found mines. I have experimented with many supposed psychics, and with some of them many times. From most of them I never get anything which, taken in bulk, is evidential; with others I sometimes get enough to surmise or even to think there is something in them which the first class do not possess; and there are a few who, along with occasional barren tracts, reveal also evidential oases, and occasional mountain peaks of complex and startling correspondence with external facts, provably unknown to the psychic. If all is guess-work and chance coincidence, how is it that with equally guarded experiments, a few persons persistently loom so much higher than the rest? Does the god chance play favorites?

Study my series of trials with Mrs. Soule, printed in *Leonard and Soule Experiments*, and observe group after group of complicated particulars corresponding almost literally with the remote facts, which could not possibly have been normally known to the psychic. Such as:

A. The description of the objects surrounding the house where I lived as a boy, as they then were, and objects on the farm and in its neighborhood: the martin-house which has been gone more than half a century; the tree out by a path, up which climbed a wild grape-vine; the sage reached by going from the house and passing the caraway, with the wall and prickly bushes near the sage; the journey back of the house which led to an ancient zigzag fence, then to a very rough pasture and a hill with a place dug in it more or less like a cellar, and bushes, bunch-plums and checker-berries growing; in another direction, iris, and trees from which we made whistles; some distance from the house a corn-field beyond which were woods whence the crows came; a spring on the farm and a railroad near enough so that the trains could be heard from the house; a group of buildings in a particular direction from the little hill, with a brook and a little pond back of them. Very few errors in detail, a number of correct ones in addition, such as the cellar on the "back road" where a fire had been. Two errors curiously suggestive, as "sassafras" when referring to something growing in a spot where sarsaparilla really grew; and a name said to sound like DeMerritt associated with the cellar over which the house of G. Myrick really once stood. A combination, with due deduction for the few small errors, incredible as the result of chance.

B. The "Mephistopheles" plus "Teddy" incident.

C. The Story of Stephen, giving the actual name of the man, saying that in my boyhood he made a charge against me which has rankled all my life, stating what the charge was, describing this man's physical appearance, his mind and his manners in detail, saying that he carried the charge to my father, with other particulars the most of which I know are correct and almost none of which I am able to contradict.

D. The prediction of a great disaster, described by many details, and the locality of it also almost unavoidably determined by the description; the disaster coming to pass exactly according to description and, moreover, taking place but three squares from where the sitter spent her girlhood. I have as yet been able to trace no other disaster in American history, which all the given details would by chance fit.

These were not all the great evidential groups. There was that, giving to an astonishing degree of accuracy a great variety of facts about a certain woman, and particularly those relating to her last illness, the latter having the curious appearance as though the stamp of *her* selection were on them, since many are mentioned which were uppermost in her sick mind, while others, of which she knew nothing or little but which are vividly in the memory of surviving relatives, are not mentioned.

Professor Henderson points to one coincidence which he estimates very extraordinary, in the course of the interaction of the innumerable items which have made up his life of more than fifty years. That is one thing, and by what some curiously call " the law of chance," it can happen. But that in material, mostly executed by the slow process of automatic writing, in the course of but a few score hours, the bell of enormous improbability, measuring from say one chance in 100,000 to one in millions, should strike again and again and again, and still again and again, is quite another thing, and it is inverted credulity to suppose it can happen—by mere guess-work.

II. BELIEF IN PSYCHIC EVENTS THE RESULT OF PATHOLOGICAL STATES

The doctrine announced in the title is implicit with one of the learned gentlemen quoted below, explicit with the rest. It may be found occasionally peeping out in other sections.

PROFESSOR B. A., a D.Sc. and Ph.D. who fills a university chair of Anatomy, author on his subject (Baptist), says:

"*Not one* man or woman who has had real training in and is *capable to grasp* the development, architecture and functions of the nervous system ever uses the stock terms of your group except in derision. The brain and spinal cord *is* an organ as much so as liver, kidneys, etc., reacting to its appropriate stimuli, and its more complicated architecture naturally allows more complicated reaction phenomena. From primitive times and in the jungle and Catholic races today ignorance of and inability to grasp structural detail as related to function has resulted in a set of secondary reactions of the apparatus known as superstition."

To Professor B. A.:

"Although not technically anatomists, I should have thought that the following persons, among others, had, in their time or now, considerable acquaintance with the development, architecture and functions of the nervous system: William James, F. W. H. Myers, F. C. S. Schiller of Oxford, Prof. William McDougall, Dr. T. W. Mitchell. They have used the terms to which you object, without derision.

" If no ' psychical ' phenomena are possible on account of the brain and spinal cord being ' an organ as much so as the liver, kidneys, etc., reacting to its appropriate stimuli, and its more complicated structure naturally allows more complicated phenomena,' it seems clear that, by the same reasoning, the mind can originate no thinking by its own activity, or, in other words, that all mental activity is the mechanical reaction from stimuli. Wundt, the founder of physiological psychology, held, at the maturer stage of his career, that the mind is an entity in itself. Would you hold that he had no real training in or was not capable of grasping the development, architecture and functions of the nervous system? Ladd, the American physiological psychologist, agreed with his old master. Do you think him lacking in the respects specified?

"I am not writing with the slightest intention of arguing or opposing your views, but only with the desire of understanding you, as I try to understand other correspondents who express themselves, as it seems to me, obscurely, or who seem to me to be facing two ways at one time. I see by *Who's Who* that you report yourself as being a Baptist. I have known many Baptists, and all I ever knew expected to survive bodily death. But if the mind is only a stream of reactions from stimuli applied to the brain and spinal cord, I cannot see any rational basis whatever for such an expectation. Furthermore, most Baptists believe that many 'psychic' facts took place in New Testament times, such as the Peter and Cornelius incident (call it the work of superior intelligences or rationalize it as an instance of telepathy). Certainly, any objection to telepathic and other 'psychic' incidents now equally shuts out such incidents in the Bible. If our inquiries whether there is anything in such claims is 'superstition,' then I suppose that holding these New Testament incidents as other than fictitious or legendary would be superstition. If not, I would very much like to know why not. Perhaps you discard everything of the sort in the accounts of the Evangelists, the Acts and the Epistles. If so, you are quite consistent in your science, but I cannot help wondering what has become of you as a Baptist!

"Really, I was glad to get the expression of your views, and am writing as above solely in the hope that you will open them up a little more fully."

The hope was in vain.

MEDICAL DOCTOR B. B. is a physician, formerly Professor of Materia Medica in a homeopathic medical college, author, permits his name to be given, but on the whole it is perhaps best not to print it. He sets forth his theory thus:

"I am of the opinion that one universal force, or mode of motion, that has been sufficiently demonstrated, operates as fear, ecstasy, hysteria, telepathy, clairvoyance and coincidental dreams, from one individual to another in a purely mechanical manner. Persons troubled with visions and apparitions are, quite certainly, afflicted with static."

This seemed to the commentator a fine piece of schizologic (to coin a word meaning a piece of purported logic consisting of an assumption and a conclusion separated by an unbridged gap), and he was curious to have it put at its best. Hence the following:

PATHOLOGICAL STATES

"I wish you would develop and clarify your statement. As it stands, it seems to me to raise as many questions as it attempts to answer, such as,

"(a) Do you mean that the one universal force or mode of motion which 'operates as fear, ecstasy,' etc., *is* fear, ecstasy, etc., or that it produces fear, ecstasy, etc.? I presume you mean the latter (though the terms would seem to imply former), after analogy of those modes of motion which precede, as causes in part of vision and sound, which are not themselves modes of motion.

"(b) Demonstrated by whom, in what treatises, for example?

"(c) Whether you are not denying that there is valid telepathy or clairvoyance or coincidental dreaming or supernormal significance, as I suppose from the derisive expression 'afflicted with static'?

"(d) If you deny the validity of telepathy, visions, etc., are you also denying the validity of fear, whether as an actual emotion, or one which often is based on adequate grounds? (I should suppose so from their being classed together as due to the one universal force.)

"(e) Whether there is more reason for classifying fear with clairvoyance, etc., as due to the operation of one universal force, than there is for including other emotions than fear which can be transmitted from one person to another by persuasion, suggestion, etc., such as courage and confidence, the opposite of fear?

"(f) Whether, to isolate one particular, your expression 'operates as fear, ecstasy, hysteria, telepathy, clairvoyance and coincidental dreams from one individual to another,' does not carry with it the admission that, in your opinion, there is such a thing as telepathy?

"(g) Whether, if there is such a thing as telepathy, in the form of transmitted dreams ('operates . . . from one individual to another') or otherwise, the phenomenon is not eminently worth investigation?

"(h) Whether this mental phenomenon's being the consequent of a 'universal force,' or its production 'in a purely mechanical manner,' makes it any the less worth study? Are not scientists seriously and worthily engaged in studying forces which operate in a mechanical manner, and their results?

"(k) Whether, if there is some interference with the one universal force or mode of motion, justifying the term 'static,' which operates to produce 'visions and apparitions,' it should not be studied? You must be aware that the static of the radio is *not* fully understood, and is being studied.

"(l) If 'persons troubled with visions and apparitions are, quite certainly, afflicted with static,' I suppose that somewhere the demonstration of that fact can be found in print. I do not mean assertion of the fact. An entire certainty can be demonstrated. I will be gratified if you will name the book or article in which this certainty is demonstrated, or any attempt is made to demonstrate it."

Dr. B. B.'s reply answered none of the questions, but reiterated his formula, and added that "mathematical processes" will probably determine the "value in these phenomena," and that taking "as a foundation measurements of vital processes operating normally in all organisms, statical or fixation points produced by specific toxic substances such as alcohol, ether, hashish, marihuana, and absinthe should be of value in checking conclusions as to the accuracy of pending calculations," thus throwing "light upon such phenomena as hallucinations, illusions and delusions, including visions and apparitions."

Presumably as an illustration of the effects of the "one universal force" the good doctor closed with an incident which was one, he says, of "presumed telepathic communication."

"At a public entertainment a man passed rapidly about the audience glancing at different objects presented to him, asking the name of each of a blindfolded woman on the stage of the theatre. I gave him a slip of paper upon which I had written a name of my invention. To his inquiry, 'What word am I looking at?' she correctly replied, 'That is a funny word, f-l-o-g—flog; I never heard of that word before.'" [It was the word written.]

Still curious to see whether the doctor could be induced to attempt the construction of a bridge over the gap in his argument, or could be made to see that the gap existed, W. F. P. wrote him as follows:

"I should have been glad if you had cared to give your reactions to all the points which I brought up in my letter, but do not complain because you did not. But, it is fair to you to admit that your second very courteous letter leaves me still puzzled. Let me put my difficulty in the simplest and most concrete way.

"For example, you think that the one universal force or mode of motion accounts for apparitions. I cheerfully admit that this might be, if only the apparition *as such* were the problem presented to us. But in many cases this is not the fact. Does it also, to your mind, satisfactorily account for *the frequent coincidences between the time of the apparition of a person and the time of his death or his undergoing some great emotional disturbance?* Would it satisfactorily explain a woman's seeing, while awake and in the daylight, the apparitions of her dead father and her living brother, at the time when he, standing on the deck of a war vessel in the North Sea watching an enemy torpedo approach the ship, saw the apparition of his father beside him? Allowing that these were facts, does your formula give any *comprehensible* solution of the double coincidence (a) in time and (b) in the persons and person seen? I do not ask you to admit that any such facts ever occurred.[1] My question is purely one of logic; if they did occur, does your formula of 'one universal force or mode of motion' explain or make a particle clearer to your intelligence how, not simply the apparitions, but the coincidences involved were brought about? Would you say that the force or mode of motion split, at a point midway between brother and sister, and went in two directions at the same time? My query is not if you still adhere to the dogma, but if it helps you to *understand?*

"I will remark that in my judgment all public performances which profess to exhibit telepathy, and which work with almost unerring accuracy, are done by cues passing from the person walking about in the audience to the person on the platform. The nature of these cues would not be recognized by one person in a thousand, previously inexperienced in this sort of thing. There are many methods known to me, and doubtless some with which I am not acquainted."

It is not worth while to print the doctor's concluding letter, as the only intelligible relevant sentence in it is one which says that "it is impossible for me to make answer to several of your requests, as I consider the field tenanted by spectres has not been covered by qualified investigators." But the one question which faced him in the last letter he received did not hinge on any confidence in either facts or investigators. It was one purely of the logic related to his formula. He perceived that it was deadly, and jumped over the fence.

PROFESSOR B. C., an E.E. and teacher of Civil Engineering in a university (Presbyterian), gives his opinion that:

"Most cases reported to you may be classed under deranged stomach or nervous system, or a desire to tell or retell something of a startling nature."

Eager to learn the process by which colic or shaky nerves could bring knowledge of a fact happening ten or thousands of miles away, the annotator wrote:

"Whatever my own opinion may be, I have no missionary spirit and no desire to convert any one to it. Therefore my only reason for writing this letter is that I hope to have your theory, which as it stands in the above sentence is, I fear, but *obiter dictum*, stated so as to be more

---

[1] But they did, according to consentient testimony unreasonable to doubt.

impressive. Just a little more clearly, *how* the deranged stomach, for example, would produce what we find in many well attested cases.

"Take that of Lord Brougham, who, as you know, was one of the greatest lawyers and finest intellects of England. He saw an 'apparition' of a friend of his who had been in India for years, and about whom he had not heard for years, sitting in a chair as fine as life, and wrote down the fact in his diary. *Afterward*, he learned that his friend had died upon that very day—it being several weeks before the news came. I can understand how the stomach-ache might produce a visual hallucination (although one seldom does), but what needs to be explained is the process by which it brought about the death of the man seen, on the same day. Out of numerous testimonies of persons of apparently good stomachs and nerves, I select for its brevity, another incident, this time relating to John Muir, the naturalist. He was high on the Sierras, when he became impressed with the feeling that Professor Butler, his old teacher, living in the East, from whom he had not heard for months, was near, and made the five-hour journey down into the valley. He found Butler's name on the hotel register, for he had arrived that day. Butler had started up the mountain, and Muir went after him, finding him lost at sundown. We have the account over Muir's signature, and Butler's endorsement. I could credit that the 'deranged nervous system' of the hardy naturalist gave him the notion that Butler was down in the valley, and caused him to do such a foolish thing as to walk five hours to find him, but it is not clear how Butler happened actually to be there and to have just come. Nor do I see how the entry in Brougham's diary is accounted for by the desire to tell something of a startling nature, while that theory applied to both the sober naturalist and the pedagogue seems to me a rather drastic application of pure dogma.

"As I glance back, it looks as though I were trying to ridicule your theory, but nothing could be further from my thoughts; it is the bare application of the theory to the facts which produces that appearance. As stated, the formula sounds neither sophisticated nor adequate. If you would explain the rationale, point out the steps in the process by which Muir's hypothetical colic or jumpy nerves or desire to tell something of a startling nature informed him that a man supposed to be three thousand miles away was near at hand, I would be sincerely grateful."

To this the professor kindly replied:

"I still maintain that my views on psychic cases is correct—'most cases reported to you may be classed under deranged stomach or nervous system, or a desire to tell or retell something of a startling nature.'

PATHOLOGICAL STATES 229

"It appears that most psychic believers forget all about the factor of COINCIDENCE in the events of human life as well as all events of the universe. Millions of coincident things are happening daily. As a simple but vivid example, automobile accidents are caused by the common coincidence of two cars arriving at a street crossing at the same time. A few seconds earlier or later for one of the cars might spoil the case of coincidence and save a few lives.

"I wish to cite a case which might be classed as psychic except for the missing factor—coincidence.

"A father, sleeping alone in his home, was suddenly roused by screams of his wife (who was several hundred miles away) calling him by his first name. He recognized his wife's voice, but it was only a dream, as the wife experienced nothing unusual. Years later the wife experienced great suffering and danger without any psychic effect on the father. Years later a daughter of the pair was almost killed in an accident (brought about by coincidence) without any psychic experience by father or mother. Now if any two or all three of these events had happened within a few hours, I suppose it would be called a most evident psychic case. But why is it that when coincidence is missing the psychic fades away?

"Take away entirely the factor of coincidence in the cases of Lord Brougham and John Muir, and what do you have left? Then go back and read the quotation relating to stomach, nerves, etc., and you have absolutely nothing left. The only reasonable way of scientifically analyzing what appear to be psychic, ghost or witch cases, is to first apply the test of eliminating coincidence."

The reply to Professor B. C., considerably revised, as it was written hastily, follows:

"I care nothing about '*most* psychic believers,' and think that your estimate may be true. The psychic investigators with whom I have anything in common by no means neglect the possibilities of coincidence. The only way we can 'eliminate it' is by mathematical computations of likelihood. No one instance could eliminate it, unless it be an instance of a great many and rare particulars, and it would still be theoretically possible that all were merely collective coincidence, as it would remain mathematically possible that once in a million or quintillion times the combination would turn up. [Here the Mrs. King case, which surpassed chance expectation 5,000,000,000,000,000 to 1, was outlined.] This is but one of many calculations which I have made or had made to estimate the *likelihood* of coincidence being the explanation.

"The case mentioned by you, of the man who was wakened with the hallucination of his wife's voice screaming his name, would not be deemed by a cautious psychic researcher as conclusive in and by itself, though it had proved that she incurred an accident at that hour. It is well recognized that hallucinations of all kinds may result from disturbed physical or mental conditions, contemporaneous sensory stimulations, etc. But if as remarkable coincidental incidents accumulate they become evidence sufficient to warrant further collection of cases and calculation of chance expectation.

"I do not think that you realize how little one or two cases such as you cite of startling and unusual experiences which do not coincide, count against a case of the same sort which does coincide within, say, the hour. Suppose it were established that on the average every person has one visual hallucination in his lifetime, or that part of it which can be remembered, in say fifty years. One of these is wakened to see an apparition of his mother, and in the same hour, at a great distance, there being no knowledge that death was impending, his mother dies. That one case would *prove* nothing. But it would defeat chance *expectation* in the ratio of 437,999 to 1. If the other nine persons had each a similar experience in his lifetime with nothing in the way of correspondence, these nine cases taken together, *being what would be expected*, would mathematically weigh almost nothing against the one absolute correspondence.

"It astonishes me that you think the 'coincidence' of two automobiles hitting each other parallel with the cases which are taken into consideration by psychical research. That seems to me a mere juggling with a word. In that sense there is a 'coincidence' equally every time a car *meets* another car. And under ordinary circumstances that 'coincidence' is *certain* to happen dozens or hundreds of times an hour at the same spot. But was it certain, when the psychic told me that I had owned a cat named Mephistopheles (a fact of long ago that no one living but myself could have vindicated), that this would be the case? In close connection with the declaration that I had owned a cat of that name, one other name came, but with no implication that it belonged to the cat. Was it certain—was it likely—that this name, Teddy, should have been as relevant to the context and to me as that the last dog I had owned (as Mephistopheles of thirty-five years ago was the last cat) should have been named Teddy? Was it certain when the eminent physicist (whose name I have not received permission to give, but whose story I have heard from his own lips) was wakened by the 'hallucination' of hearing his father call him by name, that the far-distant father, whose illness was to him unknown, should have died at that hour?

"One car hitting another car presents no problem to the intellect. But if, without knowledge of or influencing the plans of the drivers, a person should pick out a given car, say in Boston, and another in Cambridge, and put on record the statement that the two would hit each other on a given day, and it happened as stated, we would have the problem whether the coincidence of the utterance with the event was from *chance* or from some perhaps hidden cause.

"Of course; 'take away the factor of coincidence, ... and what do you have left?' Take away the factor that I had owned a cat named Mephistopheles, and a Teddy, and of course there isn't anything left. Take away the fact that the psychic whom I earlier mentioned hit the bell $33\frac{1}{2}$ times out of 34, and of course there is nothing left. One does not solve a problem by *taking away* one of the two factors which constitute it a problem. The question is whether such a tremendous percentage of hits is *likely* to have been due to *chance* coincidences. I do not think that one or a dozen cases even as extraordinary as this entirely settles the question, but the progressive accumulation of instances which are capable of some mode and degree of calculation, makes it more and more difficult to ascribe all to chance."

MEDICAL DOCTOR B. D., an M.D. and Sc.D., former university Professor of Ophthalmology, prominent ophthalmic surgeon and author, permitted the use of his name, but it is omitted lest some readers should think that a man really held in respect is derided. To the questionnaire he responded:

"Each and every one of the honestly reported so-called psychic phenomena have been, are, and will be elucidated by coincidence, the psychoses of delusions and hallucinations, the conditions of the dream state or hypnosis due to external or auto-suggestion and unconscious cerebration. Reports of such events have been impressed upon minds prepared to believe in supernatural manifestations and favored by trickery of dishonest charlatans. All such events appreciable to the senses have been duplicated, explained and exposed by well known prestidigitateurs.

"Unless the new book treats psychic manifestations as explainable by natural laws it would simply be a further contribution to superstition and subversive of science."

In the hope of moving him to further expression, this was written:

"I often wonder, when reading such comments, at the frequent belief that all persons known as 'psychical researchers' are naïvely unfamiliar with the considerations which you lay down.

"Take myself, as a humble example. It happens that perhaps no living American has printed so much explanatory, analytical and destructive of 'physical phenomena' of certain types, 'spirit photography,' 'spirit slate-writing,' fake telepathy, etc., etc., as I have done. I have never seen any mediumistic physical phenomena which convinced me. It is entirely likely that I have a much larger range of actual acquaintance with conjuring, and the psychology of deception, than yourself. My *Doris Case of Multiple Personality* has often been called a 'classical' case; you are evidently unacquainted with it, or you would not suppose that the possibilities of 'the psychoses of delusions and hallucinations, the conditions of the dream state or hypnosis due to external or auto-suggestion' are to me unknown territory, nor am I the only investigator in this field to whom such themes are familiar, and who are almost daily taking them into consideration. I confess that 'unconscious cerebration,' that incantatory term inherited from Carpenter, Beard, etc., is to me as meaningless as 'abracadabra.'

"Neither the circular letter nor the blank we are sending out has anything to do with the 'supernatural,' which is the word which I find twice in your letter. I have not the remotest idea that anything exists which is not as *natural* as anything else. But we may be forced to a wider definition of the term.

"The Society for Psychical Research in England was founded by university men, among them Professor Sidgwick, called 'the most incorrigibly skeptical man in England.' Psychical research in America was also the offspring of university training. Certain representatives have indeed in several lands been fooled by jugglery. But the field of mental phenomena has furnished instances which have been stenographically reported, critically analyzed, and thoroughly authenticated, and which, as a matter of history, no man who scorns the whole subject has boldly faced and fairly discussed, with view to explanation, in forty years.

"I do not in the least resent what you have written; and am so familiar with such sentiments that they cause me no disquiet whatever. I do not think, however, that either you or I know where 'natural laws' begin or end. But I am quite certain that it is intelligent to investigate any subject whatsoever, and unintelligent to limit the scope of inquiry, whether on the ground that it is 'impious,' or the opposite ground that looks so curiously similar, that it is 'superstitious.'"

The doctor replied, with excellent *bonhomie:*

"Since the receipt of your letter I have reread ——— and some of the psychic or rather psychiatric publications of ———. The credulity of the latter, the vermicular verbosity of ——— and the puerility of ———, Doctor of Science (from where?) only appeal to my scientific training, research in psychiatry and their application in medical practice for more than forty years. ' Can'st thou minister to a mind diseased? '

"I am heartily in favor of research, but its findings should be substantiated by something more than personal introvert testimony, which in every case may be explained as errors of observation and the conclusions reached as unsubstantiated by other than known causes. In the case of high authorities as noted in the first part of my letter, I would quote Ingersoll, ' The mistakes of Moses.'

"Do not misunderstand me in using the term ' supernatural.' That is not necessarily applied to a ghostly domain. I confine it to the ' evidence ' of those who do not either accept or who do not understand the limitations of material things and the forces moving, ions, atoms, molecules and finite bodies. I recognize the possibility that ' There are more things in heaven and earth, Horatio, than are dreamed of in thy philosophy.' Go to it, collect the material, evaluate and issue the material in terms of human understanding! *Magna est veritas et prevalibit.*

"For your own information to show experience in psychiatry and personality study: some of the titles following my name are: M.D., F.A.C.S., Sc.D. (Flight Surgeon, Air Corps U. S. A., Exam. Bureau Aeronautics Dept. Commerce, Colonel Med. Res. U. S. A.), etc."

From a letter to Dr. B. D.:

"I like you, and if we were neighbors I am sure I should like you better; I like your being from Missouri (which, if I know myself, was always my disposition), and your final admission that there may be more things in heaven and earth, Horatio, etc. I like your humor. And because you have humor, you too will probably be amused, at any rate will not take offense, at my few remarks.

"Having read my letter which stated something of the frauds I had exposed, and my poor opinion of the majority of the books written about ' spiritualism ' and psychical research, you inform me that you promptly reread ———'s '———' and ———'s book, as though giving my views another chance. Since there is no man who has proved so many of ———'s blunders and so rudely reproved him for his easy credulity as I have done in print, and since I do not in the least believe in ———'s medium, but think she was a fraud, and that his experiments were evidentially of little value, is it any wonder I smiled? It is as if I brought against ophthalmology the malpractice of a chiropractor who undertakes to cure diseases of the eye by cracking the vertebræ.

"You remarked that ' I am heartily in favor of research, but its findings should be substantiated by something more than personal introvert testimony.' I should say so indeed! But it seems strange to me that so many able men will not bring their minds to the grindstone enough to see that there are kinds of experiences which are not affected even by the fact (if fact it be), that the subjects of them are introverts. Take one actual case out of many. [Here the Osgood case was outlined, as on page 337.] Now what the heck difference does it make whether the subjects of this compound incident were introverts or not? You might take the ground that all the parties combined to lie, but that is shifting the ground.

"I don't know whether you were having fun with me in your postscript or not. It reads: 'For your own information to show experience in psychiatry and personality study, some of the titles following my name are M.D., F.A.C.S., Sc.D., (Flight Surgeon, Air Corps U. S. A., Exam. Bureau Aeronautics Dept. Commerce, Colonel Med. Res. U. S. A., etc.).'

"Now I was perfectly aware of your very high standing as an ophthalmologist and surgeon, and of your meritorious services during the war, etc., etc., but without for a moment intimating that you have not great knowledge of psychiatry

'I'll eat my hand if I understand'
how the facts that you are a Doctor of Medicine, a Fellow of the American College of Surgeons, a Doctor of Science, a Colonel and formerly connected with aeronautics and the department of commerce are supposed to demonstrate that you are. And while I am afraid that my respect for the good sense of ——— is not much greater than yours, don't you really think that, before you wrote in reference to him, 'Doctor of Science—from where,' you ought to have looked into *Who's Who*, to see if you told where you got *your* D.Sc.? *Touché!* Especially as it is the custom to do so in *Who's Who*, and not the general custom on title-pages."

Final letter by the doctor:

"Received your joshing letter of the 14th inst. which, in a way, I think I brought on myself by too much exhibition of authority. However, being hardboiled and my experience having shown that all visions are purely subjective and hallucinatory, I remain to be convinced that there is any other explanation for subjective conveyance of sensation except through the material world.

"I would certainly like to meet you and I could assure you we would have many delightful encounters which would probably prove to be a draw."

———

MEDICAL DOCTOR B. E., Alienist and Superintendent of a State hospital for the insane, thus responded to the question whether he knew of psychic incidents: "Only in psychopathic reactions and actual psychotic states."

A letter to the doctor informed him that:

"Any incident of which an insane person was the subject, and which was unexplainable by normal knowledge and faculty, would be of as much interest as such an incident in the case of a person of sound mind, for surely the mere fact of insanity would not explain it. I suppose your reference is to curious rather than to supernormal incidents, and unless I hear from you to the contrary, I will assume that this is your meaning."

He did not reply, so probably his utterance was mere raillery, a mode of argument held in high esteem by some learned men, where psychic research is concerned, since it affords satisfaction to the emotions and a minimum of mental effort.

PROFESSOR B. F., a Ph.D. and occupant of the chair of Economics in a university, also writer on that subject, answers:

"No—so far as I know no member of my family or forbears has been 'psychic,' had St. Vitus dance or gone insane. They seem to be of a very long-lived, hard-headed, rather skeptical stock who devote themselves to living in one world at a time."

Certainly the logic of these observations is that having experiences provisionally called "psychic" is on a par with having St. Vitus's dance or being insane; and that persons so unfortunate as to have such experiences are unlikely to be long-lived, hard-headed, of skeptical bent or practical.

In order that his position might not be misunderstood, the professor was asked to put a cross after each of the following affirmations which corresponded with his deliberate opinion.

Persons who have and testify to psychic experiences
  1. Tend to have short lives.
  2. Seldom appear to be hard-headed.
  3. Are usually, if not always, of credulous bent.
  4. Tend to be other-worldly (or mystical) people.

The professor maintained a dignified silence. On second thought it probably came to him that he had no proof that what he had plainly implied was not piffle, as in fact it was. Take the book *Noted Witnesses for Psychic Occurrences*, and test as to ages. The first twenty named, the dates of whose deaths were ascertained, and omitting one who died a violent death, lived to the ages of 77, 75, 66, 72, 65, 55, 71, 76, 46, 84, 75, 90, 73, 69, 71, 81, 66, 69, 77 and 75, or an average of about 71 years 8 months. Further examination in the same book will prove that the other three propositions are equally shaky.

BACHELOR OF SCIENCE B. G., member of a prominent firm of publishers and author of stories, is moved to ejaculate:

" Put the ' yes ' people in an asylum."

How can one treat so flippant an utterance with respect? A response is best couched in terms of humor, and yet humor that contains a devastating array of facts. If the " yes " people are simpletons or unbalanced, how is it that so many of them have been men of genius and shapers of history?

" I received your suggestion (with becoming modesty not signed) : ' Put the " yes " people in an asylum,' with joy, not to say with hilarity.

" Had I been for the last few centuries or so the Grand Bailiff of the race for the purpose of putting all the ' yes people in an asylum,' what a choice assortment I could have collected! Lord Brougham and Erskine, those eminent lawyers and statesmen; Chauncey Depew, the foxy man of business and after-dinner oratory; Linnæus, Muir, Pumpelly and Romanes, who they do say knew something about science; those doughty military leaders, Garibaldi, Buller and Earl Roberts; ' Ian MacLaren,' Scott, Sir Gilbert Parker, who have charmed our leisure hours; Goethe and Browning, who have lifted us on the wings of song; even Harry Kellar the magician, and Houdini, who did tell one spooky story as though he believed it (and privately told me another). The sweet strains of Schumann and Saint-Saëns would have been hushed; a heroic story of African exploration would never have been told, with Stanley kept pacing his padded cell. Burbank's amazing work with plants would have been cut short, Pickett would never have led his immortal charge, Obregon would have died not as the President of Mexico, but in a lunatic asylum. A lunacy commission would have given the Bishop of Texas attention, and a bailiff would have fetched the Bishop of London from Lambeth Palace. Time and space fail to catalogue all whom I would have to put into that asylum, which, heaven knows, would have been too much crowded. Abraham Lincoln would have had to be shut up there; there would be no statues to Jeanne d'Arc, for she would early have been hurled in willy-nilly. No German Reformation would have happened, for Luther would have been chucked in before it commenced. No doubt you are right, yet I tremble to think how history would have suffered if all the 'yeses' had been immuned as soon as their symptoms broke out. Even now I have the secrets of several scientists and psychologists of the first rank living in this country; probably they are afraid of a pogrom, for they don't tell the world, yet they have told me—I know that they are among the 'yeses,' and therefore by all rights should be in straightjackets and that asylum, and yet, we should miss 'em. I even know more than one publisher, one a confessed 'yes' but the other not—these should have been rammed into one of the cells, but how many books we should have lost!

"I hope, my dear Mr. ———, that you are not a solemn and Puritanic gentleman, in which case you probably will not mind my hilarity more than I did your apparently relentless exclamation. I don't believe that you have the spirit of a Torquemada, but rather that you are inclined to let such foolish folk as I have named run loose, after all."

III. THE ARGUMENT FROM NEGATIVED "PREMONITIONS"

In several of the following instances the word Monition would have been preferable to Premonition. Psychic research is not particularly fond of either, since both seem to imply purposed notice given, one of something happening, the other of something to happen. But in the great majority of instances, as where an apparition is seen of a person at the moment of his death, or a dream attracts attention because of its complex correspondence with a distant event, there is no evidence of intent. In many instances it has been shown that the dying person was talking about the person who, at about the same time, saw his apparition, and hence we infer probable or possible telepathy, but not that there was an effort on the part of the one dying to bring about a visual hallucination of himself.[1]

Is there any one so naïve, one wonders, as to think that, if some dreams, for instance, are telepathic, all dreams should be so. Take the case of the dream of Mr. Deering.[2] While his daughter was silently and with repugnance reading about a tall man who carried a coffin from the room in which were Marie Antoinette and some other ladies, he dreamed of a tall man in a room in which were several other dimly-seen figures, and that the man took up the coffin and was in the act of withdrawing. Or the forthwith recorded dreams of Miss Griggs, which so closely corresponded with pictures in magazines at which her mother at the same time was interestedly looking.[3] Would it affect the problem which such striking and complex parallels present to learn that Messrs. A, B, and so on to X had never experienced any such parallel dreams?

The gentlemen quoted below appear, unless for one exception, good-natured toward psychic research, but to suspect that their negative experiences damage the argument for premonition. No psychic researcher supposes that having indefinite worries or dreads, dreaming frequently that a particular person is dead, having a sudden feeling that something has happened to somebody, or even to an especial per-

---

[1] This is not to deny that there is evidence that some instances of a deliberate effort to telepathically affect a designated person so as to cause him to see an apparition of the experimenter, have been successful.
[2] *Phantasms of the Living*, I, 400.   [3] *Bulletin* IX, B. S. P. R.

son who is on a journey, having a visual hallucination in pneumonia, being prevented by accident from going on board a steamer, or apprehension of mortal danger where such danger actually exists, gives any reasonable ground for expecting the experience will prove to be a " premonition."

PROFESSOR W. F. GANONG, PH.D., who has the chair of Botany at Smith College, and has written much on his subject, says "Yes" to the question whether his name may be printed. And since he has made a real argument, there seems to be no reason why he should regret the permission.

" Several times in recent years, I have had sudden vivid impressions of something wrong with near and dear relatives,—an invalid mother, a brother on distant travel, or one of my children from whom I was then separated. It usually had something of the form of a picture of the way the persons concerned would look if injured, or in a definite kind of trouble, or dead. In one or two cases at least the impression was sufficiently arresting to make me note down the time and date. In no case, however, did anything comparable with the impression occur. Obviously if by chance it had, I could have said ' yes ' on your letter of inquiry, and would have had a fine incident to send you.

" I suppose that such sudden ' visions ' of disaster to persons much in one's thoughts (especially in cases of those who, like myself, are of a ' worrying ' temperament), are of the same genus as those sudden recollections of events, often most trivial and long past, which flash into the mind without any determinable connection with matters in conscious thought at the time (for this is characteristic of the impressions mentioned above), and if it should some time happen (as it must in time for those having many such flashes) that some mention of, old note on, or other mode of connection with, the matter soon turns up, a causal connection for the positive case would be assumed, the many negatives being forgotten or ignored in the desire to father a wonder.

" I have a sister who believes and recounts many such incidents told her by others, but I do not think that she claims to have had any such experiences herself.

" The above is written in no spirit of hostility to inquiries being made, but on the contrary with full sympathy for them. But I am of opinion that the overwhelming majority of such experiences rest in occasional chance coincidences of a real event with very many imagined ones, the coincidence needing not to be very close in view of mankind's inveterate tendency to perfect a story."

Our comments on the above are made with entire respect. Professor Ganong is undoubtedly correct in his opinion that the overwhelming majority of coincidences of which people talk, taking into account all grades of people who relate them and all the grades and types of coincidences by their narrators thought to be psychic, are significant of nothing but chance. But this affirmation gives no help in deciding whether or not there are coincidences fraught with supernormal significance, any more than the fact that the overwhelming majority of girls who think that they have the making of prima donnas negates the existence of Pattis and Galli-Curcis.

"Mankind's inveterate tendency to perfect a story" is too broad a statement to be correct. There are those "who desire to father a wonder," most certainly, and there are also those who do not, who are troubled and puzzled by being the victim of a seemingly psychic incident, or who at least tell it only to a few and shrink from its publicity.

No doubt, too, that with many persons "the many negatives" of a commonplace order are forgotten and the one hit, although equally commonplace, is remembered. But Professor Ganong is a witness to the fact that persons may remember negatives. He has had no hit and he remembers a number of his failures.

He would, in case of a chance coincidence with one of his periods of foreboding, have had a "fine incident" to send. Perhaps not so fine as he thinks. He would have received a list of queries including whether and how many times on other occasions he had had "impressions of something wrong," and whether and how many external correspondences there had been. Having admitted a number such impressions and no other correspondences of fact, his fine story would have been discounted just so much. If the hit had coincided with the death of a relative, and a query brought out the fact that he knew of the relative's serious illness, it would have suffered further discount, and so on.

His sister believes and tells many such incidents gleaned by others, but has had none herself. So the will-to-believe does not with her act as some psychologists would expect it to do. The fact is that human beings cannot be divided into just two classes. There are those who are skeptical and yet have the experiences, those who believe in them, yet have none, and vice-versa. There are those who exaggerate their odd experiences as time goes on, and those in whose memories they tend to dim.

I doubt if a large percentage of human beings ever had "very many imagined" incidents of the kind to forget. All the professor claims, in spite of that "worrying temperament" which in his case probably explains them, are "several," and he remembers them, although they were not fulfilled. The present writer cannot remember and does not believe that he ever in his life had a single picture like those described or a feeling that something was wrong with a relative or friend, unless there was an assignable reason for the feeling.

Then, too, if only once out of the " several " times, *what Professor Ganong pictured* had happened, *without any known antecedent danger that it might*, he would still have had, if not a fine story, one sufficiently beyond chance expectation to warrant attention. With that proviso, even if, in the course of the last ten years he ten times had a feeling that disaster had happened to a particular person, the chance of being correct within the day, in one of those ten cases, would be small.

But most important of all is it to observe the vast difference between types of "impressions," and the evidential quality attaching to them when they prove to be coincidental with a precisely pertinent event. Professor Ganong worries, and mentally pictures how a particular person would look if injured, etc. We do not get from his narrative the conviction that there was anything specially startling about them, although in " one or [?] two cases the impression was sufficiently arresting to make me note down the time and date." But contrast these with the incident of three persons seeing the face of a Mrs. Robinson (*Phantasms of the Living*, II, 244-7), two of them who knew her, recognizing her at the moment, and the third, who had never seen her, afterward spontaneously recognizing her portrait; Mrs. Robinson's death having taken place without their knowledge, the same afternoon. Contrast with the case of the man who died in America on the eve of departure for England, and on the date when his parents heard his voice saying, "As I cannot come to England, mother, I have come now to see you" (*Phantasms*, II, 227). The parents were so far from glorying in the incident that it was difficult to get them to say anything about it. Contrast it with the incident told me and then reluctantly written by two people whom I knew well, a hard-headed business man, and his excellent wife. He was absent some eighty miles from home. He was awakened in the night by the vivid impression that his wife had called his name, Walter, and he heard it again after he was fully awake. He saw the time by the clock, and in the morning wrote, asking if anything was wrong, and what happened at that time. It proved that their boy had been dangerously ill until past midnight, and as the crisis seemed past but she was still anxious, she went out on the veranda, noting the time as she did so, stretched out arms to the north in deep longing that her husband might be with her, and twice uttered his name.

It must be evident that such incidents, of which there are a multitude recorded and amply witnessed, are quite in a different class from the mental pictures which worry conjures up and which it occurs to one's mind may be premonitory. Such as the former cannot be forgotten by any person of sound and good mind. In many cases it is the sole experience of the kind in a lifetime. And it would hardly be possible for one to have another so strange and so vivid, even though no external event happened, and forget it. The present writer has himself once in his life experienced, in England, the hallucination of an apparition. There was no known correspondence, and therefore the incident is not in the least evidential of "psychic" quality, and yet the incident is not forgotten, and never will be.

Professor Ganong's statement is, I think, very nearly correct, so far as it goes, but it does not take into account other classes of witnesses and other classes of events, to which his criticism can be applied with great difficulty.

PROFESSOR W. C. JONES, A.M., M.D., by turns professor of Pathology, Biology and Zoology in the Universities of Illinois and Alabama, and in Birmingham-Southern College (Presbyterian), kindly gives his experience:

"I have had a good many dreams and also premonitions in the waking state in regard to future happenings favorable and unfavorable; but they never have 'panned out.' For example, for years and years throughout my boyhood, I used to dream that my father was dead; but he did not die until he had rounded out a life of eighty-four years. And during the last few years of his life when he might reasonably have been expected to be near his end, my dreaming of his death had entirely ceased.

"Furthermore, I used to dream often in my younger days of being dead myself—dream of lying in a coffin and that my relatives and friends were passing by to view the 'remains.' I am still going strong at the age of fifty-five and have every promise of living to be as old as my father.

"It may be noteworthy that my mother died very suddenly and unexpectedly; yet I had no premonition of her passing. When the news was telephoned to me away from home, I was enormously shocked.

"In my love affairs, I used to have premonitions; but they all evaporated. And finally I married a woman concerning whom I never had experienced any of these visionary phenomena.

"I am much interested in psychology and have studied and taught

ARGUMENT FROM NEGATIVED "PREMONITIONS" 243

it a great deal, and the observations and experiences of myself and my friends lead me to the conclusion that these supposed premonitions of future happenings are best explained by the fact that, according to the mathematical laws of chance, our thoughts, dreams, etc., in regard to happenings of the future *must now and then* actually coincide with the time happenings.

"Thus you see all of my experience has been negative, not because I am prejudiced, for I have an open mind."

In reply to queries, Professor Jones states that the "premonitions" were all in the form of dreams, that they did not tend to be any more vivid than dreams of a different nature, and that there did not seem to be any more reason, when he woke, to regard them as premonitory, than was derived from thinking that they concerned marriage, etc.

Two very frequent accompaniments of dreams which *do* coincide are absent here. That is to say, in a large percentage of dreams which strikingly coincide there is an emotional accompaniment to a dream seldom experienced by the same person in connection with other dreams, and, secondly, an immediate feeling of reality when the dreamer wakes.

No well-read student of such matters thinks that the fact that a dream pictures the death of any one furnishes any ground for expecting that it will prove premonitory or coincidental. But if it does coincide, it weighs more or less according to the sum of all the particulars of the dream itself and of the coinciding external fact, and then not in isolation, but as one added to a great stock of classified cases.

It is well known that some people have a great many dreams about dying. Freudians say that dreams of the death of another person signify that the person has vexed the dreamer so that the dream expresses the infantile wish that the person were out of the way with his annoyances, but Professor Jones repudiates such an interpretation, saying that his father was seldom stern and never harsh. And it is said that dreams of dying oneself are another reaction to troublesome persons, saying as a child does, "You'll be sorry when I am dead." Professor Jones does not agree to this solution, and I am not responsible for it.

But if he had *frequent* dreams of his father dying, there would have been comparatively slight evidence if his father had died near the time of one of them. This is one of the factors which psychic research always takes into account. Witnesses are asked if they have had similar coincidental or non-coincidental dreams, how often, etc. The stock objection is that dreams which do not coincide are forgotten. Many of the letters we are printing, and this one in particular, show that there is no such rule. Here is a man who can remember that he had "a good many dreams" of this character, although none of them were coincidental. Besides, there have been many persons of high intelligence who were certain that they never, or hardly ever, had another dream of such intense lifelike reality as the one which was coincidental. Without attempting to qualify for that class I may remark that my four reported,[4] I am certain, were never approached in intensity and feeling of reality by any other of my dreams. And one was not coincidental at all, yet I remember it with exactly as much clarity as the others.

PROFESSOR EDWARD EVERETT HALE [5] also relates an incident which occurred when he was a boy. He was asked by his brother Herbert to go with the latter to skate on a pond. But he declined, "*for the ice seemed rather dangerous*," and instead went down a road in another direction toward the seashore, open fields being on either side.

"I had got about half way to the beach when I heard my brother behind me calling my name. I stopped and turned round, but could see nobody. The idea came to my mind that Herbert had gone skating, had fallen in, had called to me and had been drowned, though of course I could not have heard him, for it was more than half a mile away. I paid no attention to the idea, however, but continued toward the beach. I had got almost there when I again heard my brother behind me calling my name. In each case the call must have been quite distinct, for in each case I stopped and turned round and looked back up the road. This second time I saw nothing, but the idea again occurred to me that my brother had fallen into the water and been drowned. I paid no attention to it, however, but went on to the beach, stayed there a while, and came back to the house. My brother had been skating, but he had not fallen into the water, had not called me (or thought of me) and had not been drowned. The two calls which I heard were apparently matters of the imagination, though I had not been conscious of thinking about him at all."

In response to queries, Professor Hale confirmed the impressions that his statement had made, that (1) the voice hallucination did not induce any conviction that his brother was drowned, but only the thought that he might be. (His continuing the journey to the seaside would indicate this.) (2) That there was no particular emotional accompaniment.

---

[4] "Four Peculiarly Characterized Dreams," *Journal* A. S. P. R., XVII, 82-101.
[5] See page 267.

ARGUMENT FROM NEGATIVED "PREMONITIONS" 245

The key to this experience, probably, is in the words "for the ice seemed rather dangerous." If dangerous to one so that he declined, there would certainly be consciousness that it was dangerous to the other. It is well recognized that anxiety may induce hallucinations. *Phantasms of the Living* has several pages devoted to anxiety-hallucinations.

"A sister in trouble about her brother who has had an accident, hears the words, 'Your brother is dead.' A mother nursing her son in a dangerous crisis hears an imaginary voice say, 'You can't save him.' . . . The fact that the anxiety may not have been actually dominating the consciousness at the moment of the hallucination cannot be held to remove the probability (such as it is) that the hallucination was subjectively caused, for it is the rule rather than the exception for hallucinations which can be at all connected with previous experience to be developed from ideas that are quite latent." (I, 509.)

Here we have Professor Hale's experience classified. Although anxiety was not in his conscious mind, yet it was subconsciously felt just sufficiently to produce a hallucination of his brother's voice, as if it were calling to him for help, but not sufficiently emotional or convincing to cause him to do more than to look around. Thus the incident is in strong contrast with many others, where the subject experiences a sense of emotional conviction sufficient to make him hurry to the spot and find that a death or casualty *has* happened. To the extent that the boy was right in thinking that the ice was unsafe, a real accident was likely, therefore if Herbert had been drowned that afternoon his brother's experience could count for little as evidence, unless the moment's hallucination exactly corresponded with that of the disaster, in which case it would have some, but very much less than if he had been ignorant that Herbert was skating, and that the ice appeared to be in a dangerous condition.

Thus the authors of *Phantasms of the Living* (I, 509n) refuse to accept as evidence the case of a woman who woke to see the apparition of her brother who was really killed that morning, since she knew of the impending battle in which he was to take part.[6]

---

[6] The case (I, 443) of a woman who had a vision of her husband carried off the field wounded, at approximately the time when this occurred, is accepted since she also had an auditory hallucination of his voice saying, " Take this ring off my finger, and send it to my wife," which, according to the testimony of one of the men who carried off the wounded man, and of the latter, Gen. Richardson, himself, was actually what he said.

PROFESSOR C. D. LOCKWOOD, A.B., M.D., who holds down the chair of Surgery at the University of Southern California (Union Liberal Church), writes:

"On several occasions I have had premonitions that death was imminent, but these fears have always proven fallacious. I have never observed that the laws of physiology or psychology were in any way modified by the peculiar belief or so-called experiences of my patients, and I must therefore conclude, after years of careful and sympathetic observation, that the laws of physiological psychology are in no way modified by unusual psychic experiences."

In reply to queries he adds:

"These premonitions were very vivid in character, and depressed me greatly for many days. I was contemplating a trip which involved considerable dangers, and feared I might be assassinated. The only cause I could ascribe for these premonitions was the nature of my mission on the contemplated journey and the fact that I had previously been under suspicion as an enemy in the section of the country where I was going."

Dr. Lockwood's instances have little more bearing upon the question whether there are true premonitions than has a child's fear in the presence of a menacing dog. His feelings before the journey are sufficiently accounted for as the reflex of his knowledge that he had been suspected as an enemy in the very region where he meant to go and that he was encountering actual danger. Had he actually been killed on that journey his previous feelings, being thus accounted for, would not have made it a case for psychic research.

No one who claims that "laws," whether of physiology, psychology, physics or nature, would be "modified" or "interfered with" by psychic experiences has, to my knowledge, made it clear what he means, and I doubt if any such person has his meaning clear in his own mind. Much pondering upon these claims has not revealed to me such a result any more than that if a spider crept into the midst of a delicate piece of apparatus and affected its operations, this would modify or interfere with the *laws* of mechanics. To be consistent with such talk it should be held impossible, or obnoxious, or at least "interference," for any physical effect to be initiated by human intelligence and will, but every human being and every animal is constantly bringing about physical effects which would not have taken place except for such intelligence and purposefulness as he or it exercises. The chain of physical causes and effects is complete, to be sure, and yet intelligence and will get in and *choose the links*. Not without them would an aeroplane come into existence, nor a man present the deceptive appearance of defying the law of gravity, in a million years. It is an absolute mystery today why the thought that it is desirable that the arm should lift is followed by its actual lifting; there seems to be a link missing, and we vainly seek to discover it. We are *accustomed* to such facts— that is all. My own experience has been rather barren of the sight of tables and chairs rising without physical contact, but if it should be proved to scientific men generally that these events occur, then laws would be discovered or imagined just as successfully, or unsuccessfully, to account for them as for the everyday effects of human will and intelligence upon—its interference with, if you please—matter.

The professors awe laymen with that word " laws," but must smile to each other as did the augurs of Rome. For they know that some of the " laws " of yesterday are not " laws " today, and that some which reign today in scientific thinking will yield the scepter tomorrow. For *laws* are nothing more nor less than *current* views as to what the invariable uniformities of nature are. As Webster puts it: A law is " a statement of an order or relation of phenomena which, *so far as is known* [my italics], is invariable under the given conditions."

Let us read what a learned physiologist, W. H. Manwaring, professor of bacteriology and experimental pathology in Stanford University, has recently said [7] about basic discoveries which have within twenty years altered " laws," or at least enlarged their number, and made the formerly impossible, possible. He refers first to physical science generally, and then to physiological science.

"About twenty-five years ago there were introduced into certain fields of physical science radically new basic concepts, particularly in reference to atomic structure and radiant energy. Within one decade the general acceptance of these new hypotheses rendered obsolete a thousand previous conscientious researches. For two decades the new theories have been the accepted basis for a hundred hitherto *impossible* practical applications. Today we are apparently at the beginning of a similar basic revolution in certain biological sciences, particularly in those fields of physiology and biochemistry bearing on the phenomena of infection and bodily resistance.

" Within the last five years there have been introduced in America, Germany, Russia, France and Czecho-Slovakia radically new immuno-chemical hypotheses, which, if generally accepted, will render inconclu-

[7] *Science,* July 11, 1930.

sive half of forty years' accumulated immunological literature. The suggested theory of biochemistry relativity casts doubt on a hundred current therapies, challenges a score of physiological orthodoxies, suggests a new perspective in ecology and genetics, has invaded the field of educational psychology and *has already led to at least one previous chemical impossibility.*"

MR. RICHARD F. MAYNARD, A.B., Portrait Painter and short story writer, sends an instance of supposed and frustrated " premonition."

" One evening I was alone in my studio when I had a premonition that a model who had been posing for me was in trouble of some kind. I thought this was absurd and that I should pay no attention to it, but the feeling that the girl was in distress or was ill persisted and I could not shake it off. Finally I decided to give in to my premonition, and call her up on the telephone. I was considerably relieved to hear her voice. She seemed not a little surprised at my inquiry, and said she was perfectly all right and there was nothing the matter at all."

Mr. Maynard could not be expected to know that, even if the girl had telephoned that she *was* in trouble, the incident would not be reckoned by psychic research as evidential for " premonition " or " monition " or telepathy. Suppose she were and had been for days in a condition of despondency because jilted by her lover, with all effort to appear as usual, it is quite likely that the artist might perceive some change in her face and in her tones and manner. He would put the thought away, beguiled by her artificial gaiety, and forget it, but it would still linger in his subconsciousness and be worked over there. Then, at ease in his studio, perhaps in a reverie over his pipe, something reminds him of this girl and in the passive state of his mind that feeling that she is in trouble comes up. That would be the probable though not certain explanation. Even if the girl committed suicide a few days after her telephone reply (since people do not always acknowledge their trouble, especially if it relates to a love affair) the incident would remain very doubtful as evidence. If she were at the *moment* the artist telephoned on the point of suicide, it would have *some* weight, on account of the close temporal coincidence. These principles are always kept in mind in any careful comment on cases (witness such works as *Human Personality* and *Phantasms of the Living*).

An apparition of a person or a vivid dream of the person's death counts for nothing if the seer or dreamer knows that the person is expected to die within a few days, and the death in fact comes a few days later. If the death is coincidental in time with the vision or dream, the incident has weight, but nothing to what there would have been in the absence of any knowledge of sickness.

PROFESSOR S. C. SCHMUCKER, M.S., PH.D., for many years instructor of Biology in State Normal Schools, relates two frustrated " premonitions."

"At fifteen, while very low with pneumonia, a 'ghost' appeared and pointed in my face. It was laughed over when I awoke from the delirium or sleep (whichever it was) and I had no bad effect from it.

" While my mother was an invalid in a town some distance away I awakened with the clear impression of my name being called in my mother's voice. I noted the hour and wrote next day to her nurse, who reported a comfortable night and no change.

" If either of the above had 'turned out'—that is, if I had died shortly before first, or mother had died after second—they would be considered good testimony."

Letter to Professor Schmucker:

" It is quite true that both incidents would have been regarded as ' good testimony,' if they had ' turned out '; that is to say, they would have been so regarded by some people. But it is quite a revelation to me that men of such high intelligence as yourself should be under the impression that the incidents would have passed as good evidence with scientific psychic researchers, or, if you happen to be among those who think there ' ain't no such animal,' then let us say, the more nearly scientific psychic researchers. I refer to such men as the late F. W. H. Myers, Dr. Hodgson, Dr. Hyslop, and, if I may venture to say so, myself.

" Let me tell you what I would have been compelled to say, as I have similarly said in print regarding so many instances.

" 1. It is well known that in fevers and certain other forms of disease, visual and other hallucinations are very common. The appearance of faces is a frequent pathological symptom. That being the case, how could death, *another* consequence of the illness, make the first one evidential? No one with any scientific acumen thinks that a death-bed vision, in and of itself, is proof, though we sometimes wonder, considering the cases where the mind seems otherwise unclouded, whether there is anything veridical about some of these. Where it had been carefully concealed from a little girl doomed to die that her young friend in another house was already dead, and the former, while dying, cried out with joy, saying that Milly was there before her, we come nearer evidence. But there is a flaw even in that case.

"2. You may search *Phantasms of the Living* and Myers's great book from end to end, and I do not think you will find a case like your second one which was regarded as 'good testimony.' Whether or not you remember yourself as being in a condition of anxiety for your mother, known to be ill, it would have been presumed that you were so, and that this could account for the dream of your name being called by your mother, which woke you with the impression that your name had been called. Once I found that you were aware of your mother's illness, I should regard the incident as but slightly evidential, even if your mother had died. Had it proved that she died within the hour, I should give it *some* weight, but very little compared with what would have been the case had you known nothing about her illness."

PROFESSOR WILLIAM S. TAYLOR, M.S., PH.D., of the department of Philosophy at the University of Maine and writer on psychology, furnishes the following interesting incident:

"I awoke one morning, apparently from a dream, with a surprisingly strong and definite feeling that something tragic had happened at my parental home; but whether it concerned my father, or mother, or brother, or sister, I could not tell. As I was somewhat interested in the psychology of evidence, I resolved to make a written memorandum of this 'premonition' and see whether it was borne out by any word that came from home.

"The memorandum, however, I failed to make; and the incident passed from my mind. But about a week later, in class, when a student asked 'how the psychologists explain it when you dream of something and it really does come true,' I was reminded, with a shock, of my carelessness in not recording my own dream; for I had the strong feeling that had I not been reminded in this way, and before many more days had elapsed, I would have forgotten the incident altogether. This, I think, would have been an unfortunate loss of a negative instance, because as a matter of fact nothing unusual had happened at home, nor has any calamity befallen the family during the two years that have elapsed since that time."

The substance of queries addressed to Professor Taylor and his replies:

"1. Did your dream distinctly refer to any event which you remembered, or do I understand you correctly to mean that you only woke with a *feeling* apparently based upon some forgotten dream? " *Ans.* " The latter."

" 2. If you did not remember the substance of the dream, and that dream really concerned some person of whom you were fond, not a relative, might it not be that the depth of the feeling would suggest to you by secondary elaboration that the dream probably concerned one of your immediate family? " *Ans.* " Yes."

" 3. Would it not be theoretically possible that the dream was the reflex of a telepathic impression of some kind of mental suffering on the part of a relative or friend, not necessarily of a disastrous *event?* (I am not seeking to make the dream evidential—of course it was not. But we are so used to applying every kind of obstructive hypothesis to an apparently strong coincidental case that it seems to me only fair that we should apply counter-hypotheses to negative dreams also.)" *Ans.* " True."

" 4. Did you ask members of the family whether at that time for any reason there was coincidentally any strong emotional perturbation? (On the basis of other apparently telepathic cases it would be more likely that such emotion concerned you, that your mother, for instance, for some reason was thinking strongly of and perhaps worrying about you. Even if you asked, it would be quite possible that the fact was not remembered or that one was reticent about it.)" *Ans.* " I did not ask. It may have been true."

" 5. I am interested in negative incidents. I do not think a dozen negative cases of a definite source weigh much against a striking correspondence between dream and fact practically contemporaneous. Do you? " *Ans.* " No."

" Even when the dream is definite, a lack of correspondence between it and fact does not mathematically weigh much against a case where the dream does correspond with the fact. You of course see this. An analogy is the fact that guessing right a card drawn from a pack of cards has only one chance out of fifty-two of succeeding, whereas the chance of guessing wrong has fifty-one chances out of fifty-two." *Ans.* " True."

" On the other hand, it is of course difficult to *prove* that the most perfect coincidence is not a chance one. Even a tentative conclusion must rest on a very comprehensive and protracted study with an application of delicate mathematics such as was employed by English scholars in *Phantasms of the Living.*"

There is no evasion or unwillingness to face the logic of the situation, with Professor Taylor.

J. J. Thomas, M.D., A.M., associate professor of Neurology at Harvard Graduate School of Medicine, etc., recounts:

"When about eighteen years, was in country with mother, two sisters, whom mother called home by illness of father. This did not alarm me, as illness was not severe. On second or third day of mother's absence, about 3 p. m., was reading an interesting book under a tree near house, when I heard my name called loudly in my mother's voice, so I started up and called back in reply, at once, not realizing her absence—so startling I made a note of this day and hour, and on her return asked my mother if she had called me, or wanted me much. Got the reply that she had not thought of me in any such way, nor needed help at any time during her absence."

In response to queries, Dr. Thomas added that he is confident that the experience was a hallucination, not an illusion; also that he was in excellent health, not fatigued, anxious or perturbed about anything. But psychologists and neurologists who remind us that (as we ourselves insist) memory of a state of mind experienced thirty or forty years ago must be regarded with some reserve, will not refuse to take their own medicine. It seems quite possible that time may have dimmed the recollection of a real anxiety when the mother was called home on account of the illness of the father, an anxiety reasoned with and put out of view, and hence the more likely to play tricks from the subconscious to which it was relegated. In that case, the incident would classify with similar auditory hallucination of Professor Hale, and the remarks made about that would apply here.

Dr. C. A., a prominent Physician, remembers that

"A colleague once drummed with his fingers on the footboard of my bed when I was sleeping, imitating the sound of a galloping horse. When I awoke he stated that he was trying to make me dream of galloping horses. I had such a dream while he was drumming, but I think the dream was produced by the sound rather than by his mental effort."

The annotator agrees with the doctor in his conclusion. It is an interesting instance of dream interpretation, and a tribute to the imitative skill of the drummer.

The doctor goes on:

"Very much to my annoyance, I was once prevented from making a sea trip by circumstances beyond my control. I was very greatly disappointed because I could not make this trip, but I had absolutely no premonition that something might happen. On the morning following the day the steamer sailed, I read an Associated Press dispatch stating that the steamer had sunk, and giving details."

Presumably the witness implies that being deterred by a "premonition" from embarking on a steamer, and being prevented by one of the thousand possible accidents of life are logically equivalent as relates to the subsequent sinking of the steamer. I do not think that they could, in any case, be quite equivalent, since probably a large steamer never starts on a voyage without leaving on land a number of persons who for one commonplace reason or other have relinquished their purpose to take passage, while staying off because of some sudden impression of impending danger to the vessel is probably rare, although we have no statistics to prove this.

Of course, *demonstration* of the significance of such purported premonitions cannot be attained, if at all, short of the accumulation of a vast number of cases, carefully analyzed, and mathematically tested as to chance probabilities in relation to time, etc. But it is possible for a single case of seeming premonition to be so complex and characteristic in its coincidences with an impending event as to bring the question whether it has not normal significance fairly before the mind. Take the case narrated in the *Journal* A. S. P. R. for 1923, pp. 86-89. The witness has no recollection of dreaming either before or afterward about any railroad accident. But this time he had a dream involving (1) a collision of railroad trains, (2) in a tunnel, (3) one train only in motion, (4) the stationary train just protruding from the opening of the tunnel, (5) a rear-end collision, (6) the killing or at least injuring of people at the first impact, (7) the added horror of fire or hot steam as indicated by dense clouds, (8) the consequent further damage to human beings, (9) the fact that men rushed in with axes to cut away the wreckage and make rescues *before* the clouds broke forth from which they shrank. Every particular corresponded with the newspaper account next day, and two more features must be added: (10) temporal proximity, the tragedy occurring less than six hours after the dream, and (11) comparative spatial proximity, the tragedy occurring not in some foreign land or remote part of the country, but seventy-five miles away, at a place familiar to the dreamer. An additional factor which adds to the suspicion that something more than chance may have been involved is the fearful vividness of the dream, so great that for many minutes after waking the after-effect of the frenzied screams seemed still to be heard, and the dream has remained in memory as a real event would do. The still other fact that this witness has had exactly four dreams characterized by such vividness, and thus remaining in memory, as would actual events, and that another of these was equally marked by coincidences of unusual character, including proximities of time and place, causes one the more to ponder. Those who suppose that the dreams were remembered as real events only because they happened to coincide with realities should take note that one of the four which stand out in the witness's memory as a class apart because of their awful vividness, had no known counterpart in actuality. Seven years have passed since these four dreams were published, there have been no more of that class, and the witness hereby declares his firm conviction that he never could have had a dream so marked by vividness and tremendous emotional stress, and have forgotten it.

Would Dr. C. A., after deliberation, conclude that his failure, owing to "circumstances" to take passage in the vessel which sank within a day afterward, could counterbalance a dream of the vessel sinking, with many particulars, afterwards realized in order and detail?

Mr. C. B., an A.M., in the United States Forest Service (Congregationalist), writes a letter, the substance of which follows:

As a boy he was cared for after the death of his mother by one Sarah, to whom he continued to feel affection, and she spent her last years in his brother's home. When she was old, and known by him to be in feeble health and "liable to pass out most any time," and at a time when he was doing a surveying job, one night he dreamed, "realistically," that she was dead. The next day, in the deep woods, he and others heard a shout repeatedly, traveling from north to south. After the sounds ceased, it occurred to him that someone might be trying to locate him and inform him that Sarah was dead. Again the shouting sounds began, this time traveling northward. It dawned upon him that they were moving faster than a man could travel. And then he remembered hearing, years before, a wounded bear uttering cries which could not be distinguished from those of a man. Nothing happened to Sarah at this time.

"Thought transference, dream warnings, etc., there may all be for all I know. Had my daylight surmises proved true, no doubt I should have been a believer in dream warnings at least. I suspect that numerous beliefs of that kind have arisen from unusual circumstances and coincidences."

It is quite true that unsophisticated and simple persons have often assigned to merely "unusual circumstances and coincidences" significance beyond any logical warrant. But had Sarah died about that time and had the shouts been those of a man, this case would not have been regarded a strong one by psychic research. Of course the shouts of the man would add nothing to it, since his coming would have been the normal sequence of the death. And since Mr. C. B. knew that Sarah was feeble and "liable to pass out most any time," his thinking about it or rather his trying not to think about it, would tend to bring on the dream. Had she died at that very hour, a small evidential value would have attached;[8] had she died only within a day or two, the value would have been very little indeed.

In the next volume a case will be given where the narrator did *not* know of illness or likelihood of dying, where death *did* occur and coincide in time, and where messengers *did* go to the woods.

PROFESSOR C. C., a Ph.D. and university teacher of Mathematics, says:

"I have had premonitions of accidents or death happening to relatives, always finding that no sort of harm has come to them at or near the time of premonitions. On the other hand, relatives or near friends have died without my having had any premonitions."

In a later letter he says:

"I ought to preface any statements by giving you this much of an idea of my background. Mathematical training has given me a rather unusually rigorous conception of what evidence and proof should be, and perhaps a skeptical tendency. On the other hand, I think it has also given me an instinct for fair play, and a wish to consider all possibilities.

"Still, I remember being impressed by a remark of Woodrow Wilson's, in his course in jurisprudence which I attended while a student at Princeton. He remarked that the favorable cases of premonitions

---

[8] Of course I mean as one of a mass of cases; no case taken alone, no matter how many and how extraordinary the coinciding particulars, can be proof of anything soever.

were usually recorded and given currency, while little attention is given to cases in which nothing happened to correspond to the premonitions.

"As to my actual experiences, they have none of them been recent. I do recall the fact, however, of three or four times having the feeling come over me with pretty convincing force that something serious had happened to my father, a brother, or my wife (in each case to a specific person dear to me). In fact, the experience was sufficiently vivid to make me remember it for a long time, and to remember the fact of its occurrence today. In no case was there any occurrence to justify the premonition. These were waking experiences, and came without my thinking, at the moment, of the person involved. I have had more or less frequent dreams that injury has come to a loved one, though I recall none recently. Such dreams were always vivid, and resulted in a great feeling of relief upon awakening, and upon realizing that they were but dreams.

"Dreams of a different character have been those in which a dead person was alive in my dream. This has frequently occurred—and I think it has been invariably my father who was concerned. I adored my father, in spite of some faults I saw in him. Sometimes in the dreams these faults would be accentuated, and sometimes they would be prominently absent. Usually, he would appear as he had in the flesh."

The professor was impressed by the remark he heard, "that the favorable cases of premonitions were usually recorded and given currency, while little attention was given to cases in which nothing happened to correspond." That remark had been, in substance, made by various people many times before, and has been made many times since. Yet it lacks little of being "merely an article of faith." From long experience I know that, alas! favorable cases are *not* "usually" recorded, and that at least three out of four are withheld from publication and from any use by a student of psychic research. And it is a bit droll to read approval of the view that non-correspondent cases are given little attention in the same letter which so distinctly states that the writer remembers many experiences, none of which had any external counterpart.

If I were to guess, it would be that Professor C. C. passed through some very emotional and trying experience in his early life, most likely his childhood, involving an injury to a relative or dear friend, or the fear of it, and when, in subsequent years, anxious about anything, not necessarily a person, and at the same time one of his family was away subject to possible danger, that anxiety was liable to stir up the subconscious elements of the old shock, and result in a feeling as of im-

ARGUMENT FROM NEGATIVED "PREMONITIONS" 257

pending injury or misfortune bubbling up into the conscious. Of course there would not be any logical implication that such was to be expected in fact. And yet, although the number of these apprehensive episodes would weaken the force of any coinciding instance, I suspect that if, just once, the professor had a "premonition," so detailed and so immediately realized as many which have been set down by responsible persons and in some cases amply corroborated, he would be impressed, though perhaps not convinced, the rest of his days. For example, if he found himself in a reverie after waking in the morning, thinking what a pity it was that a statue had fallen and broken during the night, and odd that the head should have been so neatly knocked off and no fracture anywhere else, and later had gone into the garden, not visible from any window to which he had access, and, realizing that he could not have walked there in his sleep without being soaked by the rain, found the statue just as he had seen it.[9] Or if he had been wakened by the auditory hallucination of hearing his daughter-in-law say, "Oh, I wish papa only knew that Robert is ill," and it proved that Robert was dangerously ill on that night three hundred miles away, and his daughter-in-law did utter those words.[10] Or if he dreamed that he saw his father on a sledge attempting to pass a cross-road, and another traveler coming at right angles so near that his horse reared with his hoofs above the father's head, and learned in the morning from two witnesses that this was exactly what happened during the night.[11] And incidentally, the dreamer testifies that she is *not*, like the professor, in the habit of visioning horrors about her relatives. " I have never had any other dream of this kind, nor do I remember ever to have had a dream of an accident happening to any one in whom I was interested." She does not declare that certainly she never once had dreamed of an accident, etc. Will the professor, who remembers his unfulfilled day dreams and night dreams be the one to say that this intelligent witness probably had many such but forgot them?

Judging by the remarks of a number of learned gentlemen, they have the notion that a coinciding dream or apparition is balanced by one which fails to coincide. This is curious, but it is surprising that a professor of mathematics should suppose that his experience of having had, "three or four times" the feeling come over him that something serious had happened to a particular relative when in fact nothing of the kind corresponded, has any appreciable bearing in rela-

---

[9] *Human Personality,* I, 381.
[10] *Human Personality,* I, 396. The amply-corroborated statement of the Rt. Hon. Sir John Drummond Hay.   [11] *Ib.,* I, 395.

tion to a definite factual and temporal coincidence. And yet he would laugh if from a bag containing a hundred marbles he three times in succession drew the one black marble, and some one else should say, " That signifies nothing; I drew twenty times yesterday and never got the black marble once." He would instantly recognize the fact that since the objector's total bad results were according to expectation 4 to 1, the results of his own trials were against expectation to the degree that there was 1 chance in 1,000,000 of achieving it, and that the twenty failures of the other man, as set over against his result, would not appreciably affect it.

Again, the professor's so-called " premonitions " consisted each, it appears, of a *feeling* that *something* serious had happened to some specific person. As I have hinted, it is likely that, if he were psychoanalyzed, his tendency to have such recurrent feelings could be explained. But at any rate, the failure of his *feeling*, in three or four instances, that *something* had happened, weighs practically nothing against such an instance as that beginning on page 424, volume I of *Human Personality*, and told by another college professor. His wife woke terrified and told him that she had seen in a dream her *headless* brother standing with his *head lying on a coffin*. She was so impressed that she looked for sad news of her brother, about whose movements she had no knowledge to cause apprehension. And it proved that a Chinaman cut off her brother's head at or very close to the hour of the dream, and, furthermore, that only his head was recovered by his friends who, of course, buried it.

If a hundred professors should every one three or four times *feel* as though *something* serious had happened to somebody, the total of all these feelings would weigh almost nothing against this one definite, complex and supremely unlikely coincidence of the fact with the dream. The principle governing the marble-drawing illustration would apply, although of course we can here make no exact mathematical measurement.

The correspondence closed with a request on the part of the commentator:

" Would you be willing to read fifteen pages of a book I will loan you, prepaying return postage, and to give your opinion as to the mathematical weight of the evidence on the supposition that my experiment was without flaw or to point out any flaw in the methodology of the experiment which you can either see or theoretically assume short of my consciously lying?

"Please do not let the expression 'give your opinion as to the mathematical weight' frighten you. I do not mean that it calls for a lot of time and effort on your part, or that it admits of any exact mathematical valuation. But it does, within limits, and I think an opinion could be formed without much trouble, and it is possible that you might find the case interesting enough to warrant that very little pains. I am not seeking your opinion to publish it with your name."

It was thought that the professor's expressed "wish to consider all possibilities" might make the opportunity offered a welcome one. But this was evidently not the case.

PROFESSOR C. D., an M.S. and Ph.D., college professor of Mathematics (Presbyterian), says:

"Recently dreamed that there was a hole in leg of my trousers. While brushing myself the following morning, before starting to my office, I looked down and found that the cloth in knee of my trousers was worn entirely through. I exclaimed to my wife, telling her of my dream of just a few hours before.

"As a death in the family next door engaged my attention, I paid so little attention to the matter that I cannot recall whether or not the details of the dream very closely coincided with the reality (as to character of hole, etc.). The only point I have in mind is this: If the coincidence had occurred in connection with some important event (like a death) it would have been remembered as a very striking and important incident."

Letter of W. F. P. to Professor C. D.:

"I don't think your parallel holds good.

"1. A particular person dies but once, while one has a hole in the knee of his trousers perhaps a hundred times in a lifetime.

"2. And (far more important) your dream probably did not correspond with the fact by mere coincidence, but was caused by having taken abstracted or subconscious note of the hole before the dream. That is, there was a normal *causal factor*. But what would be the normal causal factor in dreaming a person was dead or in seeing his apparition the moment he died, there having been no knowledge of danger?

"No scientific psychical researcher supposes that one or a dozen even such cases prove a supernormal causal relation, but they may be too many statistically to be credible as mere coincidences. That is one of the things we are trying to learn.

"If you have any criticism to make I should be glad to learn wherein my reasoning is faulty."

PROFESSOR C. E., a Ph.D. and former university professor of Mathematics, now of Vital Statistics, author on his subject, has also had what he thinks ought to have been "premonitions," if there are such things:

"I have had a few striking incidents which would have been treated as 'psychic' by bad statisticians and credulous folk if it had not happened that the coincidences failed to occur or the premonitions to be justified by events."

Response:

"So long as I am studying the possibilities of illusion, hallucination, delusion, erroneous inference, the possibilities of chance, etc., etc., with as much interest as I study cases which present problems of a very different character, I would have been glad if you had described the striking incidents which some bad statisticians and credulous folks would have treated as 'psychic,' in case there had been factual coincidences. There is no question whatever that bad statisticians and credulous folk are inclined to reason from very insufficient premises and in entire disregard of mathematics. I have shown this in print many times, and am always glad to get new instances. Even if there are apparent premonitions as judged by after events, it does not necessarily follow that there was any real premonition. Many particulars have to be taken into consideration, and no one case could prove anything. It is all a matter of evidence and logic, like anything else. This subject does not stand alone in being one where some people judge rashly and foolishly. That there are facts and experiences which the principles of science as now understood do not fully explain I personally have no doubt, but I did not come to this conclusion until after many years of inspection of the evidence. I am not impatient with any one who differs with me, knowing every man has his specialty and scarcely time for anything else. I do think that it would pay, in times of leisure, to look at some of the real evidence."

The professor did not furnish any instances, so we may not know what sort of day dreams or night dreams, worries or inferences he thinks psychical researchers should think "premonitions," the non-fulfilment of which hopelessly damns all our evidence under that head.

IV. THE COINCIDENCE ARGUMENT

The plea that coincidence is the great solvent of the purportedly psychic crops up incidentally in other sections; it is most prominently displayed in this. Professor Hale really offers no plea, but simply hands over two incidents, and agrees that they are probably due in the one case to chance coincidence, and in the other to apprehension for reasonable cause.

MR. D. A., an A.M. and Botanist, writer on his specialty (Congregationalist), gives his opinion:

" I have never known of any experiences on the part of others or in my own experience that could not be fully explained by known natural laws. I do not believe that there are any such events."

To which the annotator replied, after the usual courteous preliminaries:

" 1. Have you become familiar with the evidence reported in the *Proceedings* of the [London] Society for Psychical Research; have you read the books of Sir William Barrett, Myers's *Human Personality*, Holt's *Cosmic Relations*, Thomas's *Some New Evidence for Human Survival*, Pagenstecher's *Past Events Seership*, Warcolier's *La Telepathie*, or any even of my own books and reports, or anything at all equivalent in rating?

" 2. Assuming that a woman of intelligence and good standing, while fully awake, for once in her life sees an apparition, or rather the apparitions of her deceased father and of her brother then upon a war vessel in the North Sea, relates the vision to her mother and sister the same day, and later it is ascertained that on that day and that hour the brother, at the moment that an enemy's torpedo seemed to be about to strike his ship, saw the apparition of his father beside him, in accordance with what known natural law would you explain it? Note that this question is put in a hypothetical way and does not call for any belief on your part that the facts are authentic. You can even maintain that if they are authentic the explanation is to be found in what someone called the law of chance coincidence."

And D. A. responded, in part:

"I am not familiar with the books enumerated in your letter, but I have read a great many articles relating to psychical research.

"It is my opinion that all psychical occurrences, which are supposed to transcend natural law, may be explained as due either to hallucinations or 'the law of chance coincidences.' Hallucinations of sight and sound are common, and may be induced in various ways. One is apt to see, as well as believe, what they want to. Conan Doyle wanted to see fairies, and he tells us that he did so.

"Remarkable coincidences occur in the life of everyone. Some years ago my father was reading a newspaper and came upon the Latin of the sentence, 'Let the shoemaker stick to his last,' which he requested me to translate. At the same moment I met with the same sentence in the book I was reading. Such a coincidence might not occur again in a million years. Had he been in Europe, and had the same thought in regard to some mutual friend occurred to both of us at the same moment, very likely some would have regarded it as a case of telepathy.

"The erratic nature of the phenomena and the numerous impostors and credulous people connected with them must also receive consideration.

"I have not the slightest objection to believing that events occur which cannot be explained by known natural laws. If there are such events I should be glad to have proof of them, and I should be glad to read any evidence you may send to me. Perhaps telepathy is possible. A recent statement was made in *Science* to the effect that certain animals and plants emit waves or rays. But, if they exist at all, they conform to natural law."

He has read none of the books mentioned, he has no acquaintance with the accumulated material of the S. P. R., but he has read a great many *articles*, presumably meaning in newspapers and popular magazines! He is ignorant of the evidential situation, but has his firm opinion, this being the one branch of research whereon a multitude of otherwise intelligent men make up their minds without knowing much about it.

It is quite true that credulity makes some people see things that are not there, and so does incredulity cause other people to remember things which never happened. Conan Doyle wrote a book in defense of fairies, but did *not* profess to have seen them himself.

It is evident that the incident cited to Mr. D. A. is regarded by him as due to chance coincidence. Had this been told him as a "psychical" incident it would be said that probably in the lapse of years memory had improved it, and that very likely in fact the son had come across the expression in his reading five minutes or half an hour before the father asked the question. But only on one side of the line is memory supposed to play tricks! Yet let us assume that his memory does not err. Still I do not think that father and son happening at the same moment upon a frequently-quoted phrase at all ranks with the man's having a *vision* of his father, and at the same time his sister having a *vision* of him *including the hallucination he saw*. Nor do I for a moment allow that *such* a coincidence (that is, one of this character) is likely not to occur again in a million years, whether he means to anybody in the world or to his father and himself, if they lived so long. I was once talking with a young Jew who was practically insane over the supposed significance in his life of certain names, and among the latter was Franklin. The fact that I bear that name is what brought him to me. As he entered on one of his calls I laid a reading-glass, about three inches in diameter, which I had been using, carelessly upon a newspaper. After he had talked for a while I happened to glance downward, and there, framed by the rim of the reading-glass, was the name "Franklin," and a line or two below it something about a Jew. Never for a moment did I think this other than a pure accident, although a very unusual coincidence, so unusual that I have no recollection that anything similar to it and comparable in improbability ever happened to me at any other time in my life, though I remember a coincidence as remarkable but of a different type. But if thrice more, when this man called, there should be found something framed by the reading-glass as peculiarly significant, I should certainly be unable to believe it was all chance and should look for a cause. In other words, my intellect would revolt at the notion that the only four instances of this kind in my lifetime should be concentrated within a few weeks, and all when a particular man was present, merely by chance. It would be more tolerable to think that, all unknown to my conscious self, I had laboriously searched for passages on which to lay the glass. And so when out of scores of automatic writers I find one, Mrs. Soule, who yields the results I reported in *Leonard and Soule Experiments*,[1] and she again and again and other agains rings the bell of combinations of statements coinciding with external facts to her unknown, each against probability in ratios of from 100,000 to 1 up to

---

[1] I would not have it inferred that there are not groups of evidential facts in Mrs. Allison's sittings reported in the same book. I refer to my own to save time, since they are more familiarly in my memory.

billions to 1, I again despair of chance and seek a cause. Going back to former records of the same lady's work I come upon the series of statements purporting to come from the deceased Mrs. Fischer, together with a purported interruption by Dr. Hodgson. Whoever or however these statements came, they almost without exception corresponded with the long ago facts which took place in a humble household in a distant city of which the most resolute imagination cannot suppose that the psychic ever heard. These statements were tried out upon fifty women, to see what chance would do. On the basis of the returns, most conservative estimates were made of chance probability for each of the many statements, everything was cut down to the quick, and the whole process exposed to the judgment of the reader. No criticism of the mathematics has ever reached my ears, from saint or sinner, philosopher or simpleton, or from the most belligerent skeptic. The chance of getting *all* the statements right by guess was *conservatively* found to be 1 in 4,500,000,000,000,000,000,000,000,000,000. Almost beyond belief, but true.[2]

But Mrs. Soule is not the only psychic through whom, under conditions prohibitive of any normal information, I have had these "accidental coincidences." The bell of extraordinary coincidental groups rang in several of my few experiments with Mrs. King, and once so loudly that it signaled, as we have seen, *one chance out of five quadrillions at the very least, of getting this result!* [3]

This is by no means the measure of my results through experiment. Yet is it not enough to make one stop parroting "chance" and begin to think? Correspondents can tell of one or two very unusual chance coincidences which have happened to them amid all the uncountable multitudes of minutiæ of their whole lives; of course they can, and so can I. But in that comparatively small part of my life devoted to experiments I have had, setting aside all scattered pieces of evidence, repeatedly these great evidential groups, the valuation of some of which runs into astronomical figures, and with each new added group of such enormous antecedent unlikelihood, the absurdity of clinging to chance for explanation, the necessity of positing some cause or causes, becomes more patent.

Most true it is that "the erratic nature of the phenomena" merits attention, and they have had it, exactly as in the case with volcanoes and meteorites and mathematical prodigies. Yes, and "the numerous impostors and credulous people" must receive attention, and were the

---

[2] *Proceedings* A. S. P. R. for 1923.   [3] *Proceedings* A. S. P. R. for 1924.

botanist familiar with psychic research he would know that its leaders have been very busy with these considerations for many years.

Mr. D. A. is by no means hide-bound, and at the end of his letter thinks that telepathy may be possible. Only it must "conform to natural law." What other law is there to conform to? And what do we mean by conforming to law? The word does not really signify some force or power outside of and higher than the phenomena of nature themselves. "Laws" is only a convenient but somewhat mythological term for the uniformities of behavior or action that we discover in nature. If telepathy *is*, the ways in which it acts will be its laws, and of course it will conform to them. But even as the "laws" of the human mind are elusive and hard to define, so, and probably for the same reason, may be those of telepathy.

MR. D. B., a noted chemical investigator and author on Chemistry, B.S., M.Sc., writes:

"I have never personally seen or heard an entirely credible case which could not be explained on (1) chance, (2) worry, or similar mental states or a combination of these. As an example of a curious *coincidence*, I once (at an ∅. B. K. meeting) heckled a German-American exchange professor—*about 1909*. In 1917, when I went to register under the draft, the president of my local board (whom I had never personally met) recalled the incident to me about 9:30 P. M. That same evening I went to Washington, and next morning about 8:15 A. M. another man whom I had never met stopped me in the dining-room of a Washington hotel and also recalled the incident. *Both* these men had been at the ∅. B. K. meeting and believed that my questions had indicated that I foretold the war. Thus by *mere chance*, twice in eleven hours, two men I had never met spoke to me of an incident eight years old. But there were perfectly good reasons why they should remember the incident."

Reply to above:

"As I have in mind commenting upon this testimony, though without giving your name, and I wish to treat everybody with fairness, I will tell you how this instance strikes me.

"It seems to me that there is a little confusion of thought here, as though there were *two* singular coincidences involved. There certainly was nothing remarkable in your meeting one man who had been present at the society meeting years before, nor was there anything remarkable about this man remembering the incident, as you yourself observe, since that was the last previous time you had met him and his memory would be likely to go back to it. Had that factor existed alone you would never have thought of anything odd, because there was nothing odd. The one curious coincidence is in your meeting *another* man who had also been present, and while this was curious enough to attract attention we should certainly expect that a few times in a lifetime such a coincidence should take place by chance. I do not think that the fact that he also spoke of the society meeting is at all remarkable, seeing that that occasion was the last time that he, also, had seen you, and you appear to have furnished a graphic incident on that occasion, one likely to remain in memory. It was, therefore, the most natural thing that both should speak of that meeting.

"I have an impression that you will agree with me, but it is probably your idea that the kind of coincidences which give psychical researchers pause are just as liable to be general coincidences. That is a perfectly legitimate theory, but I think that it falls down in practice. Such a case as yours does not weigh much in the balance against the case of a man who once in a lifetime sees an apparition and it proves that the person seen died within two minutes at the most of the time that this apparition was seen. I do not think, however, that any scientific psychical researchers would think one even such remarkable instance conclusive. It is the number of such cases that gives rise to great doubt whether, by mathematical calculation, these coincidences could be the result of chance."

It should be added that psychical researchers are alert to discover any relation which "worry or a similar mental state" can possibly have to a reported incident. I can remember none ever printed as evidence by, for example, the S. P. R. or B. S. P. R., where the assumption of any such state of mind would have any explanatory force. When Mrs. Leonard tells a whole series of facts relevant to an unknown experimenter, how can worry or a similar state of mind, either on her part or that of the sitter, affect the problem? Conceivably it might make telepathy easier—that is all—but telepathy itself is "psychical" or supernormal. The same as to her famous book-tests. If a man sees the apparition of his mother at the hour of her death at a distance, and it is found that she had been ill but a short time and that he knew she was desperately ill, then the evidentiality of the apparition is put almost at the disappearing point. But if the mother was not known to be ill and for the first and only time in his life the man sees an apparition, and it is of his mother and at the moment of her death, we may indeed assume that he began to worry at that moment, but the problem why he suddenly began to worry so intensely that it caused the apparition at that coinciding moment, would be exactly as great as the problem of the unique apparition of the particular person at the particular moment, in the absence of worry.

PROFESSOR D. C., a Ph.D. whose university subject is Philosophy, has "noticed some rather striking coincidences, explicable without appeal to supernormal explanation." Quite so, and who has not? But he would not relate one of them.

EDWARD EVERETT HALE, PH.D., professor of English at Union College, author, supplied a curious coincidence. While walking among the hills he was naturally reminded of the Biblical passage, "I will lift up mine eyes unto the hills." Returning to his residence, on the way to his study he passed a case filled with books whose backs had been damaged by fire so that they were unrecognizable. He casually took one out, and it happened to be a Latin version of the Psalms, and the first words which met his eyes were "*Levavi occulos ad monticolas,*" the Latin of the same passage. The book, which had come from the library of his father, Rev. Edward Everett Hale, was one he had scarcely ever looked at.

Extract from a letter by W. F. P. to Professor Hale:

"I am as interested in steering away from the pitfalls of chance coincidence, etc., as I am in establishing incidents which seemingly defy the doctrine of chance. I take it that your interpretation is that this case must conservatively be treated as a probable one of rather remarkable chance coincidence. You know the extraordinary one (perhaps the most extraordinary in history) which may be stated thus:

"John Adams and Thomas Jefferson, first political foes and then personal friends for many years, both on the Committee which brought about the Declaration of Independence

1. Died on the same day.
2. That day was the anniversary of the day when the Declaration of Independence was adopted.
3. And that 4th of July marked exactly one-half century of independence.

"I, Walter F[ranklin] Prince, born and then living in Detroit [Maine], learned of a Walter F[rancis] Prince, who was on the Detroit [Mich.] baseball team.

"Of course, you *may* have been impelled to take down the book and open to the passage, but we can hardly urge this. On the other hand,

I am convinced that there have been many complexly coincidental cases which cannot reasonably be ascribed to chance."

To this Professor Hale responded, saying that he fully agreed.

PROFESSOR Ḍ. D., a Ph.D., etc., a Psychologist and President of a university (Methodist), says:

"A certain type of dream (about dark water, or flood) has occurred more than once in my father's experience (deceased 1917) and in my own, prior to the death, unanticipated, of relatives or friends. However, I am prone to explain these verified happenings upon the basis of (1) coincidence, (2) a kind of conditioned reflex, (3) summation-effect of heads, anxiety, (4) retroactive amnesias."

The annotator tried to get a fuller and clearer explanation, but got only the statement that he had had the dream several times prior to the deaths of relatives and friends, and thinks that they were " due to the factors already indicated."

The professor differs from many people (including myself) in that their attention has never been attracted to *any* particular type of dream as having occurred repeatedly before the unanticipated deaths of relatives and friends. How an unanticipated death could condition a *previous* dream as its reflex, or how anything whatever could time dreams of a particular type so that they would come just before entirely unexpected deaths, I cannot claim to understand. Nor, although I can easily understand why dreads and anxieties should produce dreams of a particular type, is it plain why these should be timed so as to be the prelude to unanticipated deaths. Of course the professor has a right to impeach his own memory, but one would think that, being of scientific trend, and having noted in his own case more than once coincidences of the same peculiar type related by his father, his attention would be alert to discover and his memory impressed to retain, any instances where this type dream was *not* followed by the death of a friend or relative. And that his attention being thus attracted, as a psychologist desirous to know something about his own retroactive amnesias he would record every such dream. It is doubtful if guesses furnish better evidence, really, for the negative than they do for the affirmative of a question.

V. PSYCHIC (?) INCIDENTS EXPLAINED

The reporters of experiences in this section have discovered or are able to conjecture explanations thereof. It is possible that every one supposed that, had he not given or conjectured an explanation, his incident would have been accepted as possessing credentials entitling it to be regarded as probably psychic in character. Not once, however, is this the case. In every instance, unless fuller and guarding details were obtained, any careful psychic researcher would have assumed a normal explanation, since a normal explanation is not excluded by the terms of the narration.

PROFESSOR WILLIAM H. ALLISON, PH.D., who teaches Ecclesiastical History at Colgate University (Baptist clergyman), sends an illustration of mental mechanics.

" The nearest approach [to a psychic incident] was the *clear vision of a landscape* as I was sitting on right side of railroad train looking across the Merrimack River *above* Hooksett, N. H. I tried to locate it in my memory. On return trip, later in the day, I recognized the same landscape (Hooksett Pinnacle) *below* Hooksett, and on opposite side of train. I had earlier been over that railroad a good many times, but had not for two years and in the meantime had traveled extensively in Europe. The two landscapes are perhaps one-half mile apart. Subconscious association in memory is my explanation of it."

Dr. Allison's wording is not entirely clear, and he neglected to answer the letter asking him to make it so. Presumably he means that the landscape seen on the return journey was the actual one, previously seen mentally when about a half a mile from the actual spot. He does not necessarily imply that psychical researchers would interpret the experience as a supernormal one, and they certainly would not. Surely, as he intimates, the scenery above Hooksett roused a subconscious memory of the Pinnacle, probably the most striking object in its neighborhood, and this rose in his upper consciousness in the form of a picture.

Neither Myers nor any one governed by his canons of research would regard the vivid visualizing of a landscape, even if a man experienced it in his arm-chair, wrote down its detailed description at once and afterward came upon the actual landscape, as "psychical," once it were found that the percipient had visited the spot before. It would be assumed that some emotional association revived a memory image so energetically that it became, so to speak, exteriorized.

Professor Samuel Avery, Ph.D., B.Sc., etc., Chancellor emeritus of the University of Nebraska, chemist and author of technical bulletins, writes:

"Some eighteen years ago I was riding through a valley in Virginia when the thought came to me, 'I am revisiting a familiar scene'; yet, I 'knew' that I had never been in Virginia before. For several days I suffered some mental distress on the subject. At length I thought it through. I had actually visited, a time or two, a very similar valley in Germany not far from Heidelberg. In each valley was a tannery and the odor of the bark created the illusion. Thus a subtle odor permeating a lovely valley almost created for me a 'psychic experience.'"

This classifies with Professor Allison's incident. The actual spot was not close at hand in Chancellor Avery's case, and he had no mental picture. But there was a haunting feeling of familiarity. Probably the visual resemblance would not have been enough to cause this; there he may have seen a dozen valleys more or less similar. Olfactory sensations are, at least with some people, powerfully operative in rousing memories. Thus the odor of tansy always brings to the mind of the annotator the picture of a spot by a brook where tansy grew, since he lingered there once when a boy, experiencing emotion because of the death of a relative.

Even had the writer of the incident not traced the explanation, this book would have been far from accepting the incident as evidential of a "psychic" quality.

Mr. Edgar Rice Burroughs, Novelist, relates that in 1899 he suffered a blow upon the head, so severe that for a number of weeks thereafter he saw figures, usually shrouded, standing by his bedside, at the time fully recognizing that they were hallucinations. It was at this time that an incident occurred which he thinks due to a subconscious act on his own part.

"It was my habit at this time to carry my keys, three or four in number, on a red silk cord about an eighth of an inch in diameter. The ends of the cord were tied in a hard knot and then cut off so closely to the knot that the ends were not visible. I had carried my keys in this way for some time, with the result that the silk, which was originally of a very bright color, was much darkened by use, though that portion inside of the knot must have been as fresh and bright as when first tied."

One morning, the keys having been in a locked room with him, he went to get them, and

"found that one of them had been removed from the cord, though the knot was still tied in precisely the same way that it had been; the ends were not protruding, nor was there any of the clean, bright-colored portion visible. This key could have been removed only by untying the knot and then retying it precisely as it had been, which would have been practically impossible for any one to accomplish without evidence of the knot having been tampered with being apparent.

"While the above appears to have not much bearing upon the subject of your investigation, it has suggested to me, when considered in the light of the fact that it is the only occurrence of its kind in a lifetime of over fifty years, that much other, perhaps all, so-called supernatural phenomena are the result of injured or diseased brains. Prior to my injury I had no hallucinations; subsequent to my recovery I have had none."

I do not have to urge that "practically impossible" does not mean the same as "possible," for Mr. Burroughs himself thinks that his own hands performed the act subconsciously, and as the result of a temporarily injured brain. Even had Mr. Burroughs been of another opinion, that this was a psychical performance, no scientific researcher would have been convinced. Without further testimony, one would not have been certain that the whole incident was not a hallucinatory one, owing to the morbid condition, involving paramnesia of time sequences regarding the removal of the key and cutting the ends of the cord. Nor does the narrative give any assurance that there remained, on the morning the key was found to be off, any "clean, bright-colored portion" left anywhere on the string. Working on the string to retie it might have soiled the spots, or this might have been done out of some subconscious purpose, and the slightly protruding ends cut off and concealed. Or by a rare good chance in making the knot at first loosely and then pulling in the ends, it may have settled down on the old lines. This would have been a rare chance, but not an impossible one.

Only the other day a lady brought several sheets of paper at the top of which she had typed words, and she was mystified to find faint replicas of a part of a line in each case above. She said that persons familiar with typewriters told her that it was impossible for the machine to produce such a double effect, and she came to ask me if I could explain the matter or was it a "spirit" phenomenon. I have no idea how the effect could have been made in the course of the ordinary typewriting process. But it could easily have been made by shifting the carriage back to the beginning of a certain word, turning the roller up for five single spaces, then typing the words again, striking the keys very gently. The faint replicas in every case were found immediately above and at the same distance. The lady *could* have invented the "phenomenon" with the purpose of seeing whether I would accept it as a heavenly one, or it *might* be that she executed it in an altered state of consciousness. I by no means fix on either theory, but neither am I convinced that there is anything supernormal in the matter.

It is quite pardonable that Mr. Burroughs, presumably not familiar with the data of psychic research, should wonder whether all its phenomena are not "the result of injured or diseased brains." But, in the first place, the indications are that in but a small percentage of instances had the subjects of noteworthy phenomena suffered injury, or were their brains diseased. Mrs. Piper, while she was being investigated, appeared to be quite normal as to health; there is not the least reason to suppose that Mrs. Soule has not been—barring colds and other small illnesses, such as few escape, she has seemed the very picture of mental and physical poise and vitality. Mrs. Leonard made the impression upon me of being a woman sound and vigorous in mind and body, and I never heard any rumor contradicting this impression. Mrs. King, whose astonishingly evidential psychometric work I have reported, has shown no indication of "diseased brains." And even in cases, reported by critical investigators, where the subject was not in good neural condition, that condition affords no key to the phenomena, no possible explanation. Sra. Maria de Z., it is true, was a great sufferer from insomnia, which may or may not have affected her brain, although her mentality to all appearances was sound. But were she as mad as a March hare, how could that fact explain her holding a sealed envelope containing a note written by a man just before his ship went down, carrying all its passengers and crew to death, and then describing, while in hypnotic trance, a scene of terror and confusion on a crowded deck, correctly describing a man, picturing his tearing a leaf from a notebook, enclosing it in a bottle and flinging it into the waves, and finally the going down of the ship?[1] The assumption of injury to or disease of the brain proceeds not one inch in the direction of explaining the acquisition of knowledge otherwise than through the known senses.

DR. LAURENCE LAFORGE, PH.D., of the United States Geological Survey (Congregationalist), testifies:

"When I was a lad of about thirteen and sleeping with a brother two years younger, we had an identical dream on waking one morning. As, however, it was a *waking* dream, and each spoke to the other during it, it seemed to me entirely probable that the dream was 'directed' by the circumstances, rather than being due to any metaphysical intercommunication of brain processes."

And the commentator entirely agrees with the conclusion.

PROFESSOR C. A. NEYMANN, A.B., M.D., Professor of Psychiatry in the Northwestern University, has attended numerous so-called séances held without financial recompense on the part of the medium.

"These could all be explained as hysterical manifestations. The *pencil rappings* were produced by crossing the legs and making the leather of the medium's shoes squeak," etc.

So far as appears, these numerous séances were with one medium. The annotator has attended hundreds of sittings with dozens of mediums of which it could be said that "all could be explained as hysterical manifestations, and many more where all could be explained as fraudulent manifestations. And he has had many experiments with a comparatively few mediums, of which neither could be said. The method of producing fake raps (presumably "pencil rappings" means sounds like the tapping of a pencil) stated above is one of the clumsiest of dozens.

PROFESSOR F. C. PRESCOTT, A.B., of the department of English at Cornell University, author (Episcopalian), relates:

---

[1] See Dr. Pagenstecher's "Past Events Seership" in *Proceedings* A. S. P. R., XVI, also Prince's report of experiments with the Senora, *Ib.*, XV. Both present many other evidential results.

"Some twenty-one years ago I was called home by the very serious illness of my brother. I had not been at home for a year or two. On arrival (twenty-four hours before his death) I learned that he had had a brain lesion and was only dimly conscious. As it was late at night he had not been told of my coming and I was not to see him until the next morning. I went upstairs to bed in a room next his, and as I did so heard him calling my name in what seemed to me a tone of surprise and dismay. This, which seemed very strange at the moment, might be explained by supposing that, though I entered by a distant door, he had heard my name spoken as I was greeted, or that he recognized my footstep on the stair."

Exactly so. Furthermore, were the possibility of the sick man's knowledge through hearing excluded, the psychic researcher would still have to recognize that a dying man, "dimly conscious," would not be very unlikely to call his absent brother's name, and that the tone interpreted as "dismay" more appropriately would signify dissatisfaction because of the brother's absence than joy because of his presence.

PROFESSOR F. W. SARDESON, M.S., PH.D., formerly professor of Geology in the University of Minnesota, afterwards geologist of the United States Geological Survey, reports that when

"Between twenty and thirty years of age, I several times saw 'ghosts' when I was greatly overworked. They were seen in each case out in the open, under clear sky, etc. But in each case retracing my steps and returning the matter solved itself."

Asked to give a sample, he says that when on a geological journey in Iowa, as he started to walk over a railroad trestle he saw at a little distance from the further end what he thought was a man in his shirt sleeves, standing on the railroad. He crossed the trestle, of necessity watching his step, and when he had got over looked up, and the man was gone. He retraced his steps and again saw the "man." But now it is recognized that the "man" is really "a reflection of the sky in a pond some one thousand feet beyond," which disappears as one advances.

"A number of such incidents of which this one is the last, convinced me that my carrying a pistol was making a coward of me. I laid it aside and have never been annoyed [in like manner] in the thirty-five years that followed."

The professor explains that he had taken up the practice of carrying a pistol as " these were days of tramps and ugly farmer's dogs," and he was traveling alone as a geologic field worker.

His " ghosts," it will be recognized readily, were not hallucinations, but illusions, misinterpretations of visual impressions made by real objects. Any one is liable to an occasional illusion, but in his case the general liability was increased by an over-worked condition and consequent nervous tension, and also by apprehension of possible attack. As attack would most likely be from a man, the illusions tended to take the form of a man. Carrying a pistol seems to have operated powerfully in the way of direct suggestion.

Of course no psychic researcher would think of ascribing evidential weight to any such experience, even had it had no explanation. Though it had been purely a visual hallucination, merely as such and apart from any correspondence with an unrecognized event, it could have no evidential weight. On the other hand, it is quite conceivable that an illusion might have evidential value, but a hallucinatory factor would need to mingle with the illusion. Professor Gilbert Murray tells us (*Proceedings* S. P. R., v. XXIX, pp. 59-60) that some of his apparently telepathic deliverances were meditated by sense impressions. While the " agent " was thinking of Savonarola and the people burning their luxurious possessions in the public square of Florence, a bit of coal tumbled out of the fire. Murray " smelt oil or paint burning," and so got the whole scene. At another time the subject of the experiment was: " Mr. Z. . . . galloping along a beach in Greece." In part the correct response of Professor Murray, according to his testimony, was mediated by his " *happening* (?) to hear a horse galloping in the street outside." But in each instance the attention somehow selected and fixed upon one sense impression out of the many experienced at the time. And probably, while other experiments were in progress, bits of burning coal tumbled, and doubtless horses galloped in the street, but only when they could serve as a bridge, apparently did these particular sense impressions come to the forefront of attention. These and many other of the experiments seem to indicate that knowledge in the subconscious struggled (so to speak) to emerge into the conscious, and if the " percipient " chanced to experience any sense impression, visual, auditory, olfactory or other, *similar* to some factor of that subconscious, knowledge of the subject set, it served as an easier path to conscious expression.

So one might seem to see a man, and then discover that, generally speaking, it was but the reflection of a cloud upon water. But if the reflection for a moment was, particularly if with emotional shock, recognized as the face of the subject's father, and it was afterward found that the father died at that hour while calling for his son, the impression would not be without evidential weight, although its *point d'appui* was a mere illusion.

The Hon. E. A., former Associate Justice of a State Supreme Court (Roman Catholic), says that he formerly thought that he had experienced a premonition or apparition. Traveling in an automobile on a country road by night, he seemed to see some cows in the road ahead, shouted to the driver to slow up, they disappeared, and later, he cannot now say how long, they again showed up. The facts could, he says,

" be rationally accounted for several ways: (1) fear on my part, (2) did actually see them and light may then have gone dim, or remained dim and rebrightened, (3) error in vision, (4) some coincidental factors may have been at work creating the illusion, or many things, if one takes time to work at possible suggestions."

The annotator agreed, but preferred another explanation, and wrote, inquiring:

" May not the automobile have swerved on a curve of the road after the headlights revealed the cows, so that the beams left them for a few moments?"

And the judge answered " Yes."

Professor E. B., Botanist of a university, a Ph.D., sent this statement:

" From my family I have heard much concerning ' rapping.' However, the ' rapping ' was most emphatically not psychic but of *definitely known origin*. I can give details if you wish."

A number of persons besides wrote that they could give details, but when wooed to do so, even repeatedly, retreated into the vale of silence. One wonders whether they supposed that " normal " explanations would be unwelcome, and lost their zest for exposition when the fact was found to be otherwise. The commentator would have delighted to learn of some method of trick rapping of which he previously had no conception.

BACHELOR OF ARTS E. C., Dramatist (Episcopalian), reports:

" While engaged in the long sustained and absorbing study and in the intense imaginatively creative work of dramatic writing, I have not infrequently felt, seen, or heard one or more of my characters actually present and talking with me, and even at times critically considering my work. They were sometimes quite as vividly clear to me as if they had been truly objective, but if I chose to reflect on their nature I was never deceived into thinking they were objective rather than subjective. I have therefore always believed that I was justified in regarding these ' visions ' or whatever they might be called not at all as abnormal phenomena but as quasi-objective visualizations quite within the range of the normal imagination."

Exactly so, imagination cultivated to the point of causing at times, probably usually after protracted dramatic labor, more or less of hallucinatory objectivation. Dickens, it is said, often had similar experiences. Tissot, after imaginative living for years in the New Testament period, sometimes saw a Biblical scene so static that he painted from it as one would from posing models.

No species or instance of hallucination can in itself be evidence for the supernormal, however vivid. The evidence, if any, is to be found in the relation of the hallucination to something else, with no discoverable causal link connecting them. The hundreds of recorded instances of apparitions of persons seen at or near the moment of their unexpected deaths at a distance are to the point. In none of these cases is it the hallucination of seeing a person not really present which is reckoned as evidential; the evidence is in the (1) *identity of the person* (2) with the person *then dying or just died* (3) *without knowledge* on the part of the percipient that the person is in any danger of death. Take the case of a man who once in his life experiences an apparition, and it is then of the person whose unexpected death occurs at a distance within the hour—one such case is sufficient to cause an intelligent mind to wonder if there is nothing more than accidental coincidence involved. One such case should not produce any conviction or any reaction stronger than curious speculation. But when such cases have accumulated to hundreds, it should be evident that we have a problem of real importance on our hands, in which mathematics dealing with the calculus of chance must play a part.

PROFESSOR E. D., an A.B., Mathematician and university teacher of Mathematics (Baptist), writes:

278   THE ENCHANTED BOUNDARY

"The only thing approaching this [the 'psychical'] is the occasional solution of a mathematical problem, which before was wholly obscure, without even a conscious clue to analysis."

Recognizing that we have here ordinary subconscious processes exercised at their best, it was of interest to know whether, as in some other cases, the result appeared in a dream or on waking. The witness responded to the inquiry:

"Neither dream nor waking from a dream nor early in the morning nor any other particular time. To my mind it is perfectly normal, and belongs to the same kind of experience as an effort to recall a lost name. It will not come. You cannot get the least clue to it. You throw it off your mind, and in a half hour or six hours after it comes to you like a flash of light from nowhere so far as you can trace it. You perhaps call the process 'unconscious cerebration,' and perhaps say, 'The mind once started on the trail of the name never quit the pursuit while we were conscious of other matters, but now having retrieved the name presents it to our consciousness.' But where was it the while? What blind trail did this unconscious mind (or film of mind) follow? Who can tell? So a mathematical puzzle recalcitrant and unaccommodating to conscious reason integrates in the dark and emerges as insight and reason does the rest."

Very well put, for a layman in psychology! When the conscious mind labors strenuously and vainly on a problem for a considerable time there is a tendency for the subconscious mind to continue the effort, bringing out from its storehouse the various necessary items of mathematical fact and logic, and fitting them together, the result or the essential clues to it afterward flashing up into consciousness. Calling the process "unconscious cerebration," equivalent to *unconscious braination*, however, does not make the matter any plainer, consoling as Carpenter and others have found that empty expression.[2]

PROFESSOR E. E., former teacher of English in a university, Litt.D., author, at the age of eight dreamed that he found " more Bible " in the shape of a book " Monboddin," which began:

"O King, thou shalt be slain
And Israel shall reign
Thus spake the seer Monboddin."

---

[2] See Wm. McDougall's *Outline of Abnormal Psychology*, pp. 209 ff., 253 ff.

He dreamed many times in verse, when a child, and, as time passed, the verses improved in literary quality. Once he dreamed:

"Alas, in childhood treasuring bits of heaven,
How oft we end our days in hoarding earth,"

which he now pronounces "sententious but not poetical."

Without denying that the remarkable literary genius embodied in the "Patience Worth"[3] poetry may be the sudden outflowering of her subconscious, I have yet maintained that if it is, hers is a case *sui generis*, and have invited psychologists to find in all the history of literature a single other person, who has, at a mature age, suddenly begun to produce poetry much of which is worthy of poets of first rank, after never having manifested any literary talent whatever, or had any literary ambition, or even any noticeable literary taste or special fondness for literature, up to the age of thirty years. I doubt if there can even be found the case of a child that broke out into passable verse without previous fondness for and considerable acquaintance with poetical productions.

Let us turn to the case of Professor H. He did not dream of finding "more Bible" until he had read the Protestant Bible through and had then discovered that there is, in addition, an Apocrypha. He also says:

"Where this queer name came from puzzled me, until years later I came upon a bound volume of *Harper's Magazine* of the year preceding the dream, and found in the Editor's Drawer, which being ostensibly 'the funny part' I read as a child, a skit in verse on Lord Monboddo, a predecessor of Darwin in belief of the animal origin of man. But the metre of my verse was different. I must have got it from the narrative poems of Sir Walter Scott, which I was reading at the time of the dream.

"I used to dream quite often in verse, which I thought remarkably good, but which I laughed at when I awoke, and found my 'fairy gold' dried leaves. Still, it grew better and better, as my taste in poetry improved in my waking hours, and as I read better models. Once I remember two lines of poetry that did not rhyme, and were evidently the conclusion of a poem. So I wrote a sonnet ending with them."

There we have it; he saturated himself with poetry, before he began to produce it in the subconscious dream-state. The dream verses im-

---

[3] See *The Case of Patience Worth; a Critical Study of Certain Unusual Phenomena*, Boston Society for Psychic Research.

proved in proportion as he " read better models." In answer to queries it was learned further that, having learned to read at the age of six years:

" Thereafter reading aloud was an æsthetic joy to me, and by the time I was eight years old I had read all of Milton, dipped into Shakespeare, could repeat by heart numerous passages from these, and many short poems of Burns and other poets whose works were in our home. Before I learned to read I could repeat rhymes taught me by my mother and my paternal grandfather. He died when I was five years of age, but I remember still his rhyme of the ' Borrowin' (Borrowed) Days,' which he brought from County Donegal, Ireland, and which version, handed down by word of mouth, is much cleverer than the literary one found in ' The Compleynt of Scotland.' Father would recite such heroic poems as ' Balaclava.' "

This is just about such an answer as had been expected. I still maintain that the sudden bursting forth in 1914 of the literary splendor associated with the name " Patience Worth " is, considering Mrs. Curran's history, psychologically unaccounted for; that if the case were put only as a hypothetical one it would be regarded as contradictory of the laws of the human mind. I make no assertion as regards precocious children, but wonder if the case can be found of a child who has either dreamed or consciously written passable verses, previous to warming himself at the Promethean fire and borrowing a spark therefrom—or, to forsake mythology, previous to reading or hearing considerable poetry and experiencing æsthetic gratification therefrom.

PROFESSOR E. F., a Ph.D., of the department of Latin in a college (Congregationalist), has had no psychic experiences:

" Save for occasionally finding that a person in the same room with me was thinking of a subject of which I was, sometimes not at all suggested by our previous conversation and not (apparently) growing out of any observation we were making in common. Doubtless it was due to some suggestion unrecognized by either of us."

If at a loss to find any nexus, it does not seem quite logical to say that " doubtless " one existed. Of course it may have, and something, also, should be allowed for chance coincidence.

PROFESSOR E. G., an M.E., holding the chair of Electrical Engi-

PSYCHIC (?) INCIDENTS EXPLAINED

neering at a technical institute, furnishes an amusing explained mystery. At the age of fourteen he was preparing to go to bed in a room over that in which the dead body of a favorite uncle lay, several times he heard " a long-drawn-out sigh," rejoined the family but did not inform them, an hour later returned to his room and again heard the sounds. This time he reported the facts, another uncle went to the room with him. After a short wait the sighs began to be heard again. The room below was examined without any result. The sounds in the bedroom recurred at short intervals, and all was mystery, until a very tiny dog crawled out from between the sheets at the foot of the bed.

The proper course in such a case is to assume some normal causation and diligently to seek for it. A person at all familiar with investigation would have listened in different parts of the room and thus soon have located the sounds. It is to be expected that sometimes sounds should be heard, simple as to their source when the source is discovered, but puzzling until then. It is evident that the explanation of such an incident as the above has no logical bearing on another case, any more than the discovery that a body of land in the Arctic zone, at first thought to be an island, is really a part of the mainland, has upon the question whether another body of land in the Antarctic zone is or is not an island, or any more than the exposure of a wild-cat mine swindle *explains* the Comstock mines. In *The Psychic in the House* is the account of mysterious sounds which efforts continued unremittingly for weeks and months failed to explain, but the writer remained fully aware that people are sometimes mystified by sounds which a very little of suitable investigation would trace and explain.

MR. E. H., a prominent Bacteriologist (Unitarian), replies " No " to the query whether he has had any psychic experiences, but he is a bit perplexed, for all that, by his experiences with a certain noted medium for mental and physical phenomena.

He could not see the lights that some others saw, he had an animated conversation with " maternal great-uncle John " who never lived (nor was the matter helped when this spirit switched himself to the paternal side), his living " mother " communicated, other " relatives " whose names could not be recognized greeted him, the boast that spirits can see in the dark seemed to be negated in his case, and the bringing of an inoffensive scientific instrument stopped phenomena. No evidential statements are mentioned, except that the professor's wife's " father " was introduced by his last name, with the direction to "mention the locket" to his daughter. He had in fact once given "a cheap locket" to her. If this fact had only been stated! But if her mother had owned a locket, or she herself had when a girl, or she had bought a locket with money given by the father, etc., etc., the mention would still have had its very limited evidentiality, and probably most women and their fathers share memories of some locket in the family. Presumably the medium knew the professor's name. He attended a number of times in the course of several years. *Who's Who in America* is a handy volume of reference, and it prints the family name of the father of Professor E. H.'s wife. It does not reveal his first name, and that was not given by the "spirit."

Again, the professor thought that he heard his grandmother's pet name for his mother pronounced, but, oddly, it did not purport to come from the grandmother but from the mother herself, then living! The mother's name also was in *Who's Who*, but with no sign whether she was living or dead. The chances were, judging from the professor's age, that she was not living. Now, while the annotator is on record as convinced that names have come in some cases and under some circumstances, which were quite protected and had considerable evidential value, yet he is obliged in this case to point out possibilities in connection with that diminutive name which have escaped the professor.

(1) The medium could have learned the name in *Who's Who*, where it appears as that of the professor's mother, and gambled on a diminutive of it, with great likelihood that *someone* had employed it. (2) Or, since the medium apparently whispered the name, only the first half of it, almost identical with the pet name, may have been caught by the listener.

If *Who's Who* rendered no help at this point, there are other possibilities, as observation has shown. (3) There is a tendency on the part of sitters (and the most learned is not necessarily exempt), if a name is pronounced obscurely, in whispers or indistinctly through a trumpet, and it *resembles* that of a relative, to "hear" it as if it were given correctly. The name Annie, for example, may be understood as Anna, Amy, Fannie, Nannie, Emma, or the pet name of E. H.'s mother. (4) The stated condition that "the sitter must talk freely to get the best responses" is suspicious. It is what we meet often in fraudulent work, especially where physical factors mingle with the mental. The talk serves to cover up betraying noises. But it also serves another purpose. If one talks freely with the "spirit," it is very difficult to avoid saying something at some point from which the medium may at least draw inferences, and it becomes practically impossible to remember all one has said and just according to what sequences he said it. Here is a case. Through a trumpet came a name which seemed to some present to be Mary. But the person apparently addressed had a sister, then deceased, whose name was Cary. He responded. " Did you say 'Cary'?" Now through the trumpet came the name again, this time clearly and unmistakably "Cary." A conversation ensued. The sitter afterwards cited the incident as evidential, especially since Cary is an uncommon name. In such sittings common names are purposely pronounced obscurely, since the medium has learned that sitters may thus be caused to imagine that a similar name which fits some one of his deceased relatives or friends, was the one given, and add as a highly evidential feature that the name was peculiar and no one else present knew that it belonged to him.

Contrast all the conditions with their great liabilities of illusion, on the one hand, with those of a standard experiment chosen by the experimenter, on the other. Light instead of darkness, clear pronunciation instead of obscure whispering or trumpet speaking, no necessity to "talk freely," stenographic record of all said on both sides instead of vain efforts to remember exactly what each said and in what order, etc.

PROFESSOR E. I., a Ph.B., university teacher of one branch of Mathematics, and author of books on his specialty (Methodist), has been impressed but not convinced by personal incidents which might suggest telepathy.

"The thought of some person has so often come suddenly to my mind very shortly before receiving a telephone call from that person, that the frequent repetition of the experience has come to appear surprising to me. I consider it subject to a 'normal' explanation, however, as I so frequently think of some one without receiving a call, that I put it down to the law of averages—and doubt the explanation."

One can but doubt when the witness doubts. Such coincidences certainly could be no more than the law of averages would account for, or a person could have had them due to some telepathic capacity too small to give assurance of its existence.

VI. THEN WHY HAS IT NOT HAPPENED TO ME?

This is the question which seems to underlie all of the following six statements. Two persons desired messages from the dead and did not receive them, the grandfather of another " promised to return," but did not, the fourth is agnostic to all evidence of the supernormal furnished by others, since his own life has been barren of it; the fifth does not disregard the testimony of others but thinks it " dubious " for the express reason that he has had no such experience, and the professor who is bold or indiscreet enough to allow his name to appear has had no phenomena, although " keen " in his interest.

PROFESSOR F. A., a Ph.D., who holds forth on Chemistry in a university, author on his subject, writes:

" Since the death of my wife in ———— I have been perfectly confident that she would have communicated with me if she could. No such communication has been received, even in a dream."

Reply to Professor F. A.:

" I wonder if, in your mind, the assumed power of some spirits to communicate argues that necessarily everyone should be able to do so? It seems to me like assuming that, if the evidence which has been offered for telepathy between the living, some of which is very cogent, is sufficient to prove that phenomenon, every two persons ought to be able to produce the phenomenon of telepathy between them. We know that this is far from being the case, that in fact there are very few persons who have the experience to a demonstrated degree. If there is communication from the dead, it is probably of a telepathic order (at least for the most part), and it probably implies conditions, part of which may be mental or temperamental, on the part of both the ' agent ' and the ' percipient.' It might be that you yourself are not a good receiver.

" I myself have never had the slightest feeling as though my deceased wife were attempting to communicate with me, not the slightest feeling of her presence, which some describe. Yet in a book which is

THEN WHY HAS IT NOT HAPPENED TO ME? 285

out today, entitled *Leonard and Soule Experiments in Psychical Research*, there is printed a great deal of what appeared like, and is offered as, evidence of communication from her, through another person—a 'psychic.' I would not take this series alone as evidence, no matter how difficult it would be to account for it, but on the background of other evidence and connection with it, I think that the spiritistic hypothesis is not to be lightly set aside. Yet I have no idea whatever that the time is or is likely to come when everybody can get such evidence. I am about as critical and hard-boiled as they make them, and previous to the experiments with this particular psychic, I have had very little that I could regard as evidential purporting to come from Mrs. Prince. But explain it as you may, the evidence to which I refer is very striking indeed."

MEDICAL DOCTOR F. B., Professor of Pathology and writer on his subject (Episcopalian), gives similar testimony to the preceding.

"In spite of the fact that I have always had more or less interest in psychic investigation, and right after the death of a scientific friend tried to put myself in a receptive mood, in a dark room, after having asked him to reply to my question, I never received the slightest indication of attempted communication."

Reply to the above:

"I wonder if you regarded and now regard this experiment as decisive? It appears to me that a negative result in a single case could not be accepted as an indication in one way or another, any more than a failure to get telepathic results between two designated living persons would in the slightest tend to disprove the evidence which has been offered, that between certain persons telepathic phenomena have appeared. On the spiritistic theory it would be most probable that any so-called communications from the dead would be of a telepathic character, and not at all, as many people naïvely seem to think, after the fashion of a conversation between two persons whose powers of communication have no limit.

"I wonder, also, if, in case you had, 'right after the death' of your friend, apparently received a reply to your question, unless the question were one which you could not yourself answer, you would now regard that experience as evidential, and not an hallucination due to emotion? I know a man who had arranged with his wife that she would communicate with him if possible after death, and had considerable expectation of her doing so, but for eleven months he had no experience whatever that gave him the impression of even the effort.

Then, in a distant city, in a hotel, one night, entirely without expectation or without any introduction of which he was aware that could give any possible hint of a normal explanation, he had a startling experience as of his wife conversing with him, which is convincing to him unto this day. I do not offer this case as proof, but simply as something we would not expect."

PROFESSOR F. C., an Artist who teaches Art in a university (Unitarian), makes an objection, somewhat like the two preceding it:

"My paternal grandfather on his death-bed promised to return. He was a minister in a New Bedford Seamans' Bethel. No manifestation has been received."

Letter to Professor F. C.:

"Of course I have no right to put you to any further trouble, and yet I am curious to know if the facts you state seem to you in any degree to argue against the spiritistic theory.

"While there is much in psychic research that has no apparent connection with the spiritistic claim, and while I am decidedly not a propagandist for spiritism, I personally am unable to see that such a failure to keep such a promise had very much value as evidence. Admitting there is such a thing as telepathy between the living, if a particular person should promise that a message would go from him to another person, and if nothing happened to verify the promise I do not think that it would in the slightest invalidate the evidence for telepathy which actually exists. On the other hand, I should say it was very imprudent on the part of the persons to make such a promise. Apparently there are only a few who can act as an ' agent ' successfully. We are apt to assume that if a person survives after his death he ought to be able to do anything. But we have no reason to make this assumption. For aught we know, assuming that there is any such thing as spirit communication, the spirits capable of ' telepathing ' messages to those on earth might be very few in number."

PROFESSOR F. D., an M.D., Librarian and professor of Library Methods in a university, testifies:

"Particularly during my college years and a few years after I was very much interested in the whole question of psychical research and was more than unusually on the lookout to observe any such phenomena as you describe in your letter. I was educated at Haverford, a

Quaker college, dominated largely by the tenets of a religious body which has always stood for mysticism and other-worldliness. I grew up in a Pennsylvania-German neighborhood where belief in the supernatural still persisted, even though there was a large body of skeptics also resident in the section. In spite of all these predilections to the receipt of impressions of a psychical or unexplainable nature, I cannot honestly say that I have ever had any experience which actually belongs in this class. You will draw your own conclusions. Perhaps it is a natural tough-mindedness which William James describes, or perhaps some other reason. It is not skepticism, but at most simply agnosticism."

From response to Professor F. D.:

"It is of interest, of course, that you grew up under such influences and yet have had no such experiences, and yet the fact does not in the least surprise me. It would surprise me, possibly, if I thought that all such experiences were the effects of credulity. As a matter of fact, there are many persons who have grown up under influences which stimulate faith, imagination, etc., and even have been themselves firm believers in psychic occurrences, and yet have never had any themselves. On the other hand, there are many others, including men of science, whose environment has been just the opposite, who breathed the very air of distrust of them, and yet such an experience has suddenly come to them. It may be interesting to you to know that very few psychical researchers of the more scientific order appear to have had any such experiences themselves. It is difficult to show that clergymen, the most of whom base their teachings upon purported supernormal facts, tend to have these experiences more than unreligious men.

"Therefore I should say it was not necessarily 'natural tough-mindedness' or 'agnosticism' in your case which prevents your having such experiences, but that it is something as much a part of yourself as your complexion. There apparently are some persons who have demonstrable telepathic power, but most people have not, irrespective of whether they are credulous or incredulous, scientists or ignoramuses."

PROFESSOR CLYDE W. VOTAW, PH.D., who has the chair of Biblical Literature at Chicago University, author of books on the Bible and religion, writes:

"I am now at the age of sixty-five years. Graduate of Amherst College and Yale Divinity School. Then for thirty-seven years at the

University of Chicago as Professor of New Testament Literature. All these years I have been a special student of philosophy, psychology, and biological science. I am critical, not credulous; matter of fact, not fanciful or mystical. I have been *keen* for forty years as regards the phenomena here under consideration, but have never experienced anything of importance in this line, and have never personally known of anything important."

We hear much of the "will to believe," and theologians are supposed to be particularly liable to it. To be interested in psychical claims has been declared quite enfeebling to intellectual poise, while long interest in the subject has been pronounced fatal. But here is a man who graduated from a divinity school, which throughout maintains a super-sensible world, and, moreover, has had a " keen " interest in the subject of psychic research for forty years; and yet has had no psychical experience in his life and no personal connection with one. The annotator has met a multitude of cases of such men, open-minded or, more, benevolently inclined, toward psychical experiences, or even desirous of having them, yet who have never experienced one. On the other hand, they have come, like lightning out of the blue sky, to many persons indifferent to or even prejudiced against such claims.

PROFESSOR F. E., an M.D. and M.S., prominent Oculist and Aurist, former university professor of diseases of the eye and ear (Episcopalian), writes a thoughtful letter, which furnishes the text for a somewhat extended discussion.

"I think that testimony, bearing within itself something of the character of opposition, is not undesirable in viewing any big problem. It may have, in itself, some elements of the constructive.

"All of my life—especially my more mature life—I have watched myself and my contacts with my environment, to see if there were ever a realization that I was a receptor to immaterial stimuli. After the death of my mother, between whom and myself there existed an unusual understanding and mental intimacy, I was particularly interested. I felt sure, owing to this unusual sameness of mental and spiritual values, that I would have some consciousness arising from her. I carefully watched and receptively waited any form of reaction from this source. It has never come. It has been possible for me *in my own psychic* world, to build up a contact, but I have always been assured that this was *purely* subjective, and lacked entirely the corroboration of any evidence that any one acquainted with the rules and methods of reason would insist upon. I have also had many other intimate relationships broken by death, or such that even in life, may have been manifested, but I have never been able to assure myself that I was 'listening in' with satisfactory results, to an outside separation from a spiritual or body presence. My attitude in these cases has been a willing, and not an unwilling frame of mind and spirit. It has never been one of excluding doubt. But the results have been, in all cases, the same.

"It is presuming too far, simply from this personal experience, to cast aside all evidence submitted by others as not valid and authentic. But from the exercising of rules of reason and judgment, the only source that *I* can judge from—myself, I have held these reports as at least dubious. From an analysis of them, with a knowledge that should be possessed by one who has studied much and written much on neurology, I have the suspicion that the phenomena arose *purely from within*, and not from external environment. There is nothing so disreputably tricky as the human brain, for it is the inheritor of the sum total of all the environments that have surrounded its ancestors back to the first living cell. The nervous system in its entirety may reflect all of these phases, but our inability to interpret them correctly may lead us to very false conclusions, and, what may appear to be resulting from the present, may be only a purely materialistic reflection of the past. Our minds are great storehouses of unconscious experiences. I am led to believe that its function is a purely material matter, *even into the realms of the highest psychic phenomena*. I believe what we would designate as psychic is very often nothing but physiology unrecognized and not understood.

"One thing that is often entirely forgotten, or not recognized, is the undoubted fact that our thoughts and entire mental processes *are largely pictorial*. The pictorial enters into the functioning of every other sense. For example, the memory concerned with the sense of hearing nearly always has, if not always, the *background of a picture*. This applies to taste, to touch, and to hearing. We are not conscious of this until after careful analysis. With the memory of the actual pain is the picture of that instant. I believe that these pictorial backgrounds constitute almost the entire mental complex of our memories.

"The phenomena of hallucination is also interesting in considering the subject you are investigating. These are purely and entirely from within us. They are different from illusions which are perceptual realizations of things from without, but wrongly interpreted. It is my belief that all of these processes are purely physical and physiological, just as I believe *all* manifestation of the mind's activity is physical and mechanistic. No report that I have ever read regarding visions, premonitions, and the like, have ever been such that their apparent reality was as vivid or more vivid than the pictorial play of the brain in the case of what we fully realize is a pure hallucination. The individual may not be conscious that he has ever experienced such pictures before, and does not know where they come from. But it will be noticed that they never possess any element or character that does not find their material counterpart. We cannot conceive of the beauty of heaven, except in the terms of such figures and values as our earthly experience has presented to us. If we go beyond these values, the pictures become pure mists or nebulous formations. The extremely delicate and highly organized state of certain minds render them extremely susceptible to the most marvelous development of the pictorial. With this, the sense of hearing also offers its dispositions. I believe that these mental reactions, resulting in visions and similar experiences, are just as actual when there is no external stimulus of any kind, as when such exist; that is, in some individuals. As much of a mystery as thought itself is, I believe it is no mystery, but simply something we do not yet understand—of course, in this sense, a mystery. From these remarks, it is very evident that I am not persuaded in my own mind that those who have passed beyond the portals influence us, except through our own subjective memories that concern them in the realities of the flesh. Their influences upon us, whatever they be, are such influences as were exerted in life, and which have become a part of our being. They are not pressing immaterial stimuli, being received from an actual immaterial source.

"My dear Dr. Prince, I am very much interested in your investigations, and hold an entirely open mind. Nothing will please me more than to find I am entirely mistaken. In fact, I yearn to discover that I am entirely in error, for the implications in my arguments are unavoidably connected with doubts. I shall be very pleased indeed if you will be so gracious as to give me the opportunity to see the results of your investigation. It is possible that there are more things in this world than are dreamt of in our philosophies, and that others are attuned to certain things that some of us are not."

The first thing to remark is that here again is a man with at least the wish-to-believe, one who fairly "yearns" to have his belief that "*all* the manifestation of the mind's activity is physical and mechanistic" refuted, but he has had no experience which in the least tended to that end.

The expression that "all manifestation of the mind's activity is physical" is not a lucid one; presumably it means that all the content of consciousness is purely a product of the brain. In that case the death of the brain is the extinction of the mind, and one wonders how such a view escapes extinguishing the professor's Episcopalianism.

Once admit that mind is a real though impalpable entity, and its working mechanistically is irrelevant to the discussion. Hallucinations would be mechanisms though they were, some of them, instigated from without. Telepathy would be mechanistic, yet telepathy still, with all its supernormal significance. If the mind can out of its own energy determine that the hand shall grasp an object, some mechanism of its own which we do not and may never understand comes into play which acts upon the efferent nerves; then come two mechanisms, one of the nerves which makes a nexus with the muscles, the other a mechanism by which the muscles contract so that the object is grasped. Thus, if there is such a thing as a spirit and if it can ever get a message through a psychic, mechanisms are involved, and while we cannot picture or comprehend that by which the spirit affects the psychic's brain, we can do so as easily as we can picture or comprehend the mechanism by which the mind calls into play the mechanisms of nerves and muscles which result in picking up a ball.

As the professor has stated, the phenomena of hallucination are also interesting in consideration of the subject we are investigating; more than that, they are vital to it. And we assume that a hallucination is what he says it is, an immaterial visual or auditory image arising from an interior mechanism. But it cannot be granted that this mechanism is always initiated from within. The spark, so to speak, which starts it may be from without. Professor Hale tells us that after his brother said that he was going skating, and he himself feared the ice was not safe, he experienced the hallucination of hearing his brother call his name, as if for help. Another witness tells of anxiety caused by news of a mother's illness, followed by a like hallucination of hearing her voice. A very susceptible person, smelling the powerful odor of flowers commonly found at funerals, sees a coffin.

Since a hallucination may be initiated by some cause without the sensorium, it seems to follow that it might be initiated by telepathy, if there is such a thing as telepathy, and partake of the character of something existing beyond the reach of the ordinary sense, exactly as the odor of the flowers caused the hallucination of the coffin which formerly existed in the experience of the percipient. And if we were persuaded by independent evidence that spirits exist, it would not be difficult to suppose that now and then a spirit might stimulate the mental mechanism of a susceptible person to produce an apparition of itself.

It almost seems as if the professor supposed that a hallucination, apparition or whatever it may be, is regarded by psychic researchers as being in itself evidential of something supernormal. This is not the case, any more than they regard a dream as such evidential, or automatic writing as such. The question rises, in view of the peculiar content of a few dreams, and the peculiar content of a comparatively few examples of automatic writing, whether or not, in these particular instances, some unusual factor has been injected. So in regard to hallucinations, visual and other. Certain instances are so characterized that the question is forced upon one's attention, if he thinks of them at all, whether or not the picture-exteriorizing mechanism has been utilized, automatically or under intelligent direction, to produce a supernormal result. And I point particularly to the correspondences between the visual hallucination of seeing persons, or auditory hallucination of hearing them speak, and the time of their deaths, or near it. It is a pity that everyone who has occasion to say anything on these matters, either pro or con, will not read and reread Chapter XIII of *Phantasms of the Living* until he thoroughly understands and appreciates its overwhelming mathematics. I am convinced by the calculations in that chapter and others which have been made, that coincidences between hallucinations and the deaths of the persons specifically seen or heard occur with frequency millions of times in excess of the expectation of chance. I am equally convinced that the mathematics of certain concrete groups of work, in their entirety, done by Mrs. Soule and by Mrs. King, and which I have published to the world, will not in the future any more than in the past be attacked other than by innuendo, however they may be evaded and ignored. I mention these groups because they happened to be of a character unusually susceptible of mathematical testing.

The late work *Leonard and Soule Experiments* was loaned to Professor F. E., out of curiosity to observe the reaction. The results therein reported are not mathematically appraised, but they are, for the most part, exceedingly impressive. After reading the book, the professor was frank to admit that it seemed to present a weighty problem, but one thing especially bothered him. That was that the purported " communications " were so exclusively occupied with " mundane " affairs, and said so little appropriate to the presumed environment of the communicators.

This was about the last objection which I had anticipated from my friend who had said, and justly, that " we cannot conceive of the beauty of heaven, except in the terms of such figures and values as our earthly experience has presented to us," and that the human mind is forever making pictures founded on experience. In the first place, if there are in " heaven " no end of things and states quite unrelated to

THEN WHY HAS IT NOT HAPPENED TO ME?

figures and values which our earthly experience has presented to us, they could only be described to us symbolically by means of the terms of our earthly experience, since we are incapable of conceiving any other. Supposing the book had contained a quantity of such attempts to describe, would my friend have been impressed? Not so; he would have pointed out that every item of the description may be traced to memories of mundane sensory experience, and is therefore unevidential.

Further, the book, in reporting an experiment, often gives notice that unevidential matter is omitted. There had been so much work of Mrs. Soule reported in its entirety by Dr. Hyslop, that it was judged proper in this particular book to omit material which could not bear on the evidential problem. It should have been explained in the introduction that part of this omitted material related to " heaven." On page 283 it is said that a sitting contained " little besides remarks about the alleged life beyond and mental healing."

It was well understood that I much preferred " mundane " statements such as would serve the purposes of identification, etc., and the spirit, the control, or the subconsciousness of Mrs. Soule—whichever the reader prefers—sought to accommodate me.

If spirits are attempting to get their thoughts through to us they must by this time be bewildered by the difficulties of telling us anything that, in case we are ingenious in imagining hypotheses, will be regarded as at all satisfactory. If they tell us what we are at the moment thinking of, we pronounce it telepathy under the very conditions by which we appear to have had successful results between the living; if they tell us what we are not at the moment thinking of, we say that the medium has read our subconscious mind; if what they declare we cannot remember ever to have known but find by inquiry it is true, we say that our latent memories have been explored; if it proves that we never knew what is declared, but Grandfather Robinson in Missouri knows one item of it, Aunt Dorinda in New Hampshire knows another item and Cousin Gladys in Saskatchewan knows a third, we say that something has traveled from the medium to these widely separated relatives, dug out the facts from their memories while they were busy about their occupations, and brought them back, or that something has attracted these memories like a magnet and brought them to the experiment room from Missouri, New Hampshire and Saskatchewan; if no living person to whom it was of any concern knew of the matter, but a man in Iceland or Timbuctu may have read it in a book of which he has the sole surviving copy, we say that the telepathic current found its way to that man; and all else failing, there are those of us who will say that it is a case of memory " embryologically " transmitted from dead and gone generations, or else the medium has been angling in the Cosmic Reservoir.

Or let us, if only for the humor of it, assume that my father *was*, as claimed, trying to give me evidence in the story of " Stephen," and that he carefully chose that incident from a thousand others with view to its being entirely convincing to me that his memory survives. He would think it quite a triumph to project through the psychic's consciousness a description of a man familiar to me in my early years—a description so detailed and accurate that if a man unknown to me because of the changes time had made should come to me and give it, I should almost irresistibly be compelled to believe that he was familiar with the neighborhood fifty years ago, from that description alone. Then my father would think that getting the name through, considering that the name is far from being a common one and that there was not another person in all the range of our acquaintance who possessed it, ought to convince me. When he further told me that this person, so described and so named, lied about me, stated the nature of the lie, said that " Stephen " had a conference with him about it in the open air and that afterwards he (my father) informed me of the charge which I denied, admitted that he never afterwards expressly told me he was convinced of my innocence, and added other particulars, he might naturally think that no doubt whatever could remain in my mind that he had proved his identity by his memories.

So it seems to him, but I proceed to reason as follows: That complex of facts given—the name and the description of the man who bore it, and the unique incident of my boyhood related to this man—is a nut which no man who rejects both spirit communication and telepathy between the living can crack; not even by charging forgery and wholesale falsehood, for the record of the automatic writing through which the statements were made is producible, and witnesses can be produced to testify to the man's name and description, after which my testimony to the particular incident will hardly be questioned. But if one does not deny telepathy, I reflect, then all this, although a stupendous feat, may have resulted from the psychic lady's getting the content of my mind. Continuing our effort to see how a spirit trying to give evidence would feel, what would my father say on these reflections becoming known to him? He might say: " But I told many things that could not have come from your mind, such as details of what passed between me and ' Stephen,' in the field and on the way from the field to the carriage house. Cannot you see that the story is told from my point of view, not yours? For instance, again, I told of the talk of the neighbors because I knew of that. I said nothing of what you had to suffer in consequence from the derision of boys in school since you never told me of that, and a man of forty fails to imagine such juvenile troubles."

But I think: "There is that surface appearance, but it may be only dramatization. Further, I do not know that the details said to have taken place in the field and on the way to the carriage house actually occurred. What I can test could have been derived from my own mind, and what could not have been derived from my own mind I am unable to test."

Here my father might show some little irritation, and say: "You talk about your experiments for telepathy and of successes when a couple, rarely adapted to each other, are engaged, one actively in concentrating his attention upon a particular diagram, sensation, word, thought—whatever it may be, and the other passively waiting for impressions. And I start by giving you the name "Stephen" and a number of items of description, when you had not been thinking of him at all; then when, as you admit, your mind concentrated on a particular detail, which I had not told, thus creating an ideal situation for your telepathy, you got nothing."

But I think: "I wonder why, when I asked what happened next, referring to my being sent to a lot to pick stones, I got nothing." And my father, could he be aware of the thought, might retort: "I really thought you could reason better than that. Suppose you had received, just at that point, a statement about the stone-picking, would you have been satisfied? Would you not have regarded it a brilliant indication of telepathy by Mrs. Soule, that she wrote this directly after your mind concentrated on it? You ought to see, also, the weakness of your intimation in regard to 'dramatization' in view of your telepathic explanation. The two dramatic scenes which have always lingered in your memory and which were in your field of consciousness while I was getting my memories through, were my taking you out of school and our talking on the way home, and your gloomily picking stones on the lot, while you had scarcely ever pictured anything of my talk with 'Stephen.' Answer; why did you get the last, and fail to get the two former scenes, unless it was because the incident of 'Stephen's' coming to me when I was in the field and accusing you, was the most dramatic scene in *my* memory?"

But I think: "The meeting me at the schoolhouse door and our talk in the carriage on the road home would be remembered by my father as well as myself. Why did I not get these?"

And my father would be justified at this point if he fairly lost patience and said: "Surely you are not so unobserving as that. In the first place I did give the substance of our talk in the carriage, that 'Stephen' accused you of throwing something at him, saying something and laughing, that you denied it, and that I was puzzled since the story did not accord with what I had known of your conduct and yet I could not see why 'Stephen' should have told it unless there was something in it. And did you not see in my references to 'school,' 'School,' 'schoolhouse,' 'roads,' 'roads,' that I was probably trying to complete that part of the story, but could not get it fully expressed through the psychic?"

I repeat that the way of a spirit is hard, assuming that there are spirits and that they do try to get identifying memories across to the living.

Now that the extraordinary "Stephen" incident has been used by way of illustration, I am tempted to try and give it a certain degree of mathematical valuation. Any exact measurement is of course impossible, but it is not impossible to give a mathematical valuation below which it cannot possibly be rated.

Because of persons now living it is inexpedient to give the actual name of the man referred to as "Stephen." But if there is any person in the world who is disposed to test the figures which follow I will disclose the name to him in confidence, and *Who's Who in America*, as one of the bases of calculation, is as open to him as to me.

In *Leonard and Soule Experiments* (p. 334) it is said that Stephen is about of equal rarity as the concealed name, the former occurring in a list of 3,200 *standard* " Christian " names as they run from the beginning of *Who's Who* eight times, the latter seven times. Another set of 3,439 standard names lately examined gives six Stephens and seven of the other name, making their number equal for the combined lists. The selection of the name Stephen to represent the one which must be suppressed is an instance of the laborious pains taken to exhibit facts and relations justly.

Since these two lists of names, not far from the same in number, 3,200 and 3,439, each yield seven of the name, which for convenience we will hereafter call " Stephen," it will be fair to give exclusive attention to the latter list, as there is not time to analyze so carefully as I intend to do, the two combined. It is likely enough that the first list could have been pursued 239 names further without finding another

THEN WHY HAS IT NOT HAPPENED TO ME? 297

Stephen. That number, 3,200, was arbitrarily selected. But the second ended at 3,439, so as to close with the seventh " Stephen." This, if not just, was eminently conservative.

This list begins with page 1000 of *Who's Who in America*, edition of 1926-7, and ends with page 1201. The whole number of first and middle names until the seventh Stephen was reached is 5,590. A person either unregardful of the factors involved in calculation of probabilities or anxious to magnify the importance of giving the name of the person so minutely identified, might say that Mrs. Soule had one chance in 798 + of getting it by guess.

But many persons have a " front " or middle name derived from a surname. Thus, on page 1000 of *Who's Who* we find DeWolfe, Heber, Flint, Burnett, Hart, Carr and Clay. Now if one should guess the name by which an unknown man was familiarly called, she would probably not select any name usually found only as a surname; at least the range of such possible selection would be comparatively small, being prompted by her memories of persons so named. Therefore I exclude from the account all such names, except the few which were originally surnames but have been fully adopted into the family of standard " Christian " names, such as Franklin and Harvey.

Furthermore, since the medium might assume (with danger, but in this case correctly) that there would have been within my boyhood environment very few persons not descended from the stock of the British Islands, I proceed to weed out nearly all the names which rather imply origin from one of the countries of Continental Europe. About the only ones retained are the Louis', of whom more than a third, and the Ottos and Maxes, of whom a part, are attached to names which have no continental flavor. Any country village and its environs is likely to have one or two if not a number of families descended from Germany, France, etc. Besides, the omission of the names Alpha, Alanson, Clare, Cassius, Dennis, Myron, Theodosius, Lucian, Cæsar, Calvin, Irwin, Hector, Benedict, Erastus, Dugald, Basil, Hilary, Justin, etc., is a counter-balance.

Also, on the supposition that a medium might have at her tongue's end only a limited number of the less frequent Biblical names for guessing purposes, I have left out of account the greater number of these: Darius, Lucius, Justus, Herod, Absolom, Uriah, Zebulon, Eleazar, Elisha, Asahel, Alpheus, Clement, Gideon, Philetus, etc.

Thus there are left 202 different " standard " Christian names, from the list totaling 3,439, whence we have taken our seven " Stephen's." One might think that we are now prepared to calculate the medium's chance of guessing that "Stephen" would fit the man so minutely described in his physical and mental characteristics, and further identified by a specific and peculiar act, and find the chance one in 491.

Not so, for many *persons* have two of the names in our now very much diminished list, and what we want to find out is how much chance there was of the name "Stephen" being actually that of the *person* described.

I found that of *persons* sharing the 3,439 names

1286	had two names of which one was "standard".....	1286
376	had only one name, and that a standard one......	376
195	had two names, one standard, the other represented only by an initial letter.....................	195
791	had two names, both standard.................	1582
2648	persons	3439 names

As the 791 have, as it were, two throws of the dice relatively to their 1,582 names, we must halve that number to get the chance of one throw, like the rest.

Now we are ready but for one particular; we do not know what the other name is with respect to 195 persons. True, in only two cases is there any chance of its being the name given in the trance of Mrs. Soule, since in only two cases out of the 195 is the initial the same as that name. The necessity of concealing the name represented by "Stephen" prevents me from proving what I now assert, that the chance in either of those two cases that the name is that given by the psychic is very small. But there is a chance, so let us throw all the 195 names of this set overboard.

Will any one question that we are now down to hard pan, if not deeply in it? Very well, then; $\dfrac{1286 + 376 + 791}{7}$ gives 350 +. So calculated, on the most conservative basis, there was one chance in 350 of striking the right name, "Stephen," by guess.

Now we are prepared to move more swiftly. As soon as the name "Stephen" was given, he was described. An unimportant person of poor mentality who however took himself seriously though he was a character who made the neighbors laugh; wore awful clothes, and in particular a queer "scrunched" hat; looked "like the old Harry, face and everything," and as if he never took a bath; had a peculiar walk which alone identified him almost as far as he could be seen; was sometimes seen by W. F. P. crossing the field; a character familiar to W. F. P.'s father and to W. F. P. in boyhood, etc. What value shall we give this? Almost everyone has casually seen such a figure sometimes in his life, but to have familiarly known one in boyhood in whom all these points converge—I doubt if there is one chance out of five that it would hit. I am unable to recall any one else whom I ever knew well and listened to and watched, in all my sojournings in seven States, who fills all the requirements of that description. But the " Stephen " I knew, in my boyhood, in my home neighborhood, as stated, did so completely. My father used to stand at the window and grin when he saw " Stephen " in the distance, waddling along up the road, and I used to run to the window to watch him, and we would remark about his awful " scrunched " hat and clothes and odd walk. Every farmer about, however he might dress for work in the field, would wash up and make himself tidy for various occasions, but " Stephen," Sundays and week days was the same, a living scarecrow. I cannot be persuaded that there was more than one chance in five that all the particulars of the description would photographically fit a particular period in a particular country neighborhood. But put it 1 chance in 3.

As a part of the story, the psychic declared that in my boyhood a lie was told about me which had such an effect that, to quote her language, " the acid of the wrong done to the youth . . . ate into the peace of mind of the boy," " his spirit was in rebellion and he has never thought of the incident since without a feeling of momentary injustice done to him," and the accusation gave " so much pain that it will not be forgotten after forty years." Of course it is common enough for lies to be told about lads, and of course many a man, if he thinks back, can remember of being lied about. But in most cases the pain of boyhood is evanescent and such things become shadowy memories in mature life. The wrong done me, however, was so unfounded and the hopelessness of proving to my father that I was innocent was so complete, that, as it were, a sore spot remained in the depths of my consciousness, and even after half a century the memory rankles when it comes to mind. From all of my youth only one other experience (not associated with death) remains in memory with anything like the same poignancy, and no falsehood was mixed with that. I have inquired of a number of persons whether they remember any lie told about them in childhood which is still vivid and painful in memory, and have not yet been answered in the affirmative. But I put the chance of such a guess proving correct in relation to a given person as 1 in 2.

The psychic declared that "Stephen" was the person who told that lie about me, which has haunted my memory all my life. What was the chance of her guessing that? From the point of view of my actual environment there was no more reason to expect that such an act should come from him than from any one of at least a hundred persons whom I knew before my 'teens ended. The lie which was to make a lasting scar might as easily have been told by a boy or girl as by a grown person, and this would have seemed more likely. If a boy or girl had told that lie and my father and others had for a time believed it true and I had seen no way to clear myself, the feeling of disgrace and injury would have been as great and the effects would have been as lasting. I knew at least sixty persons in my own and surrounding towns, old enough to have lied about me. It might have been somebody whom I did not know, or some stranger visitor to the neighborhood, who lied and departed. I went to a boarding school in my 'teens where there were two hundred scholars. From term to term I knew at least a hundred of them, and any other boy, for example, could have attempted to clear his skirts by asserting that he saw me do something. "Stephen" had appeared inoffensive, and I do not recall hearing of his telling another false story either before or after, and why he lied about me, or if it was a case of mistaken identity, I never knew. Not with any justice can the chance of guessing that the described "Stephen" was the author of that memorable lie be put at more than 1 in 50.

The psychic gave the substance of the lie, which was that I had "thrown or done something to him," and "there were words and laugh." The fact was that "Stephen" said I threw stones at him and derided and laughed at him. If a lie was to be told, was it necessarily to that effect? I might have been accused of being the guilty one when tricks were played on the teacher, of stealing, of attempt at arson, of myself lying, of swearing, of destroying a neighbor's property, of waylaying and attacking a schoolmate, of stopping the schoolhouse chimney by night and smoking the school out (that was actually done, but not by me), of throwing a dead cat into some one's well, or any one of dozens of other things. "Throwing something," "words," and "laugh" sum up the actual accusation. It seems to me conservative to put the chance of such a precise guess at 1 in 4.

Then, it was declared: "Stephen" made the false accusation to my father. Person for person he was the most likely person to go to. But undoubtedly he might have found my father absent and made his mendacious charge to my mother. He might have said to my older brother

THEN WHY HAS IT NOT HAPPENED TO ME? 301

or sister, " You tell your father that your brother W—— has done thus and so and should be punished." He might simply have spread the story among the neighbors. But we will put the chance of a guess on this item at the moderate figure of 1 in 2.

The psychic said that " Stephen " had the conference with father out of doors. I should say the chance of this being correct was not more than 1 in 2.

Also that the conference was in the Fall. As stated in the book, this almost certainly is correct. It was not in Summer, for then I did not go to school, and it was to the schoolhouse that my father went and fetched me. It was not in Winter, for he would not then have been engaged as he was in the field. It was probably not in the Spring, as he would probably then have been busy preparing for the crops rather than engaged in the slow operation of splitting a rock with drills. If certain that it was in the Fall, then the chance of guessing the season would be 1 in 4, as one can lie in one season as readily as in another. But the uncertainty exists, so we make it 1 in 2.

The declaration that I denied the accusation was almost certain to be correct, on the assumption that the charge was a false one. That I " could not retract and was not made to do so " would also be most probable, although there have been many cases of young persons so overborne by authority and punishment that they have confessed what was not true. But, considering that the charge was a lie, that I bitterly resented it, that I was not on the spot if any such scene was enacted (all these particulars stated by the psychic), the chances surely favor my having been able to prove my innocence. But the words, " You wanted to prove you were right and you couldn't," are true. Being a boy, and a shy one, I saw absolutely no way to vindicate myself and no express vindication ever came. But put the chance of the statement being right at 1 in 2.

There are plenty other correct details. It is true, as stated, that the attitude of my father (although in view of the strange answer I made him—see book—probably justified that attitude) troubled me more than the accusation itself. To the best of my belief it is true as stated, that the incident powerfully influenced me in after life, in the way of wishing to " hear all sides " before forming a judgment. It is true that when " Stephen " accused me to father, I was " not far away." It is true that the accusation became known throughout the neighborhood. It is true that after the accusation was made father walked away and at the end of the walk stepped " on to wood—almost like a platform." This would not be the language to employ about entering a house through an ordinary door. Father went from the field and got the carriage out of the carriage house with its broad entrance revealing the " platform," and either went directly to the schoolhouse or more likely went somewhere—I do not know where— and on the return trip took me from the school. It is true, and is not true of all men, that " Stephen " was surly and showed temper at times. It is true, in a particular sense, that his life was its own punishment. For he was supposed to have told the lie about me in revenge for some trouble I had had with a boy of his family, and not many years afterward his whole family deserted him. The description of my father's manner, conduct and words and mental processes, both at the interview with " Stephen " and that with me which followed (See pages 347, 348 and 350 of *Leonard and Soule Experiments*) are remarkably like him. It is true that I had never harmed " Stephen " in any way. It is true that no other neighbor, to my knowledge, had ever had reason to complain of my conduct or had done so. But let these and other true particulars go unweighed, to more than counterbalance the few minor details which are not correct. That the latter cancel out and leave a balance I think no candid and careful reader can doubt. Then we have left the particulars of which we have calculated the probabilities cautiously and conservatively, as 1 in 350, 1 in 3, 1 in 2, 1 in 50, 1 in 4, 1 in 2, 1 in 2, 1 in 2, 1 in 2. The chance of guessing all these correctly was, then, of course, one in six million, seven hundred and twenty thousand (6,720,000).

If any one thinks that any of the ratios do not favor chance sufficiently, let him alter according to his judgment and *give his reasons for doing so.*

I very much doubt if any living person in the world but myself remembers that incident, or any part of it. It was one of a thousand incidents to those of the country neighborhood in Maine more than fifty years ago; to one lad only it was a tragedy. I can think of but three persons who might possibly have some dim scrap of remembrance of it. Two of them to a certainty never saw Mrs. Soule nor had any communication with her—they are older living relatives of mine. The residence of the third has been unknown to me for many years. Let us imagine that this man *chanced* to meet her and did such a grotesque thing as to tell her this incident of long ago, in more detail than he ever could have known. Did the medium also *happen* to run upon someone else who knew the topography of the home farm, just where various growing things were located on it, and details of what was in my grandfather's garret, etc., etc.? For much of this the man referred

THEN WHY HAS IT NOT HAPPENED TO ME? 303

to certainly never knew. The only people knowing these things in detail are those same two relatives. And whom did the psychic *chance* to meet, capable of telling her the true incidents which happened in the hospital in New York during my wife's last illness? And the person—for it could not have been the same one—met by *chance*, who knew so intimately matters relating to her in a New Jersey town? And what other person was it whom Mrs. Soule *chanced* to discover so familiar with my household of thirty-five years ago in a fourth place, and so blest with memory, that she told of my owning a cat named Mephistopheles? To the best of my belief, no living person except myself could have vindicated that statement. And who was that sixth person who knew so intimately the interior arrangements of my foster-daughter's girlhood home in Pittsburgh, and *happened* to give the psychic a description of them? To put these questions is to show the palpable absurdity of supposing that the psychic was loaded with information in any such fashion.

Nor is there any help in the thought that many sitters themselves give facts away without meaning so to do—which is quite true. I do not stand on any reputation for skill and caution in such experiments which I may possess, but say: " The experiments were stenographically recorded; the book shows what was said and what was not said."

And my friend the professor deplores that what was given an investigator seeking evidence was so " mundane "—that there was not more about heaven!

VII. MISCELLANEOUS ARGUMENTS AND OPINIONS

Some of the nineteen men represented in this section make their statements or present their objections seriously; in other cases what they have to say is, as Artemus Ward would put it, " write skarcastic." But sarcasm implies that he who employs it has good reasons at hand for its justification. Therefore attempt was made to get those reasons stated,—with what success will be seen.

Professor Max F. Meyer, Ph.D., of the chair of Psychology in the University of Missouri, prolific writer on his subject (Presbyterian), had with the Research Officer a good-natured exchange of spicy letters. He answered the first query of the blank thus: " This cannot be answered by Yes or No. I have had many experiences which ordinary folks would call so. But I think it ridiculous to call them by such terms." To query 4 he replied: " Yes, I once broke my right arm before I had time to eat my lunch, I think this is the reason why I am so skinny."

Since he expressed his willingness to answer questions, the following were proposed:

" 1. Will you explain the logic of your response, ' This cannot be answered by Yes or No,' as related to the query, ' Have you ever experienced an incident of the kind indicated in paragraph 2 of the accompanying letter, a ' normal ' explanation of which is not to you apparent? ' etc.? Do you mean that you have had experiences the ' normal' explanation of which is to you neither apparent nor unapparent? I have a curiosity to know what such an incident could be. If you have had a coincidental dream, for instance, of such a nature that you are unable to answer either yes or no to the query whether there was any apparent explanation, I should be much more interested to learn the reasons of that inability than to know the explanation for your being, I regret to quote, ' skinny.'

" 2. Do you not think it was irrelevant to bring in what ' ordinary folks ' would think, when I am interrogating extraordinary folks, yourself and others?

" 3. The reasonings of some psychologists are so tenuous that, for

MISCELLANEOUS ARGUMENTS AND OPINIONS 305

aught I know, your remark that you think you are so skinny because you broke your arm before lunch, may be intended seriously. It may be your theory that the disaster created a complex, a *trophaphobia*, which has prevented your eating sufficiently since. But why, may I ask, should you regard your becoming skinny a 'psychic' phenomenon, if such phenomena there be?

" 4. If, however, your remarks in relation to your much-to-be-deplored condition of skinniness were written as burlesque, have you found burlesque a valuable aid to a tabulation of guaranteed and analyzed facts? "

Letter by Professor Meyer:

" To your first question I reply with Hamlet: 'There are more things in heaven and earth, Horatio, than are dreamed of in your philosophy,' interpreting ' dreamed of in your philosophy ' as meaning ' explained in terms of natural science.' Therefore, not being divine, I, for one, as a mere man of science, leave those ' more things ' alone.

" To your second question I reply thus: It is distinctly unethical to increase the interest taken by the credulous populace in 'ghost stories' (like those published in the Psy. Res. Volumes) by covering such stories with the prestige of *Who's Who*. Being in *Who's Who* does not qualify a man for being shown up as an authority in scientific methodology. (The Psy. Res. methods have not the faintest resemblance to the methods of natural science.)

" To 3 and 4: The coincidences in the Psy. Res. stories are just as 'burlesque' (I am glad you used the word, which I adopt as most fitting) as the coincidence of my 'skinniness' with my breaking my arm 'just before lunch.'

" If you could give me a definition of ' a psychic phenomenon,' I should be glad to know what that definition is. I know none which can be accepted by a man of science except during temporary madness.

" You are entirely free to quote in its original content anything I have ever said or written. If I am more emotional (as you seem to think) than you, my emotion consists only in pity that good money should be thrown away on Research like that in question. I readily admit, of course, your good intentions."

Reply to Professor Meyer:

" In reply to your fervent request for a definition of a 'psychic phenomenon,' I should say that it is about synonymous with what you mean in your first paragraph (if I am successful in making out its meaning) : ' There are more things in heaven and earth, Horatio, than are dreamed of in your philosophy,' ' interpreting " dreamed of in your philosophy " as meaning " explained in terms of natural science,"' without the implication that one must be ' divine ' in order to attempt their more precise definition and classification.

"' Psychic phenomenon ' is, to me, a provisional term, and applies to authenticated facts which have the appearance of not being explainable in terms of• ' natural science,' or the science of the present day. Whether such a phenomenon is in fact thus unexplainable is what I am trying to find out; it is not to *me* a matter of faith.

" I am so shameless as to be willing to remain in the company of William James, F. W. H. Myers, F. C. S. Schiller, William McDougall, etc.

" I never before knew that science was deterred by fear of ' unethical ' consequences, from continuing its search into the meaning of facts. It seems to me that I have heard that same warning in reference to evolution, etc.

" Of course, being in *Who's Who* does not qualify a man for ' being shown up as an authority in scientific methodology ' and no one that I am acquainted with ever dreamed that it did. There are some big fools in *Who's Who*, no doubt, as there are many outside of it. ' It will all come out in the wash '—of course, I cannot write a book to make plain to a small but worried minority that the horrific things they imagine are plotted will not take place.

" I don't admit that it is scientific to credit me with good intentions. Why not remain an agnostic on that point? Only if you are, you will also have to be agnostic as to whether my methods and my writings on psychic research are trash, for I fear you know as little about the one as the other.

" When a psychologist admits that there are more things in heaven and earth than are explained in terms of natural science he is close to the kingdom of psychic research."

PROFESSOR G. A., a Ph.D. and university instructor of Psychology, responded:

" No: but, as I once said in the ———, the concept of the supernormal is meaningless to me (and should be, I think, to all). If supernormal = that-which-is-not-explained, then of course every problem of research in the psychological laboratory, to which I devote my life, is supernormal when it is first attacked. I obviously do not reply YES to questions 1 and 4, because I know that this logical conviction of mine cannot be shared by the author of this questionnaire."

The professor evidently thought that the words in Census query 1,

MISCELLANEOUS ARGUMENTS AND OPINIONS

" an incident . . . a 'normal' explanation for which is not to you apparent," signified that in my view, any and every such incident would be supernormal. Not so, that question was shrewdly devised to invite not only incidents of evidential character, but also incidents which were simply puzzling, to see how the narrators reasoned about them and also whether I could assist to solve the puzzles. And also to draw just such remarks as those by Professor G. A.

From a letter by W. F. P. to the professor:

" I recognize the liability of the word ' supernormal ' to criticism, and have long done so, though I think I should have no difficulty in defining ' supernormal ' if some one would define the word ' normal ' so that this, too, would escape a similar reproach. ' Supernormal ' was chosen, as you know, to escape the implications of ' supernatural.' It seems as though people were beginning to project into it all the content of the latter word.

" I sometimes think we shall have to adopt a hieroglyphic to designate those categories now embraced under the objectionable word.

" We do not mean by it that-which-is-not-natural, for I suppose that everything which is, is embraced in the scheme of nature. But ' nature,' too, is an equivocal and ambiguous word. If we can imagine persons existing in space and reasoning on matters concerning this planet, it might well appear to them any physical changes or manipulations arising out of human intellect and will (such as leads to the running of railroad trains, the production of light and power by electricity, the phenomenon of airships, etc., etc.) would be subversive of the 'laws of nature,' and hence unthinkable. Any claim that there had been noted evidence of action upon the earth implying mental manipulation would be a claim of the ' supernormal.' The word therefore is to be understood *relatively*. . . .

" I cannot help thinking that psychologists sometimes, like other people, amuse themselves with a harmless game of logomachy, that they take a naughty pleasure in throwing a fog-screen of *words* about the poor psychical researchers, all the while knowing what the *facts* at issue essentially are.

" If the inhabitants of Boston saw ' an angel come down from heaven, having the key of the bottomless pit and a great chain in his hand,' and if the angel cried ' Boston is fallen, is fallen,' I am nearly certain that you, living elsewhere and hence escaping the cataclysm, would admit that there had happened something radically different in kind from what you had hitherto acknowledged as actualities. Angels which fly down from somewhere in the sky would henceforth have a place in your scheme of nature though they did not before, and though there would still be in the phenomenon ' that-which-is-not-explained.'

"If it should be established, as some think it already is, that thoughts can somehow slop over beyond the periphery of the brain, so as to be demonstrable though rarely, in persons related to each other in a way not understood, after the manner known as telepathy, there again, I think you will admit, we would have something which is *different* in kind from the great range of facts which are universally acknowledged. Even though to define that difference is difficult, the difference is there.

"Whether there is such a thing as telepathy or not, that is a different matter, one of evidence only. It is such things which university men of England, more than forty years ago, began seriously to investigate, in order to see if there could be any residuum of truth in all the age-long and world-wide stories which people have been telling, and to shut the door against them for all intelligent people if reason in the light of tested evidence showed them to be mere superstition. *They have not been able to shut the door.* In fact, the only safety for thinking men from becoming convinced that there is at least *something*, different in kind, meriting study, as Dr. Beard said long ago, is not to give much attention to these matters in the way of serious study, but to cut and run.

"This is in no sense a retort, or a remonstrance, or anything but a chat. Only, how could you be so cruel as to say that you know that your 'logical conviction' that, 'if supernormal = that-which-is-not-explained, then of course every problem of research in the psychological laboratory, to which I devote my life, is supernormal when it is first attacked,' cannot be shared by me? 'This was the most unkindest cut of all!' I am prepared, now, to hear from some quarter that of course I do not agree that a whole is equal to the sum of its parts."

Partial as I am to psychologists, I cannot help noting that of all scientists (if it be lawful to call them scientists) they are the most likely to draw hasty inferences from incomplete data. Thus it seemed to Professor G. A. that my letter was an emotional reaction. He did not know that at the very beginning of the questionnaire project it was planned to draw correspondents out, to study their reactions to the general subject of psychic research, to get their objections in intelligible form, to see whether they could convict me and my colleagues of unreason, and whether their own logic, in this particular field, was entirely sound. No more emotion necessarily lurked in such a task than would if one was making entomological researches, except that men are infinitely more amusing than bugs. Professor G. A. wrote:

"The real reason that I do not like psychic research is that there has been so much personal disagreement that the mere discussion of its facts gets colored with emotion, and emotion is unfriendly to research. I am not criticizing you, but I do note that a casual, half-whimsical answer to a questionnaire has produced two pages of single space typed by your own hand. There is some unusual spring of energy for it to be released so easily.

"But let me accept your challenge to define the 'normal.' I think with David Hume, Ernst Mach, and Karl Pearson that a scientific fact is always a statement of a relationship between terms, a correlation; and moreover, that the terms of the correlation take the form of a cause and an effect. I am not here speaking of cause and effect as implying a quantitative equivalence, but am using the broader meaning and thus allowing all the facts of psychology to come into science. The simplest facts are simple relationships between two terms, a causal term and an effectual term. The bigger facts build up into complex systems. The ideal of a science is to become a single interrelated system, but one never in practice finds this anywhere nearly complete. An isolated observation of a single term is not a fact and has no scientific meaning; it must stand in observed relation to something else, and thus the total system grows.

"We have now a well recognized body of knowledge which forms such a system or set of systems, and we call it physical science. Whether psychology could have been an entirely separate system I do not know, but the truth is that it has not gained its facts except by relation to the physical system—in terms of stimuli and the nervous system. Any new isolated observational datum that is observed in relation to terms of this system, and which therefore gains a causal meaning in respect of it, yields a new fact which is *normal*.

"There! Now you tell me what the 'supernormal' is. If my wife and I think of the same thing at the same time, it does not seem to me that I have a relationship of the causal order. It does not fit the normal system. The event is true as a particular, but it is not a fact in the scientific sense. If I find that we think of the same things synchronously only when there is a nasal whisper of the one of us or only when there are statable associations common to us both, then I am dealing with a normal fact. To say that we can do it with all normal explanations excluded is to say that we have one term in relation to nothing else, and thus to make a meaningless and useless statement as far as research is concerned."

Letter from W. F. P. to Professor G. A.:

"True, an emotion did cause me to write 'two pages' (one and a half)—the emotion of curiosity, which is the impelling force of scientific investigation. I am very curious as to human reactions to stimuli.

On the other hand, I am rather indifferent to whether my correspondents 'like psychical research' or not, being at the farthest possible removed from a propagandist. Your first paragraph was worth all the pains of provoking it.

"It would not be necessary to say more, but in courtesy I must make some response to 'Now you tell me what the "supernormal" is.' The trouble is that you have not given a stable definition of the 'normal.' It has the attribute of relativity. Had the science and inventions of 'radio' a hundred years ago been comprised in the mind of one man, and he had disclosed nothing, but simply put forward the claim that it was possible to hear the voice of a person at a thousand miles distance, there could have been to other men no assignable correlation of cause and effect. Therefore the claim would not have related to the normal, because of the then absence of any relevant known *norm*. It would not have been a scientific fact—it would only have been a fact. If telepathy should ever be universally acknowledged to be a fact, of course a cause will be assumed to exist, and probably eventually would be assigned. It is even barely conceivable that the cause might be vibrations from one brain to another, producing effects upon the brain-cells of the 'percipient.' Do not understand me to be advocating this theory.

"As already intimated, the definition of 'supernormal' is relative to that of 'normal.' Relatively to *your* definition, I should say that any facts which exist (if any do exist as facts) and which are expressly excluded from the scheme of facts which you say are 'normal,' are 'supernormal' facts. If they *are* facts and if their modes of causation become known, I suppose that they will become 'normal' facts. The term 'supernormal' was rather forced upon us, by criticisms which employed the term 'supernatural'; it is a provisional term, and a relative one.

"If I may indulge in my weakness of humor, this letter, applying your mathematical standard, is only a little more than half as emotional as yours."

And Professor G. A. finished the correspondence:

"Why of course I am as emotional as anybody else when the topic is psychic research! I was talking about the topic, and not people.

"You seem in general to agree with me, and the distinction between the fact and the scientific fact could certainly be made. Only now I do not see how the facts, that are not these related scientific facts, are ever to be selected for 'psychic research.' The majority of data about the world belong in this class, and they all become 'supernormal' on this definition. Moreover, there is the further question as to 'authentic phenomena,' and without repetition, experiment, and the consequent normalization of such facts, I should be put to it to get any meaning for 'authentic.'"

The professor is so fond of seeing his cosmos in apple-pie order that he prefers to hide any litter under a decent cover. His correspondent is so constituted that an ascertained fact or type of facts still exists, even if it at present does not give a satisfactory account of its relations. If the professor and his wife think the same thought at the same time, and he discovers that she whispered it through her nose, then he is "dealing with a normal fact." But what if she and he, a thousand miles apart, synchronously thought of and repeated ten identical poetical passages from ten different poets and he knew that they had plotted nothing? I rather think the fact would bowl him over as effectually as if the rationale of it were apparent. The same aprioristic reasoning which is now applied to psychic research kept men of science up to the close of the eighteenth century from acknowledging that meteorites fall from the sky. Heavy stones could not stay up in the air, for what would keep them from falling; or if they fell, why did they not fall before? Such a pestiferous fact which (then) seemed unrelated to any other facts, could not be allowed. Yet scores of lesser folk had seen the stones fall and knew that in fact they did come from the sky. At length the scientific world had to accept the fact, and *relations* were found for the poor orphan, and all went merry as a marriage-bell.

PROFESSOR G. B., a B.S., whose university specialty is Viticulture, responded, referring to query 1 of the questionnaire:

"'Normal' and 'apparent' require definition, but with the definition I intend my answer is No."

The annotator wrote Professor G. B.:

"I have no right to expect any further service on your part, and yet I would be pleased if you feel to give me *your* definition of the word 'normal.' I have been receiving some attempts at definition from various persons and am interested in both the attempts and their variations. It has usually begun by objecting to the word 'supernormal.' I have realized the difficulty of defining that word, and think its definition is only relative to the definition of the word 'normal,' which in my mind is exactly as shifting in its signification as used by different persons."

Professor G. B. responded in part:

"I have your letter of March 7, asking for my definition of the word normal. By its origin and general use of course it means conformable to some rule or measure. It must differ then according to the case in which it is used. Some things are incapable of exact measurement. I think the usual meanings of the word normal are—a mode—a mean—or the usual. For the purpose of my answer to your questions I define a normal cause as one which is in accordance with the immutable laws or ways of nature, *i. e.*, of the universe and its contents.

"This definition is a postulate and excludes the idea of any supernormal cause. Therefore all causes are by definition 'normal.'"

Of course anything is "normal" or not, according to definition, and if the professor is correct then the words "normal" and "supernormal" should be struck out of the dictionary. After saying that his scale of confidence runs from "I know" or "I believe" through "I think," "perhaps" and "I doubt" to "I disbelieve" (and one would suppose that to be the case), he goes on:

"There is no place in this system for supernormal causes. Causes and results are figures of speech to describe usual apparent sequences of events. When we see an unusual sequence why need we look for something supernatural. If we realize our comparative ignorance in all cases is it not better and more reasonable simply to acknowledge a little greater depth of ignorance in this case."

Letter to Professor G. B.:

"I fully concur with your remark that 'there is no place in this system for supernormal causes,' understanding the word 'supernormal' as you do. But that you do not use it in the sense which Myers and others had in mind when they adopted it for use in psychical research, is evident from your next sentence: 'When we see an unusual sequence why need we look for something supernatural?'

"It may interest you to know that the very protest you make was so fully sympathized with by Myers, Prof. Henry Sidgwick, Prof. William Barrett and others, that they adopted the word 'supernormal' as an express repudiation that there could be anything 'supernatural.' I have for years watched the growth of a tendency to suppose we mean by 'supernormal' exactly what was formerly meant by 'supernatural,' something outside of and higher than nature.

"As I understand the term 'supernormal,' it is meant to designate

MISCELLANEOUS ARGUMENTS AND OPINIONS

whatever powers, faculties, functions or phenomena, are inherent in or connected with men or animals, and which are altogether outside and transcendent of those which are generally recognized by scientific men of the day. I am not now claiming that there are, nor conceding that there are not, such powers and phenomena. And when I say, outside and transcendent, I mean in quite different categories. For instance, we may and probably shall find out much about hearing that we do not know now, but we expect it to classify with what we now know. But telepathy, if it exists, is in another category, for it supposes communication of thoughts by other channels than any we now recognize.

"If an apparition is ever caused by an intelligent something outside of the person who experiences it, and the fact becomes accepted, a new realm of reality is opened. It is not above nature, for it is in nature, but it is *something* radically different, and there is needed a word to designate the quality of that something. It would be the same were it established that some persons can look into the future. The evidence for these and kindred claims is what some of us, who have accumulated it, are discussing.

"It is no part of my wish to convince you that there is any reality in such claims. Nor have I any right to expect you to answer this letter. You may not wish to do so, and I shall quite understand. But I should be greatly interested to learn if the word 'supernormal' seems objectionable to you after the explanation I have made of its history and its use. And, in case it does, if you can think of any word which would better take its place. Without *some* general term, we should have to keep repeating the list of alleged phenomena, like 'the cornet, flute, harp, sackbut, psaltery, and all kinds of music' of the book of Daniel."

The professor's response first shifted the ground by complaining that psychic research "seems to me to be dealing with the preposterous," and ended by reiterating that "your definition of supernormal simply refers to things which to me do not exist at all; as soon as I know they exist they become normal."

The last letter in the courteous series was one by the annotator:

"I feel really grateful to you for your patience in explaining your views, and I certainly shall not expect you to take any more trouble, although I do not think that you really answered the question which I asked in my last. There are certain alleged phenomena which people talk about for and against, claim and deny as existing facts. Nevertheless, they talk about them, and my question was what term would be best to apply to them as a class or genus, so to speak. Exactly as you (and I) do not believe in little creatures that drink dew and dance on the leaves, wearing wings and clad in red jerkins and pointed hats, but we sometimes talk about their fancied existence, and agree to call them by the generic term of fairies. You seem to me to avoid the question by refusing to talk about the matters I have in mind as even hypothetical ones. I personally do not believe in 'vampires' as facts, but I know what is meant by the term, and find it easy to discuss whether or not it is the best term for what it expresses. So, too, I understand the term 'phlogiston,' that is, I know what concept it stands for, and can give the opinion that it is as good a name as any for what neither I nor any one else now thinks exists.

"As I expect to discuss your views briefly in my book, although I shall not mention your name unless I get express permission to do so, it is only fair for me to say that one point I shall make is that if you are correct in saying that whatever exists is normal, then there is no such thing as *abnormal* psychology, and that a maniac must then be a perfectly normal person, since he is as real a human being as any other."

PROFESSOR G. C., a Ph.D. and well-known university Psychologist, author of books on his subject, and crusader against the "superstitions" of psychic research, answers Query 1 of the questionnaire:

"No. By this I mean that I have no reason to suppose that a 'normal' explanation is not possible, whether I can give it or not."

If the professor has experienced or been related to any incident which puzzled him, an effort, at least, would have been made to assist him to a "'normal' explanation." No fault can be found with an attitude of agnosticism or doubt; it was only on occasions when he opposed mere dogma to evidence that the present writer has criticized him.

PROFESSOR G. D., teacher of Mathematics in a university and a Ph.D. (Episcopalian), waxed severe:

"It is my opinion that an investigation of this type can only reveal the amount of ignorance and superstition concealed under the hats of presumably intelligent persons. Furthermore, I consider the proper approach to psychic research to be through the psychological laboratory in the hands of competent psychologists."

A letter to Professor G. D., from the office of the Boston Society, proceeded on the irenic " Come let us reason together " order:

"I am interested in all such expressions of opinion, and always respond, not controversially but in the hope of getting some fuller expression. The following are some of my reflections:

"1. No one respects work done in the laboratories, psychological and other, more than I. But it seems obvious that there are classes of facts which cannot be observed at will therein, such as the fall of aerolites, volcanic eruptions, historical events (such as the memorable saving by Washington of his army by crossing East River in the night, and the influence of Madame du Barry upon the history of France), the birth of twins united in the manner of the 'Siamese twins,' and the production of a poem in a dream, as in the case of Coleridge.

"2. I should suppose that these and other classes of facts and events of importance to science or in some other relation.

"3. And that thousands of them are credited and accepted by scientific and other intellectual men who would regard it as unintelligent not to accept them.

"4. Although they are established by human testimony and collateral proofs gathered outside of the laboratory.

"5. I take it that *facts* are, as such, never too undignified for scientific attention, in some relation.

"6. And that, consequently, if it is a fact that a man sees an apparition of his father, for instance, at or near the moment of his father's death, of which he had had no warning, it would not be 'superstition' or 'ignorance' to acknowledge the fact.

"7. I take it, that there *could* be such a fact, if only by chance coincidence.

"8. And that it would not be unintelligent to mention and even discuss it, if only to illustrate the possibilities of chance coincidence, but that first it should be established as a fact.

"9. That it would be unreasonable to expect such a fact, any more than the dreaming out of the poem of which we have a fragment in 'Kubla Khan,' to take place at will, in a laboratory.

"10. So that it must be accepted, if at all, on human testimony.

"11. That, while if such a claim stood alone, or a single one were even supported by persons who testified hearing the experience related before the corresponding event, it would be more reasonable to suppose that the person lied, or the group formed a conspiracy to lie, this becomes more difficult to hold in proportion to the number of such cases, and the standing and intellectual qualifications of the witnesses.

"12. That of all classes of men, those of recognized scientific standing are the most likely to have that balance of intellectual qualifications, that exemption from the temptation to lie on a matter regarded with so much distaste by the most of their colleagues, and therefore the most likely to be impelled by regard for scientific truth to overcome their natural repugnance against relating such a story.

"13. That if *such* a person once in his life experiences the apparition (whether it be a telepathic effect, a mere coincidence or not, I do not now discuss) of a person, at or very close to the moment of that person's death, this would be such an experience as he would be likely to remember clearly and without distortion (disregarding the cases where there are corroborating witnesses).

"14. If a distinguished geologist testifies to having experienced a visual hallucination but once in his life, and that of a person who died at about that moment; if one of the most noted physicists living declared that he had an auditory hallucination once in his life, and that of hearing his name called twice by the voice of a relative who died at a great distance away in the same hour; and if the testimonies of many men and women of recognized scientific standing, including psychologists, are in hand as to experiences of a similar character, a combination of such testimonies at least intelligently justifies us in thinking that such facts do occur.

"15. And also justifies our consideration of the question whether they are mere coincidences, and if not, what the causal factor is which lies behind them.

"16. Mathematical calculation enters into the determination of that question, although there are great difficulties in the way of its application, and we can never hope for any exact results by it,—only a more or less great presumption.

"17. Neither would such calculation be a matter of the *laboratory*.

"I am not arguing, only thinking. I wish I could get many men like yourself to point out the fallacies or errors in the steps of this thinking. If you care, or are willing, to make any response, I shall be greatly obliged."

The professor is one of those too rare men who, on becoming convinced that they expressed opinions without sufficient consideration, are ready to admit it. In part he responded:

"Your letter of October 3rd seems to me to attack successfully the position which I assumed in my reply to your questionnaire. In fact the questionnaire has revealed some of the ignorance and prejudice regarding psychic research which resided under at least one hat. . . . Ghosts and kindred phenomena have troubled the minds of men for centuries. The problem they present should be studied as carefully as possible by such methods as we have. I hope that workers in this difficult field will eventually succeed in finding a scientific basis for the phenomena."

MISCELLANEOUS ARGUMENTS AND OPINIONS 317

DOCTOR OF LAWS G. E., a prominent Author and Diplomat, A.B., set down a rather drastic opinion.

" The difficulty with all of this is: Human testimony, no matter how honest, is *almost* worthless as to explicable sensations and incidents; it is even more worthless as to whatever appears inexplicable."

A copy of the letter to G. D. was sent to G. E. and his attention directed to paragraphs 10-14, in order to get his reactions. I also added that I could subscribe to his dictum if one word were added, " much," before " human testimony." In reply he coincided with my opinion by changing " almost " to " often." He added: " I am much interested in the oft-repeated phrase of those who believe that everything must be explained at once. ' It is supernatural: there can be no other explanation!' Such is the assuredness of the ego and the smaller the latter, the greater the former!" There is little fault to be found with this expression. But what deep emotion must have been awakened by the questionnaire to evoke the initial utterance! Incidents are segments of experience, for we know nothing save as part of the experience of someone, and all experience is directly through sensation, save only the experience of thinking, which derives its material mainly—some would say entirely—from sensation. All science is based on testimony of experience through the sensations. Therefore, science itself would be nearly worthless were G. E.'s dictum true. And—perhaps most dreaded of all corollaries—the excellent books of the diplomat himself, being full of incidents to which he testifies, would hardly be worth purchasing.

PROFESSOR G. F., a Ph.D. and university specialist in Physics (Unitarian), blithely remarks, referring to a partial list of reporters in the book *Noted Witnesses for Psychic Occurrences:*

" The only kind of psychic research worth while is the kind which Houdini did! I do not see his name on your list."

Response:

"As my list comprised only 50 out of the 170 persons, it should not be surprising to you that you did not see the name of Houdini, even if it were in the complete list. It will gratify you, I am sure, to know that it is. In the book referred to, Houdini is responsible for relating a story which he heard from the lips of Harry Kellar, another conjuror possibly as great as Houdini himself. It may interest you further to know that I heard from Houdini's lips another incident which occurred in his own experience and which, slightly to polish up the sentence that he employed, ' gave him a slap in the face.'

"I was friends with Houdini, knowing him very well indeed. He was a great magician and stage general, yet it has again and again surprised me that men of science should regard him as an authority upon the subject of psychic research. He knew a great deal about 'physical phenomena.' He knew very little regarding the actual evidence for certain types of mental phenomena, and when with me was frank to say so, but naturally upon the platform used the language which magicians are accustomed to use. His book, *A Magician Among the Spirits*, is literally crammed with errors. If he had lived and another edition had been gotten out, I was proposing to help him clear out a few score of these.

"It may interest you further to know that in the same book referred to, another of the persons on the ' lists ' is J. N. Maskelyne, one of the most noted magicians of England, who vouches for a ' psychic ' incident in his family."

PROFESSOR G. G., a Ph.D. and university professor of Psychology, author in his specialty (Unitarian), writes that he has dreamed of having a dream whose veridical character the primary dream demonstrated. Also in a dream obtained positive proof of both thought-transference and clairvoyance. But alas! in the waking state the phenomena all become normal. At request he narrated a very interesting and dramatically-constructed dream of proving telepathy and clairvoyance. It is not pertinent, however, to print this dream, as Professor G. G. makes no claim that it has any logical bearing on the question whether there are in fact valid claims of the psychic. All that such dreams might indicate, on the principles of psychoanalysis, is that the professor has sought to repress, for prudential reasons, a wish-to-believe, and it consequently expresses itself in dreams. The commentator cannot, by the way, remember ever having had dreams of this character, possibly because he never felt any particular desire to prove such claims true, but only to determine whether they are true or not, hence has no repressions on the subject.

PROFESSOR G. H., a Ph.D. who has a chair of Psychology in a university, testifies:

"I attended a typical spiritualistic séance. Horns were sounded, etc., but the notable thing to me was that a month or two later the organizer of this séance began to hear the voice of his dead wife—a typical hallucination—and he at once committed suicide so as to be with her."

Of course we all know that there are pathological hallucinations, but this fact does not settle the question whether or not there are veridical ones. As well would dream voices, being unreal, indicate that nobody talks.

Nor did the fact that the man committed suicide after thinking he had a communication from his wife necessarily bear upon the question of the validity of that supposed communication. If his wife had in fact risen bodily from the dead he might still have committed suicide. If it were common for suicides to occur in consequence of alleged communications, it might be best to avoid having communications, but it is not, and one swallow does not make a summer. People, insane or not, commit suicide *post*, and often *propter*, all sorts of occasions. I knew of a man who shot himself shortly after marriage, and also because of a " communication " from his (living) wife, but probably no one would cite this suicide as an argument against getting married.

PROFESSOR G. I., a Ph.D. and college teacher of Mathematics and Astronomy, utters a note of sarcasm:

" I am skeptical about almost every question except on perpetual motion and spiritualism. I think there is about the same type of reasons for believing in either."

In spite of languid interest in what the professor *believed* or *disbelieved*, yet he was thanked for reciting a portion of his creed. It is doubtful, however, if the ejaculation of disgust signified more acquaintance with the evidence of psychic research than the yokel has of astronomy when he pronounces it " all rot that these sky-sharps can tell anything about how far off the stars are." And an astronomer ought to be more of an exact observer than an intuitionalist. None of the blanks sent him had a word about " spiritualism " or named a type of alleged phenomena which has not been defended by persons who reject the spiritistic hypothesis.

PROFESSOR G. J., an A.M. and university President (Presbyterian), likewise undergoes an emotional recoil:

"My opinion I know is of little concern to you, but this questionnaire indicates to me that you must be hard put to find material for a publication. Frankly, isn't there quite enough of this sort of thing in print?"

From a letter by the annotator to President G. J.:

"First to answer your query. No, frankly, while I think there is more than enough of certain sorts of 'this sort of thing in print' already, I do not think there is enough of another sort of this sort of thing.

"Now let me pay courteous respect to your opinion. Suppose I were for the first time cognizant that this sort of thing were being discussed and had before me the stack of replies to questions concerning it. I take up yours and think, 'Since he is the President of a university, this sort of thing must be ridiculous moonshine.' But then I come upon replies by other Presidents, and many Professors—of geology, biology, physics, astronomy, mathematics, etc., etc., which relate incidents in their careers belonging to the category of this sort of thing, which they do not regard as ridiculous at all, and for which they vouch as veritable though very puzzling facts. Would I be unintelligent in pausing to consider whether this skepticism of the men who have neither had any such experiences themselves nor patience to pay adequate attention to those who have is worth quite so much as the earnest testimonies of peers who declare that they testify from personal knowledge?

"I do not intend any derision when I refer to the fact that you appear from *Who's Who* to be a Presbyterian; which implies that you place considerable reliance in the New Testament. While I do not think that the statements of the Bible, however sacred, have weight for determining a scientific question, I often feel considerable curiosity to know how one and the same person can confide in the New Testament, which, as Phillips Brooks has said in other terms, is saturated with claims of a psychic nature, and yet can view all such claims in our own day with utter contempt.

"Are the alleged facts of no value, even though they were established? On the contrary, the psychological, philosophical and ethical consequences of some of them would be illimitable. So long as there exist a great number of men and women of highest culture and standing who allege that these are facts, and they have not been shown to be fancies, I do not think the time has come to cease printing about them, whether pro or con.

"Take 'telepathy,' for instance. Its psychological and philosophical implications would be prodigious. I have before me a letter by

MISCELLANEOUS ARGUMENTS AND OPINIONS

one of the leading neurologists of this country which says, 'I have seen what seemed to be the phenomenon personally.' Much evidence for it has accumulated, enough to have convinced some scientific men, and not enough (or not sufficiently heeded) to convince others. On what grounds shall the settlement of this grave question be regarded as not worth while?"

PROFESSOR G. K., a prominent Architect and professor of Architecture, says:

"I am afraid I may be classed under paragraph 5 of the reverse page [Those who feel "dislike of the whole subject"]. The spiritual degree [sic] needs no proof to me, and I doubt if you can prove it to others by the method of 'exact science.' By others I mean those who deny it."

We are not trying to "prove" anything. We are collecting, testing, analyzing and classifying facts. "Proof" is a reciprocal process, and the facts offered have to be more or less numerous and cogent according to what the zeitgeist happens to be. And it is curious to find one who believes in a certain type of facts yet dislikes the whole subject, is not interested in seeing his faith supported by evidence. Still more curious that many others say the same.

MEDICAL DOCTOR G. L., an honorary A.M., occupant of several important medical positions, Medical Writer mostly for the general public, writes:

"Little or no value can be attached to the testimony of art, literature, clergy, army, navy, physicians, surgeons, language, 'statesmen' or *Who's Who* in a topic such as this. Pardon this expression, but it is my experience that those who report such 'authentic' experiences are of the emotional, sentimental, unscientific (objectively, experimentally) type. Most physicians and others on your list will give testimony that is worthless."

Opinions regarding the comparative reliability of classes have been and will be sufficiently attended to elsewhere. Our attention is especially called here to the effect of "a topic such as this" upon the reliability of testimony.

An attempt was made to analyze this opinion, and to induce the doctor to commit himself to its successive factors:

"Literally, as you are a member of one of the disabled classes, your negative testimony (that is, that you have had no experience which can be classified as ' in a topic like this ') cannot be relied upon. But you may mean that the inability to give reliable testimony exists only when the testimony is affirmative. May I ask:

"1. Whether you really believe that if you had the hallucination of seeing your uncle clearly at noon-day, when he actually was not there, you could not give testimony to the fact of having had that hallucination as you could to any other species of fact?"

The doctor replied: "Perhaps I could, and would describe the experience as a typical 'hallucination.'" So far, so good; I also had called it a hallucination.

"2. And if so, and you saw by the clock that the hallucination took place exactly at noon, is there any magic in 'this topic' which would make you necessarily uncertain afterwards as to the hour?"

The doctor replied: "I have no reason to say I was ever uncertain about the time a clock's hands pointed," and added that he never had experienced any hallucination. But he was not asked what had been, but whether in case he did experience a hallucination, "this topic" would render him incapable of ascertaining the time and being certain of it afterwards.

"3. And, if it afterward were proved that this uncle died at exactly the same moment or within a few minutes of it, the receipt of that news would exercise an influence to make you less certain of the fact of your hallucination and the moment when it occurred?"

Again the doctor evades the question. He knows that in the event that he saw his uncle's apparition, timed it, and then learned that his uncle had died, he would be quite capable of comparing the events as to time, and he is unwilling for the sake of argument to say that he is such a ninny as to be incapable. Also he sees how futile it would be to proclaim his own ability and the inability of other educated and intelligent persons. So he says: "Wherever confirmations of such reported coincidences have been sought from persons said to have been told of the experience, before receipt of the news of the death, it has been found that no mention of it had been previously made. The alleged 'hallucination,' 'ghost,' 'anticipation,' or what have you, has never been confirmed, checked, corroborated by unbiased objection, unsusceptible trained judges. Ask ———, Watson, et al."

I have often remarked that psychic research is the one field into which intelligent men have no fear of precipitating themselves to make skeptical affirmations without offering or knowing data to prove them. In a great number of cases confirmations have been obtained from persons said to have been told beforehand of apparitions, dreams and what-have-you of seemingly significant character, corresponding in time with the moment, hour or day of the death. They are to be found in a number of carefully compiled books.

Take *Phantasms of the Living*, for instance, and glance through it for half an hour. We find (II, 397) two persons testifying that a third in the presence of several people, one morning, on the basis of a visual experience, declared that a certain woman died at a specified hour of the previous night, that the date and hour was at once set down, and that it was afterwards found to correspond exactly with that of the woman's death. We find (II, 174) that two persons thought they heard the voice of a certain officer uttering the name of one of them, that the matter was talked over, that the officer died at about the same time, and that the confirmation sought was given over signatures. We find (II, 178) a woman who faints on seeing the apparition of her aunt, that the aunt's unexpected death took place that day, and that the witness who was told of the apparition before news of the death came, supplied her signed testimony. We find cases told beforehand, cases where two persons shared the experience and both testify, cases recorded before knowledge of the corresponding event, cases numerous and of great variety. One (II, 230) relates to a manservant Arthur, ill in St. Catherine's Home, but who was expected to live some days, so that his mistress on Friday wrote that she would visit him on Monday. That evening, at 10:30, the time he had been accustomed to extinguish the lights, his mistress and her daughter, in separate rooms, near a hall gas burner, both heard a man's tread approach it, then retire, and both emerged into the hall and remarked with surprise that the gas was still burning, and that it sounded like Arthur's step. We have both their testimonies, and also that of the woman in charge of the Home, to the fact that Arthur died at 10:30, just after asking the time.

It is really irrelevant *what* a writer's " bias " may be when we are examining the evidence he furnishes. Was not Du Chaillu " biased " by what he had seen in his African explorations, when he wrote about the pygmies and gorillas? Of course, and many authorities charged that he was romancing, but his statements were afterwards vindicated to universal satisfaction. *Phantasms of the Living* is as carefully guarded from any just liability to the charge of special pleading as any book I know. Nor is there any doubt about the standing, intelligence and character of many of the witnesses.

One is not sure whether the doctor implies that Professor Watson is one of the "unbiased," but one suspects that the professor would laugh heartily at the idea that he is unbiased on the subject of "ghosts."

"4. Or suppose the case to have been thus (and there have been many of this character): you had the hallucination, you noted the time by the clock, and you told others before the news of the uncle's death at the same time arrived. Do you still think that your testimony would be not worth taking since you belong to a blacklisted class (physicians)? If so, it must be that 'this topic' has a black magic which disintegrates the intellects of all concerned—is this your view?"

Again the doctor declines to answer the question, but says that he has examined every Baltimore case brought to his attention, and he hasn't found a valid case. But he fails to state whether his cases were more or less than a half dozen, or in what his "investigation" consisted. "No Edison, Lindbergh, Hoover, Coolidge, Mellon, Borah, Byrd, ever reported such." Appeal to some of these men is odd, seeing that the doctor had already discarded any testimony by army, navy or parliament! Borah and Coolidge are statesmen, and Hoover a statesman plus. Byrd is a Rear Admiral, and Lindbergh a Colonel, which titles should automatically disable their testimony. Probably the doctor would not limit his remark anent these gentlemen to death coincidences; he thinks that no such man would have any disgraceful "psychic" experience and be convinced of its supernormal character. Perhaps Edison could not, but Linnæus, one of the greatest scientists and closest observers of facts in his century, testified that he recognized the footsteps of his friend "precisely at that hour" when his death took place. Edison could not, but another great inventor, Hiram Maxim, could and did. Whether Hoover has ever given any attention to such matters we do not know, but we do know that the mining engineer Greenawalt, and the aeronautic engineer Dunne have, and have become affirmatively impressed. Coolidge has not told of any psychic experience, but his best friends will not claim him greater than the statesman and Lord High Chancellor Brougham, who set down in his diary that he saw the apparition of a friend who was in India, and afterwards wrote that he learned the friend died that day. And Borah may be faced by Constans, Depew, etc.; Mellon the financier by Henry

Clews; Byrd by Henry M. Stanley; and Colonel Lindbergh by other adventurous men with military titles, as General Fremont and Genérale Garibaldi.

PROFESSOR DAVID CAMP ROGERS, PH.D., who teaches Psychology in Smith College (Congregationalist), writes:

"I have been interested in the topics mentioned in paragraph two of your letter. For a number of years I have had repeated experiences myself that could be classified under these heads, and have heard repeated reports from others of similar experiences and many times have not discovered a complete 'normal' explanation. I have in my own experiences always had the impression that there were ample unknown factors so that in every case it was probable that an explanation in terms of 'normal' processes would be discovered if these factors were fully known.

"I am reporting two incidents which I regard as typical. Some years ago an unusually serious student wished to make tests of telepathy which seemed to her significant as having a bearing on the belief in immortality, and I coöperated with her in making plans for her tests.

"Her first method was to get one of her friends to relax in the corner of a darkened room while she sat in the opposite corner. When the friend signalled that she was in a relaxed and receptive condition, the experimenter would develop as vivid an image as possible of one of the four suits of playing cards and make a record. The friend in turn would wait until an image of one of the suits came to her mind and then would record her image.

"During a few preliminary tests she found that each of six subjects had either approximately the same proportion of right images as would be expected by chance, namely one-fourth, or a smaller proportion, and with a seventh subject the proportion of right images was considerably larger than the normal proportion. With the seventh subject also both the subject and the experimenter had the feeling that actual communication was occurring.

"She then dropped the six less successful subjects and continued tests exclusively with the seventh. She continued these until she had made in all 1,664 tests. Of these, the right responses amounted to 422, which is 6 more than the number which is probable by chance, a smaller deviation from that number than the probable deviation.

"This same student and others have tested their capacity to cause individuals in an audience to turn around, by themselves thinking about them and willing that they should. They found that they would not turn around any more frequently under their intended influence than without it.

"At one time when I was attending a class reunion an impressive man with swarthy skin undertook to read for us the thoughts of myself and my classmates. Each one of us was asked to write a question and the answer on a slip of paper. We were then to do anything that we chose with the slips of paper. I put mine in my pocket, and my classmates around me did the same. Later he went into a condition of extreme concentration [?], told us a question, asked whether any man present had asked that question. A classmate with whom I was well acquainted rose and said that he had. He then asked my friend whether he had ever seen him before or entered into any agreement to assist him, and my friend said he had not. Then, after further concentration, he gave the answer which my friend reported correct. This procedure was repeated with a considerable number of my classmates. I could not see that there had been any possibility of communication between the medium and these classmates with whom I was well acquainted, and so I could think of no possible explanation except telepathy and set about readjusting myself to this new experience so that I should be ready to present quite a different view of this topic than heretofore to my classes in psychology. Eventually another classmate pointed out to me something which I had entirely overlooked in my thinking, though I remembered the facts afterward when they were mentioned, namely, that the medium had given us the opportunity of putting our slips in a hat which was passed, that a hat had been passed through a small section of the audience, and that all of the classmates whose questions had been answered were in this small part of the group in which the hat had been passed. Though I had not discovered the method by which the medium had secured the information from the slips in the hat, it seemed to me there was no difficulty in supposing that it had been secured through a so-called 'normal' method."

Letter to Professor Rogers:

"Thanks for your thoughtful and discriminating letter.

"If there is such a thing as the passage of thoughts from one person to another, it seems fairly well established by this time that (a) very few persons are qualified to be agents, whether experimentally or spontaneously, in any impressive degree, *at any time;* (b) that the few who are impressively qualified at times are not so qualified at all times; (c) and that persons who in the first experiments, or the first of a series, while their minds are passive or simply mildly curious, have results greatly or considerably above chance expectation, often, as the experiments continue and their conscious minds become keenly interested and anxious to keep up the record, have less favorable results, dropping even to chance expectation or a non-significant variation from it. This was the case with the 'seventh subject' that your student tested. Whether the seventh subject actually was to some extent affected by 'telepathy' in the first experiments, and lost the necessary passivity or emotional equipoise in the succeeding ones, of course cannot certainly be known.

"Many years ago I tried some experiments with my wife, myself as percipient, and in the first eight or ten experiments got a correct result or nearly so, in the majority of cases. But the next time I had a series with her, being keenly interested, my conscious mind fully 'on the job,' and with a desire, no doubt, to 'keep up with my record,' I had no impressive results, nor had I in subsequent attempts.

"Within the year I was one of many tested by a somewhat different experiment in which the drawing of a card figured. In the first set of five trials, which I performed in a careless, amused fashion, I got something right, number of spots, suit, or color, in all five instances, a result much beyond chance expectation. But in thirty subsequent series of five trials each, on different dates, I never had one series which showed anything at all impressive. I tell you these experiences simply because they may interest you and may quite possibly be significant of the fact that a mental passivity which few people can maintain, even if they can sometimes hold it for a little, is the *sine qua non*, although my experiences *demonstrate* nothing. It would indeed require a large number of experiences, rigidly observed and recorded, of different persons, if they went no farther, to establish a strong presumption. But suppose that there were had a hundred experiments each with 1,000 people; of these 1,000 only twenty showed at any point of the series a group running far above the expectation of chance, and with all the twenty this group occurred either at the very beginning or close of it, and none at the middle or end, we should then, I think, have established a strong presumption of both telepathy and the effect of fatigue or the loss of passivity. I would be glad if you care to tell me how these remarks strike you. The more irenic discussion there is at this period when experiments are being conducted, the better for the experimenters.

"We have long ago determined that the opinion of people that they can make others turn around by staring at the back of their heads is unfounded, or, at least, that when they attempt to do it under rigidly experimental conditions, they fail. But it might still be true that out of a thousand of such persons one could do it. I am expressing no opinion that this is the case with any one, however.

"Referring to the interesting case of the 'swarthy man' who produced an effect which you now think was produced by an unperceived trick, I entirely agree with you and would judging merely from the description of act. There are a number of ways by which magicians can get possession of slips of paper gathered up in a hat or other receptacle. I could probably conjecture what method was employed if I knew exactly what was done with the hat—I mean from the time the slips were put in and the time the man spoke, and every even slightest movement, which of course no one could now be certain of. I take it that the swarthy man was not a classmate, and was a stranger. The solution would be easier to suggest if I knew whether he himself passed the *hat*, and if not, whether it was a man of the class or another stranger. Of course a member of the class *could* learn a magical trick. I have seen apparently impossible things done in broad daylight directly before me, and which no amount of learning except acquaintance with juggling methods would have enabled me to explain, mysterious tricks which baffled Muensterberg, Edison, and others.

" One remark of yours shows that you recognize a fact which many learned persons do not seem to recognize, namely, that one may entirely forget or leave out of their thinking, the most important fact within the range of their observation when the feat was performed. In your case you failed to remember or at least to think of the fact that the man had part of the slips gathered into the hat, and he answered only questions which were among those on these slips.

" I have had dozens of accounts from lawyers, business men, etc., to feats of the famous Bert Reese, all in good faith, and all supposed by them to be complete and accurate, but which were defective and inaccurate because they (as would be the case with 999 men out of 1,000 persons unversed in the methodology of conjuring) failed to notice or to remember a few very unobtrusive but all-important movements on the part of Reese."

On October 9, 1929, a letter was sent to G. M., an M.E., Army Officer and military engineer (Roman Catholic).

" In response to your letter of December 10, 1928 (which itself was in response to my questionnaire), you said in part:

" 'If I understand correctly the intent of your book is rather a one-sided one. That is, to prove by examples that there *are* manifestations for which there is no normal explanation rather than an unbiased résumé of the thoughts on both sides of the subject. If I am wrong in this and you desire to include some of my experiences, I should be glad to write them up for you. In either case I would be glad to hear from you further on the work you are doing.'

" I replied on February 20, saying that I would be glad if you would carry out your offer to write out some of the cases referred to of seeming supernormal phenomena which you had cleared up. But I have had no reply. .

MISCELLANEOUS ARGUMENTS AND OPINIONS

"I am more eager to keep my book from being a 'one-sided' one than my doubting correspondents, apparently, are to help me to that end. May I ask you to fulfil your promise?"

But he didn't.

Letters were also received from a university Law School Professor (A.B., Episcopalian), a well-known University Professor of Psychology (Ph.D.), a College Professor of Journalistics (Ph.B., Congregationalist), a miscellaneous Writer of some repute (A.B.), a Musician and composer, and a Zoologist and museum curator (hon. Sc.D.); all professing to have investigated and blasted purported cases, from one to "hundreds." The psychologist had "run down a vast number of alleged cases of this kind." All were importuned to relate one instance and its explanation, but only a single person replied, and he had forgotten.

The psychologist also said: "I have come to look on these things as explainable in principle, although I may not at the moment have a particular key in hand." Persons who have studied locks may not have in hand the particular key necessary to open a particular lock, but they can form some idea of the key that is needed. It were devoutly to be wished that the professor would describe the key which would unlock the case described in the Mrs. King hypothetical question,[1] or say if he can imagine what that key might be, short of supposing that the whole case is fiction.

---
[1] See page 209.

VIII. A VERY DOUBTING THOMAS

To one correspondent an entire section is devoted, not because his polemics are particularly novel or formidable, but because he returned to the charge again and again, and from first to last produced almost a summary of the customary objections to and dogmatic arguments against psychic research. Such good-natured persistence and ingenuity in contriving theories and surmises intended to have explanatory significance, was very gratifying. In fact, though at the end I felt increased esteem for many a correspondent, Mr. Thomas's name, as in the case of Abou Ben Adhem, "led all the rest." If of the opinion that his logic anent the theme of this book was more peccable than that relating to other subjects, I attribute the difference entirely to the enchantment of the boundary.

CHAUNCEY THOMAS, lecturer on English in Denver University, also a lecturer on literary, scientific and historical subjects, authority on frontier history and ballistics, magazine editor, etc. (Agnostic), related the following experience:

"The nearest I myself ever came to such a thing was one night in 1893, when I was on guard at the Chicago World's Fair. I was twenty-one at the time, in fine health, but having gone without my usual sleep during the day, I was very sleepy, though not bodily tired to amount to anything. It was the day after Easter, when the women had put on the large hats covered with artificial flowers. About midnight, while walking my beat in the Manufacturers' Building, I suddenly saw two girls I knew who during the day attended to the soda water booth. Apparently, there they were, outside the booth however. I looked at them closely, then slapped myself in the face and they vanished. At intervals there they were again, but always motionless and in the same position. Another slap in my face cleared the atmosphere completely for the time being, as did washing my face several times in cold water during the night. But all the time I was walking my beat as usual, and no doubt appeared normal to an observer, yet several times I found myself from about ten to sometimes about fifty feet beyond the end of my beat, practically asleep on my feet. And at times my knees would suddenly sag under me. . . .

"Now the explanation. Next afternoon, now broad day, and I

A VERY DOUBTING THOMAS   331

fully rested, I went to the same booth to unravel the matter. The two girls had the morning before put on for the first time their new large Easter hats. I recalled that then. On the wall, facing the end of my former night beat, but perhaps one hundred feet from it, some one had that same day tacked up some new advertising matter in the form of large flower clusters. My sleepy eyes had mistaken these for the girls' beflowered hats, and my sleepy imagination had slowly pictured below these 'hats' the rest of the girls themselves. When I had slapped myself they had faded instantly, except the advertisements on the wall, and I stood and watched the 'girls' slowly form beneath them, about like smoke making a shape, gradually thicker and thicker, till seemingly the solid girls' bodies were there with those 'hats' on them. They were there all the rest of the night, off and on, from 12 midnight to 4 A. M.

" Of course all this is not at all ' psychic,' but it serves, to me at least, to explain many another ' case ' as sincerely reported by others, but which, to my mind, has somewhat the same explanation."

Of course Mr. Thomas was gently informed that his experience, even had an explanation not been at hand, would have had no standing as a " case " for psychic research. No quasi-sensory effect, no matter how striking, is a " case," unless there is some conjoined feature, or approximately contemporaneous event, which gives it seeming significance. If a man " sees " the apparition of his wife, living or dead, that and nothing more, there is no " case." If he " sees " the apparition of his absent wife, and she dies by accident that same hour, there is a " case " for consideration.

Mr. Thomas's experience was an illusion, caused by extreme neural fatigue. He was, he says, practically asleep on his feet, so that his knees would suddenly sag under him. Every psychologist knows that illusions are not uncommon when a very tired and sleepy person is forced to keep awake. I myself had one experience of the sort many years ago. Going direct from long residence in a city, I walked a difficult twenty-five miles to Mt. Katahdin. While still aching from the effort I climbed the mountain, and on the way down was, with my brother, overtaken by night. We built a fire, sat by it all night, and I never slept a wink. Toward morning, while it was still dark, the burning coals of the fire transformed into a scene made up of a farmhouse, an orchard behind it, and a field with hay-cocks. It was not like the ordinary seeing things in an open fireplace, for I could not make the vision go. I turned away repeatedly, I rubbed my eyes, but the vision remained for several minutes. Later, a long stick protruding from the fire, partly charred black but here and there showing a glowing spot, created the illusion of a train of cars standing upon a bridge. The scene was realistically perfect—I could examine the details of the bridge and train, windows and all, not in miniature but as of the real thing seen at some distance. In vain I tried to banish the illusion. Only as the glowing spots on the long stick died out did it disappear. Not for one moment did I suppose the experience anything more than an illusion caused by weariness and want of sleep. Momentarily I could even note the actual *points d'appui*, but in a second the illusion was there again as vivid as ever. Still, it never occurred to me that it was a " case " for psychic research or afforded a key to the incidents in *Phantasms of the Living*, except such as are given expressly by way of illustrating unevidential illusion.[1]

My correspondent was asked what possible light his illusion cast upon the apparition seen by the great lawyer and statesman, Lord Brougham,[2] contemporaneously with the death in a foreign land of the one person with whom, in youth, he had made a compact that the first to die would try to appear to the survivor. His only response was the dictum that " history is not evidence." One wonders that the author of such an opinion should think it worth while to lecture on history, and what it means to be an " authority on frontier history." Does he have no hope of reaching *any* dependable results in his lectures, and is he an authority on that which presents *no* evidence? He probably draws the enchanted line, and means that " history " can present no evidence of *psychic* facts. What, when Brougham wrote down an account of the apparition in his diary even before the news of the death arrived, is that not evidence that he did have the experience? And his subsequent written statement that a letter announced the death of his friend on the night of the apparition was not any evidence at all?[3]

---

[1] " The slight sensory signs which Scott would normally have interpreted as the folds of coats and plaids hanging in a dimly-lit hall, were interpreted by him, at a moment when the idea of Byron was running strongly in his head, as the figure of the deceased poet." (*Phantasms of the Living*, II, 185.) Here we probably have the clue to Mr. Thomas's interpretation of the slight sensory signs in his case. He was at the romantic age of twenty-one; surely the two charming girls seen a few hours earlier were " running strongly in his head."

[2] *Noted Witnesses for Psychic Occurrences*, 59.

[3] I am aware that Lord Brougham is said not to have been always veracious in his public utterances and that he did not actually set down the facts about the letter until long afterward. Nevertheless I am convinced that he did have the experience, that he did set it down in his journal and that he did copy it later. His later attempt to minimize the importance of it by arguing that the coincidence was merely a chance one, and his effort to interpret as a dream that which originally had been described as an apparition seen while awake and taking a bath, exhibit in a manner hardly to be counterfeited the disintegrating effect of time and a rational-

Asked how his non-coinciding illusion induced by fatigue "explained" the coincidence between the apparition of his father seen by a young man on a vessel in the North Sea, and the apparitions seen of himself and his father by his sister in New Jersey, of which she told others at once,[4] Mr. Thomas responds: "Testimonials are not evidence." This contemptuous word, "testimonials," which others beside Mr. Thomas have applied to statements of psychic experiences, is probably reminiscent of testimonials to cures supposedly wrought by patent medicines. But there is no analogy. A person may think his cure due to the medicine when in fact it was due to other causes, and even when nature cured him in spite of its injurious effect. A medicine-testimonial involves a belief, a question which can be argued. But when Sir J. H. Drummond Hay, British Minister to Morocco, "heard" the voice of his daughter-in-law, three hundred miles away, saying, "Oh, I wish papa knew that Robert is ill," it was an immediate and unmistakable fact about which there was no question and could be no argument, the words clear and distinct, the voice of the speaker recognized.[5] There was therefore no reasoning, with its liability to error, from an effect back to a cause; there was direct knowledge of a fact, as startling, unique and concrete, as though a bolt of lightning had struck the house. To call Sir John's statement of that fact, which he immediately noted in his diary, a "testimonial," is a misuse of words of which a lecturer on English really should not be guilty. And I do not believe that there is any scientist in the world so ossified that had he himself had the experience and afterward received from his daughter-in-law news that her husband had been ill of typhoid fever, particularly on the night which was the night of the voice-hallucination, he also would not have written and told her what had occurred. And any man, no matter how he may look askance at the experiences of others, if his daughter-in-law, whom he knew to be honest, wrote him that she actually, in her distress, uttered those very words, would at least wonder very vigorously whether the unique experience and the double coincidence of time and verbal identity, occurred by mere chance.

Asked if his illusion really solved the problem why, as one of the greatest physicists related in my hearing, in the hour when the wit-

---

izing mentality upon a valid experience. Hardly, either, could a man of Brougham's intellect have been mistaken about the letter connected with so remarkable a unique experience. However, I could have cited many another notable witness, instead of Brougham.

[4] *Journal* A. S. P. R., XVI, 197, statements from the Osgood family.
[5] *Noted Witnesses,* 119.

ness's father died, he himself, far distant, was wakened by the hallucination of hearing his name pronounced in what he distinctly recognized as his father's voice, Mr. Thomas replies: "Greatness in one line is no proof of ability in another line. A dozen explanations possible, each more likely than that it actually occurred." But what peculiar "ability in another line" is required in order to recognize one's name and the voice of one's father? If it were a matter in which trick magic could enter, I would agree, but this is a matter requiring only sanity and intelligence. And as to the item of coincidence in the death, certainly the fact that the narrator is a physicist of distinguished intellectuality and noted for the exactitude of his work is of great value in giving assurance that he was not careless in ascertaining that there *was* temporal coincidence. I can hardly imagine one, if present when such a man gravely related the facts, expressing or even holding the opinion that, as told, the incident never "actually occurred." And although the correspondent said that a dozen explanations were possible, each more likely than that it actually occurred, he was not so helpful as to suggest one. He did, a little farther on, grudgingly admit that possibly there may be telepathy, but that explanation, which is probably the correct one as applied to this particular incident, would be an abandonment of the position that it never occurred.

The correspondent went on to say that he had "no belief in psychical research whatever." But psychical research is for the purpose of ascertaining facts, and so far as possible, explaining them. I remarked that "in my professional work I renounce all *belief*, and hardly know what the term means in application to this subject. I know only evidence and logic." My friend commented, "Both tricky tools of thought." That may be—tricks may be played with anything actual or conceivable, but *evidence and logic are the best tools we have,* nevertheless. From these alone come science—systematic knowledge—of any kind.

Then we have:

"Testimony is worthless, no matter how sincere. Read history and see the testimony about what today all men of intelligence regard as nonsense, such as the earth is flat, the snake that flirted with Mamma Eve. See the numbers who give away everything when the world is coming to an end."

My friend is a very bright man, but he has fallen under the enchantment of the boundary; surely, had he not been in full tilt against psychic research, he would not have employed what is known in logic as the fallacy of *equivocation*. In other words, he is using the word "testimony" in a sense as foreign to psychic research as it is to law. In no court would a man be allowed to testify to a belief, but only to facts within his own knowledge, through his senses. As little does psychic research bring forward as evidence any man's religious creed, or his reactions to tradition, or his philosophical notions, but only his witness to experienced facts. And there is another logical fallacy involved in the paragraph quoted above, that of the *undistributed major term*. "Testimony is worthless" is substituted for "Some [or much] testimony is worthless," which is all that can be intelligently maintained. If *testimony* is worthless, then every court in the world should be abolished. If *testimony* is worthless, then it is silly even to maintain scientific laboratories, for it is of no avail to perform experiments if testimony to their results is worthless. Let us make another syllogism after the pattern furnished us.

> Cats have tails.
> Manx cats are cats.
> Therefore Manx cats have tails.

But they haven't. And no more are we assisted one inch toward a safe conclusion by the syllogism:

> Testimony (meaning *some* or *much* "testimony," such as that one believes that snakes talked 6,000 years ago) is worthless.
> The statements of Brougham, the Osgoods, the Hays, the eminent physicist, etc. (to *facts of their experience*), are testimony.
> Therefore the statements of Brougham, the Osgoods, the Hays, the physicist, etc. (to facts of their experience), are worthless.

But no such conclusion can be drawn from the premises, any more than Manx cats were logically proved to have tails.

I have noticed that when bright men are so eager to discredit the evidence of psychic research that they utter general statements which, if true, would indict all human intelligence and honesty, they always except themselves. They become, for the nonce, of a species of solipsist, in that while they are skeptical of all other human experience and testimony, they believe in their own experiences and expect to be believed when they relate them. Thus Mr. Thomas, the same man who insists that "testimony is worthless," tells of his own illusion relating to the pretty girls and expects to be credited. Directly after he has condemned us all to external nescience by declaring that "testimony" is worthless, he also relates a remarkable coincidence that came under his notice, and says, in substance, "Say why that accidental coincidence is not as good as any of your supposedly 'psychic' cases." And it does not occur to him that, to employ the inelegant metaphor of Professor Bowne when criticizing Spencer, he has already mown the legs off from that incident offered as rebutting evidence. What do I need to say except that if "testimony is worthless," his testimony to coincidences, hallucinations and everything else which he has cited from his experience has no value whatever?

My friend says: "I find that a 'cultured' person is just as liable to get things twisted, or add to them, or omit things that mar their tale, as a ditch-digger." Certainly *a* cultured person may do that. But again the correspondent does not notice that if we are to discredit all for what some do, his own stories are discredited. "Even if correctly quoted [reported] by the parties concerned," he says, referring to the narrators of my sample incidents. Evidently he does not believe any of them. Then why should he expect any one to believe his story of an illusion? Yet it does not occur to him that I might disbelieve it, and he would have felt insulted had I expressed disbelief. I have no reason to discredit it, but let us see how the account stands between his story and another of the sort which he regards as "worthless."

(a) Chauncey Thomas,	(a) Richard Redmayne (afterwards Sir),
(b) university lecturer on English, lecturer, editor, expert in ballistics, etc.,	(b) professor of mining in a university, metallurgist, Government expert on mining,
(c) says he experienced an illusion,	(c) says that one Tonks told him that the night before he had a vision of his mother, thousands of miles away, dead, and heard her say she should never see him again; that he laughed at Tonks and quoted him to others as an example of superstition, but that news came about six weeks later, to his knowledge, that she did die as stated and did make that remark before sinking into coma.

(d) an account of which was not, so far as appears, set down at the time, and is told years afterward from memory,	(d) He wrote down all the facts in a letter and sent it to his father within a very few days of the confirmatory news, and the actual letter is quoted.
(e) without any corroboration.	(e) He also procured a corroborative statement from Tonks himself.

And yet Mr. Thomas expects his statement to be credited and to be given negative weight, but Professor Redmayne's array of proofs he would regard as "worthless"!

Again take the Osgood case. We have Miss Laura E. Osgood's account of seeing the apparitions of her father and foster brother, side by side, telling her mother soon afterwards and again talking with her mother about it the night before her brother came home, the next day hearing her brother tell of seeing the apparition of the father, that same afternoon and at least near the same hour, beside him on the deck of a vessel in great peril. We have the signed corroboration by the mother and sister. We have the statement of the brother, corroborating all that concerned him. Where was the chance of getting facts "twisted," or "added to"? On the side of the lady, there was only the fact of the figures of the two men, and the time when they were seen. On the brother's side there was only the fact of seeing an apparition of his father and the time it was seen. Take away these simple facts and there would be no reason for the mutual surprise of learning each what happened to the other, to which the four persons present testify. How, then, could anything have been added?

Presumably, Mr. Thomas's coincidence story is correctly told, but if suspicion could attach to either narrative, his is a hundred times more likely to have been "twisted," "added to," etc. He says that in a ranch in Colorado a man, who was a poor marksman, shot a coyote at about three hundred yards distance, and hit it in the left front and right rear legs, and that the next week another man, also a poor marksman, with the same rifle, shot another coyote through the left front and right rear legs. There is no corroboration. We have no knowledge whether one or both of the men referred to would have admitted that they were poor shots, or that the distance was nearly as much as three hundred yards. The skill of the shooters *could* be "twisted," a few score of yards *could* have been "added." We are not even told that Mr. Thomas was witness of either of the feats. We are not told that he saw the carcasses. For aught we know, the second man may have romanced and his romance may have been accepted, since it had an agreeable hunting flavor. Our correspondent would be indignant did we express skepticism of his story, yet writes on the margin of the far better authenticated Osgood incident an expression of contemptuous skepticism—" Testimonials are not evidence," and adds that persons of culture are likely to " get things twisted," or " add to them," whereas, if any feature of their declaration is untwisted out of it or subtracted, there is left nothing for the whole family to get excited about on that day of meeting. Why this reaction? Simply and solely, as with many other bright men, since *this* sort of an incident is not to Mr. Thomas's taste.

From a letter to Mr. Thomas:

"I quite agree with you that very remarkable coincidences can occur by chance only. That is, I agree that for something-or-other to happen to somebody-or-other at some-time-or-other against the chance of a billion to one is not proof nor even evidence. For example, there might not be one chance in a billion that a particular man living in China today would meet a particular man, or any particular man living today in the United States, say on February 1, 1925. And yet there are doubtless a number of men now living in China who will on that date meet some man in the United States. It is not proof or even evidence of anything but chance if *some* man can be found to truly testify that some event happened to him three times in succession, although this involved an improbability measured by a billion to one. For when you take into account the millions of men and the uncountable millions of events great and small that make up the existence of each of them, such coincidences are bound to happen by the strictest calculus of chance.

"An example is found in the deaths of John Adams and Thomas Jefferson. They were peculiarly associated in their lives, particularly with the great event which is celebrated on the Fourth of July; (1) they died on the same day, (2) that day the Fourth of July, (3) and that Fourth of July marking exactly half a century of their country's independence. Probably the histories of great men since the beginning of human records could be searched without bringing to light another case so remarkable in the way of coincidences *of that particular kind*. But sets of coincidences of *one or another of the innumerable possible* kinds can be found, nearly or fully as remarkable. The dice are being shaken innumerable times for innumerable men through the centuries, and *of course* amongst them all extraordinary coincidental combinations occasionally turn up.

"But, when I discovered a particular private person who repeatedly produced sets of ' coincidences ' *at call, at the time selected by me*, and *relevant to the particular stimulus which I provided*, there was a very different situation. It is not now a case of the dice coming out in an unusual way *sometime* and relating to *something* and *someone*, but we are getting results at our own time and under our own conditions. When I placed in Mrs. King's hands, folded so that only white paper showed,[6] and she made thirty-four statements (setting aside three regarding the truth or falsity of which we know nothing because the man who knew would not reply) of which thirty-three were correct, and the remaining one partly correct, all relevant to that man and his affairs, which statements, estimated by a leading mathematician, exceeded chance *probability* 5,000,000,000,000,000 to one, it is inverted credulity to say that this neither proves nor is evidence. I put to your common-sense; if a man told you as many things, some of them very unusual and striking, which happened when you supposed yourself alone, you would hardly pass the matter off as a mere set of chance coincidences, you could not be induced to accept such an explanation, but would begin to inspect the possibilities of the keyhole and of a dictaphone. If there were one person with you when these described incidents occurred, it would be very hard to convince you that the other person had not blabbed. You probably at this moment entertain the theory that the woman mentioned above had normal knowledge who wrote the letter and of the facts about him; your reason revolts at the idea that at a selected time and with a selected object a person could out of blank ignorance evolve a complicated set of facts with no ascertained error except the exaggeration of one item.[7]

---

[6] I must repeat that while it was impossible for her to read it, she would have gotten hints for very little which she said had she read the whole.

[7] Mr. Thomas's reply to the Mrs. King case was what a psychologist might call a "flight from reality." I had told him that she was a private person; he pictures her as a professional sharper. I had explicitly shown that the terms and conditions of the experiment were of my devising; he replies that "no test is possible when the medium fixes the test." I had said nothing to warrant the notion that the woman's thirty-four allegations related to what was in the folded paper she held (and very few of them did); he finds relief in picturing her as "reading those folded papers" held immovably between her palms. He says: "I'll bet she'll not read a word of mine. . . . They savor human nature usually very keenly and pick their man. . . . Pay my expenses and I'll come to Boston and dry up those mediums. . . . I've not had thirty years newspaper reporter experience for nothing, or a touch of the Secret Service years ago. . . . I think your woman folded-letter-reader would suddenly remember those biscuits in the oven and have to go straight home." He also gives me information (?) regarding certain old tricks and bunco games, having evidently pictured me as a doddering old chimney-corner theorist, who had had little contact with the hard, cold world. To get his reaction, I swapped a few autobiographical notes for his, told him that I had been rooting out frauds and tricks of various kinds since I was fifteen years old, mentioned my long-ago five years experience as the Assistant Secretary of a State organization which warred against certain crafty species of crime, my planning work for detectives and occasionally going out on some difficult job myself, the three consecutive months when

"Still further, if it was a matter of mere fortuitous coincidence that in this instance the woman got such amazing results, you would not expect her to accomplish such a feat, less astounding mathematically, but nevertheless tremendously beyond the calculus of chance, five times out of twelve trials. Seeing that she did this (by the way, she had never been experimented with until I did it), would you still say that there was no *evidence* of telepathy or some other unknown power—or (this will be just as good for my argument) of her having normal knowledge in spite of all my precautions?

"And does the fact that I followed up the experiments with her by one hundred experiments, five each with twenty other persons, and not in a single case got more than that slight sprinkling of minor 'coincidences' which were unimpressive because in company with preponderating blunders and irrelevancies—would this, I ask, have no effect upon your reasoning processes? The results of this particular woman are beyond those of the others by what I might call astronomical distances. Why were her results so different, if all was a matter of chance coincidence? Is chance so selective, consistently and persistently? Then I shall expect to hear that when in turn twenty persons are shut up in a room with a musical instrument and only discordant sounds are heard to issue therefrom except in the case of one, it was all chance coincidence and there was no real evidence that this person could play better than the others."

I brought seventy suits into court, all successful, and named certain other chapters of experience with the puzzles which animate and inanimate objects present. He replied that by no means did he (then or earlier?) think me doddering, but was still skeptical of the formidable King case, and still confident that he could reduce any psychic to impotence. Of course he could, and so could I go into a shop where clocks and watches are kept, and in half an hour cause that not one of them would tell the correct time or any time at all. And so have I expressed doubts of certain confident reports of alleged psychic phenomena, but because of defects in the reports, gaps in the conditions or evidence which could be pointed out. But every smallest pertinent detail of the experiment with Mrs. King has been printed, and I have in vain asked, begged and entreated not only the general circle of readers but a number of specific individuals of academic standing who have uttered disparaging remarks, to point out a defect in the conditions, or even to imagine any explanatory factor other than lying on the part of the experimenter. On the other hand, after having become familiar with intimations of some scientific men and other men not so scientific that the methods of that grade of psychic research which I represent are very, very bad, it has been a delight to watch some of these when they have nimbly hopped into the field of psychic research to show what they could do. I have never seen one such amateur who did not betray that he was an amateur, and have witnessed crudities which psychic researchers long ago learned to avoid.

If any one of scientific, academic or professional standing in the world will examine the printed report of the King experiment referred to, with view to its criticism and to an explanatory theory, and if the result is one grade higher than any response which has thus far reached me ("Pooh!" or "It wouldn't have taken place if I had been there"), I will gladly print it, with or without the name of the author, according to his permission or prohibitory stipulation, and will give him my thanks in the bargain. The Report is only fifteen pages long, and will be sent to any such person who may express his willingness to undertake the little task.

A VERY DOUBTING THOMAS 341

"Spontaneous coincidences also, in my judgment, *may* be evidence, and strong evidence, not, to be sure, in single instances, no matter how remarkable, and not in many instances when they are of all sorts. But when spontaneous instances of a *particular kind* occur in numbers, if, for example, out of a hundred cases of persons who have had the experience of an apparition but once in their lives, fifty of them should coincide with the time when that person died, and fifteen more with a time when that person was undergoing some very great emotional experience, if not indeed sufficient *proof* of some causal connection, it would be *evidence* of a relation between the two classes of events. It would not be evidence if the apparitions coincided with all sort of things, nor is an apparition evidential in itself. But when we consider the multitude of things which happen in a man's life, and the number of days and hours of which it is made up, for this particular kind of a coincidence to happen in so large a percentage of cases, for the coincidences to show so strong a tendency to be selective, is something which should attract notice, on exactly the same lines of reasoning by which anthropologists calculate the antiquity of human remains because of the 'coincidences' of their being found with remains of the cave bear and saber-toothed tiger.

"It is the same kind of reasoning which you yourself employ when you attempt to account for apparitions *per se*, partly on the assumption that the most of them occur in bad light. If coincidences are not even evidence, what difference does it make if eighty, or ninety or ninety-nine out of a given hundred coincide with bad light? It proves nothing, it is not even evidence. This is what you ought to say, it appears to me, to be consistent, yet I do not hear you saying it."

For what the philosopher did in 1820, and the college professor did in 1875, the lecturer on English, history, etc., boldly does in 1930—he erects dogmas on no foundation unless on his acquaintance with the "ghosts" of fiction.

"It is at least notable that most 'ghosts,' visions, etc., are seen at night, or not in clear sunlight; also most of them under unusual mental strain, which in itself tends to upset the orderly workings of the various faculties of the brain."

Having appealed to imaginary statistics, our friend could hardly object to my actual statistics on the ground that statistics are of no value anyway. "Most" must signify nearly all, since no argument can be drawn from a mere majority. In most cases, it is held, darkness or poor light prevails. In reply I cited statistics given in the division of this book entitled "Old Dogma and Later Statistics," and informed the correspondent that inspection of two hundred cases, involving two hundred and five apparitions whose appearance, whether by night or day was stated, revealed that forty-one per cent of these were seen in the daytime, and one hundred and eleven, or more than half, either in the daytime or by good light at night. Of course I do not know how many of the daylight cases were in cloudy weather, but neither does Mr. Thomas. He was also told that special search of two hundred cases shows it impossible to conclude that "most," or a majority, or even a considerable percentage, of the percipients of "ghosts," were at the time "under unusual mental strain." In a few cases they were, certainly, and it may be in more than appears. But apparently many of them—some expressly say so—were at the time peacefully and happily engaged, or waking from sound sleep. A few of them were children, "frolicking" and playing when the veridical apparition came.

One more extract:

"Incidentally, a man may have a great mind in one direction, and a childish one in another direction [several alleged examples given] . . . My good old friend, Hiram Maxim, the expert on explosives, who 'never made a mistake or I'd not be here,' wrote a big book on poetry! So it is useless, a waste of paper and time, to quote great men on anything out of their own line." [8]

Mark that, "anything"! Certainly very great, and even scientific men may, and some of them do, utter opinions without wisdom on subjects which require expert knowledge of a particular kind to handle, whether that subject be poetry or alleged spirit slate-writing. But the remark is absolutely without meaning when applied to the cases which I had mentioned by way of illustration, and which furnished the text for it. The great lawyer Brougham was certainly not a specialist on apparitions, but it is most feeble to intimate that the one which he saw and instantly recognized, the night that the man whom it represented died, is not to be credited because it was out of his line. Nor would it require a mathematician to recognize that the 19th of December which, he declares, a letter afterward announced was the date of

---

[8] The reiterated expression of skepticism to any psychic experience which is not in the line of its subject, implies that Mr. Thomas would respect such an incident if told by a man in whose line it lay. It would be in Dr. Hodgson's line, since he specialized in psychic research for many years. As a matter of fact, Mr. Thomas would as little accept it on the testimony and authority of Dr. Hodgson or any other psychical researcher, but would void his testimony on the ground that it was biased. "We have piped unto you and ye have not danced; we have mourned unto you and ye have not lamented."

the friend's death, was the same day as the 19th of December on which the apparition was seen. Or take the case of Arthur Severn and his wife.[9] He was a painter, what more she was than cousin of John Ruskin and wife of Severn does not appear. But in what particular "line" did she need training in order to test and correctly record the experience of waking with the sudden sensation of having received a blow upon the upper lip and of sitting up and pressing a handkerchief to the spot in the belief that it was bleeding, of seeing that no blood was left on the handkerchief, concluding that she had dreamed and noting by her watch that it was 7 A. M.? What possible "line" of proficiency would have made Mr. Severn any more competent to give reliable testimony that at about 7 A. M. that morning, while out sailing, the tiller of his boat swung around and gave him "a nasty blow" on his upper lip, which was still bleeding on his return to the house, where he then learned what had occurred to his wife? The experience of each, his physical, hers quasi-physical (really mental), was immediate, unmistakable, as certain as anything could be. The only other constituent of the incident was that of time, known by her to be 7 A. M., judged by him to be about 7 P. M. Provided the parties were sane and did not lie, the facts are indisputable. If there were but few such stories, with unknown names appended, one could intelligently adopt the theory of falsehood or insanity. Where an experience is, like the above, simple (free from complexities and obscurities calling for a particular training and expert judgment) and lightning-clear, it is of course in itself as weighty if told by an ordinary person of common-sense as when told by a person of recognized standing. The old fling, not yet quite silenced, was that nearly all such tales emanate from the ignorant and the unbalanced. Obviously this dogma is effectually met by citing, as in *Noted Witnesses*, or in a collection of cases drawn from people in *Who's Who*, numerous experiences of persons generally reputed to be neither ignorant nor unbalanced. It is a scientific datum that such things happen to the cultured, to the sagacious and to the scientific classes.

---

[9] *Noted Witnesses*, 246.

CONCLUDING REMARKS

We have now examined some forty books, articles and printed letters hostile to psychic research and contemptuous of its results. We have also quoted from some seventy letters specially evoked, of which by far the greater manifest general incredulity in reference to the same topic. Whenever this was the case effort has been made to induce the writer to set forth more fully his grounds for the opposition and disparagement indicated.

As stated in the preface, all this has been for the purpose of explaining the phenomenon exhibited by two groups of intelligent and cultured persons articulate on psychic research, one of which claims that there is evidence for " psychic " or " supernormal " facts, the other of which declares that there are no such facts and no valid evidence for them. We said that one of these groups must necessarily be relatively ignorant of the facts or the nature of the facts, must be swayed by prejudice or infatuation, must be employing defective logic. If the deliverances of that group should be found thus characterized in a very marked degree, herein would lie the explanation of this phenomena at the outset so puzzling.

The explanation is now before the reader. He knows that (disregarding the hot-heads who attend every movement) the affirmative has gathered a mass of evidence of which we had space only for illuminating glimpses, and that it has expended long, careful and discriminating study upon it. He also knows that the ignorance, misapprehension, evasion, haste, emotion, eccentric reasoning and unfair tactics charged in the eight numbered paragraphs on pages 19 and 20 have in fact characterized the uncompromising opposition for a century. This book has amply proved and illustrated these allegations. That being the case, no further words are necessary.

INDEX
OF PRINCIPAL NAMES, TOPICS AND ILLUSTRATIVE EXAMPLES

Capitalized names are those of persons whose opinions are subjects of comment.
Italicized titles represent theories, arguments or methods of the opposition.

ALLISON, W. H., 269-70
ANONYMOUS WRITER OF 1820, 163-179
Apparitions, 15, 24 ff., 69 ff.; psychic versus visceral, 198-206
Apparitions:
accompany visceral disease, 198-206; *affected by mood of seer*, 176; *agree with seer's notion of apparitions*, 175 f.; *always appear in familiar garb*, 175; *are morbific symptoms from excitement of renovated feelings*, 189, 191 ff.; *are seen indistinctly*, 186; *are seen rather far off*, 187; *claimed seen exactly at and dressed as at death*, 172 f.; *coincidences with deaths easily accounted for by chance*, 194 ff.; *come to terrify, kill and injure*, 169; *garments of usually white*, 179 ff.; *generally make candle burn blue*, 174; *generally seen when alone*, 173; *glide*, 184 f.; *make no noise*, 185 f.; *no coincidences of with death proved*, 174; *not authentic if they post-date the Apostles*, 189 ff.; *often appear just after light extinguished*, 174; *said to coincide with a death not told until after the death*, 171; *seen by only one of persons present, indicate mental disorder*, 177 f.; *should exhibit the "regularity of nature,"* 178 f.; *standard hour of, midnight the*, 165 ff.; *stories of as a rule second hand*, 170 f.; *supposed to come on some specific errand*, 168 f.; *tales of depend on word of single person*, 173 f.; *usually seen in feeble light*, 166 f., 180 f., 183 f., 341 f.; *usually seen when under mental strain*, 341 f.
Apostolic age, Not since, 189 ff.
Arm-chair science, 210
Arteriosclerosis, Acceptance of psychic claims the result of, 84 ff.
Assertion in face of facts, Bald, 30 f., 42, 127, 128
AVERY, S., 270.

Bailey, Charles, 157
Balfour, Gerald, 55

Beard, George M., 14
Bias, 154 f., 158, 160 f.; *Psychical Researchers disqualified by*, 99, 106 f., 322 f.
Bible against spiritism, 128
Bible and psychic phenomena, 3, 320
Billingsgate, 20
BLACK, JAMES, 131
Blackburn and Smith, 108 ff.
BLANCHARD, PHYLLIS, 83-7
Blue book, 54
Blundering misstatement of psychic problems, 66
Blunders as to questions asked on the blank, 211, 214, 218 f., 232
Blunders in factual statement, 20, 23 ff., 24, 35 ff., 40 f., 43 ff., 52 ff., 57 f., 59, 62 f., 76, 80, 84, 95, 99, 113, 121 f., 126, 131, 132, 148 ff., 153 f., 262
Blunders in figures, 33 f., 89 f.
Blunders in quotation, 53 (See "Malpractice" and "Mangling")
Blunders in spelling, 20, 77, 131, 132
Boswell, James, 22 ff.
BRILL, A. A., 113
Brougham, Lord, 228 f., 332, 342
BROWN, CHARLES REYNOLDS, 122-4
Bruce, H. Addington, 17
Burlesque as an argument, 51
BURROUGHS, E. R., 270-2

CLODD, EDWARD, 51-7
Coincidences, Chance, 41 f., 255, 261 ff., 337 ff.
Coincidences, Extraordinary chance, 267, 336 f.
Coincidences, Spontaneous and Experimental, 218 ff., 229 ff., 263 f., 337 ff.
Cock Lane Ghost, 24
Coleridge, S. T., 117 f.
Credulity, 17
Credulous incredulity, 54 f., 142 f.
Crookes, Sir William, 135
CULPIN, MILLAIS, 66-75
Curiosity would wait, Scientific, 62

DE HEREDIA, C. M., 119-121
Delusions, hallucinations, suggestion, etc., 231 f.

345

INDEX

Desire to tell something startling, 227 ff.
Dignity, Spirits would come with, 123
Dilemma, Religious, 119, 210, 224, 290, 320
Dingwall, E. J., on McCabe, 58; on Lay, 113; on Haldeman, 128
Discuss, Vain invitations more fully to, 329, (See "Hypothetical Question")
Discuss, Vain search for opponent who will squarely face and fairly, 10, 19, 41, 63, 65, 83, 340
Dogmas, Opposition by mere, 11 f., 20, 91 ff., 96 f., 314
"Doris, Mother of," 34 f., 139, 264
Dowsing, explained by subconscious muscular action and guessing, 68
DOYLE, ARTHUR CONAN, 144-162
Dream of railroad disaster, 253 f.
Duguid, David, 158
Durant, Will, 11

Ecclesiastical opposition involving logical dilemma (See *Dilemma*)
Ellsworth, Elmer, 142 f.
Emotion influencing reason, 6 ff.
Emotional reaction, Opposition from, 20, 45, 95
Environment the explanation of "telepathy," Given, 66
Eva C., 157, 159
Everett, Edward, 142 f.
Evidence, A Spirit's difficulty in giving, 293 ff.
Exorcism, 119 f.

Faith temperamentally determined, Acceptance of psychic phenomena an act of, 75 ff.
FARADAY, MICHAEL, 20-2
FARRAR, C. B., 75-82
Feeling, visualization and "perhaps," 124 f.
First Sitting suspicious, Statements not made at, 104 ff.
Fox Sisters, 148, 155 f.
Fraud under favoring conditions as explanation of cases under antipodal conditions, Successful, 137 ff.
FRAZER, PERSIFOR, 165-167, 179-188

GANONG, W. F., 239-42
Generals, Ages of, 143
Greatness in one line no proof of ability in another, 334, 342
Guessing facts, Argument by, 49, 84 f., 89, 94, 105 f.

HALDEMAN, I. M., 127-8
HALE, E. E., 245-6, 267-8, 291
Hales, F. N., on Jastrow, 96 f.
HALL, G. STANLEY, 9, 40-2

Hallucinations, 198 ff., 262, 277, 289 ff., (See "Apparitions")
HANSEN AND LEHMANN, 88 f., 134 ff.
Hawkesworth, A. S., 209
Hay, J. H. D., 333
HEAD, HENRY, 198-206
Helmholz, 11
HENDERSON, YANDELL, 217-222
HIBBERT, SAMUEL, 188-194
HILL, LEONARD, 66
Hodgson, Richard, 5, 43, 162 n.
Home, D. D., 20 ff., 52 ff., 135
HOUDINI, HARRY, 144-161
HUXLEY, T. H., 9, 22-3
Hypothetical Question, 209 ff.
Hyslop, James H., 9, 31; on Hall, 41; on Muensterberg, 43 f., 63 f.; on Newcomb, 31, 33 f.; on Scripture, 88 ff.; on Tanner, 35 ff.

Illusions, 274 ff., 330 ff., 336 f.
"Impossible," 11
Insanity, Psychic experimentation evidences or leads to, 85 ff., 235 ff., 318 f.
Insinuation, Argument of, 54 f., 56
Introvert, Psychic testimony is, 233 f.

JASTROW, JOSEPH, 10 f., 90-7
Johnson as a psychic researcher, Samuel, 23 ff.
JONES, E. H., 137-42
JONES, W. C., 242-4

Kelvin, Lord, 11
Kemble, Edwin C., on Jastrow, 91 ff.
King, Mrs., 35, 145 f.; 209, 213 f., 216, 219, 229, 264, 292, 339 f.

LAFORGE, L., 273
Lang on Hall, Andrew, 41
LAPPONI, GUISEPPE, 129-130
"Laws of Nature," Psychic Phenomena contrary to the, 11 f., 91 ff., 232 f., 246 ff., 262, 265, 307
LAY, WILFRID, 113-8
Leading by facial expression, 103
Leading by the sitter's words, 100 ff.
LEHMANN AND HANSEN, 88 f., 134 ff.
LEPICIER, A. M., 130-1
Lewes, George H., 22 n.
LOCKWOOD, C. D., 246-8
Lodge, Sir Oliver, 6, 49 f., 64 f., 68
Logic, Illegitimate, 40, 44, 49, 56, 61 f., 69 ff., 93 ff., 96 f., 97 f., 113 ff., 124 f., 127, 129, 136, 155 f., 224 f., 268
Logic of psychoanalysis compared with logic of psychic research, 113 ff.

McCABE, JOSEPH, 57-8
MACAULAY, T. B., 23-8

Magicians as judges of psychic claims, 144 ff., 317 f.
Magicians can duplicate everything, 231 f.
Malpractice upon testimony, 68 ff., 103 f.
Mangling of records, 20, 35 ff., 43 ff., 50, 57, 63 f., 68
Mathematical Arguments, 33 f., 34 f., 35, 89 f., 209, 257 ff., 263 f., 292, 296 ff., 339
MAYNARD, R. F., 248-9
Memory of psychic incidents unreliable, 336 ff.
Memory retains hits, not misses, 239 ff., 254, 255 ff., 262 f.
Mephistopheles incident, 221, 230 f., 303
MERCIER, CHARLES A., 48-51
MEYER, M. F., 304-6
Miles and Ramsden experiments, 49 f.
MILLER, A. V., 129
Mind physical, Activity of the, 289 ff.
Monck, " Dr.," 157
Motion shuts out psychic phenomena, Universal, 224 ff.
MUENSTERBERG, HUGO, 43-7
Muir, John, Experience of, 15, 228 f.
Mumler, William, 158
Mundane affairs, Purported messages deal with, 292 f., 303
Murray, Telepathic experiments with Gilbert, 42, 275
Muscle-reading, 100

" Nature," Psychic phenomena not claimed to be outside of, 98
Negative arguments easy to manufacture against evidence, 29 f.
NEWCOMB, SIMON, 30-5
NEYMANN, C. H., 273
Nibbling around the edges of evidence (unfair selection), 49-50, 63
" Normal," Meaning of, 307, 309 ff.

Osgood case, 226 f., 234, 261, 263, 333, 337

" Patience Worth," 279 f.
Personal experience, Edison, etc., had no, 324
Personal experience, No, 123, 284-303
Physical phenomena, 273, 281 ff., 318 f.; Peculiar difficulties in observation and recollection of, 109, 111
Physiology rules out psychic phenomena, 223 f.
Picking cases and material, 49 f., 84 f., 108 ff.
Piddington, J. G., 198-206
Piper, Mrs., 36, 43, 57 f., 60, 100 ff.
Podmore, Frank, 14, 99, 155, 160
Prejudgment, 20 f., 21 f.
"Premonitions," Unfulfilled, 238 ff.
PRESCOTT, F. C., 273-274

Prince, W. F.:
Boyhood home of, 221, 302; Experience, etc., of, 9 f., 231 f.
Problem of the book and its solution, vii ff., 1, 7 f., 19 f., 132 f., 344
Promise to return not kept, 286
Proofs cannot convince of eternal life, 321
Pseudo-memories, Royce's theory of, 3
Psychic and Visceral apparitions compared, 198-206
Psychic claims, The proper judges of: Magicians, 144, 317 f.; Physicists, 83; Physiologists, 83, 223; Psychologists, 61; Psychologists not, 46 f., 128, 314
Psychic incidents never told before coinciding event, 322 f.
"Psychic incidents" explained, 269 ff.
Psychic phenomena:
From old times, 1; homogeneity of, 2 f.; physical, 16 f.; prevalence of, 2; spurious, 16 (See " Spiritism ")
Psychic phenomena have never been proved by proper judges, 322 ff.
Psychic phenomena mostly from the devil, 122, 129
Psychic phenomena mostly not from the devil, but wicked human inventions, 119
Psychic Phenomenon? What is a, 305 f.
Psychic Research:
And superstitions, 12; Bunglers in, 60; By-products of, 17 f.; Founding of organized, 4; Importance of, 27 f., 32; Methods of, 9, 34, 59, 95; Not condemned by Roman Catholic Church, 130; Progress of, 4 f.
Psychic Research bad, Methods of, 88 f.
Psychic Research morally wrong, 45, 134, 305 f.
Psychic Research proves temperamental slavery, Long-continued, 75, 80 f.
Psychic Researchers:
Agreements among, as to certain facts, 15 f.; Convinced contrary to prepossessions, 5; Deceived, 12 f.; Disagree in theories, 13 f.; Employ psychological concepts, 59 f.; Qualifications of, 4, 7, 9 f.; Taught their A B C's, 31, 48, 102
Psychoanalysis and Psychic Research, 41
Psychoanalyst's argument, irrelevant to the issue, 113 ff.
Psychologists and Psychic Research, 41, 61, 82 f., 96 f.
Psychometry, 16, 145 f. (See "Mrs. King," " Maria de Z ")
Psychopathic reactions, 235
Public as a jury, The, 96

INDEX

Reason helpless against strain of interest in psychic research, 61 f., 79 f., 322 ff.
RINE, PROFESSOR, 121-2
ROGERS, D. C., 325-8

Salter, W. H., on Jones, 137 f.
SANDS, IRVING J., 83-7
SARDESON, F. W., 274-6
Saul of Tarsus Complex, 10 f., 90, 318 (?)
Schiller, F. C. S., 7; on Muensterberg, 44 ff.; on Lehmann, 134 ff.
SCHOFIELD, A. T., 131-2
SCHMUCKER, S. C., 249-50
SCOTT, SIR WALTER, 194-197
SCRIPTURE, E. W., 88-90
Severn, Arthur, 343
"Sherlock Holmes" not a proof of detective sagacity, Creation of, 150 ff.
Sidgwick, Henry, 4
Sidgwick on Tanner, Mrs., 37
Sinclair, Upton, 66 ff.
Slade, Henry, 156, 158
Smith and Blackburn, 108 ff.
Soule, Mrs., 138 f., 142, 221 ff., 230 f., 263 f., 285, 292 ff.
SPILLER, GUSTAV, 128-9
"Spiritism" comes down from early antiquity, 75 f.
Spiritism, Evil effects of, 130
"Spiritism" so very young, Modern, 76 f.
Spirits should count beans, 214 ff.
Statistics:
  Ages of Generals, 143; Ages of "psychic" persons, 236; Apparitions (26 sets relating to), 165-187; E. E., 142 f.; Experiments in "involuntary" whispering, 136; Feminine names beginning with S., 103 n.; Lunatics, 87 n.; Psychic vs. visceral hallucinations, 199-206; Spiritualist, 126
Stephen, Story of, 221, 294 ff.
Stewart, Case of, 153
STOCKDALE, F. B., 131
Stomach or nervous system explain, Deranged, 227 ff.

Stratford Rappings, 52 f.
Subconscious mental construction, 278 ff.
Suicide after receiving a "message," A man committed, 318 f.
"Supernormal" meaningless term, 306 ff., 312 f.
Superstition, Psychic research silly, 211 ff., 217, 218, 223, 231, 314 ff., 319 f.

TANNER, AMY E., 35-41
TAYLOR, W. S., 250-1
Telepathy, 30 f., 41 f., 49, 66 ff., 88 f., 108 ff., 134 ff., 215, 262, 265, 275, 291, 293, 308, 320 f., 325 ff.
Telepathy, Fake, 326 ff.
Telepathy vs. Spiritism, 14 f.
Testimony worthless:
  Human, 317, 334; *Of specified classes,* 321 f.
THOMAS, C., 330-43
THOMAS, J. J., 252
Triviality and Silliness of "Messages," 22 f., 32, 123
TUCKETT, IVOR L., 97-113
TURK, MORRIS H., 124-7
TYNDALL, JOHN, 21-2

Unfair tactics, 20 ff.

Verrall's testimony, Mrs., 37 ff.
Vibrations of investigators damage physical phenomena, 156 f.
VOTAW, C. W., 287-8

WASHBURN, MARGARET F., 59-66
Wesley, John, 27 f.
Whispering the explanation of telepathy, Involuntary, 88 f., 134 ff.
Will to believe, 5 f., 61 f., 94, 240, 288 ff.; *Length of study a sign of,* 75
Witchcraft, 119 f.
Wonder, Desire to tell a, 239 f.

Z, Maria de, 272 f.

PERSPECTIVES IN PSYCHICAL RESEARCH

An Arno Press Collection

Carrington, Hereward. **Laboratory Investigations Into Psychic Phenomena.** [1939]

Colquhoun, J. C. **Report of the Experiments on Animal Magnetism.** 1833

Coover, John Edgar. **Experiments in Psychical Research at Leland Stanford Junior University.** 1917

Cumberland, Stuart. **A Thought-Reader's Thoughts.** 1888

Doyle, Arthur Conan. **The History of Spiritualism.** 1926. 2 vols. in one

Driesch, Hans. **Psychical Research:** The Science of the Super-Normal. 1933

Ehrenwald, Jan. **New Dimensions of Deep Analysis.** [1952]

Esdaile, James. **Natural and Mesmeric Clairvoyance.** 1852

Fukurai, T. **Clairvoyance and Thoughtography.** 1931

Garrett, Eileen J. **My Life as a Search for the Meaning of Mediumship.** 1939

Geley, Gustave. **Clairvoyance and Materialisation.** 1927

Gregory, William. **Animal Magnetism.** 1909

Gudas, Fabian, [editor]. **Extrasensory Perception.** 1961

Haddock, Joseph W. **Somnolism and Psycheism.** 1851

Hibbert, S. **Sketches on the Philosophy of Apparitions.** 1824

Mulholland, John. **Beware Familiar Spirits.** 1938

Murchison, Carl, editor. **The Case For and Against Psychical Belief.** 1927

Myers, Frederic W[illiam] H[enry]. **Human Personality and Its Survival of Bodily Death.** 2 vols. 1954

Podmore, Frank. **The Newer Spiritualism.** 1910

Podmore, Frank. **Studies in Psychical Research.** 1897

Price, Harry. **Fifty Years of Psychical Research.** 1939

Price, Harry and Eric Dingwall. **Revelations of a Spirit Medium.** 1922

Prince, Walter Franklin. **The Enchanted Boundary.** 1930

Richet, Charles. **Thirty Years of Psychical Research.** 1923

Roll, William G. **Theory and Experiment in Psychical Research.** 1975

Salter, W. H. **Zoar: Or the Evidence of Psychical Research Concerning Survival.** 1961

Saltmarsh, H. F. **Evidence of Personal Survival From Cross Correspondences.** 1938

Saltmarsh, H. F. **Foreknowledge.** 1938

Sidgwick, Eleanor Mildred. **Phantasms of the Living: Cases of Telepathy Printed in the Journal of the Society for Psychical Research During Thirty-Five Years** and Gurney, Edmund, Frederic W. H. Myers and Frank Podmore, **Phantasms of the Living.** 1962

Thomas, John F. **Beyond Normal Cognition.** 1937

Tyrrell, G. N. M. **Science and Psychical Phenomena.** [1938]

Von Schrenck Notzing, [A.] **Phenomena of Materialisation.** 1920

Wallace, Alfred Russel. **Miracles and Modern Spiritualism.** 1896

Warcollier, René. **Experimental Telepathy.** 1938